MEMOIRS OF LIEUT.-GENERAL WINFIELD SCOTT

MEMOIRS OF LIEUT.-GENERAL WINFIELD SCOTT

EDITED BY TIMOTHY D. JOHNSON

Voices of the Civil War,
Michael P. Gray, Series Editor

The University of Tennessee Press / Knoxville

The Voices of the Civil War series makes available a variety of primary source materials that illuminate issues on the battlefield, the
home front, and the western front, as well as other aspects of this historic era. The series contextualizes the personal accounts within the
framework of the latest scholarship and expands established knowledge by offering new perspectives, new materials, and new voices.

The paper in this book meets the requirements of American National Standards Institute / National Information Standards Organization specification
Z39.48–1992 (Permanence of Paper). It contains 30 percent post-consumer
waste and is certified by the Forest Stewardship Council.

LIBRARY OF CONGRESS CATALOGING-IN-PUBLICATION DATA

Scott, Winfield, 1786-1866.
Memoirs of Lieut.-General Winfield Scott / edited by Timothy D. Johnson. —
First edition.
    pages cm. — (Voices of the Civil War)
Original edition published in 1864.
Includes bibliographical references and index.
ISBN 978-1-62190-163-1 (hardcover : alk. paper)
1. Scott, Winfield, 1786-1866. 2. Generals—United States—Biography. 3. United
States. Army—Biography. 4. United States—History—War of 1812—Biography.
5. Mexican War, 1846-1848—Biography. 6. United States—History—Civil War,
1861-1865—Biography. I. Johnson, Timothy D., 1957- editor. II. Title. III. Title:
Memoirs of Lieutenant General Winfield Scott.
E403.1.S4A3 2015
355.0092—dc23
[B]
                    2015006920

CONTENTS

FOREWORD

Within the Voices of the Civil War collection, readers will find more than fifty volumes dedicated to primary-source material, stretching across military theaters, exploring home fronts, and sweeping into borderlands. With recent scholarship attentive to long histories, the narrative lens has widened and the scope of interpretation has broadened, going well beyond traditional ways of demarking historical eras; the long nineteenth century or the long Civil Rights movement, for example, have become accepted periods in contextualizing the historical discussion. If one were to consider a "long Civil War," where themes can be threaded by years outside the standard 1861–1865 framework, this new volume will certainly complement such a notion. This volume features a historical voice that had been muted by many contemporaries, particularly those from the Civil War, but also generations afterwards, and continues to go unrecognized by the American public, until hopefully now. In reality, Winfield Scott transcended the Civil War, as his battlefield prowess, diplomatic astuteness, and systematic codification of war make him a rare military mind, relevant to understanding what happened long before the Civil War and after. Perhaps even more impressive was his ability to put such thoughts into practice. A teacher and leader, his extraordinary career has been astoundingly consigned to being considered ordinary until lately. Just now are historians finally recognizing "Old Fuss and Feathers" as one of the most important battlefield generals in American history, in the ranks of George Washington or Dwight Eisenhower, as well as the many Civil War commanders whom he had taught during the Mexican War.

Often overlooked and inexplicably ignored, Winfield Scott's personal writings have finally been brought out of silence—Scott's best biographer, Timothy Johnson, wields his editor's pen to bring Scott's antiquated memoirs from obscurity. This current volume is valuable on a number of fronts: the editor has merged the large two-volume memoir into a single manageable volume, updated Scott's outdated notes by providing a staggering six hundred additional references with much more illumination and context, serving as a valuable guide to the reader. The excellent editorial commentary comes with an updated and expanded index.

Scott's memoir is unique due to the long and valuable role Scott played throughout the nineteenth century. Near what turned out to be the end of the Civil War, he realized he must put his stamp on posterity, finishing his memoir two years before passing. Although some may contend his soldiering life reached its peak in Mexico, one thing that makes his work so valuable is how the reader gets special insight into foreshadowing the Civil War. Scott's opinions regarding slavery and abolition are noted, as well as consultations and confrontations with Andrew Jackson and John C. Calhoun, hostilities over nullification, and his foreboding over the states' rights clash. Scott's entries include his attempts at fortifying Federal forts off the South Carolina coast during the Nullification crisis, which would emerge as an ominous indicator in due time. His contemplations about sending forces into Charleston in order to quell any disturbances, as well as hoping the President Buchanan would remain on the defensive rather than supporting a forcible attack, are detailed. Scott is thinking about these challenges as a new coastal fortress, Fort Sumter, was being completed. Scott also reflects on the sequence leading to crisis, laying the framework for temporary diplomacy, and its breakdown, with eventual war. Indeed, Scott gives deep accounts of Bleeding Kansas, disputes with Jefferson Davis, reflects on President James Buchanan, analyses the 1860 election, and describes his preparation in strengthening Union coastal forts in the South once again, in preparation for the worst.

Those who might not be truly convinced of the significant influence Winfield Scott had on the Civil War should take heed of this volume's new introduction. Editor Johnson places Scott on the Civil War stage on a variety of levels, from his actions in delivering President Abraham Lincoln safely to Washington City, as well as his further deliberations with the president as the conflict continued, to his famous Anaconda Plan—much maligned by peers early in the war, but remarkably similar to what was ultimately carried out to ensure Northern victory. Johnson sheds particular light by emphasizing Scott's training of the officer corps during the Mexican War, where under his tutelage so many future Civil War leaders attempted to replicate their mentor's conquests— not only on the battlefield but also behind the lines. Indeed, Johnson painstakingly assembles some 78 soon to be Blue and 57 Gray generals, respectively, all coming from Scott's "Mexican War tree." It is also important to note that the memoir moves beyond front lines in order to describe what makes armies run, from quartermaster and commissaries, to caring for the wounded or captured; Scott's reports include some better known names that resurface in the next war, from ordinance overseer Benjamin Huger to medical men like Joseph K. Barnes or Charles S. Tripler, but even perhaps lesser known names, like Justin Dimick, the eventual overseer of Boston's Fort Warren—the editor's copious notes relate their previous training record from Mexico to their service in the Civil War.

Scott's extensive leadership during the Mexican War tended to shape the soldier during the American Civil War in a notable way. Johnson demonstrates this with an ironic scene that unfolded as George B. McClellan faced off against Robert E. Lee on the Peninsula. The "Young Napoleon," who while in Mexico as a lieutenant, "won" Scott's "admiration," imitated the latter's 1847 Veracruz campaign on the Virginia coast. McClellan even called his headquarters Camp Winfield Scott out of respect for his old general. McClellan was poised to strike against "Old Fuss and Feather's" truest protégé, someone Scott repeatedly commended while a young captain for distinguished service in his Mexican War reports, not limited to but including words like "indefatigable" and "daring." Those adjectives described Robert E. Lee, and it was no mistake Lee was his mentor's first choice in leading the Union army as the Civil War broke out. Perhaps Lee learned the most from Scott—the value of defense, security, reconnaissance, as well as counter-strikes, audacious attacks, and dividing his forces. It undoubtedly must have made Scott ponder the "what ifs" after reports of his two Mexican War "students" dueling it out on the Peninsula. McClellan was eventually driven back, the war was prolonged, and the capture of Richmond delayed by almost three years. Perhaps it may have been even more surreal to Scott a year later, when Lee undertook the boldest flanking movement of the war at Chancellorsville, echoing back to Scott's campaigns a little more than decade before. Scott must have been left in both an awkward and vexed position, perhaps feeling pride in his best protégé's feat yet fear at the potential for the destruction of the Union, all due to teaching his fellow Virginian so well.

Scott's memoir is full of nuances that contribute to a better understanding of Civil War policies that have roots in his Mexican War days. Readers might be surprised to find how his service in Mr. Polk's War levied heavily during the Civil War, and moreover, not just from his well-documented battlefield exploits. By aligning both conflicts, new interpretations may come from Scott's insights. With some current Civil War scholarship trending toward military codification, law (and lawlessness), but especially the Lieber Code and the development of war policy, readers might find it surprising to discover Scott's imprint on army codification in this volume, setting a formal standard for others to follow later. Scott's "Lessons" and "discipline and honor of the army" were outlined with his martial-law dictum, in which both parties would be punished for crimes committed while this precarious state existed. His Special Orders 53, dealing with illegal punishments of enlisted men in addition to officers' interactions with the rank and file, as well as his expectations for this class of soldier are expounded. He systematically went through these rules as well as the residuals of campaigning. In addition, Scott's General Orders 20 and 287 developed martial law and laid foundations for future conflicts. Even his issues while in Mexico in handling the untidy business of large numbers of prisoners of war, setting parole policy and its detriments, resonate in the Civil War—most strikingly, perhaps, in the challenges Ulysses Grant confronted after the fall of Vicksburg.

Having started a military career that spanned back to the War of 1812, reaching its height in the Mexican War that resulted in a run for president, and ending in the Civil War, Scott and his memoir provide an example in the truest sense of service to one's country. His account is particularly distinctive because he not only gives military assessments, but also delves into diplomacy and discernment of politicians and ambassadors. After reading this new edition, historians might be further challenged in bridging the Mexican War with the Civil War, and perhaps from Scott's words new interpretations will be sought out in future scholarship. Hopefully this new volume brings together the significant connections of these two great nineteenth-century conflicts and how they are inextricably linked by Winfield Scott.

Michael P. Gray
East Stroudsburg University
of Pennsylvania

EDITOR'S INTRODUCTION
TO THE SECOND EDITION

On March 9, 1814, Winfield Scott became a brigadier general in the United States Army. Beginning his military service only six years earlier, he was, in 1814, just twenty-seven years old and the youngest general in the army. Scott's career spanned fifty-three years, fourteen presidents, twenty-two secretaries of war, and six wars with foreign and domestic foes. Sadly, his longevity of service did not secure his place among the nation's pantheon of great military leaders. Indeed, a century and a half after Scott's death he remains relatively unknown to the general public. Some people have a faint recollection of the general but know only the 1861 image of him as an overweight old man who was in poor health and who dosed off in cabinet meetings. They remember his much maligned "Anaconda Plan" and think of it as his only contribution to the Union's Civil War effort. However, consider this assertion made by historian John Waugh in a 2001 book review published in *Civil War Times*: "There is an underground opinion unknown to the general public but held by many military historians: the greatest American battlefield general of all time is not Washington, Lee, Grant, or Jackson, or even MacArthur, Eisenhower, Patton, or Schwarzkopf, but Winfield Scott."

Rarely has a nation so thoroughly forgotten one of its greatest benefactors. Scott's contributions to the early Republic's military establishment were significant. One might even consider him the father of the United States' professional army. He was one of the strongest advocates of a trained officer corps and disciplined troops, and although he did not attend West Point, he loved the academy and was one of its staunchest supporters. He wrote the first comprehensive set of regulations to govern the army, kept the peace during Canadian border disputes, crossed swords with some of the country's preeminent politicians, commanded one of the most brilliant military campaigns in American history, was one of the principle agents of Manifest Destiny, served as commanding general of the army for twenty years, ran for president of the United States, and trained the generation of officers who fought the Civil War.

Despite his contributions and his status as one of the country's most accomplished generals, there are several reasons most Americans know so little about Winfield Scott. It is due in part to a lack of interest shown to him by biographers and by authors of American history textbooks. Also, the destruction of many of his personal papers in a house fire in 1841 no doubt frightened away would-be biographers for decades until the sudden appearance of three new studies between 1997 and 2003. Additionally, Scott's arrogance and insufferable elitism gave him a personality that repels rather than attracts attention. Erasmus Keyes, a longtime military aide to Scott, believed that ambition was a primary motivation in Scott's life. Keyes also asserted that "Scott regarded himself as the most able general of American history." He loved highbrow social events and was comfortable rubbing elbows with the nation's financial and political elites. He routinely hosted dinner parties at which, from the head of the table, he dominated the conversation with stories about himself. Commenting on one such episode, New York diarist Philip Hone wrote that the general succeeded in "making himself, as usual, the hero of his tale." Scott was indeed a social climber and wanted to be the center of attention—traits his *Memoirs* reveal. Upon publication of his *Memoirs* in 1864, one of Scott's favorite subordinates, Robert E. Lee, stated the obvious: "The General of course, stands out prominently." Like Xenophon and Polybius in ancient times, Scott wrote about himself in the third person, giving his *Memoirs* a detached feel. Ulysses S. Grant, writing in his own *Personal Memoirs* years later, explained why Scott referred to himself in the third person in both writing and speech: so he could "bestow praise upon the person he was talking about without the least embarrassment."

Scott's lack of humility did not result from an aristocratic upbringing. Born in Petersburg, Virginia, in 1786 into comfortable but modest circumstances, he lost his father at age three and his mother at seventeen. He briefly attended the College of William and Mary before embarking on a career in law, and as an aspiring young attorney, he traveled to Richmond to attend Aaron Burr's highly publicized treason trial in 1807. However, the threat of war with England following the *Chesapeake-Leopard* Affair diverted his attention to the military, and in 1808 he secured a captain's commission in the artillery, embarking upon a fifty-three-year career in the army.

His first assignment sent him to New Orleans to join General James Wilkinson's command. It was a turbulent beginning for the impetuous young officer. Wilkinson had stationed his men at Terre aux Boeufs, a marshy, mosquito-infested lowland outside of New Orleans, where the men suffered from disease and spoiled provisions. Scott quickly developed a low opinion of the officer corps' competency, and he ultimately displayed a lack of respect for his superiors, which led to trouble. His frustration resulted in his decision to resign his commission and go home—until rumors that he had embezzled his men's pay and had used disrespectful language aimed at General Wilkinson convinced him to return and face his accusers. In January 1810, the charges led to a court-martial that found Scott guilty of conduct unbecoming an officer, and he was sentenced to a twelve-month suspension. The twenty-three-year-old captain spent the year profitably, reading and studying military history, strategy, and tactics, and he emerged from his punishment armed with the knowledge that would be the foundation of future martial accomplishments.

Scott quickly rose to colonel at the outset of the War of 1812. He was captured at the Battle of Queenstown during a failed invasion of Canada in October 1812, and the following year he participated in the ill-fated Montreal expedition. However, during the war, a new generation of brave and energetic young officers emerged to replace the aging and sometimes infirm army leaders, many of whom had begun their careers during the Revolutionary War. Scott's star began its rise when he led the attack and capture of Fort George at the mouth of the Niagara River, and his ascendancy continued in 1814, when he was promoted to brigadier general. In just two years, the average age of U.S. Army generals had gone from sixty to thirty-six, a transition that infused the army with robust leadership.

In July 1814, Scott became an American hero as a result of his exploits at the Battles of Chippewa and Lundy's Lane, where he commanded a brigade in General Jacob Brown's army. At Chippewa, Scott used his tactical knowledge to outmaneuver and defeat a larger British force in a surprisingly quick victory. His leadership demonstrated an early skill in the art of the flank attack, a skill for which he would become known as a master and a trait that he passed on to a younger generation of officers. Three weeks later, at Lundy's Lane, he suffered a serious shoulder wound in a rare but bloody night battle in which he somewhat impetuously rushed his men into battle. Once again Scott's men showed themselves the equal of British regulars in what became one of the bloodiest encounters of the war. Along the Niagara River, American troops demonstrated an ability to stand firm in a heated battle against disciplined British troops, a major improvement over the war's previous engagements. Credit for the Chippewa victory and the Lundy's Lane draw is usually given to Scott, who had put his men through rigorous training in Buffalo, New York, the previous spring. Indeed, Scott and others believed that it was the discipline and skill instilled at Buffalo that transformed a ragtag army into a respectable fighting force capable of meeting British regulars on equal terms. While the fighting along the Niagara River in 1814 served as an example of the need for a professional army, Andrew Jackson's victory at New Orleans six months later seemed to prove the opposite.

A group of young and ambitious officers emerged from the war. Scott was the youngest of the new generals, and he spent the next thirty years pushing for army professionalism. He traveled to Europe on an observation tour, presided over a board of officers that published a tactical manual for infantry in 1815, wrote and published *General Regulations for the Army* in 1821, promoted the fledgling United States Military Academy at West Point, and helped devise the expandable army concept, which was enacted after military cutbacks. His *General Regulations* was the first comprehensive set of bylaws written to govern the U.S. Army. In it, Scott meticulously described army administration, the duties of staff officers, training requirements, appropriate dress, the chain of command, camp sanitation, army tactics, and numerous other categories. He stipulated the proper routines for every aspect of army life: camp organization, food preparation, frequency of clothing changes, the maintenance of company and regimental books, and so on. Concerning battlefield tactics, he stressed the advantages of going on the offensive and seizing the initiative from the enemy. Through his early-nineteenth-century contributions to the military establishment, Scott played a principle role in laying the foundation for a professional army, to which he then devoted his life.

His *Memoirs* contain a dearth of information about his family. In March 1817 he improved his social standing by marrying Maria Mayo, whose family was among Richmond's wealthy elites. Maria's father was a slaveholder who owned a considerable amount of real estate, including two houses in Richmond, one house in Elizabethtown, New Jersey, and a toll bridge across the James River. Winfield and Maria had seven children—five girls and two boys, but both boys died young and only three of the girls outlived their parents. The Scotts' union was apparently a proper Victorian marriage. Both parties faithfully adhered to their wedding vows, but it did not appear to be a particularly affectionate relationship. Scott was often away from home for extended periods, leaving Maria to raise the children alone, and as time passed she came to enjoy her own extended absences by occasionally spending considerable time in Europe. Along with the children and her now-widowed mother, she would spend months at a time away from home, mostly in Paris. Believing that the European climate helped her faltering health, she once spent five years overseas without returning home. Although the general gives no record of these extended separations in his *Memoirs*, his personal correspondence provides clues that he experienced loneliness. Although neither of the Scotts' sons lived to adulthood, one of the daughters married army officer Henry L. Scott, so there is a direct line of descendants who bear the Scott name.

The contentious personality that Scott displayed as a young officer at Terre aux Boeufs in 1809 proved to be a lifelong character trait. Throughout his career, his relationships with fellow officers were sometimes turbulent and his defiance of superiors, both military and civilian, was commonplace. He narrowly escaped fighting a duel with General Andrew Jackson, opposed Alexander Macomb's promotion over him as commanding general of the army in 1828, contended with Zachary Taylor over the allocation of troops in the Mexican-American War, and, most famously, engaged in a thirty-year feud with Edmund Pendleton Gaines over seniority of rank. In addition, Scott had acrimonious clashes with secretaries of war, most notably Jefferson Davis, and with presidents, including John Quincy Adams, Andrew Jackson, and James K. Polk. Scott's quarrelsome nature, along with his strict enforcement of regulations and his love of ornate uniforms, won him the nickname "Old Fuss and Feathers."

Scott was a political general who spent much time in Washington, where he fostered relationships with prominent politicians. He became a conspicuous Whig whose presidential aspirations put him in the crosshairs of Democrat administrations. Throughout his midcareer, he experienced ups and downs in his political relationships as well as in his military career. Scott's encounters with Native Americans in the 1830s (Black Hawk War, Second Seminole War, Cherokee removal) offered no opportunities for career advancement, but his negotiating skills along the Canadian border in the late 1830s and early 1840s bolstered his reputation as a statesman, helping to nourish his political ambition.

In 1841 Scott was promoted to commanding general of the U.S. Army, a position that he had coveted for years and one that he held for two decades. It was as the highest ranking officer in the land that he assumed field command of an army in Mexico and led one of the most brilliant, but largely forgotten, military campaigns in American history. Although he opposed "Mr. Polk's War" on moral grounds, he did not engage in the ongoing debate over its origins. Rather, he did his duty, which is what soldiers do when their country calls. From March to September 1847, Scott led an army of ten thousand on a 250-mile march from Veracruz to Mexico City, and along the way he defeated enemy armies twice his numbers at Veracruz, Cerro Gordo, Contreras, Molino del Rey, and Chapultepec before capturing the Mexican capital and ending the war. Throughout the campaign, Scott's capable staff conducted extensive reconnaissance, collecting valuable information upon which the general relied in formulating his battle plans. Scott consistently outmaneuvered his opponent, Santa Anna, maintained the initiative, and at Cerro Gordo and Contreras executed flank attacks that made short work of the enemy. The Mexico City Campaign demonstrated Scott's thorough grasp of Napoleonic tactics.

In addition to displaying his mastery of battlefield tactics, Scott devised a pacification strategy that succeeded in preventing a widespread uprising against his invading army. The key components that he used to pacify central Mexico were martial law, strict discipline of his own troops, the purchase of supplies from local inhabitants, and respect for the dominant Mexican religion, Catholicism. He was able to limit the wholesale plunder of the Mexican countryside and he made American atrocities the exception rather than the rule. Instead of leaving anger and destruction in his army's wake, Scott left law and order. The tactics and strategy that he employed in Mexico were a result of his knowledge, foresight, and self-confidence, and the execution of his plans was always steady and competent and sometimes bold and brilliant. The Mexico City Campaign was devised by a general who was ahead of his time, and it permanently placed him among the most preeminent generals in American history.

One other issue regarding Scott's generalship deserves notice here and will be treated in greater depth later. Many of the Civil War's most prominent and accomplished generals learned their first lessons of war as lower-grade officers while serving in Scott's army in Mexico. The editor has compiled a list of 135 future generals (78 Union and 57 Confederate) who fought in Scott's army from Veracruz to Mexico City, and it includes names such as Lee, Johnston, Beauregard, Longstreet, Hardee, Jackson, Grant, McClellan, Hancock, Hooker, Buell, and Sedgwick.

Following the war with Mexico, Scott weathered a storm of wrath from President James K. Polk, a Democrat who had the general placed before a court of inquiry to investigate his conduct during the campaign. The real reason for the inquiry, however, was to eliminate Scott as a Whig presidential candidate in 1848 and to vindicate the president's friend Gideon J. Pillow, a presidentially appointed major general who had been embarrassed by Scott during the course of the campaign. Although eliminated from political contention in 1848, Scott nevertheless emerged four years later as the Whig nominee. However, he carried only four states and the outcome of the 1852 election was more than an embarrassment for the general, it was a debacle that hastened the demise of the Whig Party.

By the time of secession and the Civil War, Scott was well beyond his prime physically. However, he tried without success in December 1860 to persuade President James Buchanan to send strong troop contingents to garrison the southern coastal fortifications in the hope of forestalling secession threats. As the national crisis deepened in the spring of 1861, Scott, approaching his seventy-fifth birthday, was overweight and lacked the energy and mobility that he once possessed. He could not negotiate stairs, could no longer mount a horse, and was given to dozing during meetings. Many people interpreted his physical infirmities as a sign of mental incapacity, despite the fact that he had calmly overseen security during Abraham Lincoln's inauguration in March amid assassination threats and it was to him that the new president came asking for a strategy to defeat the Confederacy. The plan he produced revealed a commanding general whose thought processes remained keen.

Scott proposed that the southern coastline be blockaded to cut off commerce through the Confederacy's Atlantic and Gulf Coast harbors. He also urged that a large army capture key locations along the Mississippi River all the way down to New Orleans, thus denying the Confederacy access to that important waterway. Scott's plan harkened back to Napoleonic strategy, wherein key geographic features were seized in order to gain a strategic advantage through superior positions. The objective was to put the opponent in a box and force him to realize the futility of further resistance. Scott's proposed strategy was also reminiscent of his Mexico City Campaign in two respects. It emphasized the use of water as secure lines of operation and communication, and its ultimate goal was political and not military. In Mexico, Scott had paused after each battlefield victory to allow the enemy government time to recognize the uselessness of continuing the conflict. Although he would have been willing to stop short of Mexico City if he could have accomplished a peace settlement earlier, it was ultimately the fall of the Mexican capital that provided sufficient leverage to force a political solution. Now in 1861, Scott's stated objective was not the destruction of enemy forces but the encirclement and isolation of the South so as to force it to recognize that prolonged resistance would be useless. The strategy, dubbed by his critics the Anaconda Plan, would take time, but eventually it would crush the Confederacy through economic strangulation. The attempt to break up the Union was a political problem, and the commanding general's Anaconda Plan illustrated his clear grasp of the relation between military strategy and political objectives. It also demonstrated his desire to avoid a bloodbath.

No one could predict how long such a strategy would take—months or even years. In 1861 Northerners and Southerners alike believed that if it came to a clash of arms, it would end quickly with minimal bloodshed. Thus the Anaconda Plan was ridiculed by impatient observers who believed that the war would end long before Scott's snake-like blockade could begin to squeeze the life out of the Confederacy. In the summer of 1861, the cry was "On to Richmond!" and talk of preparations and elaborate plans seemed an unwarranted delay. Scott's anaconda strategy seemed out of touch with this short-war illusion, further convincing observers that the aging hero's time had passed. When the president brought young Gen. George McClellan to Washington to assume command of the Army of the Potomac, Scott's days indeed were numbered. But time proved Scott right, and the death of over six hundred thousand Americans over the next four years proved the public wrong. The subsequent blockade and war on the waters ultimately vindicated Old Fuss and Feathers's foresight.

In the spring of 1861, McClellan was in Ohio commanding volunteers, but by summer he found himself commanding Union forces in western Virginia, where he enjoyed success in minor engagements. In a May letter to Scott, he referred to the commanding general as his teacher and mentor, and in later correspondence he stated his intention to emulate Scott's Cerro Gordo maneuver in his actions against the Confederates at Rich Mountain. After the North's defeat at First Bull Run, Lincoln called McClellan to Washington to assume command of the Army of the Potomac, and thereafter administration officials increasingly looked not to Scott but to McClellan for advice and solutions. As a result, McClellan began to exhibit an ego every bit as large as Scott's, and he too began to ignore his elderly superior. During the fall, as he organized his army and formulated his campaign plans, McClellan essentially orchestrated a power play that maneuvered Scott out of office and into retirement.

At 4:00 a.m. on November 1, Winfield Scott boarded a train for New York. The darkness and a steady rain provided a dreary backdrop as the seventy-five-year-old general left the capital without fanfare. The once great commander, renowned for his role in the War of 1812 and the Mexican-American War, the man who had done so much to lay a foundation for a professional army, made an unpretentious exit from the seat of power to live out the remainder of his days at his beloved West Point. His departure was both sad and symbolic. Not only was he passing from the spotlight, but his bright career would soon be eclipsed by a new galaxy of military stars who would collectively cast a large and impenetrable shadow.

Although Scott was soon relegated to obscurity by the enormity of the Civil War, the old sage nevertheless left a legacy that cannot be forgotten. The grand irony lies in the fact that Scott had trained the new generation of generals who commanded Civil War armies, and in many instances, his legacy is evident in their performances. Numerous flank attacks in the Civil War were reminiscent of Scott's tactics in Mexico, where turning movements were a staple. Confederate general Earl Van Dorn at Pea Ridge and Robert E. Lee and Thomas "Stonewall" Jackson at Chancellorsville are but two examples of Mexican War veterans who executed flank marches similar to the successful one at Cerro Gordo.

After wresting the title of commanding general from Scott in 1861, George McClellan actually tried to emulate the Mexico City Campaign in Virginia the following year. Using the Potomac River and Chesapeake Bay as a secure water route, McClellan executed a strategic turning movement by shifting military operations from north of the enemy capital to the eastern coastline, just as Scott had done when he landed at Veracruz in 1847, redirecting the center of the conflict from north of Mexico City to the east. Scott had marshaled all available resources and directed them toward the enemy capital, intending to end the war in one grand stroke, which was exactly what McClellan hoped to do in 1862. Once on the Peninsula in Virginia, McClellan named his headquarters Camp Winfield Scott and prepared to bombard Yorktown rather than assault it, once again mirroring Scott's Veracruz example. Eventually McClellan maneuvered up to the outskirts of Richmond, but he soon found himself confronting Scott's preeminent protégé, Robert E. Lee, who drove him off the Peninsula and back to Washington.

Lee had served as a staff officer in Mexico, and Scott later proclaimed him the best soldier he had ever seen in the field. It was Captain Lee who had conducted much of the reconnaissance upon which Scott had relied in determining the movements of his army. It was from Scott that Lee learned not only the value of reconnaissance but also the advantages that accrue to a commander who is bold, confident, and aggressive on the battlefield. At Cerro Gordo and Contreras, Scott had divided his army in the face of an opponent with superior numbers and in both instances won impressive victories. Perhaps those battles were in the back of Lee's mind at Chancellorsville when, outnumbered almost two to one, he divided his army not once but twice and won his most brilliant victory of the Civil War. And the knowledgeable reader will remember that in 1861 Scott tried in vain to persuade Lee to accept the Lincoln administration's offer to command the Union army.

After his retirement but before he settled in at West Point, an aged Winfield Scott embarked on a trip to Italy to reunite with Maria, who was on one of her extended European stays. When he reached England, however, he learned of the diplomatic controversy known as the *Trent* Affair, which threatened Anglo-American relations. The situation had deteriorated into talk of war. Thinking that his services might be needed back home, he cut his trip short and recrossed the Atlantic Ocean. Scott feared the worse, but a U.S.-British conflict did not materialize. In one final display of arrogance, the old general then appealed to the government to treat his trip to England as a diplomatic mission and reimburse him the cost of his travel across the ocean. He contended that his unexpected appearance in England at the height of the turmoil likely had a tranquilizing effect on the British and helped avert war. Sadly, Scott's decision to cut his trip short and return home meant that he never saw his wife again, for she died in Rome in 1862.

He spent much of his remaining four years in New York, mostly at West Point. Increasingly, he suffered from vertigo, gout, and other ailments. The volume of mail he received was more than he could read, but the fact that many of his correspondents wrote to ask his opinion of how the war was going attests to the degree of respect his military mind still commanded. More important, President Lincoln, frustrated over McClellan's handling of the war, traveled to West Point in June 1862 to solicit Scott's counsel. In his last winter, Scott traveled to New Orleans, where he enjoyed occasional walks in the French Quarter. While there, local observers commented on his frailty. Two years before he died in 1866, he published his *Memoirs*. During his lifetime, Winfield Scott believed that he was, except for George Washington, the greatest general in American history. In writing his *Memoirs* he hoped to provide a permanent record of his deeds, thereby securing his place in history. It is as if he sensed that the Civil War was already overshadowing him and that he had to do his part to preserve his legacy. The 1864 edition of the *Memoirs* was two volumes, and Scott included in each volume a likeness of himself presumably portraying the way he wished to be remembered. The image in volume one is of him at age thirty-seven, a young general in the vigor of youth. Volume two contains a likeness of an older Scott as depicted in a marble bust that conjures thoughts of great commanders and statesmen of ancient times. It is reminiscent of the bust of George Washington done by Jean-Antoine Houdon in the 1780s. Unfortunately, not even his own record of his life's events could save him from obscurity.

A century and a half after its publication, it is time for a second edition of Winfield Scott's *Memoirs*. First published as a two-volume set, the *Memoirs* now have become rare books. In 1970 a facsimile reproduction of the first edition appeared, but it too is often difficult to find. Because Scott was a participant in many of the important events of American history during the early and mid-nineteenth century, his recollection should be readily available to anyone interested in that time period. The general made no pretense at objectivity. Rather, he wrote with the purpose of preserving his own interpretation of his life's experiences, which ultimately is a common characteristic of personal memoirs. The fact that his version of events is often ego inflated actually provides a valuable window that enables readers to more accurately access the personality of this great military commander.

This second edition converts Scott's original two volumes into one, but none of the first edition was eliminated. In addition to keeping the entire 1864 edition intact, the modern reader will now find almost six hundred editorial notes at the back that attempt to provide context and identify people and events. Where possible, I have included birth and death dates by individual names. In editing Scott's *Memoirs*, I attempted to preserve them in their original form as much as possible. Therefore, I did not change his spelling of "practise" in chapter 1, or "Pittsburg" in chapter 4, or "barbacue" in chapter 5, or "unintrenched" in chapter 8, and so on. I did, however, standardize spelling when Scott spelled a word more than one way. In the first edition, Scott included several discursive footnotes at the bottom of the page, but in this edition the reader will find them embedded in the text. There is an asterisk marking the location of Scott's original citation, and his note is inserted at the end of the sentence and set apart by curly brackets. Finally, an index is included for the convenience of the reader.

While working on this project, I benefited from the assistance of numerous people, including Al Austelle, who furnished valuable technical assistance; Sarah Bland, who scanned each page into electronic format; Lipscomb University provost Craig Bledsoe, who provided financial support; and Rachel Pyle and the rest of the staff at Lipscomb's Beaman Library for eagerly offering their assistance. My wife, Jayne, as usual offered support along with her proofreading skills at various stages along the way. Finally, I wish to offer a long overdue word of appreciation to Ronald Spector, who unselfishly stepped in during unusual circumstances to provide guidance when I first began my research on Winfield Scott in the late 1980s. Without Professor Spector's generous and professional assistance, I might never have completed my doctoral dissertation or my subsequent biography of Scott. Spector's example as a scholar made a lasting impression on me. Thank you.

In chapter 31 of his *Memoirs*, after recounting his army's splendid victories at Contreras and Churubusco, Scott wrote of his wish that someday "the applause of a grateful country" would "be accorded" to his army for its accomplishments in Mexico. Writing almost twenty years after these battles had occurred, Scott still hoped that appropriate honor would be bestowed on his gallant little army, but at the time he wrote, he also felt personally slighted at the way in which his career drew to a close. The aged general certainly desired the appreciation of "a grateful country," not just for his army but also for himself. The publication of this second edition of his *Memoirs* is one way of fulfilling that wish and reminding Americans of his contributions during the formative years of the nation's history. As I write this introduction, it is the bicentennial of Scott's promotion to brigadier general (1814) and the sesquicentennial of the original publication of his *Memoirs* (1864). Scot Danforth, Thomas Wells, and the staff at the University of Tennessee Press have done Scott and the general public a service by making this resource accessible once again.

Timothy D. Johnson
Lipscomb University
2014

AUTHOR'S INTRODUCTION
TO THE 1864 EDITION

The English language is singularly barren of autobiographies or memoirs by leading actors in the public events of their times. Statesmen, diplomatists, and warriors on land and water, who have made or moulded the fortunes of England or the United States, have nearly all, in this respect, failed in their duty to posterity and themselves. Their speeches, state papers, despatches, reports, letters, and orders remain, indeed, fragmentary monuments of their patriotic deeds; but the Republican Ludlow,[1] the Roundhead Whitelocke,[2] Lord Clarendon,[3] Bishop Burnet,[4] and Sir William Temple,[5] five contemporaries, alone, of the Anglo-Saxon race, are exceptions, unless we add Swift, a sixth contemporary.* {Dean Swift, the literary executor of Temple, cites, in the preface to a part of his author's memoirs, an absurd objection that had been made to another part, earlier published, viz.: that the "author speaks too much of himself," and replies: "I believe those who make [this] criticism do not well consider the nature of memoirs. 'Tis to the French (if I mistake not) we chiefly owe that manner of writing, and Sir W. T. is not only the first, but, I believe, the only Englishman (at least of any consequence) who has ever attempted it. The best French memoirs are writ by such persons as were principal actors in those transactions they pretend to relate, whether of wars or negotiations. Those of Sir W. T. are of the same nature." Hence the necessity of naming himself at every turn—otherwise his narrative would have been like Shakspeare's *Prince of Denmark* the part of Hamlet left out!} This friend and counsellor of St. John and Harley,[6] brought them into power (and, according to Dr. Johnson,[7] dictated public opinion to England), mainly by a pamphlet—*The Conduct of the Allies*—that broke down the Godolphin ministry,[8] supported by that eminent man, Lord Somers,[9] and the wonderful series of Marlborough's[10] victories. The masterly narrative—*The Last Four Years of Queen Anne*, seems to complete Swift's claim to a place in the small category of makers and writers of history.* {It is remarkable that the *Vanity of Human Wishes* has, merely to illustrate the undesirableness of old age, hitched in a couplet the great master of the sword and master of the pen mentioned in the text:

"From Marlborough's eyes the streams of dotage flow,
And Swift expires a driv'ler and a show."}

It was otherwise with very many eminent men of antiquity. Moses and Joshua, among the sacred writers, belonged to the category of great public leaders. Xenophon saved the ten thousand Greeks who were in the expedition of Cyrus, and left us a most graceful narrative of his services. Cato, the censor, drew up the history of the first and second Punic wars, in which he served. Sylla, who passed through unparalleled scenes of blood and horror, found time to write twenty-two *Books of Commentaries*, and those of Caesar, having reached the art of printing, cannot now fail to live forever. Polybius, too, was an actor in many of the scenes we have from his historic pen. Coming down to modern times, France and Germany abound in autobiographies and memoirs (*pour servir à l'histoire*) from the hands of the makers of history—Sully, De Thou, De Retz, St. Simon, Villars, Frederick the Great, the two Segurs (father and son), Gohier, Napoleon, Suchet, Savary, St. Cyr, Chateaubriand, Lamartine, Talleyrand, etc., etc., etc.[11]

If, however, such writers had the great advantage of a personal knowledge of their respective subjects, they were, on the other hand, beset, from the beginning to the end, with some counterbalancing difficulties: 1. The danger of self-neglect, in the way of just praise or of just reproach, and 2. Unworthy partialities and jealousies for or against their co-actors.

"I place my name," says Cardinal de Retz to a friend, "at the head of this work [Memoirs of his own times], in order to lay myself under the strongest obligation not to diminish and not to magnify the truth in anything. Vain-glory and false delicacy are the two rocks which the greater number of those who have written their own lives, have not been able to avoid. President de Thou, in the last generation, steered clear between them, and, among the ancients, Caesar made no miscarriage. You, without doubt, will do me the justice to believe that I would not allege those great names, on an occasion personal to myself, if sincerity were not the sole virtue in which we are permitted—nay commanded—to equal the most illustrious examples."

In Dr. Middleton's Life of Cicero,[12] the embarrassments of that great orator and writer, on a similar occasion, are thus presented:

"In this year, also, Cicero wrote that celebrated letter* to Lucceius, in which he presses him to attempt the history of his transactions. {Epis. Fam. 12} Lucceius was a man of eminent learning and abilities, and had

---

AUTHOR'S INTRODUCTION

just finished the history of the Italic and Marian civil wars; with intent to carry it down through his own times, and, in the general relation, to include, as he had promised, a particular account of Cicero's acts; but Cicero, who was pleased with his style and manner of writing, labors to engage him, in this letter, to postpone the design of his continued history, and enter directly on that separate period, from the beginning of his consulship to his restoration, comprehending Catiline's conspiracy and his own exile.[13] He observes, 'that this short interval was distinguished with such a variety of incidents, and unexpected turns of fortune, as furnished the happiest materials both to the skill of the writer and the entertainment of the reader; that when an author's attention was confined to a single and select subject, he was more capable of adorning it and displaying his talents, than in the wide and diffusive field of general history. But if he did not think the facts themselves worth the pains of adorning, that he would yet allow so much to friendship, to affection, and even to that favor which he had so laudably disclaimed in his prefaces, as not to confine himself scrupulously to the strict laws of history and the rules of truth. That, if he would undertake it, he would supply him with some rough memoirs, or commentaries, for the foundation of his work; if not, that he himself should be forced to do what many had done before him—*write his own life*—a task liable to many exceptions and difficulties; where a man would necessarily be restrained by modesty, on the one hand, or partiality, on the other, either from blaming or praising himself so much as he deserved.'"

Pliny, the younger, another accomplished orator and writer—unwilling to take the risk of portraying himself—also, but in terms rather less unmanly, invoked the historic aid of a friend.

In a letter* to Tacitus,[14] he says: "I strongly presage (and I am persuaded I shall not be deceived) that your histories will be immortal. {Letter 33, Book vii} I ingenuously own, therefore, I so much the more earnestly wish to find a place in them. If we are generally careful to have our persons represented by the best artists, ought we not to desire that our actions may be related and celebrated by an author of your distinguished abilities? In view of this, I acquaint you with the following affair, which, though it cannot have escaped your attention, as it is mentioned in the journals of the public, still I acquaint you with it, that you may be the more sensible how agreeable it will be to me, that this action, greatly heightened by the hazard which attended it, should receive an additional lustre from the testimony of so bright a genius." (Pliny here gives some rough notes of the public transaction in question, with a speech of his which settled the matter, and thus proceeds:) "This short speech was extremely well received by those who were present; as it soon afterward got abroad and was mentioned by everybody with general applause. The late emperor, Nerva (who, though at that time in a private station, yet interested himself in every meritorious action which concerned the public), wrote an admirable letter to me upon the occasion, wherein he not only congratulated me, but the age, which had produced an example so much in the spirit (as he was pleased to call it) of better days. But, whatever the fact be, it is in your power to heighten and spread the lustre of it: though far am I from desiring you would, in the least, exceed the bounds of reality. History ought to be guided by strict truth; and worthy actions require nothing more.

"Happy I deem those to be whom the gods have distinguished with the abilities either of performing such actions as are worthy of being related, or of relating them in a manner worthy of being read; but doubly happy are they who are blessed with both of those uncommon endowments." —Pliny (*to Tacitus*), Book vi., Letter 16.

In general terms, applicable to all *contemporary* history and biography, but, mainly, with special reference to men of letters, Dr. Johnson, in his Life of Addison, finely touches the same difficulties:

"The necessity of complying with times, and of sparing persons, is the great impediment of biography. History may be formed from permanent monuments and records; but lives can only be written from personal knowledge, which is growing every day less, and in a short time is lost forever. What is known can seldom be immediately told; and when it might be told, it is no longer known. The delicate features of the mind, the nice discriminations of character, and the minute peculiarities of conduct, are soon obliterated; and it is surely better that caprice, obstinacy, frolic, and folly, however they might delight in the description, should be silently forgotten, than that, by wanton merriment and unseasonable detection, a pang should be given to a widow, a daughter, a brother, or a friend. As the process of these narratives is now bringing me among my contemporaries, I begin to feel myself 'walking upon ashes under which the fire is not yet extinguished,' and coming to the time of which it will be proper rather to say 'nothing that is false, than all that is true.'"* {In these reserves, Johnson evidently had in view mere authors, not public functionaries—persons taking upon themselves high offices, and, therefore, amenable to historic exposure and censure for great personal defects and miscarriages.}

In the *Edinburgh Review*, January, 1850, on Lamartine's History of the French Revolution of 1848—when a Government was extemporized, with the author at its head—there is a passage so much to my purpose that I cannot resist placing it in this introduction:

"The most valuable materials for the history of great events are undoubtedly afforded by the autobiographies of those who took a distinguished part in them. They perceived the importance of details which a bystander would have neglected. They knew what was proposed and what was decided at secret councils; they can tell us what they themselves did, and, what is often very different, what they intended. Such narratives, however, are comparatively rare: And those which we possess have generally been *written* long after the events—when the recollections of the narrator had lost their first vividness; while their publication is often delayed still longer, until the contemporaries of the writer have passed away,—perhaps until he has passed away himself,—so that much of the restraint, which the liability to denial and exposure would have imposed on his inventions or on his suppressions, has been removed. The memoirs of M. de Talleyrand, for example—which we are only to have twenty years hence, will not be received with the confidence which they would have deserved if they had been published in his lifetime, or even immediately after his death: And one of the great merits of M. de Lamartine's work is its freedom from these objections. It must have been written within a few months of the events which it relates; and is published while almost every other actor in that great drama can protest against its statements or supply its omissions. On the other hand, of course, this proximity has its inconveniences. M. de Lamartine cannot feel as impartially as if his work had treated of times long since passed; or speak as boldly as if it had been intended to be posthumous. In following the course of this narrative, we accordingly often wish for names where we find mere designations, and for details where we find only general statements. Much is obviously concealed from us which it would have been useful to know, but dangerous to tell. Undeserved praise, too, appears to be frequently awarded; and deserved blame to be still more frequently withheld. These objections, however, are far more than counterbalanced by the freshness and vivacity of the narrative: a freshness and vivacity which even as great a poet as M. de Lamartine could not have given to it, if he had written it ten years later."

In all narratives, the art of selecting, rejecting, and grouping incidents, is one of difficult attainment, and if not attained, length, tediousness, and confusion are inevitable. Truth may be lost under a cloud of details and multiplicity of words, as well as by material suppressions and inventions. Indeed, the size of a book, on any given subject, will always be in the inverse ratio of the talent and the pains bestowed upon it. In a brilliant essay on history in general—*Edinburgh Review*, May, 1828* {By Macaulay,[15] but omitted, with others, in his edition of his Essays, London, 1848.}—there are some fine passages on this subject. I can extract but one: "If history were written thus [giving, without judicious selection, all that was done and said] the Bodleian library[16] would not contain the transactions of a week. What is told in the fullest and most accurate annals, bears an infinitely small proportion to what is suppressed. The difference between the copious work of Clarendon and the account of the civil wars in the abridgment of Goldsmith, vanishes, when compared with the immense mass of facts respecting which both are equally silent."

I have drawn up this chart—marked with great names and solemn monitions—to present just characteristics of autobiography for my own guidance—perhaps, condemnation, in case of failure—in the execution of the task (already too long delayed) indicated in the title.

Napoleon, on his abdication, turned to the wrecks of his old battalions about him, and said: "I will write the history of our campaigns." Vindictively recalled from Mexico, but not till the enemy had been crushed and a peace dictated, Napoleon's declaration and memoirs recurred to me, and I resolved, in my humble sphere, to write also.[17] But circumstances (first bad health and next incessant occupations at Washington, etc.) have, till now, suspended my purpose. In the meantime I have carefully abstained from reading a line published on the Mexican campaign, lest I might be provoked to seize the pen before having sufficient strength or leisure for literary composition.

It will be seen that I aspire not to the dignity of a historian, but simply offer contemporary memoirs for the use of some future Prescott or Macaulay; and making no pretension to the gifts and graces of any of the great writers I have cited, I feel myself, on the other hand, to be superior to a few of them, in impartiality, candor, and firmness.

It is comparatively easy to build up a big book—always an evil. It is only necessary to pile line upon line, document on document, Pelion on Ossa[18]—and bulk is obtained. An author's difficulties, both of head and hand, as intimated above, lie in judicious culling and arranging—the *compression* of materials. My labors are now to be commenced, and in trying to fill the outline I have sketched, I hope not to lose myself in verbosity, on the one hand, nor fail to give necessary development to interesting events on the other. As Macaulay has remarked, the Reverend Dr. Nares, professor of modern history in the university of Oxford, has attained the full Brobdignagian dimensions in the Life of Lord Burleigh, Elizabeth's treasurer: two thousand closely printed quarto pages, fifteen hundred inches in cubic measure, and sixty pounds avoirdupois weight! Montesquicu's *Lettres Persanes*, the smallest of books found in libraries, is, perhaps, the more perfect by reason of its smallness. Abounding in wit, humor, and satire, as well as in profound views of morality and politics, it, and Nares's work, though in different paths, are opposite illustrations of the apothegm already quoted.

Undertaking an humbler subject, though one of numerous incidents, I shall attempt the *juste milieu* attained by Voltaire in the Life of Charles XII of Sweden; by Southey in the Life of Nelson, and by Bell in the Life of Canning. To be considered an approach to such models in the single power of compression, would satisfy the ambition of my unpractised hand.

WINFIELD SCOTT.
West Point, N. Y., July 5, 1863.

MEMOIRS, ETC.

CHAPTER I

BIRTH–PARENTAGE–SCHOOLS–COLLEGE

According to the family Bible, I was born June 13, 1786, on the farm which I inherited, some fourteen miles from Petersburg, Virginia. My parents, William Scott and Ann Mason, both natives of the same neighborhood, intermarried in 1780. William's father, a Scotchman, of the clan Buccleuch, was the younger son of a small landed proprietor, and taking part with the Pretender, escaped from the field of Culloden (1746) to Bristol, whence, by the aid of a merchant and kinsman, he was smuggled on board of a ship bound to Virginia, and buried himself in that colony before 1747, the date of the general amnesty.[1]

The fugitive crossed the Atlantic with nothing but a small purse borrowed from his Bristol cousin, and a good stock of Latin, Greek, and Scotch jurisprudence. He had now to study a new code—the English common law; but soon attained considerable eminence at the bar; married late, and, in a year or two, died.

In my sixth year, I lost my father—a gallant lieutenant and captain in the Revolutionary army, and a successful farmer. Happily, my dear mother was spared to me eleven years longer. And if, in my now protracted career, I have achieved anything worthy of being written; anything that my countrymen are likely to honor in the next century—it is from the lessons of that admirable parent that I derived the inspiration.* {I still often recall, with pain, that I once disobeyed my mother—a pain mitigated, however, by the remembrance of the profitable lesson that ensued. Being, on a Sunday morning, in my seventh year, ordered to get ready for church, I, in a freak, ran off and tried to hide myself. Pursued and brought back by a servant, a switch was sent for. Seeing that condign punishment was imminent, and that the instrument was a shoot torn from a Lombardy poplar, the culprit luckily quoted this verse from St. Matthew: "Every tree that bringeth not forth good fruit [should] be hewn down and cast into the fire." The quotation was from the regular lesson I had read to my mother a short time before. The rod was spared; but the pious mother seized the occasion to make her son comprehend that, beginning with the sin of disobedience, I, myself, might soon become a tree fit to be hewn down, etc.} Perhaps filial piety may be excused for adding a few sentences more on the parents and collateral kindred of this lady—the daughter of Daniel Mason and Elizabeth his wife, the only child of John *Winfield,* probably the wealthiest man in the colony. The latter survived his daughter, and dying intestate, about 1774, *Winfield* Mason, the brother of Mrs. Ann Scott, took, by descent, as the law then stood in favor of the eldest male heir, the whole of the landed estate of the grandfather—besides sharing equally in the personal property with his two sisters. I, his namesake, stood nearly from my birth, the principal devisee, in an uncancelled will that I read after my uncle's death, of nearly the whole of that large estate; but marriage and the birth of a child, very properly, abrogate a testament of a prior date; and Winfield Mason, though he married very late in life, left several children. His wife was the daughter of a near neighbor and very remarkable man—*Dr. Greenway,* who well deserves a separate memoir from an abler pen; but of whom it is not known that even the briefest sketch has ever been published, although he has now been dead some seventy years.* {He may be noticed in Barton's *Elements of Botany,* and perhaps by European *savans.*}

His descendants being without ambition or particular distinction, and early dispersed, the sources of a full biography in this case are, probably, forever lost. A rescue from entire oblivion is, however, here attempted upon a boyish memory that has rarely failed; for I perfectly recall the white head and florid face of the doctor as late as 1793, when he must have been fourscore and ten, and in whose library, in the time of the son, I spent many profitable hours. From the family and neighborhood traditions, annotations on books, and unpublished writings—it, however, may be safely said that James Greenway was born just within the English line, on the borders of Scotland, and inherited his father's trade—that of a weaver. Genius, however, stimulated by ambition, is difficult to suppress. The weaver boy, in a free school, over the border, contrived to make himself acquainted with the Greek grammar, and to become a better Latin scholar—languages which, with French and Italian, he cultivated, laboriously, through the greater part of his long life, as was evident from notes on his Homer,[2] Horace,[3] Pliny the naturalist,[4] Rabelais,[5] Dante,[6] etc., etc.—all originals. He early migrated to Virginia, where he wrought at his humble craft while preparing for a license to practise medicine, by which, combined with extensive milling operations, he amassed an ample fortune. His professional reputation brought him patients from a wide circumference, but, as he became rich, he gradually withdrew from the practice of medicine, and gave himself up to the culture of polite literature and natural history, particularly botany, and left a *hortus siccus* of some forty folio volumes, in which all the more interesting plants, etc., of Virginia and North Carolina, were described in classical English and Latin. His success, in that department and others of science, procured for him honorary memberships in several European Societies, and an extensive correspondence with Linnæus,[7] which, with a presented portrait of the great Swedish naturalist, were long preserved in the family library. Confident memory, at this distance of time and place, can add only a few other particulars to illustrate the doctor's great versatility of parts and pride in founding a family.

Living some twenty-odd miles from the nearest market town (Petersburg), no musical teacher could be hired by him. Hence, when the first daughter approached her teens, the doctor, after possessing himself of a guitar and harpsichord (pianos were yet unknown) had first to instruct himself in the use of their strings, which was the less difficult as he was, earlier, a scientific flutist and violinist; next he had to impart the same lesson to that daughter, laying her under the injunction not to marry until she had done as much for the next sister. In this way the whole of a numerous family were made highly musical—the father being the instructer also of the only son in the use of the flute and violin.

My school and college days were marked by no extraordinary success and no particular failure. There was no want of apprehension; but the charms of idleness or pleasure often prevailed over the pride of acquisition. Still, if I were not always the leader of classes, I was never far behind, and, as a summary of my whole life, it may be added, that a certain love of letters—sometimes amounting to a passion—has kept my mind in constant health and in the way of progress. One of my earlier schoolmasters—James Hargrave—a Quaker, labored hard to curb my passions and to mould my character to usefulness and virtue. This was in my twelfth and thirteenth years, at boarding school. It was in defence of this excellent man, of very small stature, that the pupil first discovered, some six years later, that he already possessed a great power of arm; for, turning a corner, at a public gathering, he found the noncombatant, on a charge of running (as county land surveyor) a false dividing line, undergoing a severe handling by a half-drunken bully. A single blow brought him to the ground, stunned, and nearly sobered. Being allowed to rise, he advanced upon his assailant. The Quaker, true to his principles, jumped between, and finding his friend the more belligerent party, seized and so encumbered him, that the bully partially hit him several times, when, by a sudden movement, the Quaker was thrown off and the bully again floored. The noise caused a rush of the crowd to the scene, where learning the original cowardly attack, it cost the Quaker and his pupil their greatest effort to save the bully from further punishment and perhaps death.* {On visiting home after the War of 1812–'15, I met my friend, Hargrave, at the scene of the above affray. The greeting, on one side, was quakerist: "Friend Winfield, I always told thee not to fight; but as thou wouldst fight, I am glad that thou were'nt beaten."}

Another and a more distinguished teacher—*James Ogilvie,* a Scotchman, rich in physical and intellectual gifts—is entitled to notice at the hands of a pupil.

Mr. Ogilvie professed to have a special call to the instruction of youth, and always urged upon his pupils to give two or three years each to the same pursuit on the reciprocal obligation of imparting a great benefit, and for the further reason that no one so thoroughly masters a subject as he who obliges himself to teach it methodically.

His first high school was on the Rappahannock; the last in Richmond. I was a year with him in the latter, just before entering college. Here were taught, besides the ancient classics, rhetoric, Scotch metaphysics, logic, mathematics, and political economy—several of them by lecture. Most of the pupils were approaching manhood; but as too much was attempted within a limited time, by republican short cuts to knowledge, it is feared that all who entered sciolists, left the school without the ballast of learning.

Mr. O., always eccentric, being an opium eater, often exhibited, before the doses became too frequent, phases of preternatural brightness. His last few years in America, before returning home to claim a peerage, were spent as an itinerant lecturer. Though a welcome guest everywhere, he took up collections to defray travelling expenses. He thus declaimed, from a carefully prepared *rostrum,* several brilliant compositions of his own, formed on the model of Cicero, with other illusory accompaniments—the dress, the gestures, the organ swell, and dying fall—of the great Roman orator. They were magnificent specimens of art; only the art was too conspicuous.

The student, now waxing fast into manhood, passed, in 1805, to William and Mary College, where, instead of relying on the superficialities of his high schools, he should have entered years before, and have worked his way regularly through. This blunder has been felt all his life. The branches of knowledge selected for his new studies were chemistry, natural and experimental philosophy, and the common law. These he pursued with some eagerness and success; as also civil and international law—the bar being looked to as a profession, and, at the same time, the usual road to political advancement.

This was the spring tide of infidelity in many parts of Europe and America. At school and college, most bright boys, of that day, affected to regard religion as base superstition, or gross hypocrisy—such was the fashion. Bishop Madison, President of William and Mary College, contributed not a little, within his sphere, by injudicious management, to the prevalent evil.[8] It was his pious care to denounce to the new comers certain writings of Hume, Voltaire, Godwin, Helvetius,[9] etc., etc., then generally in the hands of seniors. These writings the good bishop represented as sirens, made perfectly seductive by the charms of rhetoric. Curiosity was thus excited. Each green youth became impatient to try his strength with so much fascination; to taste the forbidden fruit, and, if necessary, to buy knowledge at whatever cost.

CHAPTER II

LAW STUDIES—THE BAR—TRIAL OF BURR

Being my own master, since the death of my mother, I next transferred myself, in my nineteenth year, from college to the law office, in Petersburg, of David Robinson, Esquire, a very learned scholar and barrister, originally imported from Scotland, as a tutor, by my grandfather. The young man, born a generation too late to come under the ferule of the family pedagogue, was now affectionately claimed as a law pupil* by this veteran of the bar, who, living, down to 1833, in the practice of all the charities of life toward high and low, within his sphere, is likely to have continued to him a great professional longevity by his able reports of the debates in the Virginia Convention on the adoption of the Federal Constitution, and the trial for high treason of ex-Vice-President Aaron Burr. {Mr. Robinson, in my time, had but two other students in his office—Thomas Ruffin and John F. May. The first of these and the autobiographer did not chance to meet from 1806 to 1853, a period of forty-seven years, when Mr. R., Chief Justice of North Carolina, came to New York as a lay member of the General Protestant Episcopal Convention. The greeting between them was boyishly enthusiastic. The chief justice, at the table of the soldier, said: "Friend Scott, it is not a little remarkable, that of the three law students, in the same office, in 1805 and 1806—all yet in good preservation—our friend May has long been at the head of the bar in Southern Virginia; I long at the head of the bench in North Carolina, and you, the youngest, long at the head of the United States Army!" The last that I saw of this most excellent man, always highly conservative, he was a member of the Peace Convention that met in Washington in the spring of 1861. Had his sentiments, the same as Crittenden's, prevailed, we should now (July, 1863) have in the thirty-four States fewer by several millions of widows, orphans, cripples, bankrupts, and deep mourners to sadden the land. Judge May fortunately for him, died before the commencement of this horrid war.}[1]

I had just ridden my first circuit, as an incipient man of law, when, like a vast multitude of others, including the flower of the land, I hastened up to Richmond to witness a scene of the highest interest. Aaron Burr, of the city of New York, a distinguished officer of the Revolution;—

at the bar and in politics, first the rival, and then, in a duel, the murderer of Alexander Hamilton;—an ex-Vice-President of the United States, and, before, an equal competitor with Thomas Jefferson in many anxious ballotings in the House of Representatives for the Presidency—was now to be tried for high treason, and, if found guilty, to receive a traitor's doom. This was the great central figure below the bench. There he stood, in the hands of power, on the brink of danger, as composed, as immovable, as one of Canova's living marbles.[2] Party spirit, out of court, had taken possession of the case, the factions having changed sides. It was President Jefferson who directed and animated the prosecution, and hence every Republican clamored for execution. Of course, the Federalists, forgetting Hamilton—the murdered Hamilton, eminently qualified to be considered great among the greatest of any age or country—compacted themselves on the other side. The counsel for the defence were equal to the great occasion. Luther Martin, a signer of the Declaration of Independence, was, in himself, another Viner's abridgment of the law in twenty folio volumes. The keen, the accomplished John Wickham was always ready with learning, eloquence, wit, logic, or sarcasm, as the case required.[3] Few men ever entered an arena so well armed. Benjamin Botts, just emerging from the provincial bar, also made his mark at this trial.[4] With little gesture, and scarce a figure of speech—conforming to Swift's notion of a good style—"proper words in proper places"—Mr. B. scarcely stood second to anybody in general power. Shrinking from no difficulty, his severe analysis shattered and dissolved the most knarled subjects, and then, with a driving logic, he sent home the main point in debate to the conviction of all hearers. With a fine, manly head, and soft manners in private, there was, when he rose to speak, an imposing solemnity on his brow, and a fearful earnestness of look—such as more recently distinguished the Scotch Presbyterian minister, Edward Irving, in his London Chapel.[5]* {Mr. Botts, the most intrepid of men, perished at the burning of the Richmond theatre, assisting the feeble to escape, Christmas week, 1811.} And yet there was another brilliant star in this forensic galaxy. William Wirt, who in his previous limited circle had not been without briefs and admirers, now stood for the first time on a stage worthy of his genius and ambition.[6] Appointed coadjutor to Mr. Hay, the United States' District Attorney, the burden of the prosecution and the defence of the prosecutor (including the President) became his burdens.[7] The necessities of the case were incessant and great. In the preliminaries of the trial—in the light skirmishing of many weeks which preceded the main shock of battle, he held his own well. Nor did he fail in any part of the trial, though as yet far from that depth in the law and mastery in argument which so greatly distinguished his later career. At every turn and effort, however, he caused himself to be felt and respected; but at certain times, when it was required to call back fugitive attention, in order to another march in the argument, Mr. Wirt could soar, for the moment, high above his subject, and by bursts of rhetoric and fancy captivate all hearers. These quickening passages in his oratory will ever command the admiration of the young; nor can age always find the heart to contemn them.

There were other counsel, on both sides, but of past, or local standing, adding nothing to the aggregate interest of the scene. Not so of many eminent men, spectators from a distance—as Commodore Truxtun,[8] General Eaton, of Derne memory;[9] General Jackson (witness);[10] Washington Irving,[11] etc., etc.* {It was there that I first made the acquaintance of this charming man and distinguished author—an agreeable acquaintance continued through England, France, and America, down to his death.}; besides distinguished Virginians—John Randolph, foreman, and Littleton Waller Tazewell, member, of the grand jury; William B. Giles, John Taylor, of Caroline, etc., etc.[12]

But the interest of the trial, eminent as was the standing of the defendant; eminent as was the forensic talent engaged; brilliant as were the surroundings, and great as were the passions excited—the hatreds, hopes, and fears of party—the interest would have been less than half, but that the majesty of the law was, on the great occasion, nobly represented and sustained by John Marshall, Chief Justice of the United States.[13] His was the master spirit of the scene.

To Congress, at the next meeting, the President submitted the case, that it might be seen, as he said, whether the acquittal of Colonel Burr of high treason was the result of a "defect in the testimony, in the law, or *in the administration of the law.*" The latter was understood to be his opinion. The calm judgment of the bar, however, has now long been, that though the crime had been committed, the prosecution broke down in its legal proofs. This is to be regretted—not that the thirst for blood was not slaked on the occasion; but because, there never having been an execution in the United States for the highest of crimes, our people were, in 1832 and 1861, still untaught a most needful lesson— that *playing at treason is a dangerous game!* Hence, to threaten treason has become an ordinary party device in nominating presidents, and in factious debates even on the floors of Congress; hence, nullification in 1832–'33, and hence the present (1863) mighty rebellion.* {It is a striking fact that three of our ex-Vice-Presidents—Aaron Burr, J. C. Calhoun, and J. C. Breckinridge—became, each in his day, a leader in treason.}[14]

CHAPTER III

CHANGE OF PROFESSION–ADVENTURE AS A VOLUNTEER–RETURN TO THE BAR–ENTERS THE ARMY

It was as a newly fledged lawyer, looking on the trial just described as a fine professional study, that a different career suddenly dawned upon me. In a single night I became a soldier. Burr's trial commenced May 22, 1807. A month later the outrage was committed by the British frigate Leopard, on the United States frigate Chesapeake, in our waters near the capes of Virginia.[1] The whole country was fired with indignation. July 2, President Jefferson issued a proclamation, interdicting the use of our harbors and rivers to all British war vessels. Volunteers were called for to enforce the interdict—that is, to prevent landings to obtain fresh water, provisions, etc. The proclamation reached Richmond late in an evening. I had not before belonged to any military organization; but early the next morning, at the parade of the Petersburg troop of cavalry (which had tendered its services in advance), I was in their ranks, mounted and fully equipped for the field, having travelled twenty-five miles in the night, obtained the uniform of a tall, absent trooper, and bought the extra fine charger under me. From that, my first parade, the troop marched off for the scene of its duties.

The route marches and encampments of volunteers have, unfortunately, become too familiar to hundreds of thousands of our people of the present day, to be worth describing in this place. One incident, however, occurred to me in the expedition, which came very near being of great national importance.

I belonged to a detached camp, in a charming grove, some two miles from Linn Haven Bay, opposite to the anchorage of the British squadron. There lay Sir Thomas Hardy, a favorite of Nelson, with several line-of-battle ships in sullen grandeur.[2] Toward the camp, the coast was studded with downs (*dunes,* sand hills), behind which our small pickets were posted. One of these was commanded by me as *lance* corporal (that is, corporal for the nonce),[3] when, learning one night that an expedition from the squadron had gone up a neighboring creek, I hastened with my guard to intercept its return. At the proper point a charge was made, and the whole crew, two midshipmen and six oarsmen, made prisoners. This was the more easily done, it is true, as they were all unarmed, and by the ebb of the tide the boat could scarcely be pushed through the mud. The picket being relieved, and returning to the pleasant camp next morning, the ex-corporal, jealous as Hotspur of his prisoners, had the exclusive charge of them conceded to him. The midshipmen sat on his right and left at a sylvan table, around which the whole troop—consisting of young lawyers, doctors, and merchants, like so many officers—took their meals and hobnobbed together. Of course, at dinner, extra wine and porter were allowed the corporal for his charge, who, astonished, inquired if all American soldiers lived like gentlemen?

This incident, which gave life to the camp, was regarded as quite an "untoward event" in Washington. The Federalists were numerous and bitter in opposition, and as a republic is never prepared for war, perhaps a little temporizing was necessary. Hence, notwithstanding the long series of British wrongs, capped by the recent outrage, Mr. Jefferson hesitated to take open and direct measures of retaliation. After deliberation and delay, orders came to restore the prisoners to Sir Thomas Hardy, with the imbecile admonition, usual in such cases: *Take care not to do so again.*

In February, 1816, I met, in London, at Lord Holland's hospitable board, one of those midshipmen, then Captain Fox. By his request he was brought up and presented. He began by apologizing for supposing that the major-general before him could be the Corporal Scott whose prisoner he had once been; but added, "the name, height, etc., etc., seem to exclude doubt." On being assured on the subject, a most cordial greeting and intimacy ensued between the parties.

The special outrage on the Chesapeake frigate was now in a train of settlement. The prospect of war seemed at an end, as the smaller wrongs would, it was supposed, follow the course of the greater. The young soldier had heard the bugle and the drum. It was the music that awoke ambition. But the new occupation was gone. He had to fall back on his original profession.

I left Virginia in October, 1807, intending to establish myself in the practice of the law at Charleston, South Carolina. I took Columbia in the way, to petition the Legislature to dispense me from the twelve months' previous residence required of non-native applicants for admission to the bar. The law makers in South Carolina, of 1807, composed the most dignified as well as the most intelligent body of the kind then in the Union. Among these were William Lowndes, the most accomplished statesman, generally, of his day—not merely in wisdom, but also in temper and powers of conciliation.[4] Langdon Cheves was already an able debater, much confided in by the House and his people at home.[5] William Drayton, mild, pensive, persuasive, was high in the law, and philosophy of legislation.[6] Caton Simmons, quite young, with a wide scope of intellect, had ready eloquence and an indomitable spirit. There was also another Lowndes and two Deases—all men of mark; and every member named, with scores of others, conspicuous for good manners, good morals, and, at least, a leaven of genuine chivalry.[7] John C. Calhoun was yet at home, in the early practice of the law.

I spent many weeks agreeably and profitably at Columbia, including the period of that session; but my petition failed from the want of time.

I next made arrangements for in-door practice in Charleston, till time should qualify me to appear in court, and went down to that city in company with, and under the patronage of a friend, a man of very remarkable gifts and virtues, Judge Wilds, a native of the State, yet under forty, and high on the bench.[8] So fine a head and stature have rarely been seen. To genius and learning was added, in his case, a temper sweet as that of a child. He it was who, in sentencing a master that had wilfully killed a slave, to a fine of a hundred pounds, currency—the penalty limited by an old statute,—wept tears of bitterness that he could not substitute the gallows, and threw out such a flood of indignant eloquence against the barbarity of the law, that it was by the next Legislature unanimously repealed. But, alas! "whom the gods love, die young."

I arrived at Charleston Christmas eve, 1807.* {A very few days earlier there came into port two slave ships filled with native Africans, the last that ever were entered at an American custom house, as the trade ceased with the year 1807. The cargoes, promptly landed, appeared to have been well cared for on the ocean, where but few had died. All were fitly clothed, lodged, and fed. A few, wasted by sickness, were placed in an infirmary, but fearing that it was intended to prepare them to be eaten, they starved themselves to death. All believed that they would rise from the grave in their native land. Several Cuban planters, visited on their estates, gave illustrations of a like superstition. One of them, who cultivated sugar on the coast, had a mountain infirmary to which he sent, out of a purchase of some forty new arrivals from Africa, seven adults, men and women, who were in feeble health. Not doubting they were intended for their master's table, all hung themselves the first night. Africans are as fond of jewelry as the *nouveau riche* among ourselves. Thus, a young woman, selected from a cargo, was kindly treated and instructed as their personal servant, by the mother and daughter of another family. Very soon the ingrate pagan stole the ladies' jewels, covered herself with them, and applied the fatal cord, in the firm belief that she would soon revive in her own African paradise, with all the stolen ornaments upon her!} I there learned that the prospect of hostilities with England had, at Washington, flared up again. Only the affair of the Leopard and Chesapeake, as it turned out, had been atoned—leaving the prior British wrongs, and many new cases of the same class, to rankle in the hearts of Americans. Hence it was believed, almost universally, at Charleston, that the embargo on all American shipping, just laid, was but the immediate precursor of a war manifesto on the part of Congress. I, strong in that opinion, promptly abandoned my new law arrangements and embarked for Washington, *via* New York, to seek a commission in some new marching regiment. A bill, indeed, authorizing the trebling of our regular forces, had followed closely the embargo act; but again, after a few weeks of excitement, the advocates of peace at any price seemed to gain the ascendant. In the mean time *the would be a soldier* had been received with favor by the President* and Secretary of War, on presentation by his neighbor and friend, the Hon. William B. Giles, and a captaincy promised, if the augmentation bill should become a law. {On waiting on Mr. Jefferson, we found with him Dr. Mitchell, of New York, and Dr. Walter Jones, of Virginia (two members of Congress), making three incessant talkers.[9] Mr. Giles was also distinguished for his colloquial powers. In a *sitting* of thirty minutes, but two monologues were delivered—the other two personages being in a state of forced silence, but making efforts to get the word. Swift, who, according to Dr. Johnson, though captivated by the attention of steady listeners, always made regular pauses in conversation, for the benefit of interlocutors, has had but few imitators in this politeness. Mr. Jefferson, one of those silenced, at length turned to the autobiographer: "Well young man, what have you seen in Washington? Have you visited the Capitol? Whom have you heard speak?" "I was, sir, in the House yesterday, and heard a part of Barent Gardenier's six hours' speech on the embargo." This was enough. Mr. G., a member from the city of New York, was bitter in opposition, and Mr. J. knew he had handled him with severity in that speech.[10] Suddenly interrupting Mitchell, the colleague of Gardenier, the president said: "Doctor, I have just thought of an object to which to compare the House of Representatives. Sir, it is like the chimneys to our dwellings; it carries off the smoke of party, which might otherwise, stifle the nation." Mr. Jefferson was now in his second term of office, and not a candidate for a third.}

Early in March, 1808, the war party being on the descending scale, and the spring term of the courts of Virginia about to commence, the postponed soldier returned to Petersburg, and began again the same circuit he had made the year before.

The great leader of the Petersburg circuit was, at that day, George Keith Taylor, an ex-judge of a new circuit bench created in February, 1801, and abolished by the Republicans in 1802, the members of which were called *midnight judges,* having been nominated and confirmed within the last hour of Mr. Adams's administration. Judge Taylor, the simplest, the most amiable and benevolent of men, had a giant's strength, both in the halls of justice and legislation, but was always most of a giant on the side of freedom, mercy, charity. He it was, the first in Christendom, who embodied the principles of Beccaria in the criminal code of a state,* and founded a penitentiary, the complement of that enlightened measure; and he it was, himself, a slaveholder, who, in the great suits of the time, brought by slaves for the recovery of freedom, without fee in hand or in expectancy, always stepped forward their honored champion and victor.[11] {Sir Samuel Romilly, in England, published a pamphlet in favor of a like amelioration in 1787, and followed up the subject, in Parliament, from the time he took his seat (in 1806) to his death in 1818. Sir Robert Peel, as Home Secretary, beginning in 1822, caused several bills to be passed which finally effected the object—some twenty-eight years after the amelioration in Virginia. It is worthy of remark that the principle of this reform is urged with great force in the *Rambler,* No. 114, of April, 1751, and Beccaria's book was not published till 1764. Beccaria was himself a periodical essayist, having established the *Caffe,* on the plan of the *Spectator,* at Milan, 1764. Was he a reader of the *Rambler?* The *Rambler* was translated into Italian, under the title of *Il Vagabondo;* but in what year is not ascertained.}

It is due to Virginia, which had slavery forced upon her against her protests, to give a slight sketch of one of those trials. By law: 1. The plaintiffs were permitted to sue *in forma pauperis,* which exempted them from all taxes and fees to the State and the officers of the court. 2. They had to prove that their ancestress, Hannah, was a free woman, in this case an Indian. This was done by several very aged witnesses, who remembered her, and swore that she was always called an Indian, and had the peculiar marks of the race; and 3. That they, the plaintiffs, were the descendants, through females, of that woman. Tradition was allowed to supply this link in the proof of each case. It being established that the ancestress was a free woman, that is, an Indian, and all presumptions in courts are on the side of freedom, the court next devolved on the defendants (masters) the burden of showing that though an Indian, Hannah had been captured in war and sold into slavery, during a certain two years when it was lawful so to deal with prisoners. (Such was the Spanish law for more than two hundred years.) Here the defendants broke down. Let it be added that, besides the counsel for the negroes, the judge, the clerk of the court, the sheriff, and every juryman at the trial, were all slaveholders.

I had a slight connection with this interesting case. My brother held a number of the plaintiffs, his coachman, Frank, being the leader of the whole. On the approach of the trial, I, the guest of my brother at the time, filled up the subpoenas for Frank, who, to serve them and to attend the court, called on his master for a horse, with money to pay expenses, which were furnished. On his success, Frank proposed to remain with his late master, on moderate wages, in consideration of the maintenance of some of the family who could not work, and did remain till death separated them.

I find a most pleasurable emotion in recalling a visit to Judge T.'s bedroom on the circuit, to beg advice on a critical point in a law paper I had in my hand; to remember how readily the fatigued judge, obese and lethargic, stopped his night toilet, and, in the kindest manner—which a life is not long enough to forget—gave all the information needed. And this great and good man also died young—under forty-five.

At length the commission of captain of light, or flying artillery came to me, dated May 3, 1808. I recruited my company in Petersburg and Richmond in the course of a few months, and next was ordered, with it, to Norfolk, to be embarked for New Orleans.

CHAPTER IV

FOUR YEARS' VACILLATION BETWEEN PEACE AND WAR–THE BAR AND THE SWORD

February 4, 1809, I embarked with my company for New Orleans, in a clump of a ship, half rotten, and with a master so ignorant that he did not know of the passage among the Bahama Islands called the *Hole in the Wall*. Hence, we had to sail around the Island of Cuba (nearly doubling the passage), and arrived at the mouth of the Mississippi (the Balize) in thirty-five days, where the ship lost her rudder on the bar. This accident causing a further delay, we did not reach New Orleans till April 1.

The excitement that caused the augmentation of the army the year before, like that which led to the embargo, soon subsided, to rise and fall again and again in the next four years.[1] So great was the calm in the summer of 1809 that I once more turned my mind toward civil pursuits, and sailed for Virginia. Before my resignation had been definitely accepted by the War Department, I heard that grave charges would be brought against me if I dared to return to the army of the Lower Mississippi. This was decisive. At once I resolved to face my accusers. Accordingly, I rejoined the main army, then at Washington, near Natchez, in November.

The army of that day, including its general staff, the three old and the nine new regiments, presented no pleasing aspect. The old officers had, very generally, sunk into either sloth, ignorance, or habits of intemperate drinking. Among the honorable exceptions were: 1. Macomb, who won the battle of Plattsburg, and died, in 1841, a major-general and general-in-chief of the army. 2. Swift, who aided in the general organizing of the new army in 1812, took an active part in the field the next year, and gained the rank of brigadier-general. 3. McRee, of North Carolina, who won the rank of colonel in the field, and died in 1832—an officer of rare merit. 4. Wood, of New York, often distinguished in the field, and brevetted; was killed in the sortie from Fort Erie, September, 1814, after attaining the rank of lieutenant-colonel, with another brevet then due him. 5. Totten, distinguished at Queenstown, October, 1812, and who won the rank of brigadier-general at the siege of Vera Cruz. He is now (1863) twenty-odd years the able chief of his corps. 6. Thayer, now long a colonel, brevetted for distinguished conduct and meritorious services in the War of 1812–'15, who, as superintendent from 1817 to 1833 of the Military Academy, gave development and great excellence to that institution—stamping upon it his own high. character. The foregoing were all engineers. 7. Moses Porter, first distinguished as a sergeant of artillery at Mudfort (afterward Fort Mifflin), and in 1779 and the following campaigns as lieutenant and captain. He died in 1822 a brigadier-general, a rank won by gallant services in the War of 1812–'15, and though deficient in science, yet by his gallantry in front of the enemy, his great practical abilities in the laboratory and workshops, combined with fine soldierly habits and bearing, he made himself invaluable. 8. Colonel Burbeck, to some extent a compeer of Porter in both wars, also a brigadier-general in 1812, and who had much merit of the same general character. 9. Captain (subsequently Brigadier) House. 10. Colonel Bomford, an engineer, but distinguished as an artillerist in the operations of the arsenals and machine shops. 11. Colonel James Gibson, killed in the sortie from Fort Erie. 12. Lieutenant-Colonel Heileman, died at Fort Drane in 1836. 13. Major George Armistead, distinguished in the defence of Fort McHenry (Baltimore) in 1814. 14, 15, 16, and 17. Majors John Sanders, George Peter, and M. P. Lomax, with Captain Samuel Spotts, artillerists, all with merit, more or less. Coming to the old infantry (1st and 2d regiments), but few officers are remembered worthy of particular notice. 18. Pike, then major, was made a brigadier-general in 1813, and soon after fell at the capture of York, Upper Canada, under Major-General Dearborn. 19. Gaines, then a captain, who won, as brigadier, the rank of major-general by the defence of Fort Erie in August, 1814. 20 and 21. William R. Boote, and Ninian Pinkney, who became colonels in the staff in 1813; and 22. William Lawrence, made lieutenant-colonel in 1814, for the defence of Fort Bowyer, on the Mobile.[2] The general staff of the army of that day was small. 23. Colonel A. G. Nicoll was the respectable adjutant and inspector of the army; but, 24. William Linnard, long "military agent," without army rank, and only made quartermaster-general, with the rank of colonel, in 1813, was a public servant of the rarest merit in his way. For thirty-three years he made, at Philadelphia, all disbursements on account of the army (saving the monthly payments to troops), amounting to fifty-odd millions, without the loss of a cent, and at the smallest cost in storage, clerk hire, and other incidental expenses ever known. He personally performed double, if not treble, the amount of ordinary labor. His integrity, at his death in 1835, had long been proverbial. 25. Simeon Knight, paymaster, and who became colonel in 1813, was a good disbursing officer. 26 and 27. Surgeon Dennis Claude, M.D., and Surgeon Oliver H. Spencer, M.D., were eminent in their profession, and highly esteemed generally.[3]

I will not here undertake to dissect, in like manner, the officers who entered the army with me in 1808 (and, of whom my name alone remains, in 1863, on the Army Register). The labor would be great, and the interest to most readers small. It may, however, be safely said that many of the appointments were positively bad, and a majority of the remainder indifferent. Party spirit of that day knew no bounds, and, of course, was blind to policy. Federalists were almost entirely excluded from selection, though great numbers were eager for the field, and in the New England and some other States, there were but very few educated Republicans. Hence the selections from those communities consisted mostly of coarse and ignorant men. In the other States, where there was no lack of educated men in the dominant party, the appointments consisted, generally, of swaggerers, dependants, decayed gentlemen, and others—"fit for nothing else," which always turned out *utterly unfit for any military purpose whatever.* These were the men, who, on the return of peace, became the "unscarred braggarts of the war," a heavy burden to the Government, and, as beggars, to the country. Such were the results of Mr. Jefferson's low estimate of, or rather contempt for, the military character, the consequence of the old hostility between him and the principal officers who achieved our independence. In 1808 the West Point Academy had graduated but few cadets—nearly all of whom are specially mentioned above as meritorious; for a booby sent thither, say at the age of 16, 17, or even 19—and there are many such in every new batch—is, in his term of four years, duly manipulated, and, in most cases, polished, pointed, and sent to a regiment with a head upon his shoulders; whereas, if a booby be at once made a commissioned officer, the odds are great that he will live and die a booby.[4] How infinitely unwise then, in a republic, to trust its safety and honor in battles, in a critical war like that impending over us in 1808, to imbeciles and ignoramuses!* {The officers appointed to the large augmentations of the army in 1812 and 1813, by President Madison, were, from nearly the same reasons, of the same general character. President Lincoln, and Mr. Cameron, Secretary of War, accepting the assistance of experienced officers near them, made, at the beginning of the rebellion, many excellent selections of officers for the new regiments then authorized. President

Jackson, in respect to the 2d Dragoons, raised in his time, and President Polk, in respect to the Rifle Regiment raised in 1846, followed the examples of 1808, 1812, and 1813. To the new regiments organized in the time of President Pierce, many indifferent officers were given.}

It has been stated that I rejoined the army in November, 1809. The officers were divided into two factions. Nearly all old in commission, and a majority of the appointments of 1808, were partisans of Brigadier-General Wilkinson, late commander on the Lower Mississippi.[5] The remainder were the supporters of his successor, Brigadier-General Hampton.[6] Wilkinson was the favorite of the new officers (all Republicans) because, as brother conspirator, he had turned *State's evidence* or "approver," against Burr, and Burr's treason had been prosecuted with zeal at the instance of Mr. Jefferson. Some of these partisans had heard me, in an excited conversation, the preceding summer, just before I sailed for the North, say that I knew, soon after the trial, from my friends, Mr. Randolph and Mr. Tazewell, as well as others, members of the grand jury, who found the bill of indictment against Burr, that nothing but the influence of Mr. Jefferson had saved Wilkinson from being included in the same indictment, and that I believed Wilkinson to have been equally a traitor with Burr. This was in New Orleans, the headquarters of Wilkinson, commanding the department. The expression of that belief was not only imprudent, but, no doubt, *at that time,* blamable; inasmuch as the 6th article of war enacts that "any officer, etc., who shall behave with contempt or disrespect toward his *commanding* officer, shall be punished," etc. But this was not the declaration that was now to be tried, but a similar one, made *after* my return to the army, when Wilkinson, though still in the neighborhood and the "superior," was no longer the "*commanding* officer" (being off duty), but Hampton. Notwithstanding the reasonable distinction between *commanding* and *superior* officer, plainly recognized in the articles of war (see the 9th), and strongly urged in the defence (made without counsel), the court found me guilty of this specification, and pronounced my "conduct unofficer-like"; but not *ungentlemanly,* as was expressly and maliciously charged by the prosecutor. This officer, a violent partisan, who lived and died a reprobate—as a blind, to cover his instigator, trumped up another matter as the leading accusation, viz.: withholding money intended for the payment of the company; and this too was charged under the head of "*conduct unbecoming* an officer and gentleman." The case was simply this: that of some $400 remitted to me as captain for the payment of my company at Richmond, no sufficient receipts, through ignorance of forms, were taken for about $47, although the greater part of this small sum had also been advanced to the individuals to whom it was due, and the remaining insignificant fraction could not be paid over by reason of the intermediate deaths of some two or three of the men. Certainly nothing could have been more irregular than those payments; but the prescribed receipt rolls had not been furnished, and of the whole company, including officers, not an individual had ever been present at a payment, or seen a roll used for the purpose. Moreover, captains are not the paymasters of their respective companies. The duty was wrongfully imposed. A proper paymaster should have been sent with the proper papers.[7] The court found the accused guilty of this specification, and pronounced "his conduct unofficer-like," and sentenced him, on the two findings, to be suspended for twelve months. *"But [it was carefully added] the court have no hesitation in acquitting the accused of all fraudulent intentions in detaining the pay of his men."* And further, the court recommended that nine months of the suspension should be remitted.

Those findings call for two general remarks: 1. The court, in each case, not only omit to add to "conduct unofficer like" the attainting words *"and ungentlemanly"*; but in the only case where corruption or dishonor could have been involved, the court unhesitatingly and expressly acquit the accused of "all fraudulent intentions." Indeed, how could fraud have been intended, or perpetrated? The Treasury charged the captain with the whole sum he receipted for. If he failed to return valid receipts for the whole amount, his pay would at once be stopped to balance the account. The Treasury, therefore, could not be defrauded, nor the unpaid men, as the Treasury would remain their debtor until the next visit of a regular paymaster. The imputation, therefore, was both stupid and malignant. 2. According to the 83d Article of War, any commissioned officer "convicted of conduct unbecoming an officer and a gentleman *shall* be dismissed the service"—leaving the court no discretion.

The earlier treason of Wilkinson, strongly suspected at the time, beginning about 1787, and continued many years after he was the commander of the United States' Army, is now fully established in Charles Gayarré's *History of Louisiana,* under *Spanish domination,* by Wilkinson's own letters, addressed to the governor of Louisiana, found in the archives of Madrid. See the 4th, 5th, 6th, and 7th chapters of the History *passim,* published by Redfield, New York, 1854. And for the manner of obtaining the letters,* see note to page 211. {They were copied under the eye of our minister (Hon. R. Saunders), by Mr. De Gayangos, for the legislature of Louisiana.} Mr. Gayarré was many years Secretary of State of Louisiana, and in 1835 elected to the Senate of the United States, an honor he declined on account of bad health. Wilkinson's object was to separate the whole Western territory from the Union, to be added to the crown of Spain, whose pensioner he was down to 1795. Burr's scheme was a little different, in which Wilkinson undoubtedly participated for a time.

The autobiographer, in 1810, again returned to his home; became domesticated with his invaluable friend, Benjamin Watkins Leigh, of Petersburg, the worthy rival, at the bar, of George Keith Taylor; a distinguished member of the Senate of the United States, and long, before his death, the undisputed head of the law in Virginia. Conservative and moral in the highest degree, this gifted man, son of a distinguished Episcopal minister, and the pupil of another—Neilly Robertson—added to his high collegiate attainments no mean acquaintance with theology. In the evenings of a twelvemonth the parties read aloud to each other, with running comments, principally by the senior, perhaps, every choice passage in English literature. To those readings, and to his conversation and example, I have owed, in every struggle and triumph of life, great and pleasing obligations.

The following letter, which the writer had entirely forgotten till he saw it in print, alludes to this period—the period of his suspension.

From the *National Intelligencer* of February 25, 1855.

"Petersburg, June, 1811.

"DEAR SIR

"I believe we have very little village news to give you, nor do I know what would please you in that way.

"*Of myself*—that personage who fills so large a space in every man's own imagination, and so small a one in the imagination of every other—I can say but little; perhaps less would please you more. Since my return to Virginia, my time has been passed in easy transitions from pleasure to study, from study to pleasure; in my gayety forgetting the student; in the student forgetting my gayety.* {If idle, be not solitary; if solitary, be not idle." An apothegm of Burton paraphrased by Johnson. My early motto.} I have generally been in the office of my friend, Mr. Leigh, though not unmindful of the studies connected with my present profession; but you will easily conceive my military ardor has suffered abatement. Indeed, it is my design, as soon as circumstances will permit, to throw the feather out of my cap and resume it in my hand. Yet, should war come at last, my enthusiasm will be rekindled; *and then, who knows but that I may yet write my history with my sword?*

"Yours, truly,

"WINFIELD SCOTT."

"LEWIS EDWARDS, ESQ., Washington."

Mr. E., a friend, to whom the letter was addressed, a native of Massachusetts, had long resided in Petersburg, and was, in 1811, a principal officer in the War Department. It is understood that his son, a respectable resident of Washington, and for many years a most exemplary Commissioner of Pensions, communicated the original letter to the *National Intelligencer* on the occasion of the writer's promotion to the rank of lieutenant-general.

In the autumn of 1811, I rejoined the army, headquarters, Baton Rouge, by the land route, in a party of five, made up in South Carolina. In the preceding spring two detachments of troops were started—one from Fort Hawkins, on the Ocmulgee, then the Indian frontier, far within Georgia, and the other from Baton Rouge, on the Mississippi, to cut through the intermediate forests a practical wagon, road, to bridge the smaller streams, to construct scows, and to establish ferries (to be kept by Indians) on the rivers. The whole space, up to the eastern line of Louisiana, belonged to, and was occupied by, Creeks, Choctaws, and other Indians, excepting two small settlements of less, together, than a dozen white families, about Fort Stevens and Fort Stoddart, both on the Mobile. The party was a little delayed, near the middle of the route, waiting for the meeting of the two detachments of troops. The wagons of the troops, with a gig and light wagon* belonging to the travellers, were the first wheeled vehicles that ever rolled over that immense tract of country of some six hundred miles in width. {This conveyed the tents, baggage, cooking utensils, and dry provisions of the travellers. Venison and turkeys were obtained by their rifles and purchase from the Indians. Corn (maize) for the horses, was also bought of the latter.}

Crossing the Ocmulgee, the party encamped a day or two near the residence of Colonel Hawkins, an officer of merit in the army of the Revolution, much confided in by General Washington, an ex-member of Congress from North Carolina, under the Constitution, and then Agent of the United States for the Creek Indians.[8] This venerable functionary, with an extensive general library, in that savage country—still cultivating letters and science—did much to introduce schools and the mechanic arts among his red men, by whom he was regarded as a father.

He gave me interesting information respecting the superstitions, laws, and customs of the Creeks—a small part of which, at least, seems worthy of record. In the administration of justice, in both civil and criminal cases, witnesses were sworn by their respective chiefs, to tell, first, all they positively *knew* of the cases under trial, and next to give their *belief* in respect to such particulars as did not directly strike their senses—circumstantial evidence. The chief of each then submitted to the judges (council) from his intimate knowledge of the witness, how much of the testimony, including *belief,* ought to be received, and how much rejected. This system of compurgation and purgation was said to have worked admirably.

But few incidents, worth being remembered, occurred during this tour of my service on the Lower Mississippi. At Baton Rouge, I was appointed special judge advocate for the trial of a commanding officer (a colonel) of considerable ability, for gross negligence under the heads of discipline and administration. He had several times before, by dilatory pleas, defied or baffled justice; but on this occasion was brought to trial, convicted, and censured.[9]

In the winter of 1811–'12, I was, from time to time, a member of Brigadier-General Hampton's staff, the commander of the Southern army, and much in New Orleans. Whilst in the city, there arrived, Christmas eve, from Pittsburg, in a cloud of smoke and steam, spitting fire, the first vessel of the kind that ever stemmed the currents of the mighty Western rivers. This steamer bore the name of a volcano—Etna or Vesuvius. Descending, she scarcely attracted the notice of creoles, except that of a few, who thought her a flatboat, of unusual size, and accidentally on fire. But in a day or two, returning from a trip made to the English Turn, fifteen miles below the city, she aroused the curiosity and fears of the natives on the coast, when all broke off from their Christmas sports, and many on horseback, without saddles, and more on foot, some without hats, flew up to the city, with a "bated breath and hair on end," to learn something of this water monster that could stem a current of six miles an hour without sails, poles, or oars!

The prospect of war being again faint, I spent, about this period, some hours daily, in reviewing my Domat, Pothier, etc., in order to be prepared for the bar of New Orleans, ruled by the civil law.[10] But, early in February (the mails at that time moved very slowly) news arrived that Congress had, January 11, 1812, added twenty-five thousand men to the army. The eyes of all embryo heroes were at once turned upon Washington and the British North American provinces. A declaration of hostilities on our part, however, was still withheld, till, at length, when the time for action seemed, certainly, to be at hand, Brigadier-General Hampton, with two of his suite—Captain Scott and Lieutenant C. K. Gardner (subsequently a staff colonel of considerable abilities in the field and in the bureau)—embarked, May 20, 1812, at New Orleans for Washington, *via* Baltimore. At that season a more stormy and tedious passage, between the two cities, was, probably, never known. But long as it was, it was most fortunate for the ship and passengers, particularly the three army officers, that it was not lengthened two hours more; for, as we entered the capes of Virginia, we had to pass close to a British frigate, lying off and on the bar. Standing on our course, in less than an hour we met a Hampton pilot boat under a cloud of canvas, going out to sea. This was the 20th of June, and that boat, it was subsequently known, was the bearer of despatches from the British Minister (Mr. Mansfield) at Washington, to say that Congress had declared war, two days before, against his country.[11] Of this fact our pilot, shipped far out at sea, was, of course, ignorant; and the master of the Hampton boat, on a trial for treason, was acquitted on the ground that he knew nothing of the war, and nothing of the contents of the despatch he delivered to the frigate.

What a happy escape for me! Had the New Orleans ship been captured, I might, as a prisoner, have chafed and been forgotten, for months—perhaps years—in a British prison!

Off North Point, some sixteen miles from Baltimore, the packet got aground, when, such was the extreme impatience for news, that several passengers, I among them, landed, to walk, or to find our way to the city as we might.

CHAPTER V

WAR DECLARED—DOUBLE PROMOTION— MARCH TO CANADA

At the end of the fourth mile we came upon a stated militia meeting, the commander of which had just received the Declaration of War, the Manifest, etc. Being in half uniform, and fired with the great news, I became the hero of the occasion. Mounted on a table, I was made to read the Declaration of War in the midst of the most enthusiastic shouts and cheers. This earned for me at once the offer of a seat in double gig to Baltimore. But to me, this, the fire day of the war, came very near being also the last; for my new friend, the driver, being drunk with the sentiment of the occasion, or the potations at the sylvan barbacue, overturned the gig twice, each time at the great peril of limbs and necks.

Thanks to my stars and the assumption of the reins, Baltimore was reached, in the dark, June 21, 1812, where I (a captain) was made perfectly happy by learning that a double promotion awaited my arrival at Washington. About the sixth in preparation for the field, among the old officers of the army, and a lieutenant-colonel in rank, at the age of twenty-six, with a hot war before me—seemed to leave nothing to be desired but the continued favor of Providence!

The stay of the travellers was but short in Washington. And here terminated the official connection of a respected friend and commander, with the autobiographer.

Major-General Hampton was a man of mark. Early in life he displayed zeal and enterprise under Sumter and Marion, and is mentioned with distinction in the battle of Eutaw.[1] The outlines of his character were sharp and well defined. In mind vigorous, prompt, intrepid, sagacious; but of irritable nerves; consequently, often harsh, and sometimes unjust; but followed, in every instance, by the acknowledgment of wrong, or the evident signs of contrition and repentance. Toward the humble he frequently made more substantial amends—appropriate benefits—money, clothes, and employments—at the promptings of his own generous nature. Toward the autobiographer, who enjoyed his inmost confidence, he was uniformly kind and considerate. An amusing case of quick temper, on his part, followed by placability, occurred at this visit to Washington.

Immediately preceding there had been quite an unpleasant official correspondence between General Hampton and Dr. Eustis, Secretary of War.[2] Nevertheless, mere coolness between the parties did not absolve the former from the official propriety of calling on the latter. Accordingly, the general, accompanied by me, made an early visit to the War Office. His name was no sooner announced than the Secretary flew to the door, with hand extended, to receive the general. The latter bowed, but to my great surprise, crossed his hands behind him. Nevertheless an official conversation ensued, after the parties were seated in the office, which, successively melted into a pleasant, and then a friendly character. The interview lasted perhaps an hour. The Secretary bowed the general to the door, when the latter turned, and offered both his hands. It was now the Secretary's turn to show a dignified resentment, and, accordingly, he exactly retaliated the crossing of hands behind! But this was now very differently regarded; for Hampton was not disposed to treat the matter as a game of *quits*. A messenger was despatched for General D. R. Williams,* M.C. from South Carolina; pistols were procured, a challenge indited, and everything made ready, on one side, for a deadly combat— if necessary. {It is impossible to name this most excellent man, without adding terms of admiration, love, and respect—notwithstanding a foolish speech (the only one of the sort he ever made) that gave him, for the moment, the sobriquet of "*thunder-and-lightning* Williams."} Dr. Eustis chose, as his friend, on the occasion, Mr. Secretary Hamilton (Navy Department), another South Carolinian.[3] These very judicious friends, looking to the advanced ages of the parties, and the ludicrous character of the quarrel, soon arranged that Hampton should, the next morning, present himself at the War Office door, to be met there by Dr. Eustis, with both hands extended, etc., in the presence of the same spectators—the autobiographer, and the chief clerk of the War Department!

The new lieutenant-colonel was soon ordered to Philadelphia, to collect the companies of the regiment as fast as recruited, and to prepare them for the field. A camp of instruction was formed,—but the recruiting advanced slowly. Early in September the impatience of this officer could wait no longer, and he obtained, by solicitation, orders to proceed to Niagara.

To perverted minds, "big wars make ambition virtue"; but let the lovers of war look upon, after a general action, the dead and the dying on the field, and visit the hospitals. No doubt some wars are necessary, as was that of 1812, on our part; and the constitutional and moral right, on the part of the Federal Union, of putting down the existing rebellion—if deemed expedient—is indisputable. Nevertheless, I cannot but sigh, with Cowper—[4]

> "For a lodge in some vast wilderness,
> Some boundless continuity of shade,
> Where rumor * * * * * *
> Of unsuccessful or successful war,
> Might never reach me more."

Dryden, too, in a dedication to the Duke of Ormond, has expressed a lively abhorrence for "those athletic brutes, whom, undeservedly, we call heroes," and adds—"cursed be the poet who first honored with the name, a mere Ajax—a man-killing idiot."

CHAPTER VI

NIAGARA FRONTIER—CAPTURE OF WAR VESSELS—BATTLE OF QUEENSTOWN— A PRISONER OF WAR—PAROLED

In this temper of mind, the battles and sieges of the following narrative are not likely to be much elaborated; to be written at the charging step or to the sound of the trumpet. How different were the feelings of the young lieutenant-colonel, on reporting to Brigadier-General Alexander Smyth,* near Buffalo, October 4, 1812. {This officer, a native of Ireland, was a respectable member of the southwestern bar of Virginia, when made, in 1808, colonel of the new rifle regiment. He had long been a laborious and useful member of the legislature, and for several years before his death maintained the same character in Congress. As a general, though well read, brave, and honorable, he showed no talent for command, and made himself ridiculous on the Niagara frontier, by his proclamations calling for volunteers. His certificate *on honor,* late in life, that he had discovered the Key to the Apocalypse, was another extraordinary blunder.}

I was sent immediately to cover the temporary yard, behind Squaw Island, a little below Black Rock, where Lieutenant Elliott, of the navy, was fitting up certain lake craft for war purposes.[1] This was the beginning of the squadron that won, under Commodore Perry, the following year, the splendid victory on Lake Erie.[2] In a few days two British war vessels were discovered early one morning at anchor under the guns of Fort Erie, opposite to the harbor of Buffalo. Lieutenant Elliott conceived the idea of capturing them, by surprise and boarding, just before daylight the following morning, and applied to the lieutenant-colonel for a detachment of troops to aid in the enterprise. Captain Nathan Towson, afterward much distinguished, was accordingly detailed for that service, seconded by Adjutant Roach, subsequently mayor of Philadelphia.[3] He (Towson) gallantly carried and saved the *Caledonia,* and Lieutenant Elliott carried the *Detroit,* formerly the United States' Brig *Adams,* surrendered by Hull.[4] There being no wind, the latter vessel was swept by the current down the Niagara, and got aground on the British side of Squaw Island, where she was abandoned by her captors, taken possession of by the enemy, and became the subject of a sharp contest during the day, between detachments of troops from both sides of the river. Finally she was burned by the Americans, as she could not be got afloat. This was a busy day (October 8) with the lieutenant-colonel, both on the island and mainland, and the first time that he was under the fire of the enemy.

Three days later he moved down the river, under orders to report to Major-General Van Rensselaer,[5] the patroon of Albany, who commanded a camp at Lewiston, opposite to Queenstown, of some 1,500 volunteers, and three small detachments of regulars under Lieutenant-Colonels Fenwick and Christie, and Major Mullany.[6]

Late in the evening of the 12th, Lieutenant-Colonel Scott, learning, accidentally, at Schlosser, that a hostile movement was on foot from Lewiston, marched down in the night to claim for his battalion a part in the expedition. He was refused, because all arrangements were made and instructions given, placing Lieutenant-Colonel Van Rensselaer,[7] the chief of the general's staff, at the head of the movement, and I, his senior, would not serve under any junior,* although Fenwick, the senior of the three, had waived his rank. {This refusal was remembered by Colonel Van Rensselaer in the Whig Convention that met at Harrisburg in November, 1839, when Harrison, Clay, and Scott were in nomination for the presidency, and it was also remembered that Scott had, in January, 1838, arrested the colonel's son at Schlosser, while attempting to invade Canada at the head of a body of Americans. The New York delegation would have been unanimous for Scott but for the colonel.} Christie was Scott's junior. As to the battalion of the latter, there were no boats fit for artillery carriages, and, indeed, as it turned out, not enough for the infantry previously designated.

The object of the expedition was to storm the heights of Queenstown, occupied by a small garrison of the 49th British Foot, supported by hosts of Indians, and to hold the same as a door of entrance for the large invading army (of volunteers) that was soon to follow. In crossing, about daylight, the boats had to sustain a direct plunging fire from the battery on the heights, and also the flank fire of several forts near the village, below. Van Rensselaer, badly wounded, scarcely stood on his feet at the point of landing; Fenwick's boat, perforated with shots and half filled with water, drifted to the enemy's shore, when he, desperately wounded, was taken out with a detachment of men prisoners of war. Christie's boat was also maltreated and he slightly wounded in the attempt to cross.* {He, however, subsequently joined Scott, and shared with him the fortunes of the day.} And now it was that Lieutenant-Colonel Scott—whose light batteries, commanded by Captains Towson and Barker,[8] had partially diverted the enemy's fire from our boats—was permitted, at his repeated solicitation, to cross over and take command of our forces in conflict with the enemy. Fortunately, he made the passage, accompanied only by Adjutant Roach, of his battalion, with but little hurt or damage. The heights and battery had been previously carried by detachments of the 6th Infantry, under Captain Machesney; of the 13th, under Captains Wool, Armstrong, Ogilvie, and Malcomb; one of the 23d, under Major Mullany; a company of light artillery, under Captain James Gibson, supported by Lieutenant Thomas B. Randolph, with one six-pounder and some New York militia.[9] Captain Wool had been disabled by a wound, in ascending the heights. Captain J. G. Totten, of the Engineers, was also with the troops, qualified and ready for any duty that might fall to him.[10] It was a little before this time that Major-General Brock, Lieutenant-Governor of Upper Canada, and the Secretary of the Province, Colonel McDonald, fell at the foot of the heights, while gallantly leading up from the mouth of the river a body of York volunteers, with a number of additional Indians.[11]

A pause ensued. The lieutenant-colonel rapidly reconnoitred the heights; took up a position for defence until joined by the great body of the forces remaining in camp at Lewiston; introduced himself and adjutant to his line of battle, and attempted to unspike the guns the enemy had left in the captured battery. While directing the latter operation the enemy's collected forces suddenly drove in our pickets, when regulars, volunteers, and Indians rushed upon our line of battle, which, intimidated, began to face about, and, in a moment would have been in full retreat, but that the lieutenant-colonel, running back from the battery, by storming and a free use of the sword, brought his whole line to face the enemy, and, in a charge, to drive him beyond reach. After, an interval, a second attack was made with a like result. Returning again to the chosen position our forces were reformed, and stood impatiently awaiting the arrival of reënforcements from the other side of the river; for the approach of a fresh column of the enemy from below could be plainly seen, under, as it proved, Brigadier-General Sheaffe, on whom had devolved all the public functions of Brock.[12] The new reënforcement of the enemy being also perceived by Major-General Van Rensselaer, be wrote to our commander on the Canada side: "I have passed through my camp. Not a regiment, not a company is willing to join you. Save yourselves by a retreat, if you can. Boats shall be sent to receive you."

The disgrace of Hull's recent surrender was deeply felt by all Americans. Those on Queenstown Heights, at the instance of their youthful commander, resolved, though with but little hope of success, to sustain the shock of the enemy, when, if beaten, the survivors might still seek an escape by means of the promised boats. The British commander approached with an awful tediousness, evidently supposing the small body in his view to be merely the advance guard of the Americans. At length the conflict came. The firings, on both sides, were deadly, and then followed a partial clash of bayonets. The Americans, by the force of overwhelming numbers were pushed from the heights toward the river, aiding themselves, in the steep descent, by means of brushwood and yielding saplings. One hundred and thirty-nine regulars, out of six hundred that had embarked in the morning, and two hundred and fifty-odd volunteers,* out of four hundred and fifty, reached the margin of the river. {This body of men, under Brigadier-General Wadsworth, supported by Colonel Stranahan, behaved with gallantry throughout the day.[13] When Scott assumed the command he did not know that there was a general officer on the ground. The latter, in plain clothes, modestly made his rank known, and insisted on supporting Scott, which he did, with zeal and valor, in every combat. This Wadsworth (William) and his brother, James, were the great farmers on the Genesee Flats.} Here all were seized with despair. No boats had arrived! Indeed, but a few that were serviceable remained, and General Van Rensselaer could not force nor bribe oarsmen enough, among his men, to take one of them to their forlorn countrymen! A surrender was inevitable. There was no time to lose. The enemy were gradually letting themselves down the precipice, which partially covered the Americans, near enough to render their fire effective.

Two bearers of flags of truce had been despatched in succession to the British commander, but there was no return, and no cessation of hostilities. It was concluded that they had been killed or captured by the Indians. Captains Totten and Gibson each volunteered to make a third attempt, but as to bear a flag had become a forlorn service, Lieutenant-Colonel Scott assumed the duty to himself, and took with him his gallant comrades, Totten and Gibson. Being uncommonly tall and in a splendid uniform, it was thought his chance of being respected by the savages, who were under but little control, the best. The party had to pass down along the margin of the river some hundreds of yards to find an easy ascent. Several shots had been fired at them, before they turned up to the left, when two Indians (Captain Jacobs and young Brant, of whom more in the sequel), after firing, sprang from a covert and seized the party. A deadly combat impended; but a detachment of regulars, headed by an officer, rushed to the rescue, and conducted the flag to the British commander, General Sheaffe. His first and second attempts to stop the Indian fire on the Americans under the precipice proving unsuccessful, Lieutenant-Colonel Scott demanded to be escorted back to his countrymen, that he might share their fate. He was prevailed upon to await another trial, which succeeding, a formal surrender was made on terms honorable to all parties, and the prisoners were put in march for the village of Newark (since Niagara), at the mouth of the river.

Nothing could have been more painful than the position of Major-General Stephen Van Rensselaer during the day of Queenstown.* {But distantly, if at all, related to the colonel, chief of his staff.} A citizen of undoubted patriotism and valor, with a weight of moral character very rare—but without military experience—he found himself helpless in his camp, by the machinations in the ranks of demagogues opposed to the Administration and the war. These vermin, who infest all republics, boastful enough at home, no sooner found themselves in sight of the enemy than they discovered that the militia of the United States could not be constitutionally marched into a foreign country!* {What so perverse and mischievous as party frenzy in a republic! I was made a prisoner at Queenstown, in a lawful and necessary war, because certain militia would not cross the Niagara to my rescue. In the winters of 1837–'8, and 1838–'9, it cost me my utmost exertions, physical and mental, all along the British frontiers, from Lake Huron to Aroostook—to prevent our people from making uninvited, unlawful, and preposterous invasions of the conterminous Provinces.} This pleasant doctrine to the faint hearted, soon found almost universal favor. The pure-minded general took an early opportunity of retiring from the command of such troops.

On reaching the village of Newark, the American officers were lodged in a small inn after being divested of their swords, which were temporarily stacked under the staircase in the entry. A strong guard was at hand, and sentries were posted. In a few minutes a servant said that there were persons at the front door who desired to see *the tall American*. Lieutenant-Colonel Scott, passing through several doors, found, on reaching the entry, that his visitors were the same two Indians met by him some hours before when bearing the flag of truce. Captain Jacobs, one of them, a man of uncommon stature, and power, speaking but little English was interpreted by his companion, young Brant, the life of whose father has been published by the late W. L. Stone, Esq., of New

York, in two volumes, octavo, a valuable contribution, to the history of the *French War,* as called in America, but known in Europe as the *Seven Years' War;*—to the War of American Independence; and to many subsequent wars between the United States and the Northwest Indians, as well as to the last war between the United States and Great Britain.[14]

The professed object of these Indians was to see if they had not in the several combats of the day hit the prisoner before them—each alleging that he had deliberately fired at him three or four times from no great distance. Their design, however, was no doubt sinister. All the surviving Indians were exceedingly exasperated at the severe loss their tribes had just sustained. Jacobs, accordingly, to begin the affray, seized the prisoner rudely by the arm and attempted to turn him round to examine his back. The savage was indignantly thrown against the wall, when both assailants, placing their hands on their knives and hatchets, exclaimed—"We kill you now!" It was an awful moment for the assailed. There was no witness nor help at hand. The sentinel near the door, who had improperly admitted the Indians, was not in view, and perhaps indifferent as to consequences. God and his own stout heart must save the American from instant butchery. With one mighty spring he seized the hilt of a sword with an iron scabbard (easily drawn), then springing back he faced the enemy and occupied the narrow space between the staircase and the opposite wall, but far enough advanced to allow a free use of his sword over the depressed balustrade. In this strong position he could not be attacked by two assailants at once, and he was sure to fell the foremost, though he might be assassinated by the second before he could recover his sword. At this critical moment—the parties standing at bay but in act to strike—Captain Coffin, nephew and aide-de-camp of General Sheaffe, entered to conduct some of the prisoners to the general's quarters where they were invited to dine. The scene spoke for itself. The captain instantly seized Jacobs by the collar with one hand, holding a cocked pistol in the other. Both Indians, with their weapons, now turned upon him, and the American closed in to slay the one left by the pistol. The gallant aide-de-camp had just time to call out—*the guard!* when a sergeant and squad rushed in and marched off the savages as prisoners. It required a strong escort to conduct the dinner guests in safety to and from the general's quarters, for the village swarmed with exasperated Indians.

At table, Lieutenant-Colonel Scott learned from General Sheaffe himself, that he was a native of Boston, the son of a civil *employé* of the crown;—that adopted, when a boy, by Lord Percy (afterward Duke of

Northumberland), then colonel of the 42d Foot, he was sent to England for his education, and that the duke continued his patron through his whole military career. The general added, that although he had never owed allegiance to the United States, yet anxious to avoid engaging in hostilities with Americans, his countrymen by birth, he had early requested to be sent to some other theatre of war. For the Battle of Queenstown he was made a major-general and baronet, and as soon as practicable recalled to Europe.

All volunteer officers and men, among the American prisoners, were paroled and sent home. The regulars of every rank were retained and embarked for Quebec. Before sailing, the remains of General Brock were buried with all the honors of war, in a bastion of Fort George, at the upper edge of Newark. Lieutenant-Colonel Scott, out of respect for the very high character of the deceased, sent over a request to the American fort (Niagara) opposite, to fire minute guns during the British solemnities, and thus there was a long-continued roar of American and British cannon in honor of a fallen hero.

In the following campaign (1813), Fort George was captured by the autobiographer, then colonel, and enlarged, in part, by him, according to a plan of the engineer, Captain Totten. Great care was taken by both not to disturb the bastion in which the remains of General Brock lay interred. A word more, in connection with the foregoing, may, perhaps, be pardoned. So late as 1860, a resident of New Jersey and the Highlands of New York (W. E. Baldwin, Esq.), presented to the autobiographer the identical pistols (as is well established by respectable evidence) that were in General Brock's holsters at the time of his fall. His body, partly under his dead horse, was, for a time, in the possession of the Americans. (Arms of every kind, gorgets,[15] sashes, and spurs are lawful trophies of war.)

CHAPTER VII

KINGSTON–PRESCOTT–MONTREAL– QUEBEC–SAILED FOR HOME–GUT OF CANSO–WASHINGTON

The regular prisoners passed at Kingston from vessels of war to rowboats, and under a strong guard descended the St. Lawrence, marching around the more dangerous rapids.* {A singular rudeness was experienced in passing around the *Long Saut,* on the edge of a Caledonian settlement—all Catholics. Their priest, attracted by the name and rank of Lieutenant-Colonel Scott, reproached him severely as a traitor to George III. Perceiving his sacerdotal character, a condescending explanation and reply was given, without effect. In 1827, Major-General Scott being at Buffalo, on board of a government steamer about to ascend the lakes, her master asked permission to receive in the cabin, for his benefit, a bishop and two priests. It was granted. General Scott at once discovered in the prelate his reviler at the *Long Saut.* Suppressing the discovery he invited the party to his separate table, and did his best to overwhelm the Right Reverend gentleman with hospitality and courtesy—a Christian's revenge.} At Prescott, opposite to Ogdensburg, I was taken into the quarters of the commander of the post, Colonel Pearson, who had just arrived from England.[1] Expecting a night attack by the militia, at Ogdensburg, opposite, the commander slept but little, and that on the prisoner's pallet—two blankets and a cloak, Pearson's own baggage not being up. No one exceeded this gallant officer in courtesy and amiability. To soothe his prisoner, depressed by his condition, and disappointed at not being rescued by the militia at Ogdensburg, he told the story of his own recent capture and noble treatment by an American privateer. On board of a transport ship, with his young wife, he fell in with the ——, Captain ——, and being without heavy guns, surrendered after the first fire. Captain ——, with a party, boarded the prize, when learning that Mrs. Pearson was thrown into a state of premature labor, he placed a sentinel at the cabin door, and left to the colonel an absolute control over all within it—giving such aid as was called for. The colonel was also desired to mark everything that belonged to him, with his name, and assured that all should be held sacred as private property. In sight of an American port, the prize was recaptured and taken to Halifax, where the colonel acquitted himself of the debt of liberality by his conduct to the American prize crew.* {At the Battle of Chippewa, in 1814, Colonel Pearson commanded the right wing of the British army, and subsequently was, as a general officer, Lieutenant-Governor of Gibraltar. He, up to his death, remained the friend of his prisoner (for a night) at Prescott.}

The Queenstown prisoners experienced much courtesy from other British commanders: from the old and infirm Colonel Leftbridge, who was at the head of the guard in the boats down to Montreal; from Major-General Glasgow, the commander of Quebec, a fine old soldier, and others.[2] The remarkable exception was in the Governor-General of the Provinces—Lieutenant-General, Sir George Prevost—who, being of an American family, behaved like a renegade in causing the prisoners to be marched, on their arrival at Montreal, along the front of its garrison, drawn up in line of battle, and by slights and neglects which excited contempt and loathing. As a soldier, he was signally disgraced, subsequently, at Sackett's Harbor and Plattsburg.[3]

A scene occurred, at Quebec, respecting the American prisoners, which led to a correspondence, to legislation, and other results of great national interest and importance. The story, though told in Mansfield's well-written life of the autobiographer, on notes and documents supplied by the latter, is necessarily reproduced in this place, but with some corrections and additions.[4]

The Americans being, November 20, 1812, paroled and embarked for Boston, a commission of several persons came on board, under the instructions of Sir George Prevost to sequester and to retain, as traitors, every prisoner, who, judging by speech or other evidence, might appear to have been born a British subject. Lieutenant-Colonel Scott being engaged in the cabin, heard a commotion on deck, when hurrying up, he found that twenty-odd of his men had already been selected for trial, and all much grieved and alarmed. He instantly stopped further examinations by commanding absolute silence on the part of the prisoners; had an altercation with the commissioners; explained to the sequestered the reciprocal obligation of allegiance and protection; assured them that the United States' Government would not fail to look to their safety, and in case of their punishment, as was threatened, to retaliate amply. Not another man was added to those previously selected, then, nor on any subsequent occasion.

To finish this story without regard to chronology: the lieutenant-colonel arrived at Washington (where he found himself exchanged) in January, 1813, on the evening of a reception at the President's. The warm greeting given him was scarcely over, when he, with some animation, mentioned to the President the case of the sequestered prisoners. Several members of Congress eagerly listened to the narrative, when instructions were given to report the whole case, officially, to the Secretary of War. Hence the following letter, dated January 13, 1813:

*Lieutenant- Colonel Scott to the Secretary of War.** {American State Papers, vol. iii., p. 634, as published under an act of Congress.}

"Sir:

"I think it my duty to lay before the Department that, on the arrival at Quebec of the American prisoners of war surrendered at Queenstown, they were mustered and examined by British officers appointed to that duty, and every native-born of the United Kingdoms of Great Britain and Ireland sequestered, and sent on board a ship of war then in the harbor. The vessel in a few days thereafter sailed for England, with these prisoners on board. Between fifteen and twenty* were thus taken from us, natives of Ireland, several of whom were known by their platoon officers to be naturalized citizens of the United States, and others to have been long residents within the same. {There were, in fact, twenty-three, as stated in the text.} One in particular, whose name has escaped me, besides having complied with all the conditions of our naturalization laws, was represented by his officers to have left a wife and five children, all of them born within the State of New York.

"I distinctly understood, as well from the officers who came on board the prison ship for the above purposes, as from others with whom I remonstrated on this subject, that it was the determination of the British Government, as expressed through Sir George Prevost, to punish every man whom it might subject to its power, found in arms against the British king contrary to his native allegiance."

This report was promptly communicated to Congress, which, followed up by the solicitations of the writer, led to the passage of the act, March 3, 1813, "vesting in the President of the United States the power of retaliation in certain cases."

It so chanced that in a few months the writer of that report, at the capture of Fort George (May 27), made a great number of prisoners, when, as adjutant-general and chief of the staff, with the rank of colonel, he selected and confined an equal number of the captured Englishmen, to abide the fate of the Americans sent to England for trial.

Earl Bathurst to Sir George Prevost. {American State Papers, vol. iii., pp. 640, 641.}

"DOWNING STREET, August 12, 1813.

"Sir:

"I have had the honor of receiving your despatch No. 66, of the 6th of June, enclosing a letter addressed to your excellency by Major-General Dearborn. In this letter it is stated, that the American commissary of prisoners in London, had made it known to his Government that twenty-three soldiers of the 1st, 6th, and 13th regiments of United States infantry, made prisoners, had been sent to England and held in close confinement as British subjects; and that Major-General Dearborn had received instructions from his Government to put into close confinement twenty-three British soldiers, to be kept as hostages for the safe-keeping and restoration, in exchange, of the soldiers of the United States who had been sent, as above stated, to England; and General Dearborn apprises you that, in obedience to these instructions, he had put twenty-three British soldiers in close confinement, to be kept as hostages.

"The persons referred to in this letter were soldiers serving in the American army, taken prisoners at Queenstown, and sent home by you, that they might be disposed of according to the pleasure of His Royal Highness the Prince Regent, they having declared themselves to be British-born subjects. Your excellency has been directed to send home the necessary evidence upon this point, and they are held in custody to undergo a legal trial.

"You will lose no time in communicating to Major-General Dearborn that you have transmitted home a copy of his letter to you, and that you are, in consequence, instructed distinctly to state to him, that you have received the commands of His Royal Highness the Prince Regent, forthwith to put in close confinement forty-six American officers and non-commissioned officers, to be held as hostages for the safe-keeping of the twenty-three British soldiers stated to have been put in close confinement by order of the American Government; and you will at the same time apprise him, that if any of the said British soldiers shall suffer death by reason that the soldiers now under confinement here have been found guilty, and that the known law, not only of Great Britain, but of every independent state under like circumstances, has been in consequence executed, you have been instructed to select out of the

American officers and non-commissioned officers whom you shall have put into close confinement, as many as may double the number of British soldiers who shall so unwarrantably have been put to death, and cause such officers and non-commissioned officers to suffer death immediately.

"And you are further instructed to notify to Major-General Dearborn, that the commanders of His Majesty's fleets and armies on the coasts of America, have received instructions to prosecute the war with unmitigated severity against all cities, towns, and villages, belonging to the United States, and against the inhabitants thereof, if, after this communication shall have been duly made to Major-General Dearborn, and a reasonable time given for its being transmitted to the American Government, that Government shall unhappily not be deterred from putting to death any of the soldiers who now are, or who may hereafter be, kept as hostages, for the purposes stated in the letter from Major-General Dearborn.

"I have the honor to be,
"BATHURST."

The haughty tone of this letter may be accounted for by remembering the disasters of the Russian campaign, in which Napoleon lost by frost in the retreat from Moscow, the flower of his army; to the victories of Wellington in the Peninsula, which opened exhausted France to invasion, and to the assembling, at the moment, of the *élite* of the armies of continental Europe upon Dresden, to give the *coup de grâce* to the falling emperor.

Much of that bitterness of English feeling prevailed, at the time, in one of the American parties. The Honorable Alexander C. Hanson, M.C., from Maryland, in a speech in the House of Representatives, February 14, 1814, after remarking that "the impressment of British seamen from American vessels was the vital point" in the war—next echoed the sentiments of Lord Bathurst, thus:

*"Mr. Chairman—upon this question of impressment, allegiance, protection, and naturalization, which has been connected with it, gentlemen here may fret, rail, and argue, until doomsday. {Carpenter's Select American Speeches, vol. ii., pp. 425–431.} They may set up new-fangled doctrines, and deny old and established principles, but as far as depends on the opinions of the ablest jurists, and the practice of the oldest regular governments, the point in controversy is long ago settled. It is immutably determined.

[Here he cited "the fundamental maxim of the law of England"—"perpetual allegiance"—"once a subject, always a subject."]

"Now, sir," continued Mr. Hanson, "I am prepared to go a step farther than has been deemed necessary from the actual case presented to our consideration. I say, that an Englishman, naturalized or not by our laws, if found in arms against his native country, is a *traitor* by the laws of his native country. I do not confine the position to British subjects naturalized here, and made captives within the dominions of their sovereign, where the arm of protection cannot be extended; but, if the armies of the enemy crossed the line, and invaded us in turn, and made prisoner a Briton found in, arms against Britain, he is as much a traitor as if taken a prisoner in the heart of the British empire.

"Such men are *traitors* in the legal, true sense of the word, and ought to be treated as such. The good of society and the safety of government require it. If, to protect them, we resort to a bloody, ferocious, exterminating system of retaliation, we shed the innocent blood of our own countrymen.

"I say, then, without reserve, if the President proceeds in the ruthless, bloody business he has commenced, he is answerable, here and hereafter, for all the American lives wantonly sacrificed. Posterity will pronounce him guilty, and heap maledictions upon his name.
* * * "When the party contests of the day are forgotten; when the passions engendered by political strife have subsided; when reason shall resume her throne, and the present generation is swept into the silent tomb, those who live after us will pronounce a judgment upon the chief actors in this tragedy of blood and murder."

These were dire denunciations of "the chief actors in [the] tragedy of blood and murder." Yet Major-General Scott, "the head and front of [that] offending"—when in the act of embarking at New York, for Europe, July 9, 1815, had the happiness to meet on a pier, in the East River, just from an English prison, twenty-one of the identical men taken from him at Quebec—the other two having died natural deaths! It was thus, and not by any subsequent diplomacy of the American Department of State, as has sometimes been claimed, that Great Britain was forced to yield the principle, "once her subject, always her subject"—on which the soldiers were seized, and hundreds of sailors impressed, out of American ships.

November 20, 1812, Lieutenant-Colonel Scott, with the remainder of the regular prisoners taken with him at Queenstown, sailed from Quebec for Boston, at the beginning of a snow storm. Such were the known dangers in the navigation of the Gulf of St. Lawrence at that late season, that the ship could not have been insured at a premium of less than fifty percent of her value. This cartel (British ship) was, however, staunch and well commanded. After being blown about at the mercy of a succession of gales, she, at the end of twenty-three days, entered the Gut of Canso—a natural canal, separating Nova Scotia from the Isle of Cape Breton—and came to anchor in a cove of the latter. Both shores were mountainous and uninhabited for an indefinite distance, except a single farmhouse in a small valley, opposite to the cove and near the water. This was occupied by Mr. Pain, a second Robinson Crusoe. He had sailed from Boston in a smack for the banks of Newfoundland and other fishing grounds, in 1774, before the outbreak of the Revolution. Having made up the cargo in the Gut of Canso, Pain begged his companions to let him remain till the return of the party the following season. They assisted in building him a hut, and left with him a good supply of personal and bed clothes, some axes and other tools, a gun, with ammunition, fishing tackle, and such other stores as could be spared—together with a Bible, "Paradise Lost," and "The Pilgrim's Progress." Prayers were said at parting, and the smack sailed for home. This was the last that our adventurer saw of "the human face divine," till the end of nine or ten years. The Revolutionary War supervened. There was no more fishing and curing of fish by Americans on those shores—the Gut of Canso at that period not being navigated except by vessels driven into it by stress of weather. There was no road and no trail across the mountains to any settlement whatever.

For the first year, and, indeed, till his supplies began to fail him, Mr. Pain, then young, did not lament his condition. But when the second and third seasons came, and again and again there was no return of his friends, it seemed evident they had abandoned him, his spirits drooped, and he was in danger of being lost in despair. Like Alexander Selkirk in similar circumstances, he might have exclaimed:[5]

> "I am monarch of all I survey,
> My right there is none to dispute;
> From the centre all round to the sea,
> I am lord of the fowl and the brute.
>
> "O solitude! where are the charms,
> That sages have seen in thy face.
> Better dwell in the midst of alarms,
> Than reign in this horrible place.

"I am out of humanity's reach,
I must finish my journey alone,
Never hear the sweet music of speech—
I start at the sound of my own.

"The beasts that roam over the plain,
My form with indifference see;
They are so unacquainted with man,
Their tameness is shocking to me."

But man is the most flexible and pliable of all animals. According to his own account, Mr. Pain soon learned to relish food without salt; the moose deer and fleecy goat were abundant, furnishing him with both food and raiment, and which he contrived to entrap after his powder and shot were exhausted. So, too, in respect to wornout hooks and lines: these were replaced by bones and slips of skins, so that there was no want of the "finny prey."[6] By the fifth year he began to like this new life as well as at first. His books were more than a solace to him, and the autobiographer can testify that he could accurately recite, from memory, entire chapters of the Bible, and many of the books of "Paradise Lost." Finally, when, at the end of the war, his old master in a smack came in search of him or his remains, he had become so attached to this new mode of existence that he refused to return to his native soil. A good supply of necessaries was again left with him. His little property at home was invested in cattle, with materials for a small house, some furniture, etc.—all of which were sent out to him, with an old sister, a farm laborer, and a lad—a relative. Before 1812, some new connections and laborers had joined him, and he had become a thrifty farmer.* {It is not known that any memoir or notice of this interesting adventurer has ever been published.}

The provisions for the paroled soldiers, by the neglect of the British commissariat, proved to be bad. The salt beef and pork had become rusty, and the bread worm-eaten. This food had been on board, perhaps, a twelvemonth, and a part of the time in a hot climate. The scurvy soon appeared among the soldiers. Lieutenant-Colonel Scott threw in his personal stores (fresh beef, bread, onions, and potatoes), too small a stock to produce much benefit. But a fine ox, some sheep, and a hundred bushels of potatoes, bought of Farmer Pain, proved a godsend, stopping the disease at once.

CHAPTER VIII

COLONEL AND ADJUTANT-GENERAL— FORT GEORGE—OGDENSBURG—HOOP-POLE CREEK—FRENCH MILLS

It has already been stated that Lieutenant-Colonel Scott, on arriving at Washington in January, 1813, found himself exchanged. After a short interval, he was ordered to Philadelphia to take command of another battalion of his regiment (a double one—twenty companies) then nearly ready for the field. In the month of March he was appointed adjutant-general, with the rank of colonel, and promoted to the colonelcy of his regiment about the same time. He continued to hold the two commissions for several months, occasionally quitting the staff for hours or a day to command his own and other troops in battles, skirmishes, and forrays. With his battalion he had joined the army under the command of Major-General Dearborn, on the Niagara frontier, early in May, and, as the chief of his staff, first organized the service among all the staff departments, several of which were new and others unknown in the United States since the Revolutionary War. In this labor he was greatly aided by an early edition of Théibault's *Manuel Général du Service des États-Majors Généraux,* etc.[1]

The first general movement of this army had for its object, by the capture of Fort George, to make the left bank of the Niagara the basis of further operations. That work, on the river side, had been much damaged, May 26, by the batteries of Captains Towson and Archer (of Scott's regiment) at Youngstown, opposite.[2] Accordingly, on the next day, an embarkation commenced from a creek three miles east of the Niagara, some time before daylight. Colonel Scott led the advance guard or forlorn hope, composed of a battalion of his own regiment acting as grenadiers, and a smaller one, under Lieutenant-Colonel McFeely[3] of the 22d Infantry, and was followed by field batteries under Colonel Moses Porter; Boyd's, Chandler's, and Winder's brigades,[4] and a rear guard (or reserve) under Colonel Macomb—making a force of about four thousand seven hundred men. The point of descent was the lake shore, a half mile (or more) west of the mouth of the river. Commodore Chauncey's fleet stood in as near as practicable, and by its fire, kept the enemy, under Brigadier-General Vincent, back a little, till the Americans, when near the shore, became a shield against that fire.[5]

The wind was fresh and the surf high. Captain Perry,[6] an old friend of Scott, who, from Lake Erie, had joined Chauncey as a volunteer, for the day, kindly took Scott in his gig and piloted the boats of the advance guard through the surf and the brisk fire of the enemy. The beach was narrow and the bank precipitous—from seven to eleven feet high, affording, generally, but slight foothold to climbers. The first attempt at ascent was repulsed by the bayonet, and Scott, among others, tumbled backward. Major-General Dearborn, a fine old soldier, saw, from the fleet, the fall, and honored the supposed loss of the chief of his staff with a tear. At the second attempt the bank was scaled—with a loss of every fifth man killed or wounded; the line of battle was reformed, and a furious charge made that drove more than twice the number of the enemy out of sight. This could not have been done but for the intimidation caused by the fleet of rowboats seen following in Scott's wake. Porter and Boyd soon landed. Not a horse accompanied the expedition; but Scott, mounted on the charger of a colonel, a prisoner, had, in pursuing the enemy, to thread the village circumspectly, which gave time for Colonel Miller of the 6th Infantry (Boyd's brigade) to unite with the advance.[7] Passing Fort George, now untenable and still under the fire of the American batteries at Youngstown, two fugitives were observed who had just escaped from the fort. Scott, singly, charged and made them throw down their arms. They informed him that nearly all the garrison had, fifteen minutes before, joined the enemy's retreat up the river, and that the few men remaining were spiking the guns and applying slow matches to the bastion magazines. Desirous to save these, he ordered that Captains Hindman and Stockton's companies (of his own regiment) should join him at the fort, and that the remainder of the column should continue the pursuit.[8] At his near approach, one of the magazines exploded. Horse and rider being both struck by splinters, the latter was thrown to the ground, with a broken collar bone and some bruises. Nevertheless, aided by his two prisoners—the detachment from the column being nearly up—Scott was the first to enter the fort. The last of the garrison escaped at the same moment. Hindman and Stockton flew to the two unexploded magazines just in time to pluck away the burning matches, while Scott took the colors with his own hands.* {The down-haul halliard of the colors had been shot away by the opposite batteries.

Hence the retreating garrison had nearly cut down the flagstaff, when obliged to fly, leaving the axe in position. With this in his hand Scott soon brought to the ground the coveted trophy.}

In a moment he was again in the saddle, and rejoined his pursuing column already in the midst of the enemy's stragglers. Opposite to the Five Mile Meadow (that distance from the mouth of the river) Scott met Colonel Burn (his senior colonel), who had just crossed over with a troop of his Light Dragoons.[9] Another troop was approaching in boats, and Scott agreed to wait for it, as Burn conceded to him the command. This enabled Brigadier-General Boyd personally to overtake and order the whole pursuing force back to Fort George, against the remonstrances of Scott, who assured him (as he had replied to a like order previously received from Major-General Lewis)[10] that, with the reënforcement of the Light Dragoons, he could capture the disorganized army then less than a mile ahead of him. Boyd, acting under instructions, insisted on an immediate return! And thus terminated the battle of Fort George, May 27, 1813.* {Early in the pursuit (near the lake) Scott came up with a wounded colonel, just made a prisoner, and after giving directions for his safety and comfort, borrowed the charger before mentioned. Calling to restore the property, and to provide for his wants, the Englishman handsomely observed: "We have reversed our relative positions of the last autumn. Allow me, in the way of apology, to say that you can now see the Falls of Niagara in all their splendor"—alluding to what he had said to Scott when the latter was the prisoner, viz.: that Scott, who had said something on the subject—must win a great battle before he could have that enjoyment. This sarcastic remark was sharply rebuked at the time, both by the offended party and the British general, Sheaffe, at whose table it was made.}

Colonel Scott now limited himself mainly to his staff duties. The disaster of the 6th of June, at Stony Creek, resulting in the capture of the American generals, Chandler and Winder, though the enemy was repulsed, caused Major-General Dearborn to send up his second in rank, Lewis, with Scott, to that headless army*—a renewed attack upon it being imminent. {This extraordinary result irresistibly brings to mind the siege of Cremona in 1702. Prince Eugene, by a singular stratagem, entered that city in the night, at the head of a competent force; but was finally driven out by the gallant French garrison, without other loss than that of their commander, Marshal Duc de Villeroi, who being captured and secured at the very entrance of the Austrians, gave the garrison its triumph. Madame de Staël, on the subject of Russian despotism, wittily said it was tempered and checked by the salutary practice of assassination—applied to odious czars. So among the French, before the Revolution, with their keen perception of the witty and the ludicrous: a *bon-mot, a jeu d'esprit,* anonymously circulated, often rebuked and held in defiance the meditated designs and absolutism of the court. Villeroi, the foster-brother and only acknowledged favorite Louis XIV ever had, was made to feel this power, when laid on the shelf and rendered harmless for a time by the following epigram:

> *"Français, rendez grâce à Bellone.*
> *Votre bonheur est sans égal;*
> *Vous avez conservé Crémone*
> *Et perdu votre général."*

Winder's was a hard fate, both at Stony Creek and (next year) at Bladensburg. With the elements of a good soldier, he, like Colonel Drayton, though poor, sacrificed to patriotism an extensive law practice, which was not recovered after the war. It is a misfortune to begin a new career with too much rank, or rather, too late in life.}

On the capture of Chandler and Winder, letters came down from that army to headquarters, at Fort George, requesting that Colonel Scott might be sent up to command it. But as he arrived with a major-general (Lewis) and a retreat was soon ordered from below, the general cry was heard—*Scott to the rear guard!* That post of honor was given him, and the march of forty-odd miles, though flanked by hostile Indians on one side, and by the British fleet on the other, was uninterrupted.

Another disaster to our arms soon followed. Colonel Boerstler, June 23, 1813, was detached with some six hundred men, of all arms, to attack a post at the Beaver Dams, near Queenstown, on the road thence to the head of Lake Ontario.[11] The same day the whole of this force, falling into an ambuscade, was captured.

These misadventures deeply affected the health and spirits of Major-General Dearborn—who, before, had been much disordered by the lake fever. An order of recall soon reached him from the War Department. The officers of his army, remembering his high moral worth, his patriotism, valor, and military distinction at Bunker Hill, Quebec, Monmouth, Yorktown, etc., etc., deeply sympathized with their venerable chief, and requested Colonel Scott to be, at the moment of separation, the organ of their sentiments. A short, emphatic valedictory did much to soothe a wounded heart.

Major-General Lewis having been previously sent to Sackett's Harbor, the command on the Niagara basis now devolved on Brigadier-General Boyd—courteous, amiable, and respectable, as a subordinate; but vacillating and imbecile, beyond all endurance, as a chief under high responsibilities. Fortunately, the British general-in-chief, then Major-General de Rottenburg,[12] and his second, Vincent, were equally wanting in enterprise and execution. The Secretary of War, General Armstrong, a great military critic and judge of character, instructed Boyd to intrench his army, and not to seek a conflict, but await the arrival of Major-General Wilkinson* from New Orleans. {The selection of this unprincipled imbecile was not the blunder of Secretary Armstrong. Wilkinson, whose orders were dated March 10, 1813, contrived not to reach Fort George till the 4th of September!}

Thus the army of Niagara, never less than four thousand strong, stood fixed, in a state of ignominy for some two months, under Boyd, within five miles of an unintrenched enemy with never more than three thousand five hundred men!

This long inactivity was slightly enlivened by two night demonstrations of the enemy, in which some of the American pickets were driven in; by one affair between Indians of the opposing armies, and by a dozen or more skirmishes, growing out of foraging operations, several of which turned out rather serious affairs. In most of these, Scott, without always seeking the service, either commanded originally, or was, at the first shot, sent out with reënforcements, when, by seniority, the command devolved upon him. Fortunately, though always attacked, he never lost a prisoner or a wagon, and always returned with a loaded train. These successes in *la petite guerre* came near fixing upon him the character of a partisan officer, whereas it was his ambition to conduct sieges and command in open fields, serried lines, and columns.

It is not remembered that the American friendly Indians were allowed to take part in that war except on the one occasion alluded to above. A little while before his recall, Major-General Dearborn assembled, in council, the Seneca and other Indian chiefs, residing near Buffalo, when they were invited to furnish a few hundred auxiliaries in the existing campaign, to serve the purposes of watching the legions of British Indians, of interpreting their movements and intentions, and specially to prevail upon them to return to their native wilds—leaving the white belligerents, alone, to kill each other in the settlement of their own peculiar quarrel. Scott opened the council on the part of the general, and was replied to by Red Jacket—the great orator as well as warrior among the red men.[13] He was perfectly ready for all enterprises of hazard promising distinction; but the sarcastic heathen—all the other principal chiefs were Christians—could not forbear, interpreting the invitation in his own way—*help us to beat the British*—producing a contradictory letter from General Dearborn, written early in 1812, as Secretary of War, in which neutrality, in the approaching hostilities, was strictly enjoined on the part of all American Indians. Nevertheless, the auxiliaries under the *Farmer's Brother,* the venerable head chief; Pollard, the leader of the Christian party;[14] and Red Jacket, the leader of the heathens, all promptly joined the army at Fort George. They contrived several interviews with many chiefs of the British Indians; but failed to persuade them to a pacific course. The Farmer's Brother,[15] in the name of all his people, then solicited permission, before returning home, to attack one of the hostile Indian camps a little distance apart from the British regulars. This was granted, though the Americans, intrenched, were now under the injunction to stand on the defensive; and Scott, as adjutant-general, was desired to instruct the Indians not to kill prisoners, and not to scalp the dead. Pollard and the other Christians readily acquiesced, and demanded cords and strings for tying their captives. Red Jacket and his pagan followers asked to be similarly prepared for success, when all set forward in high spirits, and to the great amusement, of the army. A battalion of infantry had been advanced halfway to the enemy's camp, some three miles off, to serve as a shield and support, in case the gallant assailants should be repulsed and hotly pursued. Passing the battalion, the Indians—not understanding injunctions *not* to fight, in time of war! called out—*Come along; what! are you afraid?* Conceive the deep humiliation; for the commander of the support was the distinguished Major William Cumming—brave, intellectual, and of sensibilities almost morbid.

In the American camp, all were on the tiptoe of anxiety and expectation; but soon sharp cracks of rifles were heard, followed by a more painful silence. There was not an officer, nor a man who would not have been happy, if permitted, to rush out of the entrenchments to support his red friends. In thirty minutes, however, shouts of triumph began to approach nearer and nearer. The enemy's (Indian) camp had been surprised, many of his red men killed or wounded, and sixteen made prisoners. When these were seen, each closely pinioned and led by a string, the novel spectacle produced such roars of delight as to be heard from camp to camp.

Finding his position at headquarters, for the reasons already given, disgusting, Scott, about midsummer, resigned his adjutant-generalcy, and limited himself to the command of troops—his own regiment and others.

Early in September it was determined to make a joint expedition against Burlington Heights, in rear of the British army, where it was supposed would be found large magazines of *matériel* and other important stores, guarded by a limited force; and Scott, with a competent detachment, was embarked on board of Commodore Chauncey's fleet for their capture. A landing and search were made, but nothing of value was there. It being now certain that the enemy's grand *depôt* of supplies was at York (Toronto), the capital of Upper Canada—captured and evacuated by General Dearborn in the preceding April—Chauncey and Scott resolved to make a second descent upon that place. The latter, with the land troops and marines, debarked and drove out the garrison after a sharp encounter—the fortifications had not been renewed; and formed a cordon of pickets and sentinels, while the commodore emptied the public storehouses of their abundant contents. Learning that there were many political offenders confined in the jail, Scott caused them (some were Americans) to be sent on board the fleet; but gave special instructions to leave all felons—persons charged with offences against morals—to abide their fate.

On reëmbarking, he learned that some of the sailors had brought off from the public storehouses a few trunks, belonging to British officers— the contents of which—uniforms, etc., he now saw flaunting about the decks. Causing the broken and emptied trunks to be brought to him, he found left in one, marked with the name of General Sheaffe—a mass of public and private papers. The latter, unread, were carefully separated, and sent to the British headquarters. A sailor, who witnessed the investigation, showed the colonel the miniature of a beautiful lady, set in gold, taken out of another trunk that had upon it the name of Lieutenant-Colonel Harvey. It was concluded that this must be the likeness of the lieutenant-colonel's young bride. Colonel Scott bought it of the sympathizing sailor for a small sum, and sent it to the gallant husband, with Sheaffe's private papers.* {It was Harvey that surprised and captured Chandler and Winder at Stony Creek, in June. Scott was personally acquainted with him. Each, as chief of the staff, in his own army, was the correspondent of the other on the official business common to their commanders. In that way they had personally met with escorts, and under flags of truce. The intimacy thus formed was turned to a good account (in 1839), as will be seen in the sequel.}

On the arrival of Major-General Wilkinson at Fort George, September 4, 1813, Scott, as an official obligation, called upon him and gave assurance that he should continue to execute, with zeal and alacrity, all duties that might be assigned to him. In less than a month (October 2) Wilkinson and nearly the whole regular force on the Niagara moved down Lake Ontario in the further prosecution of the campaign. Scott was left in command of Fort George, with some seven hundred regulars, and a detachment of Colonel Swift's regiment of militia.[16] One entire side of the fort—then undergoing an extension—was still perfectly open. The enemy—remaining in undiminished force, within five miles, and whom Wilkinson had declined to attack—could not be ignorant of the weakness of Scott's position. An early assault seemed, therefore, inevitable. Each officer (including the commander) and man worked upon the defences from fourteen to twenty hours a day. By the fourth night, however, so great had been the progress of these labors, that all became anxious for an attack. (The following official reports, taken from *American State Papers—Military Affairs,* pp. 482, 483, will carry forward the narrative as far as relates to the autobiographer.)

From Colonel Winfield Scott, of the 2d Artillery, to Major-General Wilkinson.
"Fort George, October 11, 1813.

"Within the last five minutes I have had the honor to receive your despatch by the *Lady of the Lake,* Captain Mix.

"The enemy has treated me with neglect. He continued in his old position until Saturday last (the 9th inst.), when he took up his retreat on Burlington Heights, and *has abandoned the whole peninsula.* Two causes are assigned for this precipitate movement—the succor of Proctor, who is reported to be entirely defeated, if not taken; the other, the safety of Kingston, endangered by your movement.

"We have had from the enemy many deserters, most of whom concur in the latter supposition.

"The British burnt everything in store in this neighborhood;—three thousand blankets, many hundred stand of arms; also the blankets in the men's packs, and every article of clothing not in actual use.

"They are supposed to have reached Burlington Heights last evening, from the rate of their march the night before. I have information of their having passed 'the 40'* by several inhabitants who have come down. {Forty Mile Creek—that distance from Niagara.} They add to what was stated by the deserters, that two officers of the 41st had joined General Vincent from Proctor's army, with information that Proctor was defeated eighteen miles this side of Malden. I cannot get particulars.

"From the same sources of intelligence it appears that the 49th, a part of the 100th, and the Voltigeurs, moved from this neighborhood the day after our flotilla left this, the 3d inst.; but with what destination is not certainly known.[17]

"It was first reported (I mean in the British camp) that these regiments had marched to support Proctor, who, it is said, wrote that he would be compelled to surrender, if not supported.* {Proctor was defeated, and the British and Indian force in the north west routed, on the 5th of October, 1813. The rumor which Scott speaks of was six days after the event, and was no doubt brought in either by officers or Indians from the defeated army.}

"I am pretty sure, however, that they are gone below. The movement of our army seems to have been known in the British lines as early as the 3d inst., together with the immediate objects in view: hence I have no difficulty in concluding that all the movements of the enemy will concentrate at Kingston.

* * * * "I had made this morning an arrangement, on application to General McClure, to be relieved in the command of this post, on the morning of the 13th inst., with an intention of taking up my line of march for Sackett's Harbor, according to the discretion allowed me in the instructions I had the honor to receive from you at this place.[18] My situation has become truly insupportable, without the possibility of an attack at this post, and without the possibility of reaching you in time to share in the glory of impending operations below. I am, however, flattered with the assurance that transports will be forwarded for my removal; and to favor that impression, I propose taking up my line of march on the morning of the 13th for the mouth of Genesee River, and there await the arrival of the vessels you are good enough to promise me. By this movement Captain Mix thinks with me, that I shall hasten my arrival at Sackett's Harbor five, possibly ten days. Captain Camp* (the quartermaster) has a sufficient number of wagons to take me thither. {Colonel J. G. Camp, a distinguished officer in the campaign of 1814, on the Niagara.}[19] I can easily make that place by the evening of the 15th. I hope I shall have your approbation, and everything is arranged with Brigadier McClure. * * * * I have, by working night and day, greatly improved the defences of this post, and nearly filled up the idea of the engineer. I flatter myself that I have also improved the garrison in discipline." * * * *

Wilkinson's abortive campaign ended, Scott was called to Washington for a day or two.

Extracts of a Letter from Colonel Winfield Scott to the Secretary of War.
"GEORGETOWN, December 31, 1813.

"At your desire, I have the honor to make the following report:—I left Fort George on the 13th of October last, by order of Major-General Wilkinson with the whole of the regular troops of the garrison, and was relieved by Brigadier-General McClure,* with a body of the New York detached militia. {On the approach of the enemy, McClure evacuated the fort and burnt the adjoining village—then Newark, now Niagara. This soon led to the devastation of that entire frontier, including Buffalo. So prone are men to imitate evil examples!}

"Fort George, as a field work, might be considered as complete at that period. It was garnished with ten pieces of artillery (which number might easily have been increased from the spare ordnance of the opposite fort), and with an ample supply of ammunition, etc., as the enclosed receipt for those articles will exhibit.

"Fort Niagara, on the 14th of October, was under the immediate command of Captain Leonard of the 1st artillery, who, besides his own company, had Captain Read's of the same regiment, together with such of General McClure's brigade as had refused to cross the river. Lieutenant-Colonels Fleming, Bloom, and Dobbins, of the militia, had successively been in command of this fort, by order of the brigadier-general, but I think neither of these was present at the above period.[20] Major-General Wilkinson, in his order to me for the removal of the regular troops on that frontier, excepted the two companies of the 1st artillery, then at Fort Niagara. And under the supposition that I should meet water transportation for my detachment at the mouth of Genesee River, I had his orders to take with me the whole of the convalescents left in the different hospitals by the regiments which had accompanied him. This order I complied with."

Notwithstanding Chauncey's promise to send transports to the Niagara, and Wilkinson's, to the mouth of the Genesee, Scott, on arriving at the latter, found only the despatch vessel, *The Lady of the Lake,* with a letter from the commodore saying that, contrary to his entreaties, Wilkinson would not allow any part of the fleet to be absent four days without throwing the responsibility, in case of a failure of his expedition wholly on the navy. Hence Scott was forced to continue his march upon Sackett's Harbor, *via* Canandaigua, Utica, Booneville, etc. The rainy season bad commenced, and the bad roads were daily becoming worse. Fortunately he met north of Utica the Secretary of War, General

Armstrong, returning from Sackett's Harbor, who had seen Wilkinson depart thence for Montreal; but thinking that Scott, by leaving his column under the next in rank (Hindman),[21] and striking off to the right, *via* Malone, might intercept the descent—gave the colonel permission to make the attempt. Riding diligently for some thirty hours, with his adjutant Jonathan Kearsley—who early won the rank of major by distinguished gallantry, but so maimed as to be thrown out of the field—Scott struck the river at Waddington many miles below Ogdensburg where Wilkinson, with his usual dilatoriness, had been making preparations to pass the enemy's fort—Wellington—opposite. After a short sleep and change of horses, Scott was again in the saddle, and reported himself at headquarters November the 6th, just in time to pass the enemy's fire in the headmost and largest craft in the whole flotilla. The scene was most sublime. The roar of cannon was unremitting, and darkness rendered visible by the whizzing and bursting of shells and Congreve rockets.[22]

The next day Scott was assigned to a fine battalion of grenadiers, in the *corps d' élite,* under the senior colonel, Macomb, who was in the advance, and thus the former became the commander of the advance of that corps—which placed him in the lead of the whole army. Hastening to his position he found the grenadiers in boats and pushing off shore. He had but time to leap aboard, when, being recognized, loud cheers welcomed the new commander.

The first object was to take Fort Matilda, that commanded the narrowest point in the St. Lawrence. Scott landed about sunset a little above the work, and was there met by a detachment of the enemy that proved to be the garrison of Matilda—believed, by them, to be untenable. A sharp affair ensued. The advance made some prisoners, among them an officer; killed or wounded many men, and dispersed the remainder.

Descending the river the advance had, on the 11th of November a more serious affair at Hooppole Creek, a little above Cornwall. Here were met, under Lieutenant-Colonel Dennis, an officer of merit, a force equal to Scott's (about eight hundred men) in position to defend the bridge.[23] Leaving Captain McPherson with a light field battery—other troops were coming up—to amuse the enemy, Scott stole a march of nearly a mile to the left, and forded the creek which, making an acute angle with the river below, gave the hope of hemming in and capturing the whole of the enemy.[24] Dennis discovered the movement in time to save by a precipitate retreat the main body of his men. The rear, however, was cut off, and many stragglers picked up in a hot pursuit that was continued into the night.

This affair, and the disaster at Chrystler's Field, fifteen miles in the rear, occurred the same day, and were the principal conflicts of Wilkinson's famous campaign—begun in boastings, and ended in deep humiliation![25] Montreal was still within the easy grasp of half the troops disgraced by their commanders at Chrystler's Field; but the fatuity of the general-in-chief (and of others) made success almost impossible. The army, in disgust, retreated out of Canada; ascended the Salmon River, and passed the winter at The French Mills—since called Fort Covington—in latitude 45°.

CHAPTER IX

REFLECTIONS ON PAST DISASTERS–CALLED TO WASHINGTON–BUFFALO–CAMP OF INSTRUCTION–CAMPAIGN OF 1814 OPENED

The patriot reader, stirred with indignation at the deplorable loss of national character, life, and property sustained by Hull's surrender; the surprise of Chandler at Stony Creek; the capture of Boerstler at the Beaver Dams; the abandonment of Fort George, by McClure; the vacillation and helplessness of at least three generals and many colonels in the disaster of Chrystler's—will ask, at every turn: What! Shall not fatuity, incapacity, ignorance, imbecility—call it as you may—in a commander—of whatever rank—be equally punished with cowardice, or giving aid and comfort to the enemy?[1] Shall a dull man, who ascertains that he can get a little money in the army—not having the ability to earn his bread at home—and, accordingly, obtains a commission? Shall a coxcomb, who merely wants a splendid uniform to gratify his peacock vanity—be allowed unnecessarily to lose his men by hundreds, or by thousands, to surrender them in mass, or to cause them to be beaten by inferior numbers;—shall such imbeciles escape ignominious punishment? In every such case, Humanity—as loudly as Justice—calls for death.

In the *Analectic Magazine* (Philadelphia) for December, 1814, there is a "Biographical Sketch of Major-General Scott," signed V.—understood to be the distinguished scholar and statesman—the Honorable Gulian C. Verplanck—containing reflections of great beauty, force, and value on the same campaign.[2] The writer says:

"From whatever cause it proceeded, individual bravery and enterprise had been uniformly rendered abortive by a long series of delays and blunders. The patriot, who, regardless of party considerations, looked solely to the national honor and welfare, still continued to turn away his eyes from the northern frontier—'heartsick of his country's shame.' Even the most zealous partisans of the measures of the administration did not dare to do justice to the numerous examples of prowess and conduct which had been displayed in our armies in the course of the campaign of 1813. It was scarcely suspected by the public, that this period of disaster had served as a touchstone on which the true temper of our army had been thoroughly tried, so that it had now become easy to select the pure metal from the dross; that in this hard school of adversity many brave and high-spirited young men had been formed into accomplished officers, and, on the other hand, many an empty, fop, young and old, who had been seduced into the service by the glitter of epaulets and lace, and military buttons, had been severely taught his incompetency. The rude northern gales of the frontier had swept away the painted insects which rise and spread their wings in the summer sun, but served only to rouse and invigorate those eagle spirits who, during the calm, cower undisturbed in solitude and silence, but as the tempest rises burst forth from their obscurity, and stem the storm, and sport themselves in the gale."

Early in 1813, the great contest on Lake Ontario commenced between the ship carpenters at Kingston, under Sir James Yeo, and the ship carpenters, under Commodore Chauncey, at Sacketts Harbor.[3] He that launched the last ship sailed in triumph up and down the lake, while his opponent lay snug, but not inactive, in harbor. This was (say) Chauncey's week of glory. Sir James's was sure to follow, and Chauncey, in turn, had to chafe in harbor, while preparing another launch for recovering the mastery of the lake. This contest might have been continued, without the possibility of a battle for an indefinite time. It did not end with 1814; for the treaty of peace (February, 1815) found on the stocks, at Sacketts Harbor, two mammoth ships—the Chippewa and New Orleans—pierced for more than a hundred guns each, only waiting for a thaw; and Sir James Yeo was always ready to match launch with launch.

Thus the two naval *heroes of defeat* held each other a little more than at arms-length—neither being willing to risk a battle without a decided superiority in guns and men; and if Wilkinson complained of the non-capture of the British fleet, Chauncey was ready with the retort that Wilkinson ought first to deprive that fleet of its safe refuge by taking Kingston. In fact, in the plan of operations prescribed to Wilkinson the capture of Kingston was suggested as an early object of attention. Wilkinson, however, as we have seen, preferred to take Montreal! Here then was found, in this extraordinary campaign, more than one case of (seeming) matchless imbecility, well matched.

This war was not sprung upon the United States by surprise. From time to time, and for years, wrong upon wrong had plainly admonished that base submission or resistance *à outrance* was inevitable, and the weaker party had the choice of time. Yet there was but slight augmentation of the land and naval forces, even under such powerful inducements, and no system of finance established. Loans, it is true, were authorized; but no adequate means provided for interest and redemption. Hence, from the beginning to the end of hostilities, there was a want of money and men. Indeed, seven tenths of the moneyed capital of the land were in the hands of the war's bitterest opponents. With money, men might have been obtained, and with men, victories would have inspired confidence, and thus the cupidity of capitalists allured. Hence it was that our fifty-odd regular regiments were mostly skeletons (scarcely one ever half full) during the war, and we always in our triumphs, attacked or defended with inferior numbers, except in a few instances, when equality was made up by raw volunteers or militia—oftener an element of weakness than of strength. This was extremely discouraging to commanders, like Scott, whose rank, zeal, and efficiency threw them into the front of every movement.

It has been seen that Colonel Scott, about the end of the year 1813, was called to Washington by desire of the President. He had had only three interviews with him and Mr. Secretary Armstrong,[4] when a deputation from Western New York, headed by the Hon. John Nicholas, of Geneva (ex-M.C. from Virginia)[5] arrived, to demand that Scott might be sent to make head against the enemy on the Niagara frontier, which had just been devastated by Major-General Riall,[6] in retaliation (as alleged) for McClure's burning the village of Newark. Riall having, by a rapid movement, dismayed and scattered the militia from Lake Ontario to Lake Erie almost without firing a gun, it was not known how far he might extend his triumphant march into the interior. For a time the alarm extended as far east as Geneva and Canandaigua. Scott was hastily despatched accordingly; but instructed to stop a moment at Albany, in order to make requisitions upon the Governor for fresh levies of militia; to prepare field trains, with ammunition, etc., etc., for his new mission, and in order that the appointment of brigadier-general might overtake him, as, without promotion, he could not command any militia general officer. But it was soon known at Washington that the enemy had quietly recrossed the Niagara, and as the War Department wished about this time to make a number of new generals at once, Scott's promotion was made to wait for the selection of the other names. In the mean time he continued to assist in the Albany arsenal in the preparation of the *matériel* of war for the impending campaign, under the valuable instructions of Colonel Bomford, who was well skilled in such operations.[7]

At this dark period of the war, Albany, rather than Washington, was the watchtower of the nation, and here Scott, during this hindrance on the route to Canada, was, by the desire of the President, and their cordial reception, in frequent consultation—on high political and military matters—with those distinguished statesmen and patriots—Governor Tompkins and Judges Spencer and Thompson—ever afterward his special friends.[8] Two other eminent citizens—Messieurs Jenkins and Bloodgood[9]—were often present, and indeed it was at the board of some one of the five—all hospitable—that these confidential interviews were usually held. In the North Judge Spencer was, truly, very like Judge Spencer Roane in the South the master spirit of the war;—a man that never doubted, when duty called, or shirked an opinion.[10] With him, it was but a word and a blow. "*Down with that man!* a poltroon, a traitor." "*Up with this man!* the country needs his services." And the result was, very generally, in accordance with the *dictum*.

It may be mentioned, in this connection, that the late ex-President Van Buren—then just emerging into distinction, a State senator and adjunct counsel in the prosecution of Hull, before a general court martial—now began to make time, from the labors of the Senate and the bar, to mix a little in the reunions alluded to. He ably supported the war, and had the confidence of all its friends.

Finally, about the middle of March, 1814, Scott received, at the age of twenty-seven and nine months, the long-coveted rank of brigadier-general.[11] His preparations had been made in advance, and the next morning he was in the saddle for where

"Niagara stuns with thundering sound."

Major-General Brown,[12] appointed to command the entire frontier of New York, had marched some days earlier from the French Mills for the same destination, with the 9th, 11th, 21st, 22d, 23d, and 25th regiments of infantry (not one of them half full); several field batteries and a troop of light dragoons. Scott joined him some miles east of Buffalo, March 24, 1814. Brigadier-General Ripley,[13] Scott's junior, was with those troops.

The major-general, though full of zeal and vigor, was not a technical soldier: that is, knew but little of organization, tactics, police, etc., etc. He, therefore, charged Scott with the establishment of a camp of instruction at Buffalo, and the preparation of the army for the field by the reopening of the season.[14] In the mean time—and while waiting for the recruits (which, never came) to fill up the regiments—Major-General Brown returned to the right wing of his department—then called *District,* No. 9—headquarters, Sackett's Harbor.

The spring, in the region of Buffalo, is, till late in May, inclement, and March quite wintry. No time, however, was lost; the camp was formed on very eligible ground; the infantry thrown into first and second brigades—the latter under Ripley, and the service of outposts, night patrols, guards, and sentinels organized; a system of sanitary police, including kitchens, etc., laid down; rules of civility, etiquette, courtesy—the indispensable outworks of subordination—prescribed and enforced, and the tactical instruction of each arm commenced. Nothing but night or a heavy fall of snow or rain was allowed to interrupt these exercises on the ground—to the extent, in tolerable weather, of ten hours a day, for three months. As relaxation, both officers and men were thus brought to sigh for orders to beat up the enemy's quarters; but the commander knew that such work could not be effectually done without the most laborious preparation. His own labors were heavy and incessant. Take for illustration *infantry tactics;* the basis of instruction for cavalry and artillery as well. As Government had provided no text book Brigadier-General Scott adopted, for the army of the Niagara, the French system, of which he had a copy in the original, and there was in camp another, in English—a bad translation.[15] He began by forming the officers of all grades, indiscriminately into squads, and personally instructed them in the schools of the soldier and company. They then were allowed to instruct squads and companies of their own men—a whole field of them under the eye of the general at once, who, in passing, took successively many companies in hand, each for a time. So, too, on the formation of battalions; he instructed each an hour or two a day for many days, and afterward carefully superintended their instruction by the respective field officers. There was not an old officer in the two brigades of infantry. Still, if the new appointments had been furnished with a text book, the saving of time and labor would have been immense.

The brigadier-general's labors were about the same in respect to lessons on subjects alluded to above, other than tactics (measures of safety to a camp, near the enemy; police, etiquette, etc.). No book of general regulations or *Military Institutes,* had been provided.

This great want he had to supply orally and by written orders. (It will be seen that text books on all the foregoing subjects were subsequently prepared and published by the autobiographer.) The *evolutions of the line,* or the harmonious movements of many battalions in one or more lines, with a reserve—on the same principle that many companies are manoeuvred together in the same battalion, and with the same ease and exactness—were next daily exhibited for the first time by an American army, and to the great delight of the troops themselves, who now began to perceive why they had been made to fag so long at the drill of the soldier, the company, and the battalion. Confidence, the dawn of victory, inspired the whole line.

Toward the end of June, 1814, Major-General Brown returned from the right to the left wing of his district, to open the campaign on the Niagara, though it had become rather the expectation, if not the desire of the War Department, that that service should be left to Scott, the immediate commander. The regiments from the failure to obtain recruits, were still but skeletons. Their high instruction on all points of duty won for them, however, the major-general's admiration.

With a view to the *prestige* of the day, Scott rather wished to make the descent on our national anniversary; but Brown's impatience being equal to his vigor, we anticipated a day, although the means of passing the foot of Lake Erie to attack the fort of that name opposite to Buffalo, were not all quite in position. For the preparation of those means, the army was indebted to the extraordinary zeal and abilities of its quartermaster, Captain John G. Camp, who, with other high claims to promotion, continued the chief in that branch of the staff throughout the campaign, without other reward than compliments.* {He was disbanded in 1815; made and lost fortunes in Buffalo and Sandusky; was several years Marshal in Florida, and died in 1860.}

Scott, with his brigade led, followed by Major Hindman's artillery, Brigadier-General Ripley's brigade of regulars, and Brigadier-General P. B. Porter's brigade of militia;[16] Ripley was ordered to land above the fort.[17] Scott, in the first boat, with some one hundred and fifty men and accompanied by his staff—Captain Camp, the quartermaster (a volunteer for the nonce), and Lieutenants Gerard D. Smith, W. J. Worth, and George Watts—steered for the shore, a little below the point of attack.[18] The place of landing proved to be a cove, swept by a whirlpool. The night (about 2 o'clock A.M.) was rather dark; but the enemy, perceiving the approach, planted a detachment to oppose the landing. Near the shore, when the enemy's fire began to be a little galling upon the crowd in the boats, Scott had a most critical adventure. Sounding with his sword, he found the water less than knee deep, when personally leaping out, instead of giving the command—*follow me!* had scarcely time to exclaim—*too deep!* to save hundreds from drowning; for, at the instant, before leaping, his boat had taken a wide sheer, and he had to swim for his life, equally in jeopardy from fire and water—encumbered with sword, epaulets, cloak, and high boots. It was a minute or two, still under fire, before the boat could be brought back to pick him up. Again the first in the water, and promptly followed by detachments of his brigade, the shore was cleared at once, and the fort invested below just as the other troops were landing.

The fort, like its garrison, being weak, and no known succor at hand, a formidable resistance could not be offered. Some heavy pieces of artillery were placed in battery and a few shots exchanged, when the major-general asked Scott to name an officer to bear, under a flag of truce, his demand for a surrender. Major Jesup, of Scott's brigade, was selected for this honorable service, and articles of capitulation were soon agreed upon.[19]

CHAPTER X

RUNNING FIGHT–CHIPPEWA

The night had been rainy; but a bright sun cheered the invaders on the morning of the glorious Fourth of July. To seek the enemy below, Scott was early detached with his brigade—the 25th Infantry, commanded by Major T. S. Jesup; the 9th by Major H. Leavenworth,[1] and the 11th by Major J. McNiel,[2] together with Captain S. D. Harris's troop of light dragoons,[3] and the light batteries under Major Hindman, of Captains N. Towson and Thomas Biddle[4] of Scott's late regiment of artillery.

Early in the march, a little above Blackrock, a considerable body of the enemy was discovered. It proved to be a corps of observation under the command of the Marquess of Tweedale.[5] All hearts leaped with joy at the chance of doing something worthy of the anniversary, and to cheer our desponding countrymen at home—something that might ever, on that returning day—

"Be in their flowing cups, freshly remembered."

The events of the day, however, proved most tantalizing. An eager pursuit of sixteen miles ensued. The heat and dust were scarcely bearable; but not a man flagged. All felt that immortal fame lay within reach. The enemy, however, had the start in the race by many minutes; but his escape was only insured by a number of sluggish creeks in the way, each with an ordinary bridge, and too much mud and water to be forded near its mouth. The floors of those bridges were, in succession, thrown off by the marquess, but he was never allowed time to destroy the sleepers. Taking up positions, however, to retard the relaying the planks, obliged Scott to deploy a part of his column and to open batteries. The first bridge, forced in that way, the chase was renewed, and so was the contest at two other bridges, precisely in the manner of the first and with the same results. Finally, toward sunset, the enemy were driven across the Chippewa River behind a strong *tête de pont,* where they met their main army under Major-General Riall.

This running fight, of some twelve hours, was remarkable in one circumstance: in the campaigns of the autobiographer, it was the first and only time that he ever found himself at the head of a force superior to that of the enemy in his front: their relative numbers being, on this occasion, about as four to three.

The Marquess of Tweedale, a gallant soldier, on a visit to the United States soon after peace, made several complimentary allusions to the prowess of our troops in the war, and particularly to the events of the 4th of July, 1814, on the Niagara—among them, that he could not account for the impetuosity of the Americans, in that pursuit, till a late hour, when some one called out—*it is their National Anniversary!** {Scott passing through London, in 1815, to Paris, met the Marquess of Tweedale in the street, when the parties kindly recognized each other. The latter was on the point of setting out for Scotland, and the former for France. Scott was assured of a welcome at Yester House, the seat of the marquess, if he should visit Scotland. This meeting soon became strangely misrepresented, on both sides of the Atlantic, to the great annoyance of the parties.}

The proximity of Riall reversed the strength of the antagonists, and Scott, unpursued, fell back a little more than a mile, to take up a strong camp behind Street's Creek, to await the arrival of the reserve under Major-General Brown. The junction took place early in the morning of the 5th.

Brown lost no time in giving orders to prepare the materials for throwing a bridge across the Chippewa, some little distance above the village and the enemy at its mouth. (There was no travelling *pontoon* with the army.) That work was put under the charge of our able engineers, McRee and Wood—the wise counsellors of the general-in-chief.[6] This was the labor of the day. In the mean time the British militia and Indians filled the wood to our left and annoyed the pickets posted in its edge. Porter's militia were ordered to dislodge the enemy, and much skirmishing ensued between the parties.

The anniversary dinner cooked for Scott's brigade, with many extras added by him in honor of the day, happily came over from Schlosser[7] on the 5th, and was soon despatched by officers and men, who had scarcely broken fast in thirty-odd hours.

To keep his men in breath, he had ordered a parade for grand evolutions in the cool of the afternoon. For this purpose there was below the creek, a plain extending back from the Niagara of some hundreds of yards in the broader part, and a third narrower lower down. From the dinner, without expecting a battle, though fully prepared for one, Scott marched for this field. The view below from his camp was obstructed by the brushwood that fringed the creek; but when arrived near the bridge at its mouth, be met Major-General Brown, coming in at full gallop, who, in passing, said with emphasis: *You will have a battle!* and, without halting, pushed on to the rear to put Ripley's brigade in motion—supposing that Scott was perfectly aware of the near approach of the entire British army and going out expressly to meet it. The head of his (Scott's) column had scarcely entered the bridge before it was met by a fire, at an easy distance, from nine field guns. Towson's battery quickly responded with some effect. The column of our infantry, greatly elongated by the diminution of front, to enable it to pass the narrow bridge, steadily advanced, though with some loss, and battalion after battalion when over, formed line to the left and front, under the continued fire of the enemy's battery. When Scott was seen approaching the bridge, General Riall, who had dispersed twice his numbers the winter before, in his expedition on the American side, said: *It is nothing but a body of Buffalo militia!* But when the bridge was passed in fine style, under his heavy fire of artillery, he added with an oath: *Why, these are regulars!* The gray coats at first deceived him, which Scott was obliged to accept, there being no blue cloth in the country. (In compliment to the battle of Chippewa, our military cadets have worn gray coats ever since.)[8] Two hostile lines were now in view of each other, but a little beyond the effective range of musketry.

It has been seen, that the model American brigade, notwithstanding the excessive vigor and prowess exerted the day before, had failed in the ardent desire to engraft its name, by a decisive victory, on the great national anniversary. The same corps again confronting the enemy, but in an open field, Scott, riding rapidly along the line, threw out a few short sentences—among them, alluding to the day before, was this: *Let us make a new anniversary for ourselves!* Not finding his name in the official paper (Gazette) after his handsome services at the capture of Bastia and Calvi, early in his career, Nelson with the spirit of divination upon him, said: "Never mind; I will have a Gazette of my own."[9] A little arrogance, near the enemy, when an officer is ready to suit the action to the word, may be pardoned by his countrymen. And it has often happened, if not always, when Fourths of July have fallen on Sundays, that Chippewa has been remembered at the celebrations of Independence on the 5th of July.

The brigade had scarcely been fully deployed, when it was perceived that it was outflanked by the enemy on the plain, besides the invisible force that had just driven Porter and the militia out of the wood. Critical manoeuvring became necessary on the part of Scott; for the position and intentions of Brown, with Ripley and Porter, were, and remained entirely unknown to him till the battle was over. The enemy continuing to advance, presented a new right flank on the widened plain, leaving his right wing in the wood which Scott had caused to be confronted by Jesup's battalion, the 25th Infantry, which leaped the fence, checked, and soon pushed the enemy toward the rear. At the same time having ordered that the right wing of the consolidated battalion (9th and 22d Infantry) commanded by Leavenworth, should be thrown forward, with Towson's battery on the extreme right, close to the Niagara, Scott flew to McNiel's battalion, the 11th Infantry, now on the left, and assisted in throwing forward its left wing. The battalions of Leavenworth and McNiel thus formed, pointed to an obtuse angle in the centre of the plain, with a wide interval between them, that made up for deficiency of numbers. To fire, each party had halted more than once, at which the Americans had the more deadly aim. At an approximation to within sixty or seventy paces, the final charge (mutual) was commenced. The enemy soon came within the obliqued battalions of Leavenworth and McNiel. Towson's fire was effective from the beginning. At the last moment, blinded by thick smoke, he was about to lose his most effective discharge, when Scott, on a tall charger, perceiving that the enemy had come within the last range of the battery, caused a change that enfiladed many files of the opposing flank. The clash of bayonets, at each extremity, instantly followed, when the wings of the enemy being outflanked, and to some extent doubled upon, were mouldered away like a rope of sand. It is not in human nature that a conflict like this should last many seconds. The enemy's whole force broke in quick succession and fled, leaving the field thickly strewn with his dead and wounded. The victory was equally complete in front of Jesup. A hot pursuit was continued to within half gunshot of the batteries at Chippewa Bridge, to gather up prisoners and with good success. Returning, Scott met Major-General Brown coming out of the forest, who, with Ripley's regulars and the rallied militia of Porter, had made a wide circuit to the left, intending to get between the enemy and the Chippewa, and this might have been effected if the battle had lasted a half hour longer; but suppose that Scott in the mean time had been overwhelmed by superior numbers!

The term *charge* occurs several times above, and often in military narratives. A word to explain its professional meaning may be acceptable. General Moreau,[10] when in America, remarked that in all his campaigns he had "never known anything approaching to a *general* conflict of bayonets"; though perhaps in all battles between infantry, a few files at a time, or small parts of opposing lines (as at Chippewa) come into the deadly rencounter.[11]

"A *charge,* in military phrase, is said to be made, when either party stops firing, throws bayonets forward, and advances to the shock, whether the enemy receive it or fly. An actual crossing of bayonets, therefore, is not indispensable to the idea of a charge. To suppose it is, is a mistake. Another popular error is, that the parties come up to the shock in parallel lines. Such a case has rarely, if ever, occurred. Each commander always seeks by manoeuvring to gain the oblique position, and, if possible, to outflank his enemy. With superior forces both advantages may easily be gained; but with inferior numbers the difficulty is extreme. The excess on the part of the enemy can only be overcome by celerity of movement, accuracy, hardihood, skill, and zeal."* {This paragraph is taken from Mansfield's life of the autobiographer, but was originally furnished (substantially) in the notes of the latter.}

Few men now alive are old enough to recall the deep gloom, approaching to despair, which about this time oppressed the whole American people—especially the supporters of the war. The disasters on the land have been enumerated, and now the New England States were preparing to hold a convention—it met at Hartford—perhaps to secede from the Union—possibly to take up arms against it.[12] Scott's brigade, nearly all New England men, were most indignant, and this was the subject of the second of the three pithy remarks made to them by Scott just before the final conflict at Chippewa. Calling aloud to the gallant Major Hindman, he said: "*Let us put down the federal convention by beating the enemy in front. There's nothing in the Constitution against that.*"* {The third, addressed to the 11th Infantry, at the last moment, was this: *The enemy say that Americans are good at long shot; but cannot stand the cold iron. I call upon you instantly to give the lie to the slander. Charge!*}

History has recorded many victories on a much larger scale than that of Chippewa; but only a few that have wrought a greater change in the feelings of a nation. Everywhere bonfires blazed; bells rung out peals of joys; the big guns responded, and the pulse of Americans recovered a healthy beat.

CHAPTER XI

INVESTMENT OF FORTS—BATTLE OF
NIAGARA OR LUNDY'S LANE

The enemy being again in the strong position behind the Chippewa, the preparation of materials for the bridge was renewed early on the 6th, but before they were quite ready, Major-General Riall decamped; sent reënforcements to his works at the mouth of the Niagara, struck off to the left at Queenstown and returned with the remainder of his army to Burlington Heights at the head of Lake Ontario. So it turned out, as we learned, in a day or two. Scott's brigade was again despatched in pursuit. He crossed the Chippewa Bridge early on the 7th and reported from Queenstown the ascertained movements of Riall.

Major-General Brown determined to attack the forts (George and Messassauga) at the mouth of the river, and accordingly marched his whole force upon them—Scott always in the lead. Perhaps it had been better, after masking those works, to have moved at once upon Riall. But arrangements had been made between the general-in-chief and Commodore Chauncey for siege guns to be brought up by our ships of war; for the Niagara army had not a piece heavier than an 18-pounder. The forts were invested: Messassauga, built since McClure evacuated George, the year before.

The investment was maintained till the 23d of July, when Chauncey reported that he could not comply with his promise. The reason, being that it was Sir James Yeo's turn to hold the mastery of the lake.

Major-General Brown, thinking it would be more difficult to find than to beat Riall in the Highlands about the head of the lake, now resolved to try the effect of a stratagem to draw him out of his snug position. Accordingly, the Americans on the morning of the 24th assumed a panic; broke up camp and retreated rapidly up the river. There was only a moment's halt at Queenstown—to throw the sick across into hospital at Lewiston, until all were securely encamped above the Chippewa. The following was to be a day of rest and to give Riall time to come down in pursuit. It was further arranged that Scott's brigade, reënforced, should early in the morning of the 26th return rapidly upon Queenstown, and if the stratagem proved a failure, then to trace up Riall and attack him wherever found. Consequently, it was intended that the 25th of July should be to the army a day of relaxation—without other duties than cleaning of arms, the washing of clothes, and bathing, except that Scott's troops were ordered to fill their haversacks with cooked provisions.

While all were thus unbuttoned and relaxed, a militia colonel, whose regiment occupied several posts on the American side of the river, sent a specific report to Major-General Brown that the enemy had thrown across, from Queenstown, to Lewiston, a strong body of troops, and as it could not be to disturb the small hospital at the latter place, Brown concluded the movement had in view the destruction of our magazines at Schlosser, and stopping the stream of supplies descending from Buffalo. Of course, Riall must have come down from the Highlands; but as one of our brigades had beaten his entire force, twenty days before, it was difficult to believe he had risked a division of his weakened army so near to the superior numbers of Brown; for not a rumor had reached the latter that Riall had been reënforced. Indeed it was only known, from Chauncey, at Sackett's Harbor, that Sir James Yeo had possession of the lake; for Brown's means of secret intelligence, if any, were of no avail. In this state of ignorance, but confidence in the report received, Brown ordered Scott, with his command, to march below, to find the enemy and to beat him. It was now in the afternoon, and all had dined. In less than thirty minutes, the splendid column—horse, artillery, and infantry—had passed the bridge at the village of Chippewa, and was in full march for Queenstown (nine miles below), intending no halt short of that point. But *l'homme propose et Dieu dispose*.[1] Turning the sweep the river makes a mile or two above the Falls, a horseman in scarlet was from time to time discovered peeping out from the wood on the left, and lower down, the advance guard, with which Scott rode, came upon a house (Forsyth's)[2] from which two British officers fled just in time to escape capture. Only two inhabitants had been seen in the march, and these, from ignorance or loyalty, said nothing that did not mislead. The population was hostile to Americans.

From such indications it seemed evident that there was a corps of observation in the neighborhood, and Scott so reported to headquarters; but from the information on which he had advanced, it could only be a small body, detached from an inferior army that had committed the folly of sending at least half of its numbers to the opposite side of the river. There was, therefore, no halt and no slackening in the march of the Americans. Passing a thick skirt of wood that crossed the road nearly opposite to the Falls, the head of the column emerged into an opening on the left in full view, and in easy range of a line of battle drawn up in Lundy's Lane, more extensive than that defeated at Chippewa.

Riall's whole force was in the lane; for, it turned out not only not a man had been thrown over the river, but that the night before Lieutenant-General Sir Gordon Drummond[3] had arrived by the lake with a heavy, reënforcements and had pushed forward his battalions (sixteen miles) as they successively landed. One was already in line of battle, and the others were coming up by forced marches.

The aches in broken bones feelingly remind the autobiographer of the scene he is describing, and after the lapse of nearly fifty years he cannot suppress his indignation at the blundering, stupid report made by the militia colonel to his confiding friend Major-General Brown.

Jesup's battalion (the 25th), marching in the rear, was detached to the right, covered by brushwood, between the road and the river, to turn the enemy's left. Hindman, with Towson's and Thomas Biddle's batteries, the 9th and 22d consolidated under Colonel Brady,[4] and the 11th (McNiel's) were, as they preceded Jesup, deployed to the left in the open space, when a tremendous fire of all arms responded to that of the enemy. At the discovery of the formidable line, Scott despatched another staff officer to the general-in-chief, who was still in his camp (nearly three miles off) with a promise to maintain his ground till the arrival of the reserve. Nothing was more difficult.

At the moment of this promise—whether it might not be his duty to fall back? was rapidly considered. But for some particular circumstances that alternative should have been adopted; but the brigade was, from the first, under a heavy fire, and could not be withdrawn without a hot pursuit. Being but half seasoned to war, some danger of confusion in its ranks, with the certainty of throwing the whole reserve (coming up) into a panic, were to be apprehended; for an extravagant opinion generally prevailed throughout the army in respect to the prowess— nay, invincibility of Scott's brigade.

By standing fast, the salutary impression was made upon the enemy that the whole American reserve was at hand and would soon assault his flanks. Emboldened, however, a little by its non-arrival, an attempt was made to turn Scott's left. The 11th, that occupied that position, threw forward (under cover of a clump of trees) its right, and drove the enemy beyond reach.

Jesup, too, on our right, had brilliant success. In making the sweep around the enemy's left flank, he captured Major-General Riall and cut off a segment of his line. Sir Gordon Drummond, also, was for a moment a prisoner, but he contrived to escape in the dusk of the evening. Hindman's artillery, Brady's battalion, consolidated with Leavenworth's, had suffered and inflicted great losses under a direct fire, unremitted, till dusk. The 11th, partially covered, suffered less.

At this moment Major-General Brown and staff came up a little ahead of the reserve—of course, each with the bandage of night on his eyes for it was now dark—after nine o'clock in the evening. Scott gave the general the incidents of the battle, and the positions of the hostile forces on the field. It was known from prisoners that further reënforcements, from below, were soon expected. Not a moment was to be lost. By desire, Scott suggested that the heaviest battalion in the reserve, the 21st, which he had instructed at Buffalo, and was now commanded by Colonel Miller, should, supported by the remainder of Ripley's brigade, charge up the lane, take the enemy in flank, and roll his whole crumbled line back into the wood.

To favor this important movement, Scott, with the added force of Jesup, now back in line, ordered the attack, in front, to be redoubled; guided Brown, with Miller, through the darkness, to the foot of the lane, and then rejoined his own forces Here he was assisted by the fresh batteries which came up with the reserve. The enemy, thus furiously assailed in front, remained ignorant of Miller's approach till the bayonets of his column began to be felt. The rout was early and complete, a battery captured, and many prisoners made.

Positions on the field had become reversed. The American line, reformed, now crossed that originally occupied by the enemy at right angles, and facing the wood, with backs to the river. Here it took a defensive stand. The British slowly rallied at some distance in front. Being again in collected force and in returning confidence, they cautiously advanced to recover the lost field and their battery—the horses of which had been killed or crippled before the retreat. By degrees the low, commands, *halt, dress, forward!* often repeated, became more and more audible in the awful stillness of the moment. At length a dark line could be seen, at a distance, perhaps, of sixty paces. Scott resolved to try an experiment. Leaving his brigade on the right, in line, he formed a small column of some two hundred and fifty men, and, at its head, advanced rapidly to pierce the advancing enemy's line, then to turn to the right, and envelop his extreme left. If pierced, in the dark, there seemed no doubt the whole would fall back, and so it turned out. Scott explained his intentions and forcibly cautioned his own brigade, and Ripley's on his left, not to fire upon the little column; but the instant the latter came in conflict with, and broke the enemy, Ripley's men opened fire upon its rear and left flank, and caused it to break without securing a prisoner. The column resumed its place in line, and another pause in the battle ensued.

After a while, a second advance of the enemy was made with the same slowness as before. When within short musket-shot, there was an unexpected halt, instantly followed by the crack of small arms and the deafening roar of cannon. Each party seemed resolved to rest the hope of victory on its fire. The welkin was in a blaze with shells and rockets. Though both armies suffered greatly, the enemy suffered most. The scene, perhaps, including accessories, has never been surpassed. Governor Tompkins, with a keen perception of its splendor, said, in presenting a sword of honor to Scott: "The memorable conflict on the plains of Chippewa, and the appalling night-battle on the Heights of Niagara, are events which have added new celebrity to the spots where they happened, heightening the majesty of the stupendous cataract, by combining with its natural, all the force of the moral sublime."

It was impossible that this conflict should be endured for more than a very few minutes. The lines at some points were separated by only eight or ten paces. Nothing but a deep, narrow gully intervened in front of the 25th Infantry. Scott, inquiring of the commander (Jesup) about a wound (in the hand) heard a call in the ranks—*Cartridges!* At the same moment a man reeling to the ground, responded—*Cartridges in my box!* The two commanders flew to his succor. The noble fellow had become a corpse as he fell. In the next second or two Scott, for a time, as insensible, lay stretched at his side, being prostrated by an ounce musket ball through the left shoulder joint.[5] He had been twice dismounted and badly contused, in the side, by the rebound of a cannon ball, some hours before. Two of his men discovering that there was yet life, moved him a little way to the rear, that he might not be killed on the ground, and placed his head behind a tree—his feet from the enemy. This had scarcely been done, when he revived and found that the enemy had again abandoned the field. Unable to hold up his head from the loss of blood and anguish, he was taken in an *ambulance* to the camp across the Chippewa, when the wound was stanched and dressed.

On leaving the field he did not know that Major-General Brown, also wounded, had preceded him. By seniority the command of the army now devolved on Brigadier-General Ripley. It must then have been about midnight. Ripley, from some unknown cause, became alarmed, and determined, in spite of dissuasion, to abandon the field, trophies, and all.[6] The principal officers despatched a messenger to bring back Scott, but found him utterly prostrate. Toward day, some fragments of the enemy, seeking the main body, crossed the quiet field, and learning from the wounded that the Americans had flown, hastened to overtake Lieutenant-General Sir Gordon Drummond below, who returned, *bivouacked* on the field, and claimed the victory!

CHAPTER XII

HORS DE COMBAT–PRINCETON COLLEGE–
PHILADELPHIA–BALTIMORE–WASHINGTON

The following morning (July 26) Scott—for the next forty-one years a major-general—embarked for Buffalo, with some thirteen officers of his brigade, all badly wounded. Among these were two of his three staff officers—Brigade-Major Smith, and Aide-de-Camp Worth; Colonel Brady, one of the best soldiers and men of his day, etc., etc. The row-boat was large and unwieldy, and the soldiers (militiamen) selected as oarsmen, feeble and inexperienced; for Scott would not allow any man, effective in the ranks, to volunteer for the service. Two of the consequences were that on leaving the mouth of the Chippewa the boat narrowly escaped passing over the Falls, and next, the row up the river was most tedious and distressing. The rest at Buffalo was short, and also at Williamsville, eleven miles east. Here Scott was joined by Major-General Riall, badly wounded when captured, and his friend (worse wounded) Lieutenant-Colonel John Moryllion Wilson,* one of the Chippewa prisoners. {This gallant officer, always (since) an invalid and friend of Scott, who was, in the time of William IV, in the household of the queen, and since in the government of Chelsea Hospital, still lives. He invested his little savings and wife's dower in Mississippi bonds, repudiated, mainly, by Mr. Jefferson Davis.[1] It was Scott's strong statement of this interesting case, at the time, in a published article, that brought upon him afterward the persecutions of Mr. Davis as Mr. Pierce's Secretary of War. When it is added, *upon knowledge,* that the statements of Sir Phineas Riall and Sir John Moryllion Wilson, on their return home, contributed not a little to the liberal instructions given to the British Commissioners who signed the Treaty of Ghent, perhaps it may not be extravagant or too late to say, that generous Americans should make up, to Wilson's family, their losses by the Mississippi repudiation. Our distinguished countryman, George Peabody, London, is their friend.}

These officers Scott placed on formal parole and obtained for them, from Government, as a special favor to himself, permission to return to England, after all like indulgences had ceased on the part of each belligerent. His forced sojourn was longer at Batavia, in the comfortable house of his friend, Mr. Brisbane, where he was well nursed by the kindness of his excellent sister, afterward Mrs. Carey.[2] But Batavia, exhausted of its comforts, became, in August, very sickly, and Scott's wounds were no better. For the same reason that he took the poor oarsmen, at Chippewa, he had selected an invalid surgeon for himself and wounded companions, who had not strength for hospital duty, and hardly enough to half dress the wounds of three officers twice a day. Without change, it became evident that the senior could not live. He procured a litter, and hired eight men (two reliefs) to bear him on it; but some of the principal citizens drove off the hirelings, and shouldered the litter themselves. It was thus, more than half dead, he was taken in triumph, by the gentlemen of the country, who relieved each other at the edge of every town, some seventy miles, to the house at Geneva, of another dear friend, the Honorable John Nicholas.

Here, besides the fine air, were "all appliances and means to boot," needed by Scott, except the higher skill in surgery. To obtain this he was most anxious to reach Doctor Physick, at Philadelphia.[3]

Having by the kind nursing of Judge Nicholas's family gained some strength, the new major-general was enabled to travel in an easy carriage, on a mattress, to Albany, where honors, as elsewhere, on the road, awaited him, and thence he had the benefit of steam to New York. Here another long journey, on a mattress, was to be undertaken. At Princeton College (Nassau Hall) a very interesting scene occurred. The invalid chanced to arrive at that seat of learning on *Commencement day* in the midst of its exercises, and made a short halt for rest. He was scarcely placed on a bed when a deputation from the Trustees and Faculty did him the honor to bear him, almost by main strength, to the platform of their body. This was in the venerable church where thousands of literary and scientific degrees had been conferred on pupils from all parts of the Union. The floor and galleries were filled to overflowing with much of the intelligence, beauty, and fashion of a wide circle of the country.

All united in clamorous greetings to the young wounded soldier (bachelor), the only representative that they had seen of a successful, noble army.

The emotion was overpowering. Seated on the platform, with the authorities, he had scarcely recovered from that burst of enthusiasm, when he was again assailed with all the powers of oratory. The valedictory had been assigned to the gifted and accomplished Bloomfield McIlvaine, of the graduating class, the younger brother of the present most venerable bishop of Ohio. He had, without reference to any particular individual taken as his theme, the duty of a *patriot citizen in time of war;* in which *soldiership* was made most prominent. In a whisper, he obtained at the moment, permission of the Faculty to give to the whole address, by a few slight changes, a personal application. Here again there was a storm of applause, no doubt in the greater part given to the orator.* {Though Mr. McIlvaine died very young, it was not before he had greatly distinguished himself at the Philadelphia Bar.} Finally the honorary degree of *Master of Arts,* conferred on the soldier, rounded off his triumphs of the day.

Flattered and feeble, the soldier at length reached Philadelphia. Dr. Physick, eminent as a physician, more eminent as a surgeon, and not less distinguished as a patriot, left a sickroom, for the first time in months, with his most accomplished and amiable nephew, Dr. Dorsey, to visit and heal his new patient.[4] Before this great effort of science had been accomplished, Scott, in the command of the Philadelphia Department (district) was, early in October, ere he could walk or mount a horse without help, ordered to the district of Baltimore, then threatened with another joint attack by the army and fleet which had been so handsomely repulsed the month before. Here, Dr. Gibson, another eminent surgeon, at the end of some months, finally finished the case so happily commenced, without fee or reward, in Philadelphia.[5]

Scott found a large force of militia assembled for the defence of Baltimore, which he was glad to discharge as the winter approached and the danger subsided. He visited, in the course of the winter, Washington and Fredericksburg, threatened by the enemy, and, as at all the points further north, was handsomely greeted and distinguished. But the crowning honor was conferred upon him in a resolution penned by the accomplished and rising statesman, William Lowndes[6]—in which it is ordered that a gold medal "be struck, with suitable emblems and devices, and presented to Major-General Scott in testimony of the high sense entertained by Congress of his distinguished services in the successive conflicts of Chippewa and Niagara (or Lundy's Lane), *and of his uniform gallantry and good conduct in sustaining the reputation of the arms of the United States.*" It is believed that the second clause of this resolution contains a compliment not bestowed by Congress on any other officer whatever.

Early in December, and before he had visited Washington, inquiries were made of him and his physician, whether he could bear the journey to New Orleans, in order to assist Major-General Jackson in the defence of the Mississippi delta. Dr. Gibson replied that the principal wound of his patient was still open, requiring the most critical treatment, and moreover that he had not yet the strength, to sustain a long journey. Thus the soldier of the Niagara lost the opportunity of sharing in Jackson's brilliant victories near New Orleans. He might in the beginning of the campaign, when he preferred the Northern frontier, have gone South if he had so chosen. But, as is said in Rasselas, "No man can, at the same time fill his cup from the source and from the mouth of the Nile."[7]

His headquarters remained in Baltimore. When his health had improved a little, he was called twice to Washington for consultation on plans of campaign for 1815, and under a resolution of Mr. Lowndes— who, though he "never set a squadron in the field," and experimentally knew nothing of "the division of a battle," was, as his correspondence with Scott showed, well acquainted with the subject—the latter was made president of a board of tactics, with, as associates, Brigadier-General Swift, Colonels Fenwick, Drayton, and Cumming.[8]

About the same time he was appointed president of a court of inquiry in the case of Brigadier-General Winder.[9] Both bodies sometimes met, at different hours, the same day. The treaty of peace arrived before the tactics were quite finished. The war was at an end. Scott's breast was violently agitated by opposite currents of feeling—joy for the country, whose finances were exhausted; disappointment at being cut off from another campaign in the rank of lieutenant-general; for it was in contemplation to confer that grade on Brown, Jackson, and himself.

CHAPTER XIII

REDUCTION OF THE ARMY—VISIT TO EUROPE—ENGLAND—FRANCE

The army had now to be reduced to a peace establishment—from, nominally, some sixty-five thousand, to ten thousand men; that is, we had officers for the larger number, but the regiments, as in the campaigns, were still skeletons. The reduction could not fail to fall heavily on the commissioned officers, as less than one in six could be retained in service.

The board, ordered for this painful duty met in May, 1815, and consisted of the six general officers previously selected by the President for the new establishment, viz.: Major-Generals Brown and Jackson, with four brigadiers, each a major-general by brevet—Scott, Gaines, Macomb, and Ripley. Jackson and Gaines did not appear at all, and Brown arrived after the board had made good progress in its labors. In the mean time Scott had presided.

Mr. Monroe, since the previous autumn, had been alternately Secretary of State and acting Secretary of War, or the reverse. Wise, firm, patriotic, and indefatigable in the performance of every duty, his strength at length gave way. The Secretary of the Treasury, the Honorable Alexander J. Dallas, without neglecting one of its duties became acting Secretary of War, and it was under his judicious instructions that the board reduced the army.[1] He it was, also, who put the new establishment in operation as smoothly as if he had been all his life a soldier. The autobiographer has known men as able as Mr. Dallas, but never one who combined so much talent for the despatch of business, with the graces of a gentleman and scholar.

At the ratification of the treaty of peace there was a strong inclination on the part of some members of Congress to make Scott Secretary of War, which he discouraged, emphatically, and next to engage him to act in that capacity, until the arrival of the new Secretary, Mr. Crawford, from his mission to France.[2] This proposition he also declined from a feeling of delicacy toward his seniors, Major-Generals Brown and Jackson, who would, nominally, have been under the command of the acting secretary.

At length, charged with limited diplomatic functions, for the execution of which on his return home, he was handsomely complimented by the Executive, Scott sailed for Europe, July 9, 1815, before the news of the battle of Waterloo had reached America. That great event burst upon him on the arrival (in eighteen days) at Liverpool, together with the astounding fact that Napoleon was a prisoner of war in an English port. After a partial glance at England, Scott hastened to cross the channel to see the assembled troops of Europe, for *la belle France* did not then belong to Frenchmen. A great nation, exhausted by the victories of mad ambition, had, in its turn, become conquered and subdued.

It was authentically ascertained that the foreign armies in France amounted to five hundred thousand men, besides another hundred thousand hovering about the frontiers. Nearly all these troops Scott saw reviewed at different points.

Dipping a little into society—French, Dutch, German, and Italian, as well as English and Scotch—when returning homeward;—visiting theatres and libraries; glancing at the wonders of architecture, sculpture, and painting;—seeing a little of the interior of Oxford and Cambridge, and paying devotion to many scenes of historic fame—not one of which objects need be here described, first, because that has been done by scores of better pens; and next, because this is not a book of travels— Scott recrossed the Atlantic in 1816, a little improved both in knowledge and patriotism.

There were, however, a few incidents in his rapid tour, a slight notice of which (the greater number being more or less connected with America) may be interesting to his countrymen.

It was the fortune of the American to be almost daily in the galleries and halls of the Louvre, for weeks, immediately preceding the restoration of the foreign objects of the fine arts—trophies of French victories—where the frequent spectacle of emperors, kings, princes, dukes, marshals, and the rest of the *élite* of Europe, male and female, were seen passing along, as if in review, admiring the *chefs-d'oeuvre* to the right and left. First came Alexander, as affable and courteous as a candidate for office, and his brother emperor, Francis, grave to sadness. He had received heavy afflictions from the arms of France; had shifted sides at a critical moment, making his daughter a political widow, and his grandson, Napoleon II, an alien to France. These were ample grounds for shame and sorrow. The King of Prussia,[3] too, had his griefs; was glum, incapable of any lively emotion, and goaded by his people to acts of revenge. Old Blucher, always by his side, had made secret preparations for blowing up the bridge of Jena, a beautiful object of art and of the greatest value to Parisians.[4] Baron Humboldt,[5] long a resident of Paris, and master of the civilization of the age;—high in the pride of all Prussians, and the associate of crowned heads, hastened to the king and implored that the hand of the barbarian might be stayed—adding, if not, he would, in shame, renounce his country for ever. The bridge was saved by a few minutes.

During the weeks in question, no person, born in France, was seen in the Louvre, save a few female artists mounted on high steps, busily engaged in copying some of the master paintings before their early departure. These *patriotes* did not condescend to glance at the moving world below—all enemies of France. Even the passing compliments of Alexander met with no response from one of them in word or look.

The dismounting of the Corinthian horses from the triumphal arch, in the *Place du Carrousel,* to be sent back to Venice, was also witnessed. On this occasion, the autobiographer said to his friend standing by him, the Honorable Thomas Bolling Robertson—a descendant of Pocohontas, a member of Congress from Louisiana, and otherwise distinguished[6]—"Very well; these wonders in bronze, have already made journeys and changed masters several times, and as

'Westward the course of empire takes its way,'

they, may, in time, adorn the capital of our country." That prediction has already been sadly defeated by the existing rebellion in the United States!

Scott corresponded with, though he failed to see, the venerable Kosciuszko;[7]—spent some days at La Grange, on a visit to General La Fayette, dear to all Americans. He made the acquaintance of several of Rochambeau's officers who were at the surrender of Cornwallis— among them the venerable and distinguished Count de Ségur,[8] the elder, author of the memoirs of the greatest interest, in three volumes, the second of which is devoted to America. The Baron Humboldt, who had visited the United States, and who took a lively interest in the cause of freedom, did the autobiographer the honor to make him several visits of usefulness—to spread his acquaintance among literary and military men—himself a man of the world, and a most instructive companion. Master of many languages, he, in rapid conversation, unconsciously, mixed up several of them in the most amusing manner.

Another highly interesting acquaintance, made in Paris, was Barbé Marbois, who accompanied, as consul-general, the first French minister to the United States.[9] Being a moderate liberal, he was now (1815) minister of justice. His very amiable daughter, the wife of the Duc de Plaisance (Lebrun, third consul in 1799), who presided at his hospitable board, was half American—her deceased mother having been a Philadelphian. M. Marbois gave to Major-General Scott many anecdotes of the Congressional Government of the United States, some of which may appear in this narrative—the greater number having been published by Sevelinge from the portfolio of M. Girard, the minister.[10] M. Marbois had some time before published his *Conspiration d'Arnold,* a copy of which he presented to the American.

An event of poignant interest to Americans occurred in September. The British troops were all quartered in and about Paris. Some of the regiments that assisted, under that freebooter,* Admiral Cockburn,[11] and the gentlemanly, but pliant General Ross,[12] in burning the civil edifices at Washington—the Capitol, the President's mansion, and other executive buildings—hit upon the pleasant conceit—being in the occupancy of the capital of Europe, to celebrate, in it, the anniversary of their vandalism in the capital of America. {This is a harsh term to apply to an officer of high rank; but Cockburn made war a trade of profit as well as of vengeance, in the true barbarian spirit of Lord Bathurst's letter to Prevost, given above. The late J. S. Skinner, Esq., of Baltimore, chanced to be at Ross's headquarters, under a flag of truce, when a sailor reported that he had discovered some hogsheads of tobacco in the barn of a farmer. The indignant general replied: "Begone! I'm no freebooter like Cockburn!!" This admiral had been living ashore at free quarters for some time, in General Greene's last residence, Dungenness, Cumberland Island, Georgia, when the published treaty of peace was received, early in March, 1815.[13] Cockburn prepared to return to his flagship. Mrs. Shaw, the widowed daughter of the great general, said to Cockburn: "Your servants are packing up all my plate—silver urns, pitchers, cups, spoons, forks, etc., etc." "The servants," he replied, "have mistaken their orders. My steward shall correct the error." In a short time she flew to him again, to say: "There goes, in the boxes leaving the door, every piece of my plate—presentations to my father, and all!" "Madam, on board, your property shall be carefully separated from mine and sent back." Nevertheless, the whole was carried off, together with some of her colored servants, who, no doubt, were sold in some of the British West India Islands! This story the autobiographer had from Mrs. Shaw herself, at Dungenness, in 1826.} Accordingly, full of their "*laudable* ignominy," the officers of those regiments founded a grand entertainment, to which were invited many principal officers of the same army, including the Duke of Wellington, together with a thick sprinkling of French hungry courtiers, recently back from a long emigration, and all, of course, idolizers of British troops.

It is not now distinctly recollected whether the great duke was present or not. The documents are not at hand. He certainly did not interdict the celebration, nor warn his officers not to make a vaunt of their shame in respect to the burnings.

The founders and their guests, had it all in their own way. Forgetting that Washington had no defenders when Cockburn and Ross approached, except mobs of militia, hastily collected,—but half of whom had had time to obtain arms, or to learn the names of their officers;—forgetting, too, how British troops had been, the year before, repeatedly beaten and dispersed in Canada, and (still later) repulsed and disgraced at New Orleans—poor Americans! how shockingly were they maltreated by those Washington heroes, and their friends! Such victories, however, aside from "the iron harvest of the field," are, but a cheap indulgence.

Fired with indignation, the Americans at hand resolved on a retaliation. It was the general wish to select the anniversary of some conflict in which Scott had been a principal. To this he objected, begging a postponement to the New Orleans victory—the 8th of January. As the time approached, grand preparations were made. The Hôtel Robert, Rue Grange Battelliére, where the sovereigns habitually hobnobbed before they dispersed homeward, was selected as the place of meeting. A sumptuous dinner for seventy Americans besides their guests, to be served on silver and by waiters in livery, was ordered. The ostentation was intended to give increased publicity to the occasion, and for the same purpose, the Americans everywhere, dropped the *expectation*—many, the *hope,* of being jostled; for that Hotel continued to be the resort of the higher English, and "the bucks and bloods" of the English army.

The morning of the dinner, Count Woronzow[14]—lieutenant-general and aide-de-camp to the Emperor Alexander; also then commander of the forty thousand Russians, part of the foreign army of occupation (one hundred and fifty thousand) under the Duke of Wellington—chanced to make one of his agreeable calls upon Scott. Through an accidental opening of the bedroom door, he caught a view of the American's uniform, and being young, playful, and tall, he seized upon the coat, put it on, and with the companion-sword in hand, charged about the apartment, and slew British troops in much finer style than the weapon had ever known before. The acting was perfect.

The ventilation of the uniform led to the story of the provocative and retaliatory dinners, and to the remark that a possible conflict might ensue; for Lord Hill's quarters, with a battalion of troops, were nearly opposite to the Hôtel Robert. The Russian impulsively offered to send a battalion of the emperor's guards to protect the meeting. On a little reflection Scott declined the distinguished honor, as it would almost certainly have caused a coolness, if not something more grave, between the count and his commander, the Duke of Wellington.* {It was at the same visit that his Russian friend gave to Scott this anecdote:—"After exiling Napoleon to Elba, in 1814, the allied sovereigns went over to England to make the regent (subsequently George IV.), a visit. The latter had prepared a naval combat, on the Serpentine River, between a British and an American frigate (diminutives) for his imperial and royal guests— Brother Jonathan, in a 'fir frigate, with a bit of bunting for a flag," stood the distant fire pretty well; but when John Bull laid his ship alongside, poor Jonathan struck his bunting and ran below! The regent, etc., were charmed with the victory, when the Emperor Alexander whispered into the ear of his aid, Woronzow: 'This is contemptible—when an American sloop-of-war, on the coast of Ireland, and an American privateer in the channel, are sinking or destroying scores of British vessels.'"}

The Americans, in a respectable column entered the hotel, and mounted the grand staircase. Scott, Colonels Drayton, McRae, Thayer, Archer,[15] etc., etc., in uniform, with swords by their sides, and some others with pistols in pocket. The crowd was as great as usual in the evening; but not a jostle, interruption, or insult was experienced. Scott presided, assisted by the principal officers named, and Mr. Jackson, late United States' Chargé d'Affaires,[16] but not accredited to Louis XVIII at this time. A band of music gave the national airs of America and France. The cloth being removed, the toasts followed in quick succession: Our Country; the President of the United States; Memory of Washington; La Fayette (then sick in bed), and nine others. The Fifth was:—Major-General Jackson *and his heroic army, who, this day a year ago near New Orleans, defeated thrice their numbers of the best British troops, commanded by Sir Edward Pakenham, the brother-in-law of the Duke of Wellington!*

This toast, introduced with some sharp remarks, by Scott, on the provocation that had led to the dinner, was drunk with the utmost enthusiasm, and the company dispersed at a reasonable hour, in perfect order and quietness.

A report, in French, of the meeting and toasts, specially stating the provocation, was drawn up and sent by a committee to the *Constitutionnel* (a liberal paper) for insertion. M. Le Censeur of the press, a crabbed old *emigré,* running his spectacled eyes down the page came upon the great disparity of the belligerent forces, at New Orleans, and the statement that the defeated commander was the brother-in-law of the Duke of Wellington, when he gutted the toast of the "perilous stuff" that could not fail to give offence to the English. The toast in compliment to La Fayette was by this official, entirely expunged—frankly saying the French Press was not open to the praise of that patriot hero. In revenge, Scott, at the cost of a few guineas, caused the unexpurgated report to be published in a London paper.

CHAPTER XIV

ENGLAND–LONDON–BATH

Soon after the dinner, Scott recrossed the channel. The second Adams was then the honored American minister in London, who showed every attention to his soldier countrymen, and of whom more will be said in the sequel.

Under the self-imposed restrictions, given above, the autobiographer has but few more European occurrences to add to this narrative.

The English Parliament was in session. Among other distinguished persons, Scott dined several times with Lord Holland—high in literature, high as a political leader, and, like his illustrious uncle, Charles James Fox, a decided friend to "the cause of freedom throughout the world."[1]

Persons of like sentiments and liberal pursuits, of whatever country, were easily admitted into his family circle; for Lady Holland, an American, had also high gifts and accomplishments. At one of those dinners, present several of the higher nobles, and the more distinguished commoners—Sir James Mackintosh[2] and Sir Samuel Romilly[3] (both of whom were very kind to Scott on many occasions), an incident occurred, too characteristic of English feeling toward America, at the time, to be omitted.

This particular dinner was given in special compliment to the Earl of Lauderdale, who had a near relative at table, unknown to Scott, the captain that received Napoleon on board the Bellerophon. The naval officer, loud and rude as Boreas at sea; but coming up to London, as a "blood," fell under the fashionable code of Bond Street, and had to lisp and mince words, to stammer between syllables, and even letters in the same word, like the rest of the coxcombs of the day. When the ladies had retired, this fop inquired of Scott, whether "the Americans continued to build line-of-battle ships, and to call them frigates?" Anywhere else the offensive question would have been very differently answered. The American bit his lips and replied: "We have borrowed a great many excellent things from the mother country, and some that discredit both parties—among the latter is the practice in question. Thus when you took, from France, the *Guerrière,* she mounted forty-nine guns, and you instantly rated her on your list a thirty-six gun frigate; but when we captured her from you, we found on board the same number, forty-nine guns!" "General Scott," said the Earl of Lauderdale, "I am delighted with your reply to my kinsman. Please take a glass of wine with me."[4]

A short visit to Bath was not without interest. Among his letters of introduction, Scott had one to John Parish, Esq., of that city, whose son David, a resident of Philadelphia, had been the agent of certain Dutch and Hanseatic bankers, in loans to the United States, to an amount of half the expenditure of the recent war with Great Britain. The father, an *octogenarian,* had, in fifty years, as a merchant at Hamburg, made an ample fortune, and now lived in a superior style among the throng of dowager ladies, half-pay generals, and admirals who constituted the resident population of that remarkable city. He had contrived to send to America, during the Revolutionary War, many cargoes of arms, ammunition, and clothing, and subsequently became consul of the United States. His obsolete commission as such, in frame, signed by President Washington, hung conspicuously in one of his apartments. General Bonaparte, about to sign the preliminary treaty of Campo Formio,[5] chanced to remember La Fayette, then three years in an Austrian dungeon (Olmutz), and withheld the pen until a formal order was given, by the Emperor Francis, for the liberation of the Franco-American patriot. He was personally delivered to Mr. Parish, American Consul.

Another introductory letter from a belle of Philadelphia, to her great aunt, Lady J., wife of Sir Henry Johnson, Baronet, residing at Bath, and a senior general of the British army, led to an interview which, at this distant day, cannot be recalled without emotion. This lady, in 1779, and some years before, was, as Miss Franks, the belle of Philadelphia— handsome, witty, and an heiress.[6] She was also high in toryism and eccentricity. Many amusing sarcasms of hers, levelled at revolutionary men of eminence, were in circulation in Philadelphia down to the autobiographer's early days. One of them, of a practical nature, was too offensive to be amusing. Mrs. General Washington gave a ball to the French minister, M. Girard, in honor of the recent alliance between Louis XVI and the United States, which had led the Americans to unite the cockades of the two countries—white and black. Miss Franks caused this token of alliance to be tied to the neck of a dog, and by a bribe to a servant, got the animal, thus decorated, turned into the ball room.

The equally eccentric, Major-General Charles Lee, wore, in the saddle, long pantaloons lined from the crotch to the ankle with buckskin to prevent abrasion—after that example, much worn in America by military men down to within forty-five years. Miss Franks charged that they were "green breeches, *patched* with leather." In his celebrated reply* to her, filled with coarse wit and humor, he denies the patching, and adds that his pantaloons are "legitimate *sherry vallies,* such as his majesty of Poland wears"—on whose personal staff he had recently served. {See his Life and Memoirs, New York, 1813, and Memoirs of the Life, etc., London, 1792. Both anonymous.}

This brilliant young lady married, about this time, Major Johnson, a British officer, made prisoner at the capture of Stony Point (of which he was the commander) and sent to Philadelphia. In 1816 she had become, from bad health, prematurely old—a very near approach to a ghost, but with eyes still bright, and other remains of her former self.

On the receipt of the letter of introduction, Lady J. despatched her amiable husband—a fine old soldier, to fetch the stranger. Scott, as has been seen, was fortunately a little acquainted with her eccentric manner. She had been rolled out in an easy chair to receive him. On presentation, he was transfixed by her eager, but kindly gaze. "Is this the young rebel!" were her first words. "My dear, it is your countryman!" etc., said Sir Henry, fearing that Scott might take offence. "Yes, it is," she quickly added, "the young rebel; and you have taken the liberty to beat his majesty's troops." Scott, by a pleasant word or two, parried the impeachment as well as he could; but the lady followed up the accusation, with specific references, which surprised not a little. Scott soon found himself seated by her side, with a hand clasped in both of hers—cold and clammy, as in the article of death. Taking a sudden turn, she exclaimed, with emphasis: "I have gloried in my rebel countrymen!" Then pointing to heaven, with both hands, she added, in a most affecting tone: "Would to God I, too, had been a patriot." A gentle remonstrance was interposed by the husband, who had been carried away by sympathy up to this moment. Turning now upon him, she said, with the earnestness of truth: "I do not, I have never regretted my marriage. No woman was ever blessed with a kinder, a better husband; but I ought to have been a patriot before marriage." Hers were the only dry eyes of the party.

CHAPTER XV

REFLECTIONS ON PEACE AND WAR—
THE CANKER ABOLITIONISM—STATE
RIGHTS—NULLIFICATION—REBELLION

A s has been said, the autobiographer returned home in 1816, when he resumed his duties in the army. Thence to the Mexican War, in 1846, there is a gap of thirty years to be bridged over in this narrative. In this long interval he was not idle, and a few of its scenes and events with which he was connected will be sketched in this narrative.

Always preferring peace to *unnecessary,* and of course to unjust wars, he never made his own the distracted cry of poor Constance, in King John:

"War! war! no peace! peace is to me a war!"

Yet, perhaps, the thesis might plausibly be maintained that war is the normal or natural state of man.

*Homo homini lupus.** {Erasmus.}

Amid the woods the tiger knows his kind,
The panther preys not on the panther brood,
Man only is the common foe to man.* {Motto to Caleb
Williams.}

Milton sings:

—Peace hath her victories
No less renown'd than war.

This fine couplet, addressed to the great warrior and statesman—the Lord General, Cromwell—often quoted by civilians as a taunt to soldiers, will not, in that sense, bear a philosophic analysis; for what has been accomplished in peace, that might not have been as well done in a state of war? Sunday schools, Bible societies, missions to the heathen, vaccination, the steam engine, the electric telegraph, etc., are the great human triumphs of recent times. Several of these blessings had, as is known, their beginning and maturity in time of war; and what a flood of Christian light followed, and is likely to follow, the recent march of European armies into the interior of China? And Shakspeare, the deepest of human observers, recognizes "the cankers of a calm world and long peace." Perhaps, an occasional interlude of *foreign* war may be even necessary to the moral health of a people rapidly increasing in population, wealth, and luxurious indulgences.

In this interval of peace, certain speculative, moody minds at the "North, Northeast, and by East,"* like Loyola, brooding over their want of occupation or usefulness—and being as tired of prosperity as Athenian demagogues were with the name of Aristides *the just;*[1]—these dreamers, struck out the idea of abolishing, at "one fell swoop," negro slavery in the other half of the Union. {Shakspeare.} By a singular aptitude this idea coalesced at once with religious fanaticism, when a "charm of powerful trouble" became "firm and good." The ambitious leaders of a political party eagerly made court to this great and growing element of strength; succeeded in the wooing, and were placed at its head.

Now it is the nature of a new hallucination to shut out from the mind facts and principles—everything that conflicts with the one ruling idea. Hence the work of agitation now went bravely on. The fact was entirely ignored that slavery, in several States, was happily undergoing a gradual but sure amelioration, and could not fail to be more and more spontaneously accelerated, without the danger of reaction, if it were left to God's own time to educe good from evil, in his own way. So were forgotten that His great work—even the creation of the world—was one of time and deliberation, instead of a simple fiat, which, if He had pleased, would have been all sufficient;—that more years were allowed to intervene between the promise made to Abraham and the advent of our Saviour, than Africans had been in America—the chosen people of God being, meanwhile, slaves in Egypt and Babylon;—that the monarch oak and lofty pine—fit "to be the mast of some great ammiral"[2]—require centuries to mature them; forgetting, too, that, as has just been shown, hundreds of years, more or less, in divine estimation, but as a moment in the life of a people or race of men;—forgetting all those high considerations, the reckless reformers rushed in "where angels" might "fear to tread," at the imminent peril of setting owners and slaves to the mutual slaughter of men, women, and children of the opposite color. That this would have happened, since the rebellion, no white woman, in putting her children to bed would have doubted, but for the wide spread of troops, Union and Confederate, over the South; and, indeed, a like danger and a like nervous apprehension existed—not without cause, in Southern families—created by external, pragmatic missions and missiles—beginning some twenty-odd years before.

The first great error of the South, *after* the agitation began, was, in causing abolition petitions to be laid upon the table in Congress, instead of referring them to committees for due consideration and respectful reports on the same. The alleged ground of this treatment was, that the petitioners asked for what Congress had no power, under the Constitution, to grant. Agreed; but why not have allowed a committee (or committees) to find that fact and solemnly report that finding? Such report—say from Mr. Adams, who was prepared so to report—would have taken from abolitionists more than half of the fuel needed to keep up their excitement to fever heat; for the abstract right of petition had, by the events immediately preceding the revolution, become *hallowed,* more particularly in the public mind of the New England States. Thus action and reaction, error and outrage went on, each producing its like—Caliban, his Caliban[3]—as certainly as if the propagation had been commanded in the book of Genesis. And, unhappily, the parties seem still (January, 1864), as desperately bent as ever, on playing out the game—*All for HATE, or the World well Lost.** {"All for Love, or the World well Lost"—the title of Dryden's Antony and Cleopatra.} Hence "all our woe."

Now it cannot be doubted that if it had pleased God, but a few years before, to have taken away only some ten or fifteen of those zealots from one half of the Union, and as many of the hot-brained Southerners—mainly intent, on president-making and the increase of slave property—the South would not already be a scene of general desolation—one "house of mourning";—nor the North filled with widows, orphans, cripples, and another evil of large dimensions—swarms of rich contractors—many of them fraudulent—whose low manners, high pretensions, pomp and extravagance, excite the contempt of the philosophic, the pity of the good and envy of legions of weak-minded men and women.

But this inductive history of present calamities would be incomplete—nay, unjust, without a further glance at men and measures hostile to the Union—of an earlier period. The stream of bitter waters, here alluded to, had its source in the connection of President Washington and his first Secretary of State, Mr. Jefferson.

Dr. Johnson has supposed Socrates and Charles XII of Sweden,[4] to address an assembly of some pride of character. The great founder of moral science, with persuasive eloquence, commends the beauty of virtue.

The heroic Swede, in his turn, draws his sword and flashing it in the eyes of the multitude; calls out—*Follow me and let's dethrone the Czar!* Johnson doubts whether many listeners would remain with Socrates.

The same moralist puts another case to illustrate the same feeling, which he holds to be quite common in the breasts of men. Lord Mansfield is brought into a circle with a Blake or a Marlborough, and is made to feel, in such presence, that his learned decrees on the bench, and terse eloquence in the Senate, are of but little worth.[5]

There is, no doubt, much exaggeration, but a basis of nature, in those illustrations. Hence, as revolutionary worthies assured the autobiographer fifty and sixty years ago, Mr. Jefferson, the author of the Declaration of Independence—highly ambitious; a man of genius, of literary culture, and with a fine turn for philosophic inquiries—always felt himself uneasy—nay, rebuked—in the presence of Washington—not so much at his calm dignity, wise statesmenship, and moral weight of character; as at the recollection of his being the great general and hero in the war that achieved independence. To recover himself from the painful sense of inferiority, Mr. Jefferson was forced to set up an opposition, and leave the cabinet, when his party pretended to find that man is too much governed; that property, and liberty, with law and order, had nothing to fear from popular judges and universal suffrage; that Washington had imparted too much centripetal force to the Union—to meet which they opposed the centrifugal tendency, or the doctrine of *State Rights*—the first fruits of which have been seen in nullification—almost identical with rebellion; both in part, the posthumous works of Mr. Jefferson.

Mr. Calhoun, of pure morals and high intellect—only a little too much imbued with metaphysics—followed in the same career, not from the beginning of his political life, but was forced into it by circumstances. No one was more eminently conservative* in politics till after his election to the vice-presidency, when President Jackson (toward whom he always stood in awe) learned that he had, as Secretary of War, in Mr. Monroe's cabinet, suggested the hero's recall—perhaps, punishment, by a court martial, for the conquest of Middle Florida during a state of profound peace with Spain.[6] {Mr. Calhoun's mind had a strong tendency to extremes. He was, at first, in favor of making, by the authority and at the expense of the United States, Appian highways from the centre to the frontiers in every direction; of a high tariff and a bank of the United States. To illustrate his genius and early doctrine, this anecdote may be added:—At a dinner of six or eight, all officers of the army, but himself, he spoke of the party contests at the beginning of this century, and continued: "When the Republicans, headed by Mr. Jefferson, stormed and carried the citadel of Government, in 1801, they were not such fools as to spike the guns."} This late discovery of a meritorious act, brought down upon the second functionary of the Government the utmost wrath of the first.

There was no recovery from this blight, but, as it seemed to Mr. Calhoun, in an abrupt change of party. Accordingly, to recover himself, he took refuge in *State Rights;* stereotyped the doctrine on the Southern mind, and hence nullification, and next rebellion.

As to the abstract right of man to hold any human being in slavery, except in the way of punishment for established crime, the sentiment of the civilized world is fast waxing to unanimity on the negative side of the proposition. The recent abolition of serfdom in Russia was a mighty stride in that direction, and it may at this time be safely assumed that all the chairs of moral philosophy throughout Christendom, except, perhaps, a very small number in slaveholding countries, deny all claim of right on the part of masters. But as to the *manner* of mitigating, to extinction, the evil of negro slavery,—whether by degrees, more or less slow or fast, or at once, in districts where it actually exists, in masses—these are very different questions, involving difficulties within difficulties.

There is no intention of doing more, in this place, than to glance, very slightly, at some of those points, not developed in the foregoing pages, nor fully in the autobiographer's recorded views (his Atkinson letter)[7] on the same subject, published in newspapers in 1843, reproduced in Mansfield's able work,[8] and which paper may be repeated in these memoirs. From those sources it will plainly appear that the autobiographer's wishes have been to hasten emancipation only as fast as might be found compatible with *the safety of both races.*

The color of the American slave is the first difficulty. When a Roman placed the cap of liberty on the head of his white slave, the latter, himself, or at least his children, readily passed into the general population without any brand of former servitude upon him. Not so with the negro freedman. His color will always be certain evidence that he, or his progenitors, had once worn the yoke of the white man.

Immediate and wholesale abolition of negro slavery cannot be dismissed without a few additional remarks.

In this war, how many hundreds of thousands have already been liberated—men, women, and children—and are now fed and clothed

---

by the United States, besides the colored troops who are also receiving pay as such; and how many millions of the same people, the Government may, in all, take under its wing by the close of the war—it would, it is thought, be difficult to say within a million. The numbers will be numberless. How long will these be paid, lodged, clothed, and fed in like manner with those first named? And, in the end—where colonized, and how distant the colony? Transportation is a heavy item of cost. Is the territory obtained or designated? The climate and soil—are they good or bad? How make those work, who have, for a time, lived without labor, and who have never worked except when compelled by a master? And last and mightiest—how discharge the grand aggregate cost of such operations—including that of the conquering armies? With all the gold mines known to commerce in its possession, Government could not, in half a century, reduce that mountain of debt, that has been piled up in less than three years.

Once more—a parting glance, in the way of contrast, at the system of gradual emancipation, with the actual system—immediate abolitionism.

In about sixty years, counting from (say) 1833, but for the pragmatists alluded to—Delaware, Maryland, Virginia, North Carolina, Tennessee, Kentucky, and Missouri, would have been, in all human probability, free States, and those farther South, by the force of example, must, in the mean time, have entered on the same career of wisdom and humanity. Virginia in 1831–'2, it ought to be remembered, came within a vote of carrying the system at the first trial, and wanted but a little more time to have brought over to its support an overwhelming majority; but just then, as has been noticed above, petitions to Congress, and missions, and missiles of violence to the negroes, agitated and revolted the whole South.

By the gradual system, of which—honor to him to whom honor is due—Mr. Jefferson was the author and uniform supporter—each slave on attaining the proper age—males (say) twenty-one—would have become a free man on the spot, where his hired labor would have been needed. Thus he would remain with the younger members of his family till their liberation in turn, or have engaged himself to work on the next plantation. In this way each freedman would have had, to some extent, the choice of employers, and each employer, to a like extent, the choice of laborers—each with a strong motive to respect the interests and feelings of the other. Thus, moreover, the labor of the country would not have been diminished, *nor its productions.*

The wise Oxenstiern said to his son: *Nescis mi fili quantulâ scientiâ gubernatur mundus.*[9] And the good old Gloster, blind, says, in King Lear:[10]

"'Tis the times' plague when madmen lead the blind."

In virtue, wisdom, talent, one of the most eminent men of his times—Rufus King[11]—already prominent at the end of the Revolution, when quite young—twice our Minister Extraordinary to London, and twenty-odd years a leader in the Senate of the United States—this American Oxenstiern, always opposed to the principle of slavery, and to its extension into new States and Territories—had in him nothing of the madness of political abolitionism. Honored by his kind attentions from early in the war of 1812–'15, to the end of his career, I, the autobiographer, am happy to cite his sentiments on the great subject under consideration, to which my own closely approximated.

Mr. King, feeling a modest assurance that his name, position, and services could not fail to carry with them due weight, with Congress, at some future day, laid upon the table of the Senate, February 16, 1825—fifteen days before he finally left that body—a benign resolution to the effect that as soon as the remnant of the national debt should be discharged, the net proceeds of the whole of the public lands, "then and thenceforth, shall constitute and form a fund which is hereby appropriated, and the faith of the United States is pledged that the said fund shall be inviolably applied to aid the emancipation of such slaves, within any of the United States, and to aid the removal of such slaves, and the removal of such free persons of color in any of the said States as by the laws of the States respectively, may be allowed to be emancipated or removed to any Territory or country without the limits of the United States of America." The resolution stands a national record.

Here is statesmanship—far-sightedness, seeking to disarm the muttering clouds which threatened to burst upon and overwhelm the land. Here is magnanimity, considering the hostility of the South on account of Mr. King's powerful resistance to the admission of Missouri into the Union with slavery. Here is a Christian's revenge—returning good for evil! All honor to a great deed and a great name!

Hearing of the noble act, I, a Southern man, waited upon Mr. King the same evening to return him my hearty thanks, and added that the time could not fail to come when the whole South would be equally grateful. The rebellion ended, the first tranquil moment will be that time.

I place in juxtaposition with the foregoing, a kindred sentiment that gleamed in the same body on a more recent occasion.

It had been proposed, without due reflection, by one of our gallant commanders engaged in the suppression of the existing rebellion, to place, on the banners of his victorious troops, the names of their battles. The proposition was rebuked by the subjoined resolution, submitted by the Hon. Mr. Sumner to the Senate, May 8, 1862:[12]

"Resolved, That, in the efforts now making for the restoration of the Union, and the establishment of peace throughout the country, it is inexpedient that the names of the victories obtained over our own fellow citizens should be placed on the regimental colors of the United States."

This was noble and from the right quarter.

CHAPTER XVI

MARRIAGE—RECEPTION OF SWORDS AND MEDAL

Soon after his return from Europe, the autobiographer married Miss Maria Mayo, the daughter of an eminent citizen, John Mayo, Esq., of Richmond, Virginia—a young lady more admired in her circle than her soldier husband, who, however, was highly feasted and honored everywhere—in Richmond by the whole State—that is, by the governor, legislators, judges, and many other of her first citizens united. She died, June 10, 1862. Of this marriage three daughters remain, of seven children—two sons and two daughters having died quite young.[1]

The medal voted by Congress was presented in a handsome address, by President Monroe, a few days before his descent from power. The following short extracts from the recipient's reply may show his manner of feeling and expressing himself at that period:

"With a deep sense of the additional obligation now contracted, I accept, at the hands of the venerable chief magistrate of the Union, this classic token of the highest reward that a freeman can receive—THE RECORDED APPROBATION OF HIS COUNTRY.

"And you, sir, whom I have the honor officially to address for the last time; you who bled in the first, and powerfully contributed to the second War of Independence; you who have toiled fifty years to rear and to establish the liberties of this great republic—permit an humble actor in a much shorter period of its history, to mingle his prayers with those of millions, for the happy but distant termination of a life, of which, as yet, others have enjoyed the distinguished benefits, whilst the cares have been all your own."

This medal chanced to be temporarily in the City Bank of New York, for safe-keeping, when two thieves, in a night's work, took from that institution $260,000. The medal was lying in a trunk of gold. All the coin was stolen, but the medal, though taken out of its case (marked with the owner's name) to gratify curiosity, was left. A few years later, when the robbers had served out their sentences in the State prison, or been pardoned by the Executive, Scott was, in a steamer, on the Hudson, robbed of his purse by pickpockets who did not know him. The principal of the bank robbery hearing of the loss ($140) bestirred himself among the fraternity; threatened to cause the whole body to be sent to the State prison if the money was not returned, and added, "When in the City Bank I saw the medal, but was not such a villain as to rob a gallant soldier." In a day or two the money was returned by Hays, the high constable, with that report, received from a third party. To show that he did not himself pocket the money, Hays was required to produce Scott's written receipt for its return—which was given.

A handsome sword was, about the same time, though voted years before, presented to Scott in a complimentary address by the Governor (Pleasants, bred a Quaker) of Virginia.[2]
A part of the reply, to illustrate the character of the autobiographer, is here inserted:

"The law which gave my name to a county; the thanks voted by the General Assembly; and this sword which I now have the honor to receive at your hands, in the presence of the executive council, are the precious evidences of that partiality. Sir—they are appreciated by me in the spirit in which they are bestowed, as inculcating the first lesson of a citizen—soldier, that, as liberty is the greatest of blessings, so should he ever hold himself armed in her defence, and ready to sacrifice his life in her cause!"

A similar presentation was earlier made to Scott by the amiable and devoted patriot, Tompkins, Governor of New York.[3] His address, very partially quoted above, written *con amore,* is too splendid as a composition, to say nothing of its flattery, to be much abridged in these memoirs:

"In adverting, sir, to your claims to distinction, it would be sufficient to say, that on all occasions you have displayed the highest military accomplishments, the most ardent attachment to the rights and honor of your country, and the most intrepid exertions in their support. A rapid and unprecedented succession of promotions at an early age, has been the well-earned fruit of your talents. The distinguished notice by your Government is the best encomium on your character, and the highest reward to which the virtuous and the great aspire.

"But, sir, your military career is replete with splendid events. Without descending into too much minuteness, I may briefly refer to your exploits in the most interesting portion of the American continent. The shores of Niagara, from Erie to Ontario, are inscribed with your name, and with the names of your brave companions. The defeat of the enemy at Fort George will not be forgotten. The memorable conflict on the plains of Chippewa, and the appalling night-battle on the Heights of Niagara, are events which have added new celebrity to the spots where they happened, heightening the majesty of the stupendous cataract, by combining with its natural, all the force of the moral sublime. The admirers of the great in nature, from all quarters of the globe, will forever visit the theatre of your achievements. They will bear to their distant homes the idea of this mighty display of nature, and will associate with it the deeds of you and your brothers in arms. And so long as the beautiful and sublime shall be objects of admiration among men; so long as the whelming waters of Erie shall be tumbled into the awful depths of Niagara, so long shall the splendid actions in which you have had so conspicuous a share, endure in the memory of man."

This paragraph closed the reply of Scott to the Governor of New York:

"On an occasion like this, declarations would but feebly express the volume of obligation contracted. Permit me to assure your Excellency, and through you, the Legislature and people of the proud State of New York, that I am sensibly alive to the duties of a republican soldier, armed by the hands of his countrymen to support and defend their national honor and independence; and if my personal services had been more worthy of the distinction bestowed, I should have no wish left me, at this moment, but that the glory and liberties of the republic might be eternal."

In 1817 quite an angry correspondence took place between Major-General Jackson and Scott, then entire strangers to each other. In Parton's life of the former,[4] and Mansfield's of the latter—two works of considerable ability—the particulars of this quarrel are given. A passing notice of it in this compressed autobiography must suffice.

The Secretary of War, acting in the name or by the authority of the President, had sent an order, direct, to a topographical officer, in the Southern division (half of the United States) under the command of Jackson, telling him to go on some duty elsewhere. This slight irregularity was caused by the wish to save time, for the officer's post office was at a considerable distance from Jackson's headquarters. If notice (always proper in such cases) had been given of the order in question, to Jackson, the irregularity would have been cured; but this was not done by the acting secretary, Mr. Graham.[5] The want of courtesy, on the part of the Executive, was met by a grave offence—a severe rebuke of the Executive, in an order addressed to his division by the hero of New Orleans, in which all his officers were peremptorily instructed not to obey any mandate whatsoever, from whomsoever, that did not pass through his (Jackson's) hands. This was, no doubt, the production of one of his numerous young staff officers—madcaps—to whom was usually abandoned, as was well known to the whole service, all labors of the pen. The penman, no doubt, proud of his commission, very dogmatically, laid down on the subject a code of military doctrines, most of them juvenile crudities, but well suited to the violence of the chief. The order was ostentatiously thrown into many newspapers at once, soon to be taken up by all, and become a subject of universal conversation. Just then, June, 1817, Scott chanced to meet Governor Clinton, present two or three other gentlemen.[6] Being interrogated, professionally, by his Excellency, on what he termed the "extraordinary order," the soldier entered fully and methodically into the subject, and necessarily pointed out several grave blunders, with many regrets, and added the hope and belief that, in consideration of great services, an *admonition*—and not what the governor thought—a *court,* would terminate the matter. That high functionary, had about him, necessarily, many politicians of inferior grades—one of them, a sort of *familiar,* the editor of a paper devoted to his Excellency as a candidate (a second time) for the presidency. To this editor Scott's comments on the order were casually mentioned, and this was repeated, by the latter, in the same way, to a scribbler in the same paper—a former aide-de-camp to a rival general. This ingenious miscreant, from vicarious hostility, a love of mischief, or some hope of personal benefit, addressed General Jackson, anonymously, giving Scott's comments, but suppressing the praises of Jackson, and enclosing a newspaper slip, of his own writing (which he attributed to Scott), attacking Jackson! The entanglement thus produced was slowly unravelled in the next ten or twelve years. Jackson enclosed to Scott a *copy* of the anonymous letter (refusing the original) and the contemptible printed article, demanding, etc. In reply, Scott (also suppressing his praises) acknowledged and repeated his comments on the order, but spurned the printed squib. Then came the rejoinder full of bad temper, bad writing, and bad logic, but containing no challenge—only intimating that Scott might, if he pleased, call him to the field! Now this was as arrogant as absurd; for the law of the *duello* requires that the party, first conceiving himself to be insulted, should make such call—otherwise there would be a mere competition in vulgar abuse, as in the quarrels of fishwomen. Scott, however, for the sake of a conceit that forced itself upon him, chose for the moment to consider the rejoinder as a challenge, in order to add that he declined the combat as his "ambition was not that of Erostratus"[7]—intimating that being without distinction, he waived his only chance of acquiring any by killing a defender of his country. Jackson, probably, not understanding the compliment, hugged the pleasanter conceit to his bosom, that he had won another personal victory by bullying! It seemed cruel to disturb so much happiness, and Scott left his enemy in all his glory.

In the next six years the report often reached Scott and down to a late day, that Jackson had declared he would cut off Scott's ears (his usual threat against offenders) the first time they should chance to meet. They first saw each other in Washington, December, 1823. Jackson had just taken his seat in the Senate, and Scott was en route for the Western Department, headquarters, Louisville, Kentucky, and thence to the Gulf of Mexico, etc., etc. During his short stay in Washington, Scott—having the privilege of the floor—was every day in the Senate chamber (when open)—unarmed;—for he never has worn a concealed weapon—always declaring it would be the smaller evil that he, or any other person should be slain, than to set so bad an example. He frequented the Senate not to attack, or to insult, but simply to put himself under the eye of Jackson—contriving to pass out the chamber, on adjournment, just ahead of him.

Wearied with this state of things, and impatient to proceed to his duties in the Southwest, this letter was written:

General Scott to General Jackson.

WASHINGTON, D. C., December 11, 1823.

SIR:

One portion of the American community has long attributed to you the most distinguished magnanimity, and the other portion the greatest desperation, in your resentments. Am I to conclude that both are in error? I allude to circumstances which have transpired between us, and which need not here be recapitulated, and to the fact that I have now been six days in your immediate vicinity without having attracted your notice. As this is the first time in my life that I have been within a hundred miles of you, and as it is barely possible that you may be ignorant of my presence, I beg leave to state that I shall not leave the District before the morning of the 14th inst.

I have the honor to be, sir,
Your most obedient
servant,
WINFIELD SCOTT

The Hon. General A. Jackson, Senator, etc.

The following answer was promptly returned:
General Jackson to General Scott.

Mr. O'Neil's, December 11, 1823.

SIR:

Your letter of to-day has been received. Whether the world are correct or in error, as regards my "magnanimity," is for the world to decide. I am satisfied of one fact, that when you shall know me better, you will not be disposed to harbor the opinion, that any thing like "desperation in resentment" attaches to me.

Your letter is ambiguous; but, concluding from occurrences heretofore, that it was written with friendly views, I take the liberty of saying to you, that whenever you shall feel disposed to meet me on friendly terms, that disposition will not be met by any other than a correspondent feeling on my part.

have the honor to be, sir,
Your most obedient
servant,
ANDREW JACKSON.

General W. Scott.

Scott, though prepared for the worst, was pleased with Jackson's reply, and, as the younger man, lost no time in waiting upon the honorable Senator. He was graciously received, and the next day took the road to the West. It is painful to reflect that so amicable a settlement only meant, with one of the parties, a postponement of revenge to a more "convenient season."[8]

CHAPTER XVII

TEMPERANCE MOVEMENT—MILITARY INSTITUTES—TACTICS—DEATH OF GENERAL BROWN—MACOMB PROMOTED—ANIMATED CORRESPONDENCE

In the *National Gazette* of Philadelphia (September 22, 1821), I published a *Scheme for Restricting the Use of Ardent Spirits in the United States,* in which I gave a glance at the history of intemperance from the earliest times, and its frightful statistics among ourselves. Mr. Walsh, the able and accomplished editor, published the essay in a supplement of thirteen columns, and heralded it with high praises in the *Gazette* itself.[1] The following is the opening paragraph giving the origin of the essay:

"It is now many years since the writer of this essay was first made to reflect, with some intensity, on the vice of drunkenness, whilst endeavoring to apply a remedy, in a small corps, to that greatest source of disease and insubordination in the rank and file of an army. Having the attention so awakened, and subsequently being much accustomed to change of place from one extreme of the Union to another, he has been led to observe, with a more than usual keenness, the ravages of the same habit among the more numerous classes of the community. The conviction has thus been forced upon him that, of all *accidental* evils, *this* is the most disastrous to our general population."

The principal merit of the essay is that it led to the formation of temperance societies, since so general, throughout the United States.

A little before that time, I had become a member of societies for *the prevention of pauperism, and the suppression of vice and immorality,* to which the essay was a contribution.

True to my motto—*when solitary, be not idle;* and to the maxim, *in peace, prepare for war;*[2] I conceived the idea, in 1818, of preparing a system of General Regulations or *Military Institutes* for the army. After a wide study, begun long before, I made a rigorous analysis of the whole subject, and submitted it to the War Department, which being approved, and provided for by Congress, I duly executed.

This was the first time that the subjects, embraced, were ever reduced, in any army, to a regular analysis, and systematized into institutes. The *Législation Militaire* of France, was indeed, most copious, containing all that can be desired for an army, in the field—excepting tactics, strategy, and engineering—each of which and some other branches of war, properly requiring separate treatises. And the English book of *General Regulations,* was also composed of independent articles, without connection or system. But in the *Institutes,* besides definitions of administration, instruction, service, police, *subjects treated of—* there is a due logical connection and dependence between the parts, not found in the other books mentioned.

How the author's great labors on this and his tactical works have been obscured, mutilated, and pirated, by permission of superior authority, from 1836, down to 1861 inclusive, to the injury of the service, through, I must confess, my neglect of my own interests, may be touched upon in the sequel of this narrative.[3]

It has been seen that I was president of a board of infantry tactics when the treaty of peace with Great Britain arrived in February, 1815. Their labors were hastily and imperfectly concluded by that great event. Another board, on the same subject, of which I was again president, met at West Point in 1824. Each of these boards took, as its basis, the French tactics—the same that I had orally and practically taught in the camp of instruction at Buffalo, beginning in March, 1814.

Besides the Board of Tactics for the army, in 1824, I was president of another, in 1826, at Washington, consisting of two general officers of the militia—Major-General T. Cadwallader, of Philadelphia,[4] a very well read soldier, and who, in the war of 1812–'15, for some time, was commander-in-chief of that department—a citizen of the greatest moral weight of character—and Brigadier-General Sumner, long the intelligent adjutant-general of Massachusetts[5]—together with five army officers.[6] This board was instructed to report: 1. A plan for the organization and instruction of the whole body of the militia of the United States; 2. A system of artillery tactics; 3. A system of cavalry tactics; and 4. A system of infantry and rifle tactics—all four for the benefit of the militia of the Union. The first and fourth of those reports were from Scott's pen, and of the fourth, sixty thousand copies were printed by order of Congress at once, for general distribution.

In the third year (February, 1828) of the second Adams's Administration—a statesman of great learning and abilities; of high patriotism and conscientiousness—an unostentatious Christian—honest, and as obstinately brave as any Puritan in Cromwell's time—Major-General Brown, general-in-chief of the army, died, and Jackson had resigned to be Governor of Florida—which left me senior as brevet-major-general, from July 25th, whereas Gaines' brevet of major-general only gave rank from August 15th, and Macomb's only from September 11th—all in 1814.[7] But Macomb's *ordinary* commission was only that of colonel of engineers, to which he had been cut down at the last reduction of the army in 1821. Both Scott and Gaines, therefore, were not only Macomb's seniors, by brevet, but also, as brigadiers by ordinary commission over his ordinary commission as colonel. It is true, however, that the President has never been legally bound in making promotions, beyond the rank of colonel, to restrict himself, absolutely, to seniority. Hence the question—Who shall be selected to fill Brown's vacancy? became quite general.

An incident now occurred which, among prudes, and men like prudes, may be considered beneath the dignity of history, or memoirs, to record.

Two ladies, sisters, of great excellence—Mrs. Mason, of Anacosta Island,[8] Georgetown, and Mrs. Rush, wife of the Secretary of the Treasury, waited upon the wife of the President to solicit the appointment for Macomb, who, if promoted, as they said, had promised to make the son-in-law of Mrs. Mason (Lieutenant Cooper, then at Fortress Monroe, now adjutant-general of the Confederate army) an aide-de-camp.[9] Mrs. Adams, mistress of all the proprieties, of the sex, and her "pride of place," archly replied: "Truly ladies, though *Mesdames* Maintenon and Pompadour[10] are said to have appointed all the *generalissimos* of their times, I do not think that such matters appertain to women; but if they did, and I had any influence, it should be given to Mrs. General Scott, with whom I accidentally, in travelling, last summer, became acquainted." (The authority for this statement is the late Dr. Hunt, who, as family physician, happened to be present, and who often repeated it to many persons, several of whom are still living.) All this time I happened to be inspecting the Indian frontiers of Louisiana and Arkansas. The ladies, though defeated in their first effort, did not stop there. At their instance, a master now took the matter in hand; for Mr. Secretary Rush, a most amiable and persuasive gentleman, had not resided at a European court (London) without improvement in the arts of insinuation. The President held an evening consultation with many of his cabinet on the question—Who shall be the new general-in-chief? present, Mr. Clay, Mr. Southard, Mr. Wirt, and Mr. Rush.[11] I was named and approved without discussion or dissent. The four members of the cabinet happened to be severally engaged for the evening to the distinguished wife of a distinguished Senator (Johnston) of Louisiana.[12] All took leave of the President together; but Mr. Rush soon turned back as if he missed his gloves or handkerchief. The game was now readily won; for knowing Mr. Adams's horror of bloodshed in private combat, he pressed the strong probability, according to him, of a deadly affair of pistols between Scott and Gaines (of which there was not the slightest danger) if either of them should be appointed to the vacancy; whereas, as he argued, with Macomb at the head of the army, all would be acquiescent and harmonious! It only remains to be added, that Mr. Adams confessed to Mr. Clay and other cabinet advisers, *after the nomination,* that, to save bloodshed he had changed his mind;—that Cooper was in good faith appointed aide-de-camp, and that his most excellent wife (who has been kind to at least one Union prisoner at Richmond) was brought up to Washington and to her affectionate mother.

How nugatory are human institutions! The Salic law may be established in monarchies, and women excluded from the polls, as well as from office, in republics. It is all in vain; for there is "a higher law," "which altereth not"—the result of civilization—that bends imperial man to the stronger will of the weaker vessel![13]

A long and very animated correspondence ensued between the War Department and myself consequent on its order placing me under the command of Macomb, a junior major-general—that is, a superior under an inferior officer. As all the letters are in print they need not be reproduced in this narrative. The heads of my argument against the anomaly, may, however, be succinctly stated thus: That Macomb, though a major-general, was not *the* major-general of the whole army—there being several others of the same grade (by brevet) and no such grade, in law, as *the* major-general or general-in-chief—the latter being a designation of convenience only, and meaning, simply, the senior of several others of the same grade, like commodore, at that day, meaning the senior commander of several vessels besides his own, whether commanded by midshipmen or post captains. 2. That rank is rank, whether the same be conferred by ordinary or brevet commission—both being equally the creatures of the law—unless the *law* has made a difference to the prejudice of one or the other rank, as, in the 61st article of war, which is against brevet rank—*only* within regiments or some other similar corps, as the corps of engineers. I did not claim the right to command Macomb, unless, coming together on common duty, when one would be obliged to command the other, which it was always competent for the Executive, by arrangement, to avoid, as I might be rightly assigned to some separate command or duty, in direct correspondence with the Executive, or laid, by the latter on the shelf, as has become so common recently. I simply contended that no senior, in rank, of the same grade, whether by brevet or otherwise, had ever been, or could be, legally placed under a junior in the British or American army, except by the consent of the senior, and, that, the rules and articles of war were the same in the two armies.

Mr. Adams, as was well known, read, during his presidency, with conscientiousness, every paper, connected with every important subject, that required Executive decision, and, in this controversy, in which, by inveiglement, he had become, virtually, a principal—he did more, he wrote, himself, most of the replies to my formidable appeals and demonstrations. With the obstinacy of a Roundhead, equal to his invincible honesty, he brought to bear against me all the great resources of his rhetoric and ratiocination; and, perhaps, it may even be added—some of the tricks of the schoolmen—being hard pressed and animated to forgetfulness. One of his clever *fetches* overwhelmed me for a moment. Up to April, 1818, all brevets in the army, including mine, had been conferred by the President, without the concurrence of the Senate. *Ergo,* they had been unconstitutionally given, or were of little or no worth; for the supreme law had declared—that "Congress may, by law, vest the appointment of such *inferior* officers as they think proper in the President alone."* {This case shows that it is as dangerous to possess certain arts of rhetoric as to wear concealed weapons, as even good men are liable, under excitement, to use them improperly.} Recovering from the blow, I recollected that, in all tariffs for the exchange of prisoners of war, agreed upon by belligerents, the value of every grade of rank is estimated in privates. Thus in the cartel between the United States and Great Britain in the war of 1812–'15, a brigadier-general is put down as worth thirty privates, and a major-general at only ten more. Consequently, President Madison in making me a major-general, by brevet, had not made a major-general out and out (tinder the act of Congress), but only added the fractional value of ten privates to the grade of brigadier-general before (in my case), solemnly approved by the Senate; that is, but a fourth of the full value of a major-general. To this reply, overwhelming in its turn, I added the resolution of Congress giving me a gold medal, and two other acts, all recognizing, by express citation, my higher rank. I then turned upon my great adversary in the controversy, and triumphantly summed up by saying—if that presentation of my case amounted to nothing, "why then, the world and all that's in it, is nothing; the covering sky is nothing; Bohemia nothing [etc.], for nothing, have these nothings, if this be nothing!"

Mr. Adams confessed himself pleased with the earnestness of this rejoinder; but it seems to belong to the creed of Roundheads, notwithstanding their great characteristics for good, in the past, and for the future, never to acknowledge error.

An incident occurred in this controversy, so curious, that it seems to be entitled to a record in this place. The late adjutant-general (Jones), a good soldier and a better man, calling on business one morning, found the President reading one of my letters then just received, and laughing heartily.[14] "Here," said Mr. Adams, giving an abstract of the letter in his hand—"the general is commenting on the 61st, and 62d articles" of war—relative to rank and command, which, like the whole series, had come down from September, 1776, as borrowed by Congress from England, without change, till 1806—and charges that "some bungler, no doubt a clerk in the War Department, had ignorantly made the revision." Renewing his laughter, Mr. Adams added: "I am that bungling clerk, for being a member of the Senate's committee, to which the subject was referred, in 1806, the labor of the revision fell to me!"

CHAPTER XVIII

BLACK HAWK WAR–CHOLERA IN THE ARMY–INDIAN TREATIES–ROMANTIC TALE

In 1832, Indian hostilities of some magnitude broke out against the then frontier settlements of the Upper Mississippi. Brigadier-General Atkinson,[1] a dear friend of the autobiographer, an excellent man and fine soldier, collected such forces as were at hand—regulars, under Colonel (afterwards President) Taylor, with a much greater number of Illinois volunteers—and marched against Black Hawk and his volunteer band of confederate Sacs and Foxes, who were supported, not only by the sympathies, but material, secret aid, of their neighbors, the Winnebago tribe. As the example of Black Hawk was likely to become infectious among many other Indians in that quarter—Sioux, etc., etc., Scott, who commanded at the time in the Eastern half of the United States, was, to meet contingencies, ordered to the Northwest, with a respectable number of regulars taken from the seaboard defences. Ascending Lake Huron, the Asiatic cholera, the new scourge of mankind which had just before been brought to Quebec, found its way up the chain of waters, in time to infect the troops of Scott's expedition at different points on the lakes. In his particular steamer, the disease broke out suddenly, and with fatal violence. The only surgeon on board, in a panic, gulped down half a bottle of wine; went to bed, sick, and ought to have died. There was nobody left that knew anything of the healing art, or of the frightful distemper—only Scott, who, anticipating its overtaking him in the Northwest, had taken lessons from Surgeon Mower,[2] stationed in New York—eminent in his profession, and of a highly inquiring, philosophic mind—in respect to the character, and mode of treating the disease. Thus he became the doctor on the afflicting occasion no doubt a very indifferent one, except in labor and intrepidity. He had provided the whole expedition with the remedies suggested by Doctor Mower, which, on board his steamer, he applied, in great part, with his own hand to the sick. His principal success was in preventing a general panic, and, *mirabile dictu!* actually cured, in the incipient stage, by *command,* several individuals of that fatal preparation for the reception of the malady. It continued several days after landing, in July, at Chicago—then but a hamlet. As soon as the troops had become sufficiently convalescent they were marched thence across the wild prairies, inhabited by nomads of Potawatamies—Indians of doubtful neutrality. Scott preceded the detachments, and on arriving at Prairie du Chien, was glad to find that Atkinson, after a most fagging march of weeks and hundreds of miles, following the devious retreat of the Hawk, finally overtook him at the mouth of the Badaxe in the act of crossing the Mississippi, with his band, and in a gallant combat, killed many of his followers, made others prisoners, and dispersed the remainder. The principal chief and many hundreds of his people, men, women, and children, escaped across the river; soon, however, to be brought in by the Sioux, who were intimidated by the knowledge that reënforcements were approaching from the East. All the fugitives from the battle, on both sides of the Mississippi, were ultimately brought in.[3] Inspecting the hospital at Fort Crawford, Prairie du Chien (Taylor's post), Scott was struck with the remarkably fine head of a tall volunteer, lying on his side, and seeking relief in a book. To the question—"What have you there, my friend?" the wounded man pointed to the title page of Young's *Night Thoughts*. Scott sat down on the edge of the bunk, already interested, and learned this story:

The reader's brother, Mr. Paine, was Black Hawk's first victim. Not in a spirit of revenge, but to protect the surviving frontier settlers, the wounded man had become a volunteer. Riding into the battle of the Badaxe, he passed an armed Indian boy, not more than in his fourteenth year, whom he might easily have sabred, but that he thought him a harmless child. The incipient warrior, however, fired, and lodged a ball against the spine of the noble volunteer, who, though still suffering greatly, declared that he preferred his condition to the remorse he should have felt if he had killed the boy believing him to have been harmless. Scott soothed the Christian hero by giving him the story (told above) of the Robinson Crusoe Pain, of the Isle of Cape Breton, and took leave with moistened eyes.

Scott, with his principal forces, descended the Mississippi to Rock Island, a little above the mouth of Rock River, which he had given to all the neighboring Indians—friendly, neutral, or lately in arms—as the point of assemblage for the adjustment, by treaty, etc., of the rewards or punishments due to conduct in the recent troubles. There soon approached the confederate Sacs and Foxes, noble tribes, who reminded one of Dryden's fine triplet:

"Free as nature first made man,
Ere the base laws of servitude began,
When wild in woods the noble savage ran."

The cunning Winnebagoes were also coming in, as well as the (for a time) doubtful bands of Sioux, and the not unfriendly Menominees. But just then the cholera broke out among the troops at the island, in all the violence of a first attack. On that account, Scott sent directions to all those Indians not to approach him till a new summons. In the mean time an incident occurred, like several others of a later date, at the same place, to illustrate the manners—morals, *moeurs*—of our red men—not yet taught by his white brethren to lie, to cheat and steal, except to and from an enemy.

There were found at Fort Armstrong, Rock Island, the appointed scene of diplomacy, three civil prisoners, Sacs, confined by an Indian agent on the charge of murder—that is, surprising and killing a party of Menominees (old enemies), in exact retaliation, and according to Indian habits, of a like act on the part of the latter.

In reference to the terrible cholera, Scott said to the prisoners: "If I permit you, as you desire, to seek safety in the prairies, and, if attacked with the disease, to cure yourselves, with your own unscientific remedies—will you, when the cholera shall have left the island, return here to be dealt with—probably hung—as a civil court may adjudge?" They gave the required pledge.

It was accordingly arranged, that on the exhibition of a certain signal, hung out from a dead tree, at an elevated point of the island, they would return. Loaded with hard bread, and armed with guns, they were put ashore on the mainland. The cholera having passed away, the signal was given, when, in a day or two, the three *murderers* presented themselves! Scott placed them again on parole, to await the answer to an appeal, in their behalf, he had already made to Washington. The answer finally came and was favorable.

The new summons was now given to all the tribes before mentioned, and obeyed, when conferences and grand councils of war for the settlements, before alluded to, commenced. While these were pending, a demand came up, from a judge of Illinois, sixty miles below, for an Indian murderer, his name unknown, but who had been distinctly traced to the camp of the great body of Sacs and Foxes whom the chiefs had contrived to hold in neutrality during the recent hostilities—influenced mainly by Keokuk—not a hereditary chief, and only a principal *brave* or warrior, the sense bearer, orator, and treasurer of the confederacy.[4] The demand was communicated to this remarkable man. After a little musing, the painful truth of the story seemed to flash upon him. With candor he stated the grounds of his fears. A young *brave* of some twenty years of age, the son of a distinguished chief, had long sought to marry a handsome young squaw, the daughter of another famous chief; but the maiden repulsed the lover, applying to him the most opprobrious epithet—*squaw*—he never having taken a scalp, killed a grizzly bear, nor, by surprise, robbed an enemy of his arms, horse, or wife. Hence, she said her lover was not a *brave,* but a woman. Her sympathies were, moreover, with Black Hawk—her only brother having run off with that reckless chief. All these particulars were not yet known to the wise treasurer; for he had only been surprised, at the change of conduct in the *belle sauvage,* who had so suddenly married her lover. Keokuk, in good faith, said he would inquire, for his great care had been to save his people from destructive war and entire spoliation, with which Black Hawk's conduct had caused them to be threatened.

The next day he called at headquarters and whispered that his fears had proved prophetic; that the happy bridegroom had, for the good of the confederacy, confessed himself to be the guilty party, and was at hand; but begged the general to repeat, in a full council, the demand, etc. This was accordingly done, and as soon as Scott's peroration—*I demand the murderer!* was interpreted, the young Apollo stood up and said: *I am the man!* With a violent stamp and voice Scott called out—*the guard!* A sergeant with a dozen grenadiers rushed in, seized the offender and carried him off.

When the blacksmith began to place and rivet irons upon him he struggled furiously. It took several of the guard to hold him down. He said he did not come forward to be ironed; he did not wish to be tried, that he preferred to be shot at once. He was sent down to the Illinois court, then in session; put on his trial, and notwithstanding the strong circumstantial evidence, and that it was proven he had acknowledged the killing in a hand-to-hand fight—a tricky lawyer, well provided with the means of bribing, no doubt, by the chiefs of the confederacy, obtained from the jury a verdict of *not guilty.*

The acquitted had yet to pass another ordeal—one of fire and water. A swift horse, halfway between the court and the Mississippi (a few hundred yards off) had been provided for the occasion; but frontier men always have their rifles in hand, and their horses ready. The lawyer hastened his client out of court, and gained for him a good start. "Fly, young man, or your dear-bought Helen will soon be a widow!" In a minute, followed by some whizzing shots, he was in the saddle. In another, "horse and rider" were plunged into "the great father of waters," swimming side by side. Now came up furiously a dozen mounted riflemen, who threw away their lead at the too distant game. The last news of the romantic Sac represented him as the happy father of a thriving family of "young barbarians," by more than a "Dacian mother,"—all far beyond the Mississippi.[5]

Conferences were held with the Menominees and Sioux, and treaties signed with—first the Winnebagoes, and next with the confederate Sacs and Foxes, in separate general councils. There was a second commissioner, united with Scott, in these negotiations—Governor Reynolds.[6] But the wearer of the sword, before Indians, is the effective orator.

The spirit of forbearance and liberality, on the part of the United States, were the prominent features in those settlements. Scott opened each council with stern reproach—reminding the confederate tribes that, by their failure to restrain one of their chiefs, Black Hawk, from making an unjust war upon the unoffending white settlers, near them, the whole confederacy had forfeited as much of their territory as the conquerors might choose to claim as an indemnity; and the Winnebagoes were informed, that their secret encouragement and preparations to join in highly criminal hostilities, made them liable to like punishment.

These emphatic denunciations being made perfectly clear, through excellent interpreters, and their justice shown to be indisputable, Scott, on each occasion, proceeded: "Such is justice, between nation and nation, against which none can rightfully complain; but as God in his dealings with human creatures tempers justice with mercy—or else the whole race of man would soon have perished—so shall we, commissioners, in humble imitation of divine example, now treat you, my red brethren! who have offended both against God and your great human father, at Washington." He then, in each case, demanded a portion of their superfluous territory—from the confederates, that next to the Mississippi, now the best part of Iowa; and from the Winnebagoes the northern hart of Illinois—paying liberally for the cessions, and stipulating for the support at the cost of the United States, of schools and workshops, to teach reading, writing, arithmetic, and the more necessary mechanical arts.[7]

Grateful replies were returned in each council. That of Keokuk, on the part of the Sacs and Foxes, was full of sound sentiment, power, and pathos.

The evening after signing the last treaty, the general gave a grand dinner to the principal chiefs, and had later, a brilliant display of pyrotechnics—that is, the throwing of fire balls from mortars, and firing of single and batteries of rockets, which caused much shouting of delight from the Indians encamped on the mainland—Rock Island being in the centre of an amphitheatre of high hills—notwithstanding their usual *nil admirari*,[8] or phlegm.

The young officers of the army—all volunteers had been discharged by Scott, soon after the battle of the Badaxe—had a dance on the green turf at the same time—reels and quadrilles—with young *braves*—the Indian *mœurs*, like those of the Turks, forbidding that the red women should mix themselves up, in public, with their male superiors—barbarians! Many of the softer sex, however, were allowed to look on the dancers, and showed by their giddy chatterings that they would have been happier if whirled about in the dance by those charming young white *braves!*

Ah! how sad for man, and woman too, if not allowed, in youth and innocency, to converse, to talk, to play and laugh together.

The male partners of our officers were quick in step and imitation, as well as in loud laughter, at every turn. A band furnished the music and heightened the joy of all.

Keokuk, too, contributed not a little to the entertainment by a pantomime, which needed no interpretation, of one of his successful expeditions against a hostile party. First the tedious march; streams to swim; next the rapid run, and now the stealthy step—beckoning to his followers the discovery of the unsuspecting enemy at camp fires with rifles laid aside, waiting—a moment longer for the cooked venison they were destined never to eat;—then the rush upon the unarmed, and the slaying. In a moment all was over, but the shouting. Bigotini was never happier in pantomime at the Paris Opera.[9]

A war dance was added by the same accomplished hero in peace as in war, whom Scott had solemnly invested with the rank and broad silver medal of a chief, with the consent of the tribe, and on an equal footing with the proudest who had inherited the title through long generations.

The sequel of the late troubles were thus closed, when all, of both colors, dispersed, contented and cheerful.

It was in allusion to the cholera and the foregoing settlements with the Indians, that General Cass, then Secretary of War, now one of the most venerable of American citizens, after a long life of usefulness and distinction—without one error in morals, and but few in politics—addressed to Scott a letter containing this passage:[10]

"Allow me to congratulate you, sir, upon this fortunate consummation of your arduous duties, and to express my entire approbation of the whole course of your proceedings, during a series of difficulties requiring higher moral courage than the operations of an active campaign, under ordinary circumstances."

A published letter from an intelligent officer of the army, still unknown, but supposed to have been the lamented Captain Richard Bache (a descendant of Dr. Franklin), deserves a place in this narrative.[11] It is more in detail, and better *motivé* than the Secretary's:

He says that "the general's course of conduct on the occasion should establish for him a reputation not inferior to that which he has earned in the battle field; and should exhibit him not only as a warrior, but as a man—not only as the hero of battles, but as the hero of humanity. It is well known that the troops in that service suffered severely from the cholera, a disease frightful enough from its rapid and fatal effects, but which came among us the more so, from the known inexperience of our medical men, and from the general belief, at that time, in its contagiousness. Under such circumstances it was clearly the general's duty to give the best general directions he could for proper attendance on the sick, and for preventing that spread of the disease. When he had done this, his duty was performed, and he might have left the rest to his medical officers. But such was not his course. He thought he had other duties to perform, that his personal safety must be disregarded to visit the sick, to cheer the well, to encourage the attendants, to set a example to all, and to prevent a panic—in a word, to save the lives of others at the risk of his own. All this he did faithfully, and when he could have had no other motive than that of doing good. Here was no glory to be acquired; here was none of the excitements of the battle field; here was no shame to be avoided, or disgrace to be feared; because his general arrangements and directions to those whose part it was to battle with sickness, had satisfied duty. His conduct then exhibited a trait in his character which made a strong impression on me, and which, in my opinion, justice requires should not be overlooked."

CHAPTER XIX

REJOINS HIS FAMILY–ORDERED TO CHARLESTON–NULLIFICATION–INCIDENTS– PEACE RESTORED

Scott now hastened to join his family, at West Point, in their retreat from the cholera in New York. He himself, always in its presence, experienced symptoms of the infection; but without taking a remedy, he had, so far, escaped prostration.

Passing through Cincinnati, he told the eminent Dr. Drake, judging by his usual feelings, that the evil was about to burst upon the inhabitants, which happened the next day.[1] Sleeping at Chambersburg, where he arrived late at night, he was much cramped, and learned, next morning, that a cholera patient was just dead on the same floor. At Philadelphia he told his friends, Professors Chapman and Gibson, that the disease was still lingering with them, and always well on the road, he might have said the same thing at New York.[2] Here, eating a sumptuous dinner, for the first time in many months, with wine, at Delmonico's, he took the evening steamer for West Point, with stronger premonitions than ever before; lay down to sleep, determined if, on waking up, the symptoms continued, to pass his family and die somewhere beyond them.[3] Happily, getting into a healthy atmosphere, he, at the end of two hours, found himself again well.

It was now about the 4th of November. But little rest with his family was allowed. Having done much work, more was demanded. In a few days he received an order from the War Department, marked confidential, to hasten to Washington. He passed, unknowingly, Mr. Secretary Cass on the road to the North. Scott, arriving in the evening, had no one to report to, but President Jackson himself. Waiting upon him at once, he, after a gracious reception, adverted to the certainty that South Carolina would very soon be out of the Union—either by nullification or secession. On that probability, he condescendingly invited Scott's views as to the best measures of counteraction—he himself being patriotically resolved to stand his ground—*The Union must and shall be preserved.* Scott, in reply, suggested strong garrisons for Fort Moultrie (Sumter was not quite above ground), Castle Pinckney, and the arsenal at Augusta, Georgia.[4] The latter was filled with the *matériel* of war—then easily seized and emptied by a sudden expedition across the bridge that made Hamburg, in South Carolina, a faubourg of Augusta—there being always, in both places, hundreds of cotton wagons harnessed up.[5] He added, that besides troops, a sloop-of-war and some revenue cutters would be needed in Charleston to enforce the collection of duties on foreign importations. "Proceed at once and execute those views. You have my *carte blanche,* in respect to troops; the vessels shall be there, and written instructions shall follow you," were the President's prompt orders, given orally.

In the act of taking leave, Scott was invited to wait a moment for supper. He replied that as he should proceed South in the morning, he had only that hour for calling upon his friend, Ex-President Adams, a little distance off. "That's right," said General Jackson, "never forget a friend." Mr. Adams astonished Scott not a little by two remarks: 1. "You are going South to watch the nullifiers." (There was no intercourse between him and his successor whatever.) 2. "Mr. Calhoun will be the first to give way. He will show the white feather!"[6]

Scott reminded Mr. Adams that this was about his usual time for making his regular tour of inspection along the Southern seacoast. "Yes," he reiterated, "to watch the nullifiers."

Scott reached Charleston a few days after the passage of the ordinance of nullification. On the journey he had twisted a little an ankle. This was fortunate, and he made the most of the accident to cover delays at Charleston, Savannah, and Augusta; for it was important to the interests of uninterrupted peace, that he should not, by open preparations for defence, precipitate hostilities,—the minds of nullifiers, about half of the population, being much inflamed, and on the *qui vive.*[7] As biennial inspector, he contrived, by a little hobbling, to visit Fort Moultrie and Castle Pinckney; gave confidential instructions to enlarge and strengthen the fort, etc. Orders were also sent for the handfuls of troops (single companies, from many points) necessary to complete garrisons. Thence he visited Augusta in the same way, and for a like purpose. That being accomplished, he fell down to Savannah, where he laid himself up rather more than the improved ankle required, because an early return to Fort Moultrie would unquestionably have betrayed the special purpose of his presence; have caused an immediate attempt to seize Fort Moultrie, and, probably, an intestine war, as bad as that which is now (February, 1864), afflicting the good old Union.

While lying at Savannah, awaiting a nearer approach of the impending crisis in South Carolina, the reply, below, was written to the Honorable William C. Preston, afterwards of the Senate of the United States— then a leading member both of the legislature and convention of South Carolina.[8]

No one intimately acquainted with this distinguished man can speak of him without seeming, to a stranger, to run into extravagance. With the purest morals, and a wife worthy to glide "double, swan and shadow," down the stream of life with him—they were "lovely and pleasant in their lives, and in their death [not long] divided."

He, so highly gifted in genius and fancy; highly accomplished as a scholar, a gentleman, and a statesman; with powers of oratory to enrapture the multitude, and edify the intelligent;—with a soul so genial and voice so sweet, as to win all who approached him—young and old, men, women, and children—was, at this unhappy period, given up to nullification. His good genius, however, triumphed in the end; for he lived long enough to make atonement to the Union, and to die (in 1860) faithful to the same allegiance that distinguished his grandfather, Campbell, of King's Mountain, and also his immediate parent, General Frank Preston, long a member of Congress from Southwestern Virginia.[9]

Letter from Major-General Scott to the Honorable Lewis Cass, Secretary at War.

[Extract.]

"Headquarters, Eastern Department, Savannah, December 15, 1832.
"Sir:

"I have had the honor to address you once from this place since my return from Augusta. The letter bore date the 10th or 11th instant. In it I stated that I had not the time to retain a copy.
"I now take the liberty to enclose a copy of a private letter which I addressed to William C. Preston, Esq., a leading member of the South Carolina Legislature, and a nullifier. I do this, because letters from me to individuals of that party should be seen by the Government, and because this letter contains the sentiments and topics which I always urge in conversation with nullifiers.

"It will be seen that I speak of the arrival of troops in the harbor of Charleston. I did this because I knew the movement of the troops was, or would be soon known, and because I wish to prevent the idea of offensive operations (invasion.) Such an idea might precipitate the State authorities into some act of open hostility, which would not fail to be followed by a civil war, at least among her own citizens."

Savannah, December 14, 1832.

My Dear Sir:

You have an excellent memory to remind me, after so long an interval, of my promise to visit you when next on a tour to the South, and I owe you an apology for not earlier acknowledging your kind letter. It was handed to me just as I was about to leave Charleston, and I have been since too constantly in motion (to Augusta, and back here) to allow me to write.

As to the "speculations" at Columbia relative to "the object of my visit to Charleston at this moment," I can only say, that I am on that very tour, and about the very time, mentioned by me when I last had the pleasure of seeing you. On what evils days we have fallen, my good friend, when so commonplace an event gives rise to conjecture or speculation! I can truly assure you, that no one has felt more wretched than your humble correspondent, since an unhappy controversy began to assume a serious aspect. I have always entertained a high admiration for the history and character of South Carolina, and accident or good fortune, has thrown me into intimacy, and even friendship, with almost every leader of the two parties which now divide and agitate the State. Would to God they were again united, as during the late war, when the federalists vied with the republicans in the career of patriotism and glory, and when her legislature came powerfully to the aid of the Union. Well, the majority among you have taken a stand, and those days of general harmony may never return. What an awful position for South Carolina, as well as for the other States!

I cannot follow out the long, dark shades of the picture that presents itself to my fears. I will hope, nevertheless, for the best. But I turn my eyes back, and, good God! what do I behold? Impatient South Carolina could not wait—she has taken a leap, and is already a foreign nation; and the great names of Washington, Franklin, Jefferson, and Greene, no longer compatriot with yours, or those of Laurens, Moultrie, Pinckney, and Marion with mine!

But the evil, supposing the separation to have been *peaceable,* would not stop there. When one member shall withdraw, the whole arch of the Union will tumble in. Out of the broken fragments new combinations will arise. We should probably have, instead of *one, three* confederacies—a Northern, Southern, and Western reunion; and transmontane Virginia, your native country, not belonging to the South, but torn off by the general West. I turn with horror from the picture I have only sketched. I have said it is dark; let but one drop of blood be spilt upon the canvas, and it becomes "one red."

"Lands intersected by a narrow frith
Abhor each other. Mountains interposed
Make enemies of nations, which had else,
Like kindred drops, been mingled into one."

But you and my other South Carolina friends have taken your respective sides, and I must follow out mine.

You have probably heard of the arrival of two or three companies at Charleston, in the last six weeks, and you may hear that as many more have followed. There is nothing inconsistent with the President's message in these movements. The intention simply is, that the forts in the harbor shall not be wrested from the United States. I believe it is not apprehended that the State authorities contemplate any attack, at least in the present condition of things, on these posts; but I know it has been feared that some unauthorized multitude, under sudden excitement, might attempt to seize them. The President, I presume, will stand on the defensive—thinking it better to discourage than to invite an attack—better to prevent than to repel one, in order to gain time for wisdom and moderation to exert themselves in the capitol at Washington, and in the state house at Columbia. From humane considerations like these, the posts in question have been, and probably will be, slightly reënforced. I state what I partly know, and what I partly conjecture, in order that the case which I see is provided for in one of your bills, may not be supposed to have actually occurred.

If I were possessed of an important secret of the Government, my honor certainly would not allow me to disclose it; but there is in the foregoing neither secrecy nor deception. My ruling wish is, that neither party take a rash step, that might put all healing powers at defiance. It is, doubtless, merely intended to hold the posts for the present. A few companies are incapable of effecting any further object. The engineer, also, is going on, steadily, but slowly, in erecting the new work (Fort Sumter, near the site of Fort Johnson, long since projected for the defence of the harbor), the foundation of which is but just laid.[10] When finished, some years hence, I trust it may long be regarded, both by South Carolina and the other States, as one of the bulwarks of our common coast.

There is nothing in this letter intended to be confidential, nor intended for the public press. When I commenced it, I only designed giving utterance to private sentiments, unconnected with public events; but my heart being filled with grief on account of the latter, my pen has run a little into that distress. Let us, however, hope for more cheering times. Yet, be this as it may, and whether our duties be several or common,

I shall always have a place in my bosom for the private affections; and that I may ever stand in the old relation to you, is the sincere wish of your friend,
WINFIELD SCOTT.

The time of danger at length arrived, and so had the detachments of troops in the harbor of Charleston, each company astonished to meet the others. Scott borrowed the revenue cutter of the collector, who supposed him to be bound to St. Augustine—a supposition neither favored nor denied by Scott, who giving orders not to take letters, sailed from Savannah "for parts unknown" to all but himself. Passing the Tybee bar, the astonished master of the cutter was told to *stand for the harbor of Charleston.* The next day Scott was ensconced in Fort Moultrie, where, for several days, he lay, without the knowledge of anybody in Charleston, save his friend—the great patriot and moral hero—James L. Petigru (now lately dead of a broken heart at the state of the country), and a few other friends of the Union—Poinsett, Huger, etc., etc.[11]

Finding that at a general meeting in the city, the leaders of the quasi rebellion had proposed and carried a resolution to suspend its commencement, in order to await the result of certain compromise measures before Congress—Scott again, to avoid the irritation the threatening aspect of his presence might occasion, quietly embarked in another cutter for the North, *via* Wilmington, North Carolina—intending to return before the expiration of the *quasi* armistice. Colonel Bankhead, Scott's chosen second in command—a manly, generous soldier, was left to improve, in the mean time, the discipline of the troops and the strength of the forts.[12]

In the night, late in January, Scott reëmbarked in the lower harbor of New York for Charleston—his departure unknown in the city, and also his name to the master and owners of the packet. That same day, he despatched an article to his friend, General Broadnax,[13] the acknowledged leader of the Virginia Legislature, against both nullification and secession, containing politico-military views and arguments not likely to occur to the minds of many civilians, and which, being published in the newspapers at the time and place, had a considerable effect in preventing Virginia from plunging into the South Carolina vortex, to which her State Right doctrines made her but too prone. She was then saved; but, at the second temptation (in 1861) lost in rebellion!

"The mother of States," late in January, 1833, passed resolutions recommending that the offensive ordinance of South Carolina be repealed, and requesting Congress to mitigate the tariff. The third step, taken at the same time, was to appoint a commissioner of persuasion and peace to her wayward sister—perhaps, not entirely in harmony with the spirit of the supreme law of the Union that prohibits "any agreement or compact" between States. The person selected for that duty was the Honorable Benjamin Watkins Leigh, already mentioned in these memoirs as Scott's earliest and longest-continued friend—soon after a distinguished Senator of the United States, and distinguished in every previous walk of his life for virtue, talent, and usefulness—whose motto always was: *Right ends, pursued by means as good as the ends.* Shaking hands in Charleston, the two friends exclaimed together: *How strange our meeting here, and how strange the occasion!*

In every case where there was a liability of collision between the Federal and State authorities, Scott consulted with the District Attorney, Gilchrist, with Petigru, etc., always holding himself ready to support the marshal by force.[14] Happily no collision fell out between the parties. But the duties of Scott were most critical, requiring the nicest observance and delicacy of management, to avoid the shedding of the *first* drop of blood; for failing in this, the two home parties, nearly of equal numbers, and always ready for blows, would instantly have rushed into the affray, and have filled the State with the sound of hostile arms. Nor could such calamity have been pent up within her borders; but must have raged and spread like the present dire rebellion.[15]

Perhaps the peace observances alluded to, though great in the aggregate, were, separately, too small in detail for historical record; yet nothing that tended to prevent a civil war ought, by patriots, to be regarded as trivial. Besides, the record may he valuable to future commanders finding themselves in similar circumstances. The basis of Scott's policy was *humility and forbearance* on the part of the United States' troops, officers, and men. The crews of the rowboats, which consisted of men selected on account of their intelligence and sobriety—for marketing purposes, visiting the post office, and conveying officers up and down between the fort and the city—were made to comprehend and support that policy. The general, sometimes a passenger himself, took that instruction into hand. He said to the crews, and as often as practicable to officers and others of the garrison: "These nullifiers," all known by their palmetto cockades, "have, no doubt, become exceedingly wrong-headed, and are in the road to treason; but still they are our countrymen, and may be saved from that great crime by respect and kindness on our part. We must keep our bosoms open to receive them back as brothers in the Union. If we succeed by such means in this endeavor, it will be a great moral triumph, worth much more to our country than crushing victories in the field. In walking the streets let us give place to all citizens. Bad words and even, casting mud upon us, can do no harm. We shall show our courage by quietly passing along. I rather think that I should disregard even a few brickbats, and *remember,* my gallant fellows, that *you are no better than your old commander!* But should those misguided men be driven to the field by our neglect or their own inherent madness;—should they, drop the name of Americans, and under the wing of some foreign power make war upon us, then, in tears and blood we will crush them!!" Such remarks often repeated, and falling from an officer of high rank, needed, for propagation among troops, no printing press. They ran through mouths and ears of all with wonderful rapidity.

Hundreds of citizens, respectable men, decorated with the palmetto, visited the fort in the course of every week. Scott, and many of his intelligent officers, made it a point to converse freely with those citizens, and to show to some of the seniors and most intelligent, the interior of the defensive works—always taking care to remark: "You see we have made ourselves as strong as possible, and wish it to be known to our neighboring countrymen; because it is to be feared, that in the unhappy excitement prevailing, some unauthorized multitude, by a sudden impulse, may rush upon us, in ignorance, and to their certain destruction." Some of the graver of those visitors were, on many occasions, even invited by the general to dine at the officers' mess, and treated with the highest courtesy.

At a public meeting of nullifiers—there was more than one a week—to keep up excitement—Governor Hamilton[16] in a *tirade* told the multitude that, to try the question whether the Federal authorities would dare to stop, at the fort, dutiable articles till satisfaction of all tariff demands, he had ordered some boxes of sugar from the Havana, and "my friends," he added, with great applause, "if Uncle Sam put his robber hand on the boxes, *I know you'll go the death with me for the Sugar!*" The ship soon arrived, the sugar was quietly taken out, locked up in the fort, and kept a secret from everybody in Charleston, except the importer; because, if known, consistency in folly might have caused an attempt to execute the threat.

While all good patriots were fearful of folly and madness on one side, and with aching eyes turned to Congress on the other;—that is, while all were in the agony of suspense—a great calamity fell upon Charleston, which Scott instantly sought to turn to the interests of peace. At nightfall, it was seen at the fort that a fire was raging in the city, which, aided by a fresh breeze, was likely to reduce everything combustible to ashes. The drums beat the *long-roll,* the garrison leaped from an unfinished supper, and, in a moment, all were under arms. Scott in his usual tone stated the reason for the call;—made a short appeal to the sympathies of the soldiers, and asked for volunteers to aid in stopping the fire. All stepped forward. He directed the company officers to select some three hundred men, and prepare the boats. In the mean time he despatched Major Heileman, an excellent officer and man, who, from long service in the harbor had made himself a favorite with everybody in the city—to report to the Intendant (mayor) that he would soon be followed by detachments of men anxious to help their friends in the existing calamity.[17] He was told to say that the troops would arrive *without arms,* and take care not to allow the crabbed Intendant time to retort "*D—n General Scott and his arms! I'm not afraid of them*"; but to add, in his first breath: "This is said in order that should you set the soldiers to guard banks and property in the streets, you may see the necessity of lending them a few stands of muskets." The gallant Major Ringgold (mortally wounded under General Taylor on this side of the Rio Grande) at the instant came up with some eighty lusty fellows, ready for the good work.[18] He reported himself to the sulky Intendant, unworthy of the city and his office—who made no reply to either of those officers. Just then, a citizen called to Ringgold, "Here, Major, for God's sake save my sugar refinery, for the adjoining house has caught the flames!" Ringgold turning to his men said: "*Do you hear that my lads; we'll go the 'death for the sugar!'*"—a most happy quotation from Governor Hamilton, that caused everybody to smile but the Intendant, who evidently considered the kind presence of the soldiers a most untoward event to the cause of nullification. Ringgold's party soon tore down the house next to the refinery, and mainly by the aid of the other troops and a body of United States' sailors, the devouring element was stayed everywhere.

Scott remained up to welcome and applaud his noble detachments. The good citizens, melting with gratitude, had been liberal in the offer of bread, cheese, and cider—the soldiers declining ardent spirits, and all, sober and happy, were in their own beds by one o'clock the same night.

Mr. Leigh, much with the nullifiers, to whom he had been commissioned, wrote to Scott the next day, that "a great good had been effected. It works pow[er]fully."

One other incident occurred during this same state of lingering agony that seems entitled to come upon this record. The nullifiers, though they regarded Scott askance, and with feelings bordering on honest, but mistaken hatred, had not lost all the brightness of their old chivalry, and hence, in the Jockey Club, united with the Union members in extending to Scott an invitation to attend the approaching races—a sort of annual jubilee, which always brought to Charleston, in February, most of the numerous families of wealth, refinement, and fashion in the State. The club, moreover, did him the honor to appoint a man of mark as his *cicerone* for the occasion, and in case of need, a ready, very sufficient protector. This true chevalier was the Ex-Governor Wilson,[19] a staunch nullifier, formerly a powerful editor of a newspaper;—a recent translator of certain Greek fragments into elegant English poetry;—in early life, almost a professed duellist, but of late the common pacificator in private quarrels;—not yet old, but subdued in temper, probably more by remorse than age, and now benignant in smiles and sentiments.

The two, Wilson and Scott, had hardly reached the Stranger's Stand, before Mr. Leigh, from the Governor's Stand, came almost breathless to Scott: "Why," he said, "this rash step you are about to take—a new fort at this critical moment, when the friends of peace are just beginning to hope it possible to avoid a civil war?" "My good friend, I don't comprehend you," replied Scott. "Oh, there is no use in mystery on the subject. Here's a Washington paper (received in advance of the mail) containing a letter to you from the War Department, telling you to cause Stono Inlet to be examined, with a view to a fort at that point." Now it was true Scott had, some time before, received such letter, but was astonished to find it had been published. It was certainly, under the circumstances, a most sinister publication—quite athwart Scott's peace policy and measures; for if a spade had been, about that time, put into the ground for a new work beyond Sullivan's Island, civil war would have been inaugurated on the spot. Happily Scott was enabled to say, with truth, that he had absolutely no intention of sending an officer or a man to that point, and that to occupy it by a fort or troops was entirely outside of his military views and purposes. Mr. Leigh and Governor Wilson hastened to communicate this assurance to the high officials and others on the ground, all in a state of morbid excitement, breathing defiance and war.

Considering the oral and written instructions Scott had before received from the President and Secretary of War, it is difficult to imagine the necessity for this missile. Through some babbler an inkling of the order reached the ears of a member of the House of Representatives, when, in a spirit of hostility, it was called for and thrown out, as a fire-brand among more than a million of States' Rights men south of the Potomac ready for explosion.

A while later Congress passed the Compromise Act; the South Carolina Convention reconvened and rescinded the nullification ordinance, when Leigh and Scott returned North in a state of quiet satisfaction.

Scott called at the President's mansion. Vice-President Van Buren, a temporary guest, came down to receive him, and told the visitor that he had read all his reports, official and semi-official, from the South, and kindly spoke of them with emphatic approbation. The President himself soon followed and touched lightly the same subject—deigning a few terms of measured praise.

This extreme temperance of phrase on a great occasion slightly awakened Scott's' suspicion that the reconciliation between the parties in 1823, was, with General Jackson, but external; although the habit of his, Scott's mind, was of the opposite character—he, always, accepting as sound maxims, that "more men are duped by suspicion than by confidence,"* {Le Cardinal de Retz, Liv. II.} and that—"Evils may be courted, may be woo'd and won by *distrust*."* {Proverbial Philosophy.} But more of the particular suspicion in the sequel.

Mr. Leigh, who died in 1849, in a published letter, addressed to Edward D. Mansfield, Esq., author of Scott's biography, and many works of great scientific and literary merit, said: "I was in Charleston when Scott arrived and assumed command [his last visit, about the first of February—by sea, from New York], which he did without any parade or fuss. No one who had an opportunity of observing on the spot the excitement that existed can have an adequate conception of the delicacy of the trust. General Scott had a large acquaintance with the people of Charleston. He was their friend; but his situation was such that many, the great majority of them, looked upon him as a public enemy. * * * * * He thought, as I thought, that the first drop of blood shed in civil war, between the United States and one of the States, would prove an immedicable wound, which would end in a change of our institutions. He was resolved, if possible, to prevent a resort to arms, and nothing could have been more judicious than his conduct. Far from being prone to take offence, he kept his temper under the strictest guard, and was most careful to avoid giving occasion for offence; yet he held himself ready to act, if it should become necessary, and he let that be. distinctly understood. He sought the society of the leading nullifiers [old friends], and was in their society as much as they would let him be, but he took care never to say a word to them on the subject of political differences; he treated them as a friend. From the beginning to the end his conduct was as conciliatory as it was firm and sincere, evincing that he knew his duty and was resolved to perform it, and yet that his principal object and purpose was peace. He was perfectly successful, when the least imprudence might have resulted in a serious collision."

CHAPTER XX

TACTICS—GENERAL REGULATIONS— FLORIDA WAR—CREEK WAR—JACKSON'S WAR UPON SCOTT—COURT OF INQUIRY

In 1834–'5 the autobiographer translated and adapted to the particular organization of the United States' Infantry, unencumbered with a board, the new French Tactics on the old basis. His *General Regulations* for the army, or *Military Institutes,* had, in a new impression years before, dropping his name, been blurred, mutilated, and spoiled under high military authority. This, his last edition of tactics, was soon, under the same protection, abridged and emasculated down to utter uselessness, by the present adjutant-general of the Confederate army, without the knowledge of Scott, and next pirated, in great part, under the immediate protection of Mr. Secretary Jefferson Davis, by one of his pets, now a division commander in the Confederate army, aided by another pet of the same Mr. Davis, a major-general of the United States' volunteers, who, recently, following up the old hostility of that *clique,* has entirely superseded Scott's tactics, with the consent of a loyal Secretary of War, and two loyal regular generals, all three the professed friends of Scott, but who did not chance to know anything of the particular history or the merits of the case, and through Scott's personal neglect of his own fame and interests.[1] With a single added remark, the result of an old experience, the autobiographer will dismiss this subject for ever:—*It is extremely perilous to change systems of tactics in an army in the midst of a war, and highly inconvenient even at the beginning of one.*

A slight incident occurred about this time, which, though perhaps below the dignity of history, may be tolerated in personal memoirs, which are usually of a more anecdotal character, and written with greater freedom and ease.

Scott being on a short visit to Washington, had the honor to be invited to dine with President Jackson, and was further complimented by being assigned to conduct an agreeable lady, to him a stranger, to the table, where he was desired to place her between the President and himself. Towards the end of the sitting General Jackson said to the fair lady, in a tone of labored pleasantry, that is, with ill-disguised bitterness: "I see you are pleased with the attentions of your neighbor. Do you know that he has condemned all the measures of my administration?" Mrs. —— was perfectly shocked. Scott promptly replied: "Mr. President, you are in part mistaken. I thought highly, of your proclamation against nullifiers, and yesterday, in the Senate, I was equally pleased with your special message on the French Indemnity question, which I heard read." "That's candid!" retorted the President. "He thinks well of two—*but two!* of my measures." The lady evidently regarded Scott, like the old general, as a bad subject of the realm. The most unsuspicious nature might now plainly see that the bolt was forged, and would in due time be launched.

The Seminole war, which commenced by the surprise and massacre of Major Dade, and about one hundred and ten men, December 28, 1835, may from its cost (about twenty millions) and duration (seven years) be called a great war.[2] Brigadier-General Clinch, nearest at hand, advanced on the Indians, and at the head of a small force won the battle of Withlacoochee.[3] Major-General Gaines hastily collected, at New Orleans, a body of volunteers and some companies of regulars, and soon reached Florida.[4] He marched past the scene of the massacre, buried the dead, and proceeded towards Fort Drane for supplies. His detachment, attacked by the Seminoles on the Withlacoochee, intrenched themselves, and would probably have shared the fate of Dade's party, but for a prompt undictated movement by Brigadier-General Clinch, commanding at Fort Drane—a man of singular excellence—whose sentiments had the unvarying truth of instincts, and whose common sense always rose to the height of the occasion.

Clinch liberated the beleaguered Gaines, who held a parley with the Indians, and abandoning the great and single object of the Government—their emigration, according to the treaty of Payne's Landing—he annulled that treaty, and told them if they would remain quiet, they might continue to occupy the whole country south and east of that river! This the superannuated general preposterously called *dictating a peace to the Indians!* and went off swiftly to New Orleans, rejoicing! Now as the conceit made one man happy, it would have been well enough; but that the staff officers at that city, learning that the war had been happily finished by a single *coup de maître,* failed to send to Tampa Bay the supplies for men and horses that Scott, the successor of Gaines, had ordered thither! Scott's embarrassment—throwing out the ludicrous cause thereof, was serious and irremediable.

His advance on Tampa Bay in two columns, by different routes—one commanded by General Clinch, with whom Scott marched, and the other by Colonel Linsay,[5] was unmarked by a single event of interest, except that Clinch's passage of the Withlacoochee was slightly opposed by the enemy. The whole expedition returned (again by several routes) to the northeast of Florida for these reasons: 1. The failure of supplies, already noticed, and 2. The term of service of the troops, except that of a handful of regulars, was near its expiration.

Scott was next ordered to the Chattahoochee River. The Creek Indians (much connected with the Seminoles), being also under treaty stipulations to leave Alabama and Georgia for the far West, had begun to show symptoms of resistance. He proceeded to Columbus on that river, late in May, with the Florida fever upon him. Here he soon had collected a sufficient body of Georgian volunteers; but they were without arms and ammunition. These supplies had been promptly ordered, principally from the arsenal at Augusta. There was a great delay in their arrival. In the mean time Major-General Jesup, second in command, at the head of the Alabama volunteers, on the opposite side of the hostile Indians, without waiting for the joint action prescribed by Scott—an advance from all points at once against the enemy, by which all would have been hemmed in and captured—flushed and scattered the main body of the Creeks with but small results. Jesup, who was well aware of Scott's bad standing with the President, and to indemnify himself for the complaints of his senior in an unhappy moment—a short forgetfulness of old feelings and obligations—addressed a private letter to the editor of the official paper at Washington, denouncing Scott's dilatoriness against the Creeks, and likening it to his want of energy in the Florida war.

The letter was laid before the President, who, too happy that the moment had at length arrived to launch the bolt so long held in readiness, ordered—*Let Jesup be placed in command, and Scott before a Court!* But before meeting the thunderer full face to face, it will be best to follow up the interminable Seminole war.

In Florida, Jesup succeeded Scott, who, with small numbers and inadequate supplies, had less than thirty days for operations. On Jesup, now the double pet of the President, who commanded in Florida some eighteen or twenty months, and had lavished upon him men, means of transportation, and supplies of every other kind beyond anything ever known before in war everything depended,—with full power to buy up all the Indians he could not capture. Success on any terms and by any means—it being doubly important to build up the new favorite, as that could not fail to give consummation to the blows intended for Scott. But Jesup, with all those great aids, signally failed, when, smitten with remorse, he retracted his charge of dilatoriness, etc. The *amende* lacked a little in fulness, but Scott, in time, forgave.

Brigadier-General Taylor, who won the battle of Okechobee,[6] succeeded Jesup, and was, in time, succeeded by Brigadier-General Armistead;[7] and, finally, in 1842, towards the end of the seventh year of the war, Brigadier-General Worth patched up a sort of treaty or agreement with those Indians, under which the bands of Sam Jones and Bowlegs were allowed to remain and to possess a large tract of their original country.[8]

Scott, who had failed to do that in less than thirty days, which, pets and others did not accomplish in more than six years, was now to meet before a court the unbroken power and popularity of the most remarkable man on this side of the Atlantic of the 19th century.

Establishing himself in Tennessee, after attaining manhood, in a region where civilization was but in the dawn, Andrew Jackson had the heroic characteristics suited to that condition. In the frequent strifes and conflicts among the settlers, his neighbors, he himself at that period also much of a bully, with a born talent for command, jumped in between the hostile parties, and at once, by words, silenced the feud, or became the partisan of one side and soon subdued the other. Elevated to the bench, though unlearned in the law, he knew well how to enforce order. A bully, in open court, knocked down an opponent. Said the judge: "Sheriff, seize that man, and place him at the bar to receive judgment for his contempt of the court." The sheriff soon reported: "May it please your honor, the offender is armed and won't let me seize him." "Very well," the judge replied—"Summon the *posse!*" After a time, the sheriff again reported: "Sir, the man is on horseback, at the door; I have summoned everybody, and nobody dares to touch him." "Summon me, sir!" was the next order. The *posse* of one (the judge) soon wounded and unhorsed the offender, helped to take him up bodily, placed him at the bar, reascended the bench and pronounced the merited sentence. This certainly was an effective way to civilize a rude, wild people—to break their necks to the necessary yoke of the law.

His Indian wars were well enough. But, at New Orleans, with fearful odds of British troops against him, he despaired not of success; poured his own great spirit into all around him; struck the advancing enemy a timely blow in the night of December the 23d, that paralyzed him for the next sixteen days—a great gain—and then, owing in part to the stupidity of attacking strong intrenchments by daylight, won the crowning victory of the war.

In short, such was his antithetical character that the future philosophic historian will be forced to say—"We scarcely can praise it, or blame it too much"; for, without the charm of romance to distemper the mind, he took possession of a man's wife (whom he made his own) and shot another man in a duel, leisurely and with great deliberation, after the latter had lost his fire.[9] He invaded Spanish Florida, and took Pensacola and St. Marks, without a declaration of war by Congress, or instructions from the President, as well as without necessity; and then, at the door of the Senate, within hearing of many of its members, threatened, on their adjournment, to cut off the ears of two principal committee men that had condemned his conduct toward a nation with whom the United States were at peace.

And prior to this period, at New Orleans, flushed with the great victory of January the 8th, and knowing to a certainty, though not officially, that a treaty of peace between the United States and Great Britain had been signed at Ghent, he imprisoned a Federal judge for issuing a writ of *habeas corpus* in favor of one of his (Jackson's) civil prisoners without the least color of the tyrant's plea—*necessity.*[10] Yet this eminent man, of a double nature, was only immoral in the specified instances. In all else he was mild, and temperate—*except when in passion*—and even a professor of religion, though he entirely ignored the Christian injunction, "Let not the sun go down on your wrath."

It may well be maintained that for his popularity with the multitude, he owed fully as much to his demerits as to his virtues and splendid services. Everywhere in the deep columns of his supporters the loud cry could be heard: *Washington was great, but Jackson is greater!*—just as faithful Mussulmans shout at every turn: *God is great and Mahomet is his prophet!* The enthusiasm in behalf of the American also partook largely of allegiance—bigoted idolatry; and it may be placed to his credit—to the bright face of his duality—that he did not profit by the circumstances, and intrench himself for life in the Presidency with remainder over to his heirs and assigns.

Coming up to the executive chair of a great people, he was not in the least intoxicated by power; but coolly appointed a friend, one of his secretaries, whose marriage and its antecedents were exactly like his own, and broke up his first cabinet because some of the members and their families would not associate with the tainted couple.[11] Enveloped in the fumes of the pipe, with only the occasional imprecation—*by the eternal!* he cut off the heads of more office-holders than all his predecessors put together. And this not in any sudden spasm of vindictiveness. The pleasure was economized and long drawn out, his partisans hunting up new victims; for "increase of appetite had grown by what it fed on."

Lord Byron, in 1809, visited Ali Pacha, of Yanina (or Janina), then an old man, and formed quite an intimacy with him.[12] Several years later the Pacha, in a Latin epistle, told Byron that he had just then taken a hostile town, where his mother and sisters had been insulted forty-two years before, and relates as a meritorious action, that he caused to be seized and shot, under his eye, every surviving offender, his children, grand children, and connections, to the number of six hundred! Hobhouse, the companion of Byron, describes the Pacha as "possessing a pleasing face." Doctor Holland, another traveller, compares the spirit that lurked beneath Ali's usual exterior to "the fire of a stove, burning fiercely under a smooth and polished surface." And Galt, writing about the same Turk, calls him—"That agreeable-mannered tyrant."* {Notes to Canto II., Stan. 63, of *Childe Harold,* and Canto IV., Stan. 45, of *Don Juan.*}

At length, late in the autumn of 1836, the time for the certain condemnation of Scott arrived.[13] The court of inquiry consisted of Major-General Macomb, possessed of many military accomplishments, gentlemanly manners, and a generous bias towards the right in sentiment and conduct, but not always of absolute proof against combinations of audacious power and official influence. Atkinson and Brady were walls of adamant against all political violence and injustice. Such were the three members of the court, with the amiable Cooper (the aide-de-camp of Macomb) judge advocate.

Scott in his address to the court, after the overwhelming evidence in his favor had been recorded, had still to approach the merits of the question with circumspection: for the old lion, whose power was yet to endure several months, began to growl lest he might after all lose his prey.[14]

It is repeated that Scott approached the merits of the case with circumspection: 1. From his great and undeviating respect for the constituted authorities of his country; and 2. From the reasonable fear that General Jackson, still President, might in passion dismiss the court and the subject of investigation before the verdict of honorable acquittal could be recorded. Hence the tone of Scott's address; and he never employed counsel or asked for legal advice in any military controversy. With deep feeling and correspondent solemnity he said:

"*Mr. President, and Gentlemen of the Court:*

"When a Doge of Genoa, for some imaginary offence, imputed by Louis XIV., was torn from his government and compelled to visit France, in order to debase himself before that inflated monarch, he was asked, in the palace, what struck him with the greatest wonder amid the blaze of magnificence in his view? 'To find *myself* here!' was the reply of the indignant Lescaro.[15] And so, Mr. President, unable, as I am, to remember one blunder in my recent operations, or a single duty neglected, I may say, that to find myself in the presence of this honorable court, while the army I but recently commanded is still in pursuit of the enemy, fills me with equal grief and astonishment.

"And whence this great and humiliating transition? It is, sir, by the fiat of one, who, from his exalted station, and yet more from his unequalled popularity, has never, with his high displeasure, struck a functionary of this Government, no matter what the office of the individual, humble or elevated, who was not from the moment withered in the general confidence of the American people. Yes, sir, it is my misfortune to lie under the displeasure of that most distinguished personage. The President of the United States has said, 'Let General Scott be recalled from the command of the army in the field, and submit his conduct in the Seminole and Creek campaigns to a court for investigation.' And lo! I stand here to vindicate that conduct, which must again: be judged in the last resort, by him who first condemned it without trial or inquiry. Be it so. I shall not supplicate this court, nor the authority that has to review the 'opinion' here given. On the contrary, I shall proceed at once to challenge your justice to render me that honorable discharge from all blame or censure which the recorded evidence imperiously demands. With such discharge before him, and enlightened by the same mass of testimony, every word of which speaks loudly in my favor, the commander-in-chief of the army and the navy cannot hesitate; he must acquiesce, and then, although nothing may ever compensate me for the deep mortification I have been recently made to experience, I may hope to regain that portion of the public esteem which it was my happiness to enjoy on past occasions of deep moment to the power and the glory of the United States of America."—*Reported in National Intelligencer.*

After a severe and concise synopsis of the evidence by Scott, the court unanimously approved his conduct. His plan of the Seminole campaign was pronounced to have been "well devised and prosecuted with energy, steadiness, and ability," and the court added that, in respect to the Creek war, his plan "was well calculated to lead to successful results, and that it was prosecuted by him as far as practicable with zeal and ability, until recalled from the command." (An account of these transactions and most of the events in the life of Scott, are given in greater detail and terse eloquence in Mansfield's biography of the autobiographer.)

The emphatic verdict of acquittal in this case, openly approved by hosts of his supporters, administered to President Jackson the first wholesome rebuke he had received in that office. He was made to feel that it shook the public faith in his supremacy. Hence he did not dare to set aside the well-reasoned, solemn acquittal; nor, would he—faithful to his vindictive nature—approve the verdict of the court; but left that duty to his successor in the high office.

CHAPTER XXI

HONORS TENDERED–BIDDLE FAMILY–SPEECH OF R. BIDDLE, M.C., VINDICATING SCOTT–JACKSON'S MARTIAL LAW–HIS DEATH

Returning to his headquarters, New York, a public dinner in honor of his triumph before the court, was tendered to the acquitted by a long list of prominent citizens of both parties. The following letter to a committee gives the result:

"New York, May, 1837.

"GENTLEMEN:

"Early last month I accepted the invitation to a public dinner, which you and other friends did me the honor to tender me. In a few days the commercial embarrassments of this great emporium became such that I begged the compliment might be indefinitely postponed. You, however, were so kind as to hold me to my engagement, and to appoint a day for the meeting, which is now near at hand. In the mean time the difficulties in the commercial world have gone on augmenting, and many of my friends, here and elsewhere, have been whelmed under the general calamity of the times.[1]

"Feeling deeply for the losses and anxieties of all, no public honor could now be enjoyed by me. I must, therefore, under the circumstances, positively, but most respectfully withdraw my acceptance of your invitation.

"I have the honor, etc., etc.,
"WINFIELD SCOTT."

The subscribers to the dinner held a meeting, the Hon. Cornelius W. Lawrence in the chair, and unanimously passed the following resolutions:[2]

"*Resolved,* That in the decision of General Scott to withdraw, for the reason assigned, his acceptance of the public dinner designed to testify to him our high appreciation, both of his private and public character, we find new evidence of his sympathy with all that regards the public welfare, and of his habitual oblivion of self, where the feelings and interests of others are concerned.

"*Resolved,* That we rejoice with the joy of friends in the result, so honorable to General Scott, of the recent court of inquiry, instituted to investigate his military conduct as commander-in-chief in Alabama and Florida, and that the President of the United States (Mr. Van Buren), in approving, its proceedings, acted in gratifying unison with the general sentiments of the nation."

Like honors were tendered about the same time from a number of other cities, far and near, and all declined.

About to quote a speech on the recent events, just narrated, delivered in the House of Representatives, in the session of 1837–'8, by Richard Biddle, of Pittsburg,[3] the autobiographer cannot resist the temptation to dedicate a few lines to his connection with the remarkable family of the orator, including the General Thomas Cadwallader of the war of 1812–'15, one of them, by marriage; a citizen of the greatest excellence, and like them a Federalist, but devoted in public meetings and associations, and in every other way to the support of the war *after it was declared.*

Scott's intimacy with the united families commenced with Cadwallader, a major-general of militia, but most worthy of a like rank in the regular army; next with two brothers, both majors, Thomas and John Biddle, who served with Scott in the campaigns of 1813 and 1814, and were highly distinguished for gallantry, intelligence, and efficiency. At Philadelphia, he also became much connected, officially and in society, with the venerable father of the two majors, the chairman of the *Committee of Defence,* who had been a leading patriot in the Revolution, and Vice-President of Pennsylvania, under the Presidency of Dr. Franklin; with Nicholas Biddle, an elder brother of the majors, sometime Secretary to Mr. Monroe, Minister at London, and also the same to General Armstrong, Minister at Paris, and recognized in both countries as an accomplished scholar and linguist, who was, in 1813–'14, a leader in the Pennsylvania Senate, where he carried a bill for raising ten thousand regular troops, by conscription, at the cost of the State, for the general service of the Union, when its treasury was without both money and credit. (Virginia and South Carolina had the honor of passing similar bills about the same time.) Another brother, the senior of Nicholas, the gallant Commodore James Biddle, of the United States' Navy, was early distinguished in the harbor of Tripoli and other conflicts, and crowned his valor and seamanship by the capture, in the Hornet, 18 guns, of the British sloop-of-war Penguin, of about the same force. Richard, the fifth and youngest brother, though but a lad, bore arms, under General Cadwallader, in 1813, '14, '15, in camps, formed on the Delaware, as often as his native city, Philadelphia, was threatened by the enemy in the same war. He began his profession, as a lawyer, at Pittsburg; soon became the leader of that bar, and first took his seat in the House of Representatives, December, 1837. Here, in a service of three or four years, he became the most classical and effective debater of his time. How painful it is to reflect that not an individual named of this remarkable family—all intimate friends of the autobiographer—survives! One of the family, however, standing in the same relation to Scott, remains—Charles J., son of Nicholas, brevetted a major "for gallant and meritorious conduct at Chapultepec," Mexico, that is, as the successful leader of a storming party; next an eminent member of the Philadelphia bar; and recently a member of Congress.

On an appropriation for carrying on the Seminole war, in his first session as a member of the House of Representatives, Mr. Richard Biddle said:

"It would be recollected by all, that after the war in Florida had assumed a formidable aspect, Major-General Scott was called to the command. An officer of his rank and standing was not likely to seek a service in which, amidst infinite toil and vexation, there would be no opportunity for the display of military talent on a scale at all commensurate with that in which his past fame had been acquired. Yet he entered on it with the alacrity, zeal, and devotion to duty by which he has ever been distinguished.

"And here (Mr. B. said) he might be permitted to advert to the past history of this officer.

"Sir, when the late General Brown, writing from the field of Chippewa, said that General Scott merited the highest praises which a grateful country could bestow, was there a single bosom throughout this wide republic that did not respond to the sentiment? I for one, at least, can never forget the thrill of enthusiasm, boy as I then was, which mingled with my own devout thankfulness to God, that the cloud which seemed to have settled on our arms was at length dispelled. On that plain it was established that Americans could be trained to meet and to beat, in the open field, without breastworks, the regulars of Britain.

* * * * * * * * * * * * * * *

"Sir, the result of that day was due not merely to the gallantry of General Scott upon the field. It must in part be ascribed to the patient, anxious, and indefatigable drudgery, the consummate skill as a tactician, with which he had labored, night and day, at the camp near Buffalo, to prepare his brigade for the career on which it was about to enter.

"After a brief interval he again led that brigade to the glorious victory of Bridgewater.* {Niagara or Lundy's Lane—three names for the same battle of July 25, 1814.} He bears now upon his body the wounds of that day.

"It had ever been the characteristic of this officer to seek the post of danger, not to have it thrust upon him. In the years preceding that to which I have specially referred—in 1812 and 1813—the eminent services he rendered were in positions which properly belonged to others, but into which he was led by irrepressible ardor and jealousy of honor.

"Since the peace with Great Britain, the talents of General Scott have ever been at the command of his country. His pen and his sword have alike been put in requisition to meet the varied exigencies of the service.

"When the difficulties with the Western Indians swelled up into importance, General Scott was despatched to the scene of hostility. There rose up before him then, in the ravages of a frightful pestilence, a form of danger infinitely more appalling than the perils of the field. How he bore himself in this emergency—how faithfully he became the nurse and the physician of those from whom terror and loathing had driven all other aid, cannot be forgotten by a just and grateful country."

* * * * * * * * * *

"Mr. Chairman, I believe that a signal atonement to General Scott will, one day, be extorted from the justice of this House. We owe it to him; but we owe it still more to the country. What officer can feel secure in the face of that great example of triumphant injustice? Who can place before himself the anticipation of establishing higher claims upon the gratitude of the country than General Scott? Yet *he* was sacrificed. His past services went for nothing. Sir, you may raise new regiments, and issue new commissions, but you cannot, without such atonement, restore the high moral tone which befits the depositaries of the national honor. I fondly wish that the highest and the lowest in the country's service might be taught to regard this House as the jealous guardian of his rights, against caprice, or favoritism, or outrage, from whatever quarter. I would have him know that, in running up the national flag, at the very moment our daily labors commence, we do not go through an idle form. On whatever distant service he may be sent—whether urging his way amidst tumbling icebergs, toward the pole, or fainting in the unwholesome heats of Florida—I would enable him, as he looks up to that flag, to gather hope and strength. It should impart to him a proud feeling of confidence and security. He should know that the same emblem of majesty and justice floats over the councils of the nation; and that in its untarnished lustre we have all a common interest and a common sympathy. Then, sir, and not before, will you have an army or a navy worthy to sustain and to perpetuate the glory of former days."

Before entering on a new administration, disregarding the rigors of chronology, in favor of continuity of subjects, the autobiographer adds two more notices of General Jackson. The following *review* was written by Scott, pending a discussion in Congress on a bill to refund the fine levied by Judge Hall for Jackson's arrest of the judge.

From the *National Intelligencer* of January 4, 1843.
"Martial Law, by a Kentuckian; four Essays, republished in the pamphlet form, from the Louisville Journal, 1842; pp. 14.

"This timely publication, understood to be from the pen of a distinguished ex-judge of the Kentucky Court of Appeals,* discusses, with much learning and ability, the extraordinary doctrines recently avowed in Congress and elsewhere, attributing to a commander of an army in the field, the right to proclaim and enforce *martial law* as against *citizens* (including legislators and judges) wholly unconnected with the military service. {S. S. Nicholas.}[4]

The monstrous proposition avowed has raised the indignant voice of *a Kentuckian,* and it is only necessary to read him to consign the speeches and writings he reviews to the same repository with the *passive obedience and non-resistance* doctrines of the Filmers and Hobbses of a former age.[5]

With a view to a similar discussion, I had been occasionally engaged, for a week, in collecting materials, when a friend placed in my hands a copy of the pamphlet mentioned at the head of this article. Finding it to cover nearly the whole ground I had intended to occupy, I shall now confine my humble labors to selections from my notes, planting here and there a few principles, authorities, and illustrations in such corners or blank spaces as a *Kentuckian* has overlooked.

In England, the land forces in the public service—regulars and militia, of whatever name and arm—are governed by an *annual* mutiny act, and a sub-code called *articles of war,* made by the king, under the. express authority of the former. The preamble of that act always recites:

"Whereas, the raising or keeping a standing army within the United Kingdom of Great Britain and Ireland, unless it be with the consent of Parliament, *is against law,* and, whereas, it is judged necessary by his Majesty and his present Parliament that a body of forces should be continued for the safety (etc.), and that the whole number of such forces should consist of —— thousand men, exclusive of, (etc.); and, whereas, no man can be forejudged of life or limb, or subjected to any kind of punishment within this realm, by *martial law,* or in any other manner than by the judgment of his peers, and according to the known and established laws of the realm; yet, nevertheless, it being requisite for the retaining all the before-mentioned forces in their duty, that an exact discipline be observed, and that soldiers who shall mutiny or stir up sedition, or shall desert his Majesty's service, be brought to a *more exemplary and speedy punishment* than the usual forms of law will allow; be it therefore enacted," etc. (when follow a careful enumeration of all the higher crimes which military men can commit against discipline; that is, against good order and subordination in an army. At the end of each enumeration, the act declares that every officer or soldier so offending 'shall suffer death, or such other punishment as by a court martial shall be awarded.')

The *articles of war* are entirely subordinate to the mutiny act, and originate nothing but certain smaller details for the *better* government of the forces.

It is in view of the high principles of civil liberty, consecrated by Parliament as above, that Tytler, for a long time Judge Advocate of Scotland, says in his *Essay on Military Law:* 'Martial Law was utterly disclaimed as binding the subjects in general.[6] The modern British soldier, enjoying in common with his fellow subjects, every benefit of the laws of his country, is bound by the military code solely to *the observance of the peculiar duties of his profession.*' And so Lord Loughborough,[7] Chief Justice of the Common Pleas (soon after as Earl of Roslin, Lord High Chancellor), said, in Trinity Term,[8] 1792, on a motion on behalf of Sergeant Grant: 'Martial Law, such as it is described by Hale,[9] and such also as it is *marked* by Sir William Blackstone,[10] *does* not exist in England at all.' He gives examples, in the way of distinction between Great Britain and continental Europe, as also between military persons and others at home, thus: 'In the reign of King William there was a conspiracy against his person in Holland. The persons guilty of that conspiracy were tried by *a council of officers.* There was a conspiracy against his person in England; but the conspirators were tried by *the common law.*' Therefore (adds the Chief Justice), 'it is totally inaccurate to state *martial law* as having any place *whatever* within the realm of Great Britain, as against subjects not in the line of military duty.' But (he continues), an army is established in this country (etc.); it is an indispensable requisite (etc.), that there should be order and discipline (etc.); that the persons composing it should, for all offences in their *military* capacity, be subject to a trial by their officers.' Tytler's Essay, with this opinion of Lord Loughborough, given in a note at length, was published in the last century, and was in the hands of our officers, generally, before the War of 1812.

There is in the *Encyclopœdia Britannica* an excellent *popular* view, given by an eminent lawyer, of the same general question:

'Military, or martial law, is that branch of the laws, of war which respect military discipline, or the government and control of persons employed in the operation of war. Military law is not exclusive of the common law; for a man, by becoming a soldier, does not cease to be a citizen, or member of the commonwealth. He is a citizen still, capable of performing the duties of a subject, and answerable in the ordinary course of law, for his conduct in that capacity (as murder, theft, and other felonies). Martial law is, therefore, a system of rule *superadded* to the common law for *regulating the citizen in his character of a soldier.*'

Notwithstanding those conservative views, long embodied in the laws and public opinion of England, which hold in utter abhorrence the application of martial law to any person not at the time in the military service, one general, and many eminent statesmen and public writers are found on this side of the Atlantic, who ignorantly suppose that that law, described and stigmatized by Hale and Blackstone 'as in truth and reality *no* law, but something *indulged* rather than allowed as law,' is a part of the common law in these States, because mentioned in those great common-law writers, and therefore an engine which every com-mander of an army in the field may *indulge* himself with, at his own wanton discretion, against the free citizens of republican America!

Is there anything in *our* statute book to warrant a conception so monstrous?

We have no *mutiny act,* so called. Our 'rules and articles for the Government of the *armies* of the United States' were borrowed from that act and the British articles of war (in part), July 30, 1775, before the Declaration of Independence. The code was enlarged by the old Con-gress from the same sources, September 20, 1776. In this form it was enacted by the first Congress under the Constitution; and again reën-acted, substantially the same, April 10, 1806, as it stands at present. The act consists of but three sections. The first declares: 'The following shall be the rules and articles by which the *armies* of the United States shall be governed'; and gives one hundred and one articles. Each article is confined, in express terms, to the persons composing the army. The next—the celebrated *second section*—contains the only exception; and what an exception! It is in these words:

'In time of war, all persons *not* citizens of, or owing allegiance to, the United States of America, who shall be found lurking, as *spies,* in or about the fortifications or encampments of the armies of the United States, or any of them, shall suffer death, according to *the law and usage of nations,* by sentence of a general court martial.'

'Not citizens,' because if citizens, and found so 'lurking,' the crime would be that of *treason*—'adhering to [our] enemies, giving them aid and comfort'; and is so defined by the Constitution.

The third, or remaining section of our military code, merely repeals the previous act, which adopted the resolves of the old Congress for governing the army.

There is nothing, then, in this code to give the slightest pretence that any part of it can, by possibility, be applied to citizens not attached to an army.

A *Kentuckian* further argues against such barbarian application, from the silence of the Constitution. But, in a matter so infinitely important to the existence of free government and our civil liberties, the Constitution is *not* silent. The fifth amendment expressly declares: 'No person shall be held to answer for a capital or otherwise infamous crime, unless on a presentment or indictment of a grand jury, *'except in cases arising in the land or naval forces, or in the militia when in actual service, in time of war or public danger.'* (The militia, by the previous article 1, section 8, can only be called out 'to execute the laws of the Union, suppress insurrections, and repel invasions.') And the 6th amendment is to the same effect: 'In all criminal prosecutions (the exception of military persons, as above, being understood) the accused shall enjoy the right to a speedy and *public* trial by an impartial *jury.'* (Military courts always deliberate in *secrecy.*)

If these amendments do not expressly secure the citizen, not belonging to an army, from the possibility of being dragged before *a council of war or court martial,* for any crime, or on any pretence whatsoever, then there can be no security for any human right under human institutions!

Congress and the President could not, if they were unanimous, proclaim martial law over any portion of the United States, without first throwing those amendments into the fire. And if Mr. President Madison (begging pardon of his memory for the violent supposition) had sent an order to General Jackson to establish the odious code over the citizens of New Orleans during, before, or after the siege of that capital, it would have been the duty of the general, under his oath to obey the Constitution, to have withheld obedience; for, by the 9th article of war (the only one *on orders*), officers are not required to obey any but 'lawful commands.'

General Jackson 'took the responsibility' with as little of necessity, or even utility, as of law. In this he stands distinguished from every American commander from the Declaration of Independence down to the present day. The *Constitution*—not the writ of *habeas corpus* merely—being suspended, he imprisoned Mr. Louallier; he imprisoned the Federal Judge (Hall) for issuing a writ of *habeas corpus* to inquire into the cause of that imprisonment; and he imprisoned the United States' District Attorney (Dick) for seeking to procure from a *State* judge a writ of *habeas corpus* for the Federal judge. Mr. Louallier, a citizen of the United States (by the treaty of Louisiana), a highly respectable member of the State Senate, and in no way connected with the army, was put on trial *for his life,* before a court martial, on five several imaginary charges. One of these was *for being a spy,* under the second section, given above! Whatever may be our astonishment at the fact that a court of *American* officers should have proceeded, under illegal orders, to try such a prisoner on such charges, they saved themselves and the country from that last of degradations—the finding the prisoner guilty because accused by the commanding general. Mr. Louallier was acquitted.

When Pompey played the petty tyrant at Sicily, as the lieutenant of that master-despot Sylla, he summoned before him the Mamertines.[11] That people refused to appear, alleging that they stood excused by an ancient privilege granted them by the Romans. 'What!' said Sylla's lieutenant; 'will you never have done with citing laws and privileges to men who wear swords!' Roman liberty had already been lost in the distemperature of the times. *Inter arma silent leges*[12] found its way into our young republic in the thirty-ninth year of its existence.[13]

If Pompey had gained the battle of Pharsalia, would his odious reply to the Mamertines have been forgiven by the lovers of law and of human liberty? *With such maxims of government,* it was of little consequence to the Roman world that Cæsar won the day. A Verres would have been as good as either.[14]

For the glorious defence of New Orleans, Congress voted thanks and a gold medal to the hero. That measure of justice was short at both ends. *Censure and a monument should have been added.*

That all soldiers in our republic do not concur in the maxims above reprobated, a striking example lies before me. In the general regulations for the army, drawn up in 1825 by one of our officers [Scott] and cheerfully obeyed by all, we have this head: '*Subordination to the civil authorities*'; and under it, the following:

'Respect and obedience to the civil authorities of the land is the duty of all citizens and more particularly of those who are *armed* in the public service.

'An individual officer or soldier who resists the civil authority, will do so at his peril, as in the case of any other citizen; but union or concert between two or more military men in such resistance, whether *voluntary* or *by order,* would be a much more serious offence, and is, therefore, positively prohibited.

'A civil officer charged with the execution of civil process will, on making known his character, be freely permitted to pass and repass all guards and sentinels.

'In the case of *criminal* process, issued by the civil authority against military persons, all officers are expressly required by, the 33d article of war to give active aid and, assistance.'

This article of war is too remarkable to be omitted here. Like the mutiny act of England, it speaks of 'the known laws of the land,' in contradistinction and as superior to the martial code. Under it, General Jackson's own officers were bound to aid in causing the writ of *habeas corpus* to be executed against him, as also in executing the precept for his appearance before the judge, if he had refused to appear, and to submit to the sentence of the court. The article is a part of the law of Congress and of the Constitution, being enacted in strict pursuance to the latter.

'*Article* 33. When any commissioned officer or soldier shall be accused of a *capital crime or of having used violence, or committed any offence* against the persons or property of any citizen of any of the United States, such as is punishable *by the known laws of the land,* the commanding officer and officers of every regiment, troop or company, to which the persons so accused shall belong, are hereby required, upon application duly made by, or in behalf of, the party or parties injured, to use their utmost endeavors to deliver over such accused person or persons to the civil magistrate, and likewise to be aiding and assisting to *the officers of justice* in apprehending and securing the person or persons so accused, in order to bring him or them to trial. If any commanding officer or officers shall wilfully neglect, or shall refuse, upon the application aforesaid, to deliver over such accused person or persons, *to the civil magistrates,* or to be aiding and assisting to *the officers of justice,* in apprehending such person or persons, the officer or officers so offending shall be cashiered.'

This rule and article 'for the government of the armies of the United States,' is as old, on the statute book, as our glorious Revolution of 1776, and as old in England (whence we borrowed it) as the glorious Revolution which drove out James II. and *his* martial law.* {Martial law as applied to persons not of the army has been unknown in England since that great event.} It is expressed in the very spirit of the Anglo-Saxon race—ever jealous of liberty. Under this safeguard—with spirited citizens, independent judges, and obedient soldiers, taught their duties to the civil authorities—what military officer dare to suspend the Constitution, or the writ of *habeas corpus,* or to imprison citizens—each a *capital crime* or an act of gross *violence?*

A *Kentuckian* has cited, from most of the State constitutions, express provisions placing the military, at all times and under all circumstances, in strict subordination to the civil authority. In South Carolina, during the Revolutionary War, at the moment that Sir Henry Clinton was investing the devoted city of Charleston, and the Tories were in arms everywhere, the Legislature of the State empowered her excellent Governor, John Rutledge, after consulting with such of his counsel as he conveniently could, 'to do everything necessary for the public good, *except the taking away the life of a citizen without legal trial.*' Under that exception, at a time when there was no Constitution of the United States, to shield the liberty and the life of the citizen, there was no Louallier deprived of one and put in jeopardy of the other, by martial law.

It is vulgarly supposed, particularly by those who, 'dressed in a little brief authority,' and lust for more, that the suspension of the writ of *habeas corpus* lets in upon the citizen *martial law.* The suspension by Congress would, certainly, for the time, enable power to hold any, citizen incarcerated without cause, and without trial; but, if brought to trial, it must still be before one of the ordinary courts of the land. In the suspension by *martial law,* as in continental Europe, all other writs, remedies, and rights which might stand in the way of power, according to its own arbitrary will, would be suspended at the same time. Tyrannic rule could want nothing more.

It is a curious fact that this writ has been but twice *practically* suspended—(by Generals Wilkinson and Jackson)—in both instances at New Orleans, and never once, constitutionally, anywhere in the United

States since the Declaration of Independence. The Constitution declares that 'the privileges of the writ of habeas corpus shall not be suspended, unless when, in case of rebellion or invasion, the public safety may require it,' in the opinion of Congress.

During Burr's conspiracy, Mr. Giles, in the Senate, upon a, message from the President, introduced a bill for a three months' suspension of that great writ. It was, in a panic, immediately passed, and sent to the House, January 26, 1807. The House, all on the same day (January 26), refused to deliberate in secrecy; and, on the question, 'Shall the bill be rejected?' the votes stood—ayes, 113; noes, 19; a great triumph of civil liberty over panic and outlawry!

This is the only constitutional attempt at suspending the writ of *habeas corpus* ever made in free America. May we never hear of another in Congress or elsewhere!

A SOLDIER OF ONE WAR."

It has been seen that the autobiographer, being in Paris, got up, under very extraordinary circumstances (see above, p. 166), the first celebration of the 8th of January—the anniversary of the great defence of New Orleans. So, being President of the Board of West Point visitors, in June, 1845, news came to him, while a class was under examination, which caused him to make this short address: *"Major Delafield, Superintendent.*[15] I suspend the further labors of this examination till to-morrow, in honor of an event interesting to all Americans. A great man has fallen among us. Andrew Jackson, after filling the world with his fame, and crowning his country with glory, departed this life on the 8th instant. It is not for any authority inferior to the President, to prescribe the special honors to be paid to the illustrious dead by the military posts and troops of the United States. No doubt, orders on the subject will soon arrive from Washington."—And so ended Scott's relations with the hero of New Orleans.

CHAPTER XXII

PRESIDENT VAN BUREN—FINE TEMPER—CANADIAN AGITATIONS—BURNING OF THE CAROLINE—SCOTT SENT TO THE FRONTIER—THE TURMOIL QUIETED—SCOTT SENT TO REMOVE THE CHEROKEES

MR. VAN BUREN succeeded to the presidency. With a very respectable degree of moral firmness, all his other qualities were in happy contrast with those of his predecessor.

Few men have ever suffered less wear and tear of body and mind from irascible emotions. Hume,[1] in his *unique* autobiography, says of himself: "I am, or rather was" (for being at the end of life, "emboldens me the more to speak my sentiments),— I was, I say, a man of mild disposition, of command of temper, of an open, social, and cheerful humor, capable of attachment, but little susceptible of enmity, and of great moderation in all my passions," which advantages he, some pages before, puts down as of more worth than "to be born to an estate of ten thousand a year."

According to this mode of estimation, Mr. Van Buren, throughout a long life, was a *millionaire.* He entered on the presidency with right intentions toward his country and all mankind, and with the needful gifts and abilities to make an excellent practical administrator of the Executive Department—only that from the sense of gratitude to General Jackson, he felt himself obliged to work with (one exception) the old cabinet, consisting of members he never would have selected for himself; and, in the second place, he retained a little of his early and only weakness—an inclination toward the *expedient* more than either of the Catos, a Hampden, or Roland would have approved.[2]

The autobiographer became early in the War of 1812–'15 acquainted with Mr. Van Buren, an acquaintance that soon ran into intimacy and friendship; and he believes he was the first to suggest that, with his advantageous standpoint, it would be easy for the rising New Yorker to make himself the President of the United States. That friendship was cooled down—suspended, for many years—Mr. Van Buren taking an active part in behalf of Mr. Crawford, for the presidency, in the election of 1824, and Scott, though standing aloof, being, in his open *wishes,* on the side of Mr. Adams.[3] The separation continued through the contest that elected General Harrison to the presidency in 1840. The social courtesies, however, between the parties, as often as they chanced to meet, remained all the while unchanged.

As soon as elected to the presidency (November, 1836), Mr. Van Buren, highly approved of his son's (Major Abram Van Buren) wish to join Scott, then before the court of inquiry at Frederick, on the ground that he might be needed as a witness on certain points only known, as he (the major) supposed, to himself, while a volunteer aide-de-camp to Scott, in the Seminole war. Indeed, for the same delicate reason, the major had declined, some months before, against a strong inclination, to make the tour of Europe, although he and Scott (through wrongs of third parties) were not, at the time, on speaking terms; and further, although Scott had given assurances that he could, by circumstantial evidence, dispense with the major's presence.

His arrival, however, was of great value as a volunteer secretary; for Scott had been without any one of his staff (two regular aids) from the beginning of the court. Major William de Peyster, of New York, and for some time planter in Florida, had marched with Scott from Tampa Bay as a volunteer aid, and tendered him good assistance as an amanuensis at Frederick.

A word more on this subject may be pardoned the autobiographer. Major Van Buren, as paymaster, made the campaign of Mexico with Scott, and although encumbered with a military chest, containing money and vouchers, amounting to millions, he never failed, at the first gun, to hasten, mounted, to Scott, as a volunteer aid, and gallantly rode through every battle, a bearer of orders, with his accustomed quiet smile and amiability. The lieutenant-colonelcy given him at the end of this war was the inadequate reward of such heroism.

President Van Buren, while in office, never omitted on proper occasions, to show kindness to Scott, and it gives the latter great pleasure to add, that the ancient friendship between the parties became revived some twenty years before the death of the former and continued up to that event.

In the winter of 1837–'8, a singular disturbance broke out on the lake and northern frontiers of the Union. A number of radicals, in the Canadas, had, a little earlier, begun to agitate in favor of certain revolutionary changes, with an eye, on the part of many, toward ultimate annexation to the United States. The heat of the strife soon crossed the frontiers and extended, in many directions, to the depth of forty and sixty miles into the United States. More than two hundred thousand Americans took the infection, organized themselves into lodges, bound by oath to secrecy, and ridiculously enough, without ever having been in Canada, or knowing anything about the merits of the question, called themselves *Canadian Patriots!*—eager to invade the Provinces and fight for *their* rights!! Here was another of "the cankers of a calm world and a long peace."[4]

A circumstance soon occurred that exasperated to a high degree the frontier population on the American side from Lake Michigan to the borders of New Hampshire. A *mauvais sujet,*[5] calling himself Colonel Van Rensselaer (no relation of the patroons), a dismissed cadet from the Military Academy, had organized a number of those Americans whose patriotism was in a foreign country, and taken possession of a small British island called *Navy Island,* opposite to Schlosser, on the American side, about a mile and a quarter above the Niagara Falls. Here, after the Canadian people—the militia themselves—had, without regulars, suppressed an attempted revolt in that neighborhood—Van Rensselaer hopelessly awaited events. A little steamer, the Caroline, came down, December 29, to serve as a ferry boat between the island and Schlosser, and made fast for the night to the wharf of the latter. Before morning an expedition, under a Mr. McLeod, was fitted out from the Canada side, which shirked the British island, where it might easily have captured the patriot camp, and seized, by surprise, the steamer; killed several persons on board; set her on fire, and sent her adrift over the cataract— as it was erroneously believed, for a time—with wounded Americans in her hold. This was a clear violation of neutrality, involving murder, which outrages caused all along the frontiers, a very general cry for war—by, or without authority.[6]

The news reached Washington late in the day of January 4, 1838. It so happened that President Van Buren had invited to dine with him, the same evening, Mr. Clay and a large number (nineteen) Whig friends, with three or four Democrats. The autobiographer was one of the former. All had arrived, and the appointed hour had long gone by, but still the President was absent. He, it became known, after a time, was in council with his cabinet. The Whigs jestingly inquired of the Democrats if the President had abdicated or was about to resign. All were equally ignorant, merry, and hungry. At length the master of the feast came down, and whispered the news to Mr. Clay and Scott—saying to the latter: "Blood has been shed; you must go with all speed to the Niagara frontier. The Secretary of War (Mr. Poinsett) is now engaged in writing your instructions."

The circumstances, as already known, were sufficiently critical, and private letters represented that there was reason to apprehend the city of Buffalo might be seized, perhaps, sacked, by the outraged Canadians, to break up the hotbed of the *patriots* and destroy their depots.

Passing through Albany, and not knowing what number of the militia he might have occasion to call for, Scott, at his own suggestion, prevailed on Governor Marcy and the adjutant-general of the State (McDonald) to accompany him to the scene of difficulties, so that no time might be lost by a correspondence between Federal and State authorities three hundred and fifty miles apart.[7]

There were no regular troops on the Niagara. They were all in Florida, or on the Western frontiers. Journeying through New York, Scott had ordered to follow him several detachments of army recruits. To supply the needed physical force, he had ample powers to call for the uninfected militia of the Border States, including Western Virginia and Kentucky.

1. All this was quite a new scene for Scott. In 1812, '13, '14 he had appeared on the same theatre as the leader of battalions and participator in victories. Now, rhetoric and diplomacy were to be his principal weapons, his countrymen and friends the objects of conquest, and a little correspondence with the British authorities beyond the line, as an episode to the whole. Had Scott not been a soldier, though he had been the famed Athenian orator or the American

"Henry, the forest-born Demosthenes,
Whose thunders shook the Philip of the seas,"

his entreaties and harangues would have been wholly lost upon his hearers. But the memory of other days gave to him an influence which he would have sought in vain without it. The soldier of 1812, '13, '14, reappearing near the scene of his former activity, drew forth the applause of listening multitudes.

2. During the winter of 1838 and that of 1838–'9, he was busy in exercising his influence for peace, and in quieting the disturbed frontiers. This was his employment for many months of the coldest season of each year. The patriot movements were chiefly confined to the season of frost, which, bridging with ice some of the waters separating the two countries, greatly favored descents upon Upper Canada. Scott was ably

seconded in watching and counteracting those movements by distinguished officers. General Brady, on Lake Erie and the Detroit frontier, General Worth (made General 1842) on the Niagara, Lake Ontario, and St. Lawrence frontier, and Generals Wool and Eustis on the, northern side of New York and Vermont, were active in aiding Scott in his arrangements, and pacifying the borderers.[8] The troops, both regulars and volunteers, proved to be steady supporters of law and order, and were held everywhere ready, as *posses,* at the call of the United States marshals and collectors. The army officers mentioned were the district commanders.

3. Scott posted himself nowhere, but was by turns rapidly everywhere, and always in the midst of the greater difficulties. In these winter campaigns against the trespassers of the borders, lie passed frequently along the frontier, sometimes on the Detroit and sometimes on the north line of Vermont. His journeyings were made by land, and principally in the night; oftentimes with the cold from ten to twenty degrees below freezing point. Daylight he chiefly employed in organizing the means of counteraction by an extensive correspondence and the labors of direct pacification. He obtained, and pressed upon Federal district attorneys, marshals, and collectors, information of the designs and movements of the patriots, and tendered to those civil functionaries the aid of the troops. In performance of his duty as a peacemaker, he addressed, on a line of eight hundred miles, immense gatherings of citizens, principally organized sympathizers, who had their arms at hand.

4. In these addresses he declaimed with fervor, and they were often received with the loud applause of the audience. He handled every topic which could inspire shame in misdoers, or excite pride in the friends of the Government and country. His speeches were made with popular illustrations and allusions, and addressed both to the knowledge and the sentiment of the people. He reminded them of the nature of a republic, which can have no foundation of permanency except in the general intelligence, virtue, respect, and obedience of its people; that if, in the attempt to force on unwilling neighbors independence and free institutions, we had first to spurn and trample under foot treaty stipulations and laws made by our own representatives, we should greatly hazard free institutions at home in the confidence and respect of our own people; that no government can or ought to exist for a moment after losing the power of executing its obligations to foreign countries, and of enforcing its own laws at home; that that power depended in a republic chiefly on the people themselves; that we had a treaty with England,

binding us to the strictest observance of amity, or all the duties of good neighborhood with adjoining provinces, and also an act of Congress for enforcing those solemn obligations; that the treaty and the laws were as binding on the honor and the conscience of every American freeman, as if he had specially voted for each; that this doctrine was of the very essence of a civilized republic, as the neglect of it could not fail to sink us into anarchy, barbarism, and universal contempt; that an aggressive war, waged by a part of the community, without just cause and without preparation, as is common among barbarian tribes, necessarily drags the non-consenting many along with the madness of the few, involving all alike in crime, disaster, and disgrace; that a war, to be successful, must be very differently commenced; and in these addresses he often concluded: "Fellow citizens,—and I thank God, we have a common government as well as a common origin,—I stand before you without troops and without arms, save the blade by my side. I am, therefore, within your power. Some of you have known me in other scenes, and all of you know that I am ready to do what my country and what duty demands. I tell you, then, except it be over my body, you shall not pass this line—you shall *not* embark."

5. To the inquiry everywhere heard, "But what say you of the burning of the Caroline, and the murder of citizens at our own shore?"

6. In reply to these questions, Scott always frankly admitted that these acts constituted a national outrage, and that they called for explanation and satisfaction; but that this whole subject was in the hands of the President, the official organ of the country, specially chosen by the people for national purposes; that there was no doubt the President would make the proper demand, and failing to obtain satisfaction, would lay the whole matter before Congress—the representative of the public will, and next to the people, the tribunal before which the ultimate appeal must be made.

7. These harangues were applauded, and were generally very successful. Masses of patriots broke off and returned to their respective homes, declaring, that if Scott had been accompanied by an army they would not have listened, but have fought him. The friends of order were also encouraged to come out in support of authority, and at length peace and quiet were restored.

8. In the first winter, one of those incidents occurred which make history dramatic, and which illustrate how much depends on individual men and single events. Many days after the destruction of the "Caroline," another steamer, the "Barcelona," was cut out of the ice in Buf-

falo Harbor (January, 1838), and taken down the Niagara River, to be offered, as was known, to the patriots, who were still on Navy Island.* {53 Niles's Register, 337.} Scott wished to compel them to abandon their criminal enterprise. He also desired to have them, on returning within our jurisdiction, arrested by the marshal, who was always with him. For this purpose, he sent an agent to hire the "Barcelona" for the service of the United States, before the patriots could get the means to pay for her, or find sureties to indemnify the owners in case of capture or destruction by the British. He succeeded in all these objects. The "Barcelona" proceeded back to Buffalo, where Scott had immediate use for her on Lake Erie, yet navigable in all its length. The authorities on the Canada side were on the alert to destroy her.

9. As the "Barcelona" slowly ascended against the current on our side of Grand Island (belonging to the United States), three armed British schooners, besides batteries on the land, were in position, as the day before, to sink her as she came out from behind that island. On the 16th of January, Scott and Governor Marcy stood on the American shore opposite that point, watching events. The smoke of the approaching boat could be seen in the distance, and the purpose of the British was perfectly evident in all their movements. The batteries on our side were promptly put in position. The matches were lighted. All was ready to return the British fire. There was a crisis!

10. The day before this, when it was supposed the Navy Island people were coming up the same channel in other craft, and before it was known that the "Barcelona" had accepted his offered engagement, Scott wrote on his knee, and despatched by an aide-de-camp, the following note:

To the Commanding Officer of the Armed British Vessels in the Niagara.
HEADQUARTERS, EASTERN DIVISION
U. S. ARMY, TWO MILES BELOW BLACK ROCK,
January 15, 1838
11. Sir:

With his excellency the Governor of New York, who has troops at hand,* we are here to enforce the neutrality of the United States, and to protect our own soil or waters from violation. The proper civil officers are also present to arrest, if practicable, the leaders of the expedition on foot against Upper Canada.* {These men were, in strictness, not yet under Scott's command, simply from the want of time to muster them into the service of the United States—a ceremony of some hours.}

12. Under these circumstances, it gives me pain to perceive the armed vessels, mentioned, anchored in our waters, with the probable intention to fire upon that expedition moving in the same waters.

13. Unless the expedition should first attack—in which case we shall interfere—we shall be obliged to consider a discharge of shot or shell from or into our waters, from the armed schooners of her Majesty, as an act seriously compromising the neutrality of the two nations. I hope, therefore, that no such unpleasant incident may occur.

I have the honor to remain, etc., etc.,

WINFIELD SCOTT.

14. The same intimation was repeated and explained the next morning, January 16th, to a captain of the British army, who had occasion to wait upon Scott on other business, and who immediately returned. It was just then that the Barcelona moved up the current of the Niagara. The cannon on either shore were pointed, the matches lighted, and thousands stood in suspense. On the jutting pier of Black Rock, in view of all, stood the tall form of Scott, in full uniform, watching the approaching boat. On Scott's note and his personal assurances, alone depended the question of PEACE OR WAR. Happily, these assurances had their just effect. The Barcelona passed along. The British did not fire. The matches were extinguished, and the two nations, guided by wise counsels, resumed their usual way.

(The fourteen *numbered* paragraphs immediately preceding, are quoted, omitting complimentary epithets, almost literally from Mansfield's *Life and Services* of the autobiographer, from whose copious notes—omitting those epithets of the partial editor—they had been copied, including the quotation from Byron.)

The frontiers being for the time quieted by the means narrated, by the thaw of the spring, and the return of the farming season of industry, Scott was called to Washington and ordered thence to the Southwest—charged with the delicate duty of removing the Cherokee Indians, under certain treaty stipulations, to their new country on the upper Arkansas River. This work unavoidably fell upon the military, and with *carte blanche,* from President Van Buren, under his sign manual—Mr. Secretary Poinsett being very ill—Scott undertook the painful duty—with the firm resolve that it should be done judiciously, if possible, and, certainly, in mercy.

The number of volunteers called for by Scott's predecessor (Colonel Lindsay) in that special command, independent of a few regulars, was overwhelming. Hence resistance on the part of the Indians would have been madness. The Cherokees were an interesting people—the greater number Christians, and many as civilized as their neighbors of the white race. Between the two colors intermarriages had been frequent. They occupied a contiguous territory—healthy mountains, valleys, and plains lying in North Carolina, Georgia, Alabama, and Tennessee. Most of their leading men had received good educations, and possessed much ability. Some were quite wealthy in cultivated farms, good houses, cattle of every kind, and *negro slaves.* Gardens and orchards were seen everywhere, and the women graceful, with, in many cases, added beauty. Of course the mixed races are here particularly alluded to. The mountaineers were still wild men, but little on this side of their primordial condition.

The North Carolinians and Tennesseans were kindly disposed toward their red brethren. The Alabamians much less so. The great difficulty was with the Georgians (more than half the army), between whom and the Cherokees there had been feuds and wars for many generations. The reciprocal hatred of the two races was probably never surpassed. Almost every Georgian, on leaving home, as well as after arrival at New Echota,—the centre of the most populous district of the Indian territory—vowed never to return without having killed at least one Indian. This ferocious language was the more remarkable as the great body of these citizens—perhaps, seven in ten—were professors of religion. The Methodist, Baptist, and other ministers of the Gospel of Mercy, had been extensively abroad among them; but the hereditary animosity alluded to caused the Georgians to forget, or, at least, to deny, that a Cherokee was a human being. It was, however, to that general religious feeling which Scott had witnessed in the Georgia troops, both in Florida and on the Chattahoochee in 1836, that he now meant to appeal, and on which he placed his hopes of avoiding murder and other atrocities. And as will be seen that blessed sentiment responded.

The autobiographer arrived at the Cherokee Agency, a small village on the Hiawassee, within the edge of Tennessee, early in May, 1838, and published the subjoined addresses to the troops and Indians. Both were printed at the neighboring village, Athens, and to show singleness of feeling and policy, the two papers were very extensively circulated *together,* among all concerned.

Extracts from General Orders, or the Address to the Troops.

"HEADQUARTERS, EASTERN DIVISION,
CHEROKEE AGENCY, May 17, 1838.

"Considering the number and temper of the mass to be removed, together with the extent and fastnesses of the country occupied, it will

---

readily occur that simple indiscretions, acts of harshness and cruelty on the part of our Troops may lead, step by step, to delays, to impatience, and exasperation, and, in the end, to a general war and carnage—*a result, in the case of these particular Indians, utterly abhorrent to the generous sympathies of the whole American people.* Every possible kindness, compatible with the necessity of removal, must, therefore, be shown by the troops; and if, in the ranks, a despicable individual should be found capable of inflicting a wanton injury or insult on any Cherokee man, woman, or child, it is hereby made the special duty of the nearest good officer or man instantly to interpose, and to seize and consign the guilty wretch to the severest penalty of the laws. The major-general is fully persuaded that this injunction will not be neglected by the brave men under his command, who cannot be otherwise than jealous of their own honor and that of their country.

"By early and persevering acts of kindness and humanity, it is impossible to doubt that the Indians may soon be induced to confide in the army, and, instead of fleeing to mountains and forests, flock to us for food and clothing. If, however, through false apprehensions, individuals, or a party here and there, should seek to hide themselves, they must be pursued and invited to surrender, but not fired upon, unless they should make a stand to resist. Even in such cases, mild remedies may sometimes better succeed than violence; and it cannot be doubted, if we get possession of the women and children first, or first capture the men, that, in either case, the outstanding members of the same families will readily come in on the assurance of forgiveness and kind treatment.

"Every captured man, as well as all who surrender themselves, must be disarmed, with the assurance that their weapons will be carefully preserved and restored at, or beyond the Mississippi. In either case, the men will be guarded and escorted, except it may be where their women and children are safely secured as hostages; but, in general, families in our possession will not be separated, unless it be to send men, as runners, to invite others to come in.

"It may happen that Indians will be found too sick, in the opinion of the nearest surgeon, to be removed to one of the depots indicated above. In every such case, one or more of the family or the friends of the sick person will be left in attendance, with ample subsistence and remedies, and the remainder of the family removed by the troops. Infants, superannuated persons, lunatics, and women in helpless condition, will all, in the removal, require peculiar attention, which the brave and humane will seek to adapt to the necessities of the several cases."

"MAJOR-GENERAL SCOTT, of the United States' Army, sends to the Cherokee people remaining in North Carolina, Georgia, Tennessee, and Alabama this

ADDRESS.

"Cherokees:—The President of the United States has sent me, with a powerful army, to cause you, in obedience to the treaty of 1835, to join that part of your people who are already established in prosperity on the other side of the Mississippi. Unhappily, the two years which were allowed for the purpose, you have suffered to pass away without following, and without making any preparation to follow, and now, or by the time that this solemn *address* shall reach your distant settlements, the emigration must be commenced in haste, but, I hope, without disorder. I have no power, by granting a farther delay, to correct the error that you have committed. The full moon of May is already on the wane, and before another shall have passed away, every Cherokee man, woman, and child, in those States, must be in motion to join their brethren in the far West.

"My friends—This is no sudden determination on the part of the President, whom you and I must now obey. By the treaty, the emigration was to have been completed on or before the 23d of this month, and the President has constantly kept you warned, during the two years allowed, through all his officers and agents in this country, that the treaty would be enforced.

"I am come to carry out that determination. My troops already occupy many positions in the country that you are to abandon, and thousands and thousands are approaching from every quarter, to render resistance and escape alike hopeless. All those troops, regular and militia, are your friends. Receive them and confide in them as such. Obey them when they tell you that you can remain no longer in this country. Soldiers are as kind-hearted as brave, and the desire of every one of us is to execute our painful duty in mercy. We are commanded by the President to act toward you in that spirit, and such is also the wish of the whole people of America.

"Chiefs, head men, and warriors—Will you then, by resistance, compel us to resort to arms? God forbid! Or will you, by flight, seek to hide yourselves in mountains and forests, and thus oblige us to hunt you down? Remember that, in pursuit, it may be impossible to avoid conflicts. The blood of the white man, or the blood of the red man, may be spilt, and if spilt, however accidentally, it may be impossible for the discreet and humane among you, or among us, to prevent a general war and carnage. Think of this, my Cherokee brethren! I am an old warrior, and have been present at many a scene of slaughter; but spare me, I beseech you, the horror of witnessing the destruction of the Cherokees.

"Do not, I invite you, even wait for the close approach of the troops; but make such preparations for emigration as you can, and hasten to this place, to Ross's Landing, or to Gunter's Landing, where you will all be received in kindness by officers selected for the purpose. You will find food for all, and clothing for the destitute, at either of those places, and thence at your ease, and in comfort, be transported to your new homes according to the terms of the treaty.

"This is the address of a warrior to warriors. May his entreaties be kindly received, and may the God of both prosper the Americans and Cherokees, and preserve them long in peace and friendship with each other.

"WINFIELD SCOTT."

There was some delay in bringing in the mountaineers of North Carolina; but most of the people residing in Tennessee and Alabama were readily collected for emigration. Scott remained with the Georgians, and followed up his printed addresses by innumerable lessons and entreaties.

The latter troops commenced in their own State the collection of the Indians, with their movable effects, May 26. Scott looked on in painful anxiety. Food in abundance had been provided at the depots, and wagons accompanied every detachment of troops. The Georgians distinguished themselves by their humanity and tenderness. Before the first night thousands—men, women, and children—sick and well were brought in. Poor creatures! They had obstinately refused to prepare for the removal. Many arrived half-starved, but refused the food that was pressed upon them. At length, the children, with less pride, gave way, and next their parents. The Georgians were the waiters on the occasion—many of them with flowing tears. The autobiographer has never witnessed a scene of deeper pathos.

Some cheerfulness, after awhile, began to show itself, when, counting noses, one family found that a child, another an aged aunt, etc., had been left behind. Instantly dozens of the volunteers asked for wagons, or saddle horses, with guides, to bring in the missing.

In a few days, without shedding a drop of blood, the Indians, with the exception of small fragments, were collected—those of North Carolina, Georgia, and Tennessee, at the Agency, in a camp twelve miles by four; well shaded, watered with perennial springs, and flanked by the Hiawassee. The *locale* was happily chosen, as a most distressing drought of some four months—counting from about the middle of June—came upon the whole Southwestern country, that stopped any movement to the West till November; for the Tennessee, Mississippi, and Arkansas Rivers ceased to be navigable by the beginning of July; and on the land route, to the Arkansas, there were many spaces of twenty, forty, and even sixty miles, without sufficient water for the inhabitants and their cattle. The other camps of emigration were also shaded and watered. Scott caused the few sick to be well attended by good physicians; all proper subjects to be vaccinated; rode through the principal camp almost daily, and having placed the emigration in the hands of the Cherokee authorities themselves—after winning the confidence of all—was at liberty, at an early day, to the great benefit of the treasury, to send all the volunteers to their respective homes, except a single company. A regiment of regulars, to meet contingencies, was also retained. Two others were despatched to Florida and the Canada frontiers. The company of volunteers (Tennesseeans) were a body of respectable citizens, and under their judicious commander, Captain Robertson, of great value as a police force. The Cherokees were receiving from Government immense sums; as fast as decreed by a civil commission (then in session) in the way of damages and indemnities, which attracted swarms of gamblers, sleight-of-hand men, blacklegs, and other desperadoes. The camp was kept cleansed of all such vermin by the military police—a duty which, probably, would have been resisted if it had devolved on regular troops. At length, late in October rain began to fall and the rivulets to flow. In a week or two, the rivers were again navigable. All were prepared for the exodus. Power had said:

"There lies your way, due West."

And a whole people now responded:

"Then Westward—ho!"

They took their way, if not rejoicing, at least in comfort.

"Some natural tears they dropt, but wiped them soon."

Many of the miseries of life they had experienced; but hope—a worldly, as well as a Christian's hope, cheered them on Scott followed up the movement nearly to the junction of the Ohio and Mississippi, where he gave his parting blessing to a people who had long shared his affectionate cares. He has reason to believe that, on the whole, their condition has been improved by transportation.

In the foregoing labor of necessity—executed, it is felt, in mercy—the autobiographer was well supported by his Acting Inspector-General,

Major M. M. Payne (subsequently Colonel), who, if living (January, 1864), is somewhere in Virginia, bedridden, from a wound received in one of General Taylor's battles on this side of the Rio Grande;[9] by Captain Robert Anderson, Assistant Adjutant-General, since the hero of Fort Sumter, and a Brigadier-General of the army;[10] by Lieutenant E. D. Keyes, Aide-de-Camp, now Major-General United States' Volunteers;[11] Lieutenant Francis Taylor, of the Commissariat, now long deceased;[12] Captains Page and Hetzel, Quartermasters;[13] Lieutenant H. L. Scott, since Aide-de-Camp and Inspector-General, then of the United States' 4th Infantry,[14] and by Major H. B. Shaw, Extra Aide-de-Camp, Tennessee Volunteers, since a distinguished member of the Louisiana bar, residing in Corcordia and Natchez—besides Colonel William Lindsay, 2d Artillery, and Colonel William S. Foster, 4th Infantry. Colonel I. B. Crane, 1st Artillery,[15] participated handsomely in the same service.

CHAPTER XXIII

SCOTT ORDERED BACK TO BRITISH FRONTIERS—TURMOIL RENEWED— MAINE BOUNDARY

It has been said that the autobiographer had intended to accompany the emigration farther west than the Ohio, to help it through any unforeseen difficulties on the route; but short of that point he received despatches from Washington telling him that he *Canadian patriots* (taking advantage of his absence in the South) had, in great numbers, reorganized their secret lodges all along the frontiers, and would renew their attempts to break into the Canadas on the return of frost, and he was directed to hasten thither, arranging with the Governors of Kentucky and Ohio, in route, the supply of such uninfected volunteers as might be needed to maintain the obligations of neutrality toward Great Britain.

Accompanied by Captain Robert Anderson, Scott rapidly visited Frankfort and Columbus; made contingent arrangements for volunteers that might be wanted, and also with the United States' District Attorney of Ohio for the assistance of his deputies and marshals in the arrest of leading offenders. Several of these, accompanied by a deputy marshal, he pursued for days. Though he lost not a moment on the route, he arrived but in time at Cleveland, Sandusky, and Detroit, respectively, to stop and disperse multitudes of frenzied citizens, by the means used in the previous winter, and thence proceeded down the frontiers *via* the places named, to Buffalo, Oswego, Sackett's Harbor, Ogdensburg, and Plattsburg, to the northern frontier of Vermont—meeting like assemblages and successes everywhere.

At the point farthest east he heard of the forward movement of the State of Maine on the Aroostook question, and fortunately was sufficiently out of work to hasten to Washington for instructions on this new difficulty—one entirely independent of Canadian patriots and sympathizers.[1]

The autobiographer reported himself in person to the Secretary of War, without having been in a recumbent position in eighty hours.

Every branch of the Government felt alarmed at the imminent hazard of a formidable war—but little having been done in a twenty-four years' peace to meet such exigency.

Though the moments were precious, Scott was detained several days to aid by explanations and arguments the passage of two bills—one to authorize the President to call out militia for six, instead of three months, and to accept fifty thousand volunteers; the other to place to his credit ten millions of dollars *extra*. For that purpose, he (Scott) was taken into conference with the chairmen of the committees on foreign and military affairs, of both Houses of Congress, and he may add, excusably, he hopes, that but for his expositions, and the known fact that the whole management of the difficulty in question would devolve on him, the bills would not have become laws; for, besides a hesitancy in the House of Representatives, a decided majority of the Senate was opposed to the Administration.

In taking leave of Mr. Van Buren and Mr. Secretary Poinsett, in order that there might be no "untoward" mistake, Scott respectfully said: "Mr. President, if you want *war,* I need only look on in silence. The Maine people will make it for you fast and hot enough. I know them; but if *peace* be your wish, I can give no assurance of success. The difficulties in its way will be formidable." "Peace with honor," was the reply; and that being Scott's own wish—looking to the great interests of the country—he went forward with a hearty good will.

Always accompanied by the gallant Captain Robert Anderson, and now rejoined by Lieutenant Keyes, Aide-de-Camp, the autobiographer, with *carte blanche,* hastened toward Maine—stopping in Boston long enough to arrange a contingent call for militia and volunteers with the patriotic and most accomplished Governor—Edward Everett—who, at the presentation to the executive council overwhelmed the sleepless general by this address:[2]

"GENERAL:

"I take great pleasure in introducing you to the members of the Executive Council of Massachusetts; I need not say that you are already known to them by reputation. They are familiar with your fame as it is recorded in some of the arduous and honorable fields of the country's struggles. We rejoice in meeting you on this occasion, charged as you are with a most momentous mission by the President of the United States. We are sure you are intrusted with a duty most grateful to your feelings—that of averting an appeal to arms. We place unlimited reliance on your spirit, energy, and discretion. Should you unhappily fail in your efforts, under the instructions of the President, to restore harmony, we know that you are equally prepared for a still more responsible duty. Should that event unhappily occur, I beg you to depend on the firm support of the Commonwealth of Massachusetts."

The general replied most respectfully, and concluded with assuring the Governor and council that the Executive of the United States had full reliance on the patriotism and public spirit of Massachusetts, to meet any emergency which might arise.

From that scene Scott was next taken to the popular branch of the legislature, where he was also handsomely received—another life-long, valued friend, Robert C. Winthrop, subsequently distinguished in both Houses of Congress, in the chair.[3]

Arriving at Portland, Scott met his first difficulty. The whole population, it seemed, had turned out to greet him. All being in favor of war, or the peaceful possession of the Aroostook, the "disputed territory," all looked to him to conquer that possession at once, as they had become tired of diplomacy, parleys, and delays. Many of his old soldiers of the last war with Great Britain were in the crowd; and although no man is a hero in the estimation of his *valet de chambre,* the feeling is quite otherwise with a commander's old brothers in arms. These now exaggerated Scott into the greatest man-slayer extant;—one who had killed off, in the Canadas, more men than Great Britain had there in that war.

Loud calls were made for a speech, *a speech!* But, too young in diplomacy to have acquired the art of using language to conceal his thoughts, the missionary of peace took refuge in silence, being, really, much oppressed with a cold and hoarseness. The word *peace* he had to hold *in petto,* to be suggested in the gentlest and most persuasive accents to the hostile ears of the Governor and his council at Augusta, the capital of Maine.[4]

Scott found a bad temper prevailing at Augusta. The legislature was in session, and the Democrats dominant in every branch of the Government.

In the legislature the weight of talent and information, however, was with the Whig minority. Hence they were much feared; for, having recently been in power, the least error on the side of the Democrats, might again give them the State. The popular cry being for war, the Whigs were unwilling to abandon that hobby-horse entirely; but the Democrats were the first in the saddle and rode furiously.

The State of Maine and the Province of New Brunswick were fast approaching actual hostilities, and if Scott had been a few days later in coming upon the scene, the troops of the two countries would have arrived, and crossed bayonets on the disputed territory—a strip of land lying between acknowledged boundaries, without any immediate value except for the fine ship-timber in which it abounded. The cutting of these venerable trees by British subjects led Maine to send a land agent, with a *posse,* to drive off the trespassers. The agent was seized and imprisoned, for a time, in the Province. Much angry correspondence ensued between the two Governors, followed by ominous silence and war preparation.[5]

Scott soon perceived that the only hope of pacification depended on his persuading the local belligerents to stand off the territory in question for a time, and to remit the whole question in issue to the two paramount Governments at Washington and London, from which it had been improperly wrested, by the impatience of Maine at the dilatoriness of American diplomacy.

He took up his quarters at the same house, in Augusta, with His Excellency and other leading Democrats, and sat in the midst of them three times a day at the same public table. By degrees he won their confidence. He was known to them as the representative, in the special matter, of their friends of the same party at Washington.

The intrinsic difficulties to be dealt with in the mission were much aggravated by a new element just thrown in by federal authority and published at the time in all the papers, viz.:[6]

"MEMORANDUM

"Her Majesty's authorities consider it to have been understood and agreed upon by the two Governments, that the territory in dispute between Great Britain and the United States, on the northeastern frontier, should remain exclusively under British jurisdiction until the final settlement of the boundary question.

"The United States' Government have not understood the above agreement in the same sense, but consider, on the contrary, that there has been no agreement whatever for the exercise, by Great Britain, of exclusive jurisdiction over the disputed territory, or any portion thereof, but a mutual understanding that, pending the negotiation, the jurisdiction then exercised by either party, over small portions of the territory in dispute, should not be enlarged, but be continued merely for the preservation of local tranquillity and the public property, both forbearing as far as practicable to exert any authority, and, when any should be exercised by either, placing upon the conduct of each other the most favorable construction.

"A complete understanding upon the question, thus placed at issue, of present jurisdiction, can only be arrived at by friendly discussion between the Governments of the United States and Great Britain; and, as it is confidently hoped that there will be an early settlement of the question, this subordinate point of difference can be of but little moment.

"In the mean time, the Governor of the Province of New Brunswick and the Government of the State of Maine, will act as follows: Her Majesty's officers will not seek to expel, by military force, the armed party which has been sent by Maine into the district bordering on the Aroostook River; but the Government of Maine will, voluntarily, and without needless delay, withdraw beyond the bounds of the disputed territory any armed force now within them; and if future necessity should arise for dispersing notorious trespassers, or protecting public property from depredation by armed force, the operation shall be conducted by concert, jointly or separately, according to agreements between the Governments of Maine and New Brunswick.

"The civil officers in the service respectively of New Brunswick and Maine, who have been taken into custody by the opposite parties, shall be released.

"Nothing in this memorandum shall be construed to fortify or to weaken, in any respect whatever, the claim of either party to the ultimate possession of the disputed territory.

"The Minister Plenipotentiary of Her Britannic Majesty having no specific authority to make any arrangement on the subject, the undersigned can only recommend, as they now earnestly do, to the Governments of New Brunswick and Maine, to regulate their future proceedings according to the terms herein set forth, until the final settlement of the territorial dispute, or until the Governments of the United States and Great Britain shall come to some definite conclusion on the subordinate point upon which they are now at issue.

> "John Forsyth, Secretary of
> State of the United States
> of North America.
> "H. S. Fox, H. B. M. Envoy
> Extraordinary
> and Minister Plenipotentiary.
> "Washington, February 27, 1839."

This *memorandum* gave great offence to the authorities and people of Maine. They were required to withdraw their forces from the territory in dispute simply on the promise that British officers would not *seek to expel them by force!*—without any reciprocal obligation;—the other party being left free to remain; to fortify themselves; to continue their depredations, undisturbed, and for an indefinite time! This bungle Scott had first to adjust between Democratic authorities —State and Federal—he being himself a Whig! It was no easy thing to find a solvent for such knarled perplexities, foreign and domestic. Fortunately accidental circumstances in his history supplied the *desideratum.*

The Governor of the Province, New Brunswick, was, at the time, the distinguished Lieutenant-General, Sir John Harvey, of the British army, the same who in the campaign of 1813 was adjutant-general in Upper Canada with the rank of lieutenant-colonel. (See above, p. 53 and note.)

The report of Colonel Harvey's kindness to such American officers and men as fell into the hands of the enemy, made him an object of respect and kindness throughout our ranks. Harvey and Scott being leaders, and always in front, exchanged salutes several times on the field, and once, when out reconnoitring, Scott's escort cut off the Englishman from his party. A soldier, taking a deadly aim, would, certainly, have finished a gallant career, if Scott had not knocked up the rifle—saying, *Don't kill our prisoner!* But though a prisoner for a moment, Harvey, by a sudden movement, spurred his charger and escaped into a thicket, unhurt, notwithstanding the many rifle balls hastily thrown after him. This was the second time that he had escaped from captivity, and Scott now gave strict orders never to spare again an enemy so active and dangerous.

It so happened that in leaving the Cherokee country, the *major*-general received a friendly letter from the *lieutenant*-general, which, from the want of time, remained unanswered when the former arrived at Augusta.

The reply to that letter, semi-official, was followed by a rapid interchange of like communications, the Governor of Maine reading all that was written by the correspondents. By degrees Scott won over to his pacific views the dominant party—only that it hesitated lest the Whigs should shift about, agitate against any compromise and thereby regain the State. This apprehension was mentioned to Scott by the Governor, in the presence of the aged treasurer, an honest man, but a bigot in politics.[7] Scott, who had not approached the Whigs in the Legislature, who, indeed, had shunned him as a Democrat;—nor had he expressed a party sentiment to anybody after his leaving Washington—now asked permission of Governor Fairfield to speak to his leading opponents in that body—adding that he himself being a Whig, might bring them out, openly, in support of pacific measures. At this declaration of party bias, the good old treasurer was thrown into a most ludicrous attitude of surprise and consternation, which caused his Excellency, though himself, at first, a little startled, to laugh most heartily. This burst of good humor, in which the treasurer eventually joined, was a positive gain in the right direction. (All the details of this negotiation cannot yet be given. There was, however, no bribery.)

To bring those leading Whigs and Scott together required dexterous management; for if that had happened without the presence of leading Democrats, a suspicion of foul play would have been excited. Scott, therefore, induced Senator Evans, just from Washington, to invite them, the Governor and several State Councillors to sup with him at Gardiner, a little below Augusta.[8] The envoy took charge of his Democratic friends in a government sleigh. All the topics he intended to urge upon the Whig leaders were given and discussed in the vehicle. The night was brilliant, and so was the entertainment. Mr. Evans—a distinguished Whig, as everybody knew—placed his Democratic guests at his end of the table, and Scott, with the Whigs around him, at the other. The latter were sulky, and Scott's blandishments, in doing the honors of his position, failed to open the way to the main business of the evening—next to the supper—when, on a beckon, the master of the feast came to the rescue, and whispered to the Whigs (capital fellows!) that the representative of President Van Buren, near them, was as good a Whig as the best of them! Another ludicrous surprise! Compliments and cordiality ensued at once, and viands and business were discussed together to the content of all parties. The Governor understood the object of the Senator's whispers, and plainly saw that Scott had succeeded. A feast is a great peacemaker—worth more than all the usual arts of diplomacy. Scott had also, from the first, received good assistance from the Honorable Albert Smith, of Portland, afterward a member of Congress, who, happening to be in Augusta, gave him the temper and bias of many particular Democrats whom it was necessary to conciliate.

The work was done. Virtually nothing remained, but the synthetic process of gathering up all the particular results into one general act of amnesty and good will. Sir John Harvey was of a too elevated character to be fastidious about non-essentials. On being sounded, he had concurred at once with Scott on all essentials, and Governor Fairfield and council having no longer anything to fear from perversity on the part of the Whigs, now sent in a message, March 12, to the Legislature, of which this is an extract:

"What then shall be done? The people of the State surely are not desirous of hurrying the two nations into a war. Such an event is anxiously to be avoided, if it can be without dishonor. We owe too much to the Union, to ourselves, and, above all, to the spirit and principles of Christianity, to bring about a conflict of arms with a people having with us a common origin, speaking a common language, and bound to us by so many ties of common interest, without the most inexorable necessity. Under these circumstances I would recommend that, when we are fully satisfied, either by the declarations of the Lieutenant-Governor of New Brunswick, or otherwise, that he has abandoned all idea of occupying the disputed territory with a military force, and of attempting an expulsion of our party, that then the Governor be authorized to withdraw our military force, leaving the land-agent with a posse, armed or unarmed, as the case may require, sufficient to carry into effect your original design—that of driving out or arresting the trespassers, and preserving and protecting the timber from their depredations."

The Legislature, on the 20th of the same month, passed an act in accordance with the message, and the next day Scott despatched by his line of couriers, to meet Sir John's line at the border, the following papers:

From the Augusta (Me.) Journal, March 26, 1839.
"The War Ended.—Important Correspondence.

"HEADQUARTERS, EASTERN DIVISION
U. S. ARMY, AUGUSTA, ME.,
March 21, 1839.

"'The undersigned, a Major-General in the Army of the United States, being specially charged with maintaining the peace and safety of their entire northern and eastern frontiers, having cause to apprehend a collision of arms between the proximate forces of New Brunswick and the State of Maine on the *disputed territory,* which is claimed by both, has the honor, in the sincere desire of the United States to preserve the relations of peace and amity with Great Britain—relations which might be much endangered by such untoward collision—to invite from his Excellency Major-General Sir John Harvey, Lieutenant-Governor, etc., etc., a general declaration to this effect:

"'That it is not the intention of the Lieutenant-Governor of Her Britannic Majesty's Province of New Brunswick, under the expected renewal of negotiations between the cabinets of London and Washington on the subject of the said disputed territory, without renewed instructions to that effect from his Government, to seek to take military possession of that territory, or to seek, by military force, to expel therefrom the armed civil posse or the troops of Maine.

"'Should the undersigned have the honor to be favored with such declaration or assurance, to be by him communicated to his Excellency the Governor of the State of Maine, the undersigned does not in the least doubt that lie would be immediately and fully authorized by the Governor of Maine to communicate to his Excellency, the Lieutenant-Governor of New Brunswick, a corresponding pacific declaration to this effect:

"'That, in the hope of a speedy and satisfactory settlement, by negotiation, between the Governments of the United States and Great Britain, of the principal or boundary question between the State of Maine and the Province of New Brunswick, it is not the intention of the Governor of Maine, without renewed instructions from the Legislature of the State, to attempt to disturb by arms the said Province in the possession of the Madawaska settlements, or to attempt to interrupt the usual communications between that Province and Her Majesty's Upper Provinces; and that he is willing, in the mean time, to leave the questions of possession and jurisdiction as they at present stand—that is, Great Britain holding, in fact, possession of a part of the said territory, and the Government of Maine denying her right to such possession; and the State of Maine holding, in fact, possession of another portion of the same territory, to which her right is denied by Great Britain.

"'With this understanding, the Governor of Maine will, without unnecessary delay, withdraw the military force of the State from the said disputed territory leaving only, under a land agent, a small civil *posse,* armed or unarmed., to protect the timber recently cut, and to prevent future depredations.

"'Reciprocal assurances of the foregoing friendly character having been, through the undersigned, interchanged, all danger of collision between the immediate parties to the controversy will be at once removed, and time allowed the United States and Great Britain to settle amicably the great question of limits.

"'The undersigned has much pleasure in renewing to his Excellency Major-General Sir John Harvey, the assurances of his ancient high consideration and respect.

"'WINFIELD SCOTT.'

"To a copy of the foregoing, Sir John Harvey annexed the following:

"'The undersigned, Major-General Sir John Harvey, Lieutenant-Governor of Her Britannic Majesty's Province of New Brunswick, having received a proposition from Major-General Winfield Scott, of the United States' Army, of which the foregoing is a copy, hereby, on his part, signifies his concurrence and acquiescence therein.

"'Sir John Harvey renews with great pleasure to Major-General Scott the assurances of his warmest personal consideration, regard, and respect.

"'J. HARVEY.

"'Government House, Fredericton,
New Brunswick, March 23, 1839.'

"To a paper containing the note of General Scott, and the acceptance of Sir John Harvey, Governor Fairfield annexed his acceptance in these words:

"'Executive Department,
Augusta, March 25, 1839.

"'The undersigned, Governor of Maine, in consideration of the foregoing, the exigency for calling out the troops of Maine having ceased, has no hesitation in signifying his entire acquiescence in the proposition of Major-General Scott.

"'The undersigned has the honor to tender to Major-General Scott the assurance of his high respect and esteem.

"'JOHN FAIRFIELD.'

"We learn that General Scott has interchanged the acceptances of the Governor and Lieutenant-Governor, and also that Governor Fairfield immediately issued orders recalling the troops of Maine, and for organizing the civil *posse* that is to be continued, for the time, in *the disputed territory.* The troops in this town will also be immediately discharged."

With Sir John's acceptance came this letter:

"My DEAR GENERAL SCOTT:

"Upon my return from closing the session of the Provincial Legislature, I was gratified by the receipt of your very satisfactory communication of the 21st instant. My reliance upon *you,* my dear General, has led me to give my willing assent to the proposition which you have made yourself the very acceptable means of conveying to me; and I trust that as far as the Province and the State respectively are concerned, an end will be put by it to all border disputes, and a way opened to an amicable adjustment of the national question involved. I shall hope to receive the confirmation of this arrangement on the part of the State of Maine at as early a period as may be practicable."

Dr. W. E. Channing, a leading philanthropist scholar, orator, and divine, of his day, in the preface to his *Lecture on War* (1839), devoted two paragraphs to the honor of the autobiographer's peace labors, in these words:[9]

"To this distinguished man belongs the rare honor of uniting with military energy and daring, the spirit of a philanthropist. His exploits in the field, which placed him in the first rank of our soldiers, have been obscured by the purer and more lasting glory of a pacificator, and of a friend of mankind. In the whole history of the intercourse of civilized with barbarous or half-civilized communities, we doubt whether a brighter page can be found than that which records his agency in the removal of the Cherokees. As far as the wrongs done to this race can be atoned for, General Scott has made the expiation.

"In his recent mission to the disturbed borders of our country, he has succeeded, not so much by policy as by the nobleness and generosity of his character, by moral influences, by the earnest conviction with which he has enforced on all with whom he has had to do, the obligations of patriotism, justice, humanity, and religion. It would not be easy to find among us a man who has won a purer fame; and I am happy to offer this tribute, because I would do something, no matter how little, to hasten the time when the spirit of Christian humanity shall be accounted an essential attribute and the brightest ornament of a public man.

"He returns to Washington, and is immediately ordered to the Cherokee nation, to take charge of the very difficult and hazardous task to his own fame of removing those savages from their native land. Some of his best friends regretted, most sincerely, that he had been ordered on this service; and, knowing the disposition of the world to cavil and complain without cause, had great apprehensions that he would lose a portion of the popularity he had acquired by his distinguished success on the Canadian frontier. But, behold the manner in which this last work has been performed! There is so much of noble generosity of character about Scott, independent of his skill and bravery as a soldier, that his life has really been one of romantic beauty and interest."

CHAPTER XXIV

POLITICS—GENERAL-IN-CHIEF—STOPS UNLAWFUL PUNISHMENTS—ATTEMPTS TO ABOLISH HIS RANK AND TO REDUCE HIS PAY—MR. ADAMS AND MR. C. J. INGERSOLL

It was about this time that the autobiographer was, without wish or agency on his part, brought into the arena of party politics, although long before a quiet Whig. A convention of delegates of that party met early in December, 1839, at Harrisburg, to select candidates for the Presidency and Vice-Presidency at the election in November of the following year.

Mr. Clay, the head of the party, and General Harrison were the principals before the convention. Scott had also a respectable number of supporters (the delegates of five States, including those of New York) in that body; but Scott wrote a number of letters to members, friends of Mr. Clay, to be seen by all, expressing the hope that the latter might, with any prospect of success, before the people, be selected as the candidate, and if not, that General Harrison might be the nominee.

So far as respects the younger, or third candidate, himself, the result is not, at this day, worth a single remark. But the accidental circumstances which finally ruled the convention, are too curious within themselves, as well as too important to the future of the country, to be longer suppressed.

There was abundant evidence from the beginning of the convention that Scott was the second choice of a great majority both of the Clay and Harrison members; but Mr. Leigh (the Honorable B. W.),[1] who led the Virginia delegation, and that led the other Clay delegations—all Southern and Southwestern men;—by a singular infelicity, contrived that those delegations should lose both their first and second preferences. The supporters of Scott, after a great many ballotings, communicated to the separate assemblages of the Clay men, that if the latter did not, after the next vote, come over to Scott, their known second choice, they, the New

Yorkers and associates, would, in that case, next vote for Harrison, their second choice. Here the strangeness alluded to must be told.

Mr. Leigh—a man of perfect uprightness of character, of high abilities; and early in life a passionate and successful cultivator of polite literature—had now, and for many years before, become the slave of his profession—without any diminution of business, but with a yearly decrease of fees and increase of family—so fagged, for twelve and fourteen hours a day, that his acquaintance with the advancing world, literature, and politics, did not extend beyond the narrow circle of Richmond. Being without a rival in that sphere, and now for the first time in his life three days north of Washington;—conscious of the purity of his intentions, and having made up his own mind that Mr. Clay ought to be the next President, he carefully avoided everybody likely to perplex and distress him with the contrary wishes or calculations.

Congress met three days before the convention. The Whig members of the former, desirous of conversing understandingly with their friends as they passed through Washington to Harrisburg, held in formal meetings, by States, and came to the conclusion, after inquiry and reflection, that Mr. Clay could scarcely carry a district represented by one of them—Mitchell, alone, being confident that his, the Lockport or Niagara District of New York, would vote for the illustrious Kentuckian; but Mitchell could not be relied upon; for he was long before the election put into the State prison as a forger.

Mr. Leigh, apprehending such interference at Washington, and true to his provincial superiority, quietly passed down the James River and up the Chesapeake Bay, through Baltimore, with a large number of dependent delegates, to Harrisburg—where he was taken possession of by two veteran and inveterate Clay supporters from the city of New York (traders in politics, but not members of the convention), who so mesmerized him that he could not believe a word said to him by men of the highest standing in the North and East. Hence, when the message, just mentioned, was received by the Clay supporters, that is, by Mr. Leigh, who was not only the organ, but the sole voice of that party, his mesmerizers told him to treat it with contempt, that it was a mere fetch, and that the Scott delegates would be obliged in a few ballots more to vote for Mr. Clay.

This assurance was speedily falsified, and then some of the dupes, including Mr. Leigh himself—wished to move for a reconsideration of the vote; but Scott's friends very judiciously said, "No; it is too late. Harrison's name, as our nominee, will, in five minutes, be on the wings of the winds to all parts of the Union, and now to nominate another would distract the party and make us contemptible."[2]

But the nomination and success of General Harrison, if his life had been spared some four years longer, would have been no detriment to his country. With excellent intentions and objects, and the good sense to appoint able counsellors, the country would not have been retarded in its prosperity, nor disgraced by corruption in high places. No one can, of course, be held responsible for sudden deaths among men. A single month in office, ended President Harrison's life, when the affecting plaint of Burke occurred to all: "What shadows we are, what shadows we pursue!"

Mr. Leigh's great error at Harrisburg is yet to be narrated, and referred to the same virtues combined with the inaptitude of one long ignorant of the world. All the able men who voted early or late for Harrison, were inclined to name Mr. Leigh, as a slight indemnification to Mr. Clay, for the Vice-Presidency;—but Mr. Tyler, of the same delegation, wept audibly for the loss of Virginia's candidate, and intrigued quietly with the weaker brethren to secure that honor for himself. Mr. Leigh being sole committee man of his delegation on the selection of candidates, and the reverenced adviser of many others, delicately hesitated about receiving the nomination, and worse, from delicacy toward a colleague, neglected to tell distant members how utterly unfit Mr. Tyler was for the second place in the Government—nobody, of course, thinking of a vacancy in the presidential chair,—a case that had never occurred.[3] Thus by the double squeamishness of a good man, the United States lost an eventual President not inferior to more than one man that had ever filled that high place.

Of Mr. Tyler's administration of the executive branch of the Government, but little will be said here. He soon committed the grossest tergiversation in politics, from the fear of Mr. Clay as a competitor for the succession, and to win that for himself, all the patronage of the Government, all the chips, shavings, and sweepings of office, down to the lowest clerkship, the posts of messengers and watchmen, were brought into market and bartered for support at the next election. To the honor of the country, Mr. Tyler was allowed to relapse into a private station.

In June, 1841, Scott was, on the death of Major-General Macomb, called to reside in Washington as the General-in-Chief of the entire army. In that capacity he made several ordinary tours of inspection, but nothing occurred in the next five years that called him to any mission of importance. Many specimens of orders might be given to show his regard for the soldier, as well as love of military discipline and efficiency; but they would not be interesting to the general reader. One only will here be inserted to exhibit his long persevering and successful efforts to stop arbitrary, that is, illegal, punishments in the army.

GENERAL ORDERS.   HEADQUARTERS OF THE ARMY,
No. 53   WASHINGTON, August 20, 1842.

1. . . . Intimations, through many channels, received at General Headquarters, lead to more than a suspicion that blows, kicks, cuffs, and lashes, against law, the good of the service and the faith of Government, have, in many instances, down to a late period, been inflicted upon private soldiers of the army by their officers and non-commissioned officers.

2. . . . Inquiries into the reported abuses are in progress, with instructions, if probable evidence of guilt be found, to bring the offenders to trial.

3. . . . It is well known to every vigilant officer that discipline can be maintained (—and it shall be so maintained—) *by legal means.* Other resorts are, in the end, always destructive of good order and subordination.

4. . . . Insolence, disobedience, mutiny, are the usual provocations to unlawful violence. But these several offences are denounced by the 6th, 7th, and 9th of the rules and articles of war, and made punishable by the sentence of courts-martial. Instead, however, of waiting for such judgment, according to the nature and degree of guilt, deliberately found—the hasty and conceited—losing all self-control and dignity of command—assume that their individual importance is more outraged than the majesty of law, and act, at once, as legislators, judges, and executioners. Such gross usurpation is not to be tolerated in any well-governed army.

5. . . . For insolent words, addressed to a superior, let the soldier be ordered into confinement. This, of itself, if followed by prompt repentance and apology, may often be found a sufficient punishment. If not, a court can readily authorize the final remedy. A deliberate, or unequivocal breach of orders, is treated with yet greater judicial rigor; and, in a clear case of mutiny, the sentence would, in all probability, extend to life. It is evident, then, that there is not even a pretext for punishments decreed on individual assumption, and at the dictate of pride and resentment.

6. . . . But it may be said, in the case of mutiny, or conduct tending to this great crime—that it is necessary to cut down, on the spot, the

exciter or ringleader. *First* order him to be seized. If his companions put him into irons or confinement, it is plain there is no spread of the dangerous example. But, should *they* hesitate;—or should it be necessary in any case of disobedience, desertion, or running away—*the object bury to secure the person for trial;*—as always to repel a personal assault, or to stop an affray—in every one of these cases any superior may strike and wound; but only to the extent clearly necessary to such lawful end. Any excess, wantonly committed beyond such measured violence, would, itself, be punishable in the superior. No other case can possibly justify any superior in committing violence upon the body of any inferior, without the judgment of a court—except that it may sometimes be necessary, by force, to iron prisoners for security, or to gag them for quiet.

7. . . . Harsh and abusive words, passionately or wantonly applied to unoffending inferiors, is but little less reprehensible. Such language is, at once, unjust, vulgar, and unmanly; and, in this connection, it may be useful to recall a passage from the old *General Regulations for the Army* (by Scott):

"The general deportment of officers toward juniors or inferiors will be carefully watched and regulated. If this be cold or harsh, on the one hand, or grossly familiar on the other, the harmony or discipline of the corps cannot be maintained. The examples are numerous and brilliant, in which the most conciliatory manners have been found perfectly compatible with the exercise of the strictest command; and the officer who does not unite a high degree of moral vigor with the civility that springs from the heart, cannot too soon choose another profession in which imbecility would be less conspicuous, and harshness less wounding and oppressive." (*Edition* 1825.)

8. . . . Government not only reposes "special trust and confidence in the patriotism, valor, fidelity, and abilities of" army officers, as is expressed on the face of commissions; but also in their self-control, respect for law and gentlemanly conduct on all occasions. A failure under either of those heads ought always to be followed by the loss of a commission.

9. . . . At a time when, notwithstanding the smallness of the establishment, thousands of the most promising youths are desirous of military commissions, the country has a right to demand—not merely the usual exact observance of laws, regulations, and orders, but yet more— that every officer shall give himself up entirely to the cultivation and practice of all the virtues and accomplishments which can elevate an honorable profession. There is in the army of the United States, neither room, nor associates, for the idle, the ignorant, the vicious, the disobedient. To the very few such, thinly scattered over the service—whether

in the line or the staff—these admonitions are mainly addressed; and let the vigilant eye of all commanders be fixed upon them. No bad or indifferent officer should receive from a senior any favor or indulgence whatsoever.

10. . . . The attention of commanders of departments, regiments, companies, and garrisons is directed to the 101st of the rules and articles of war which requires that the whole series shall be read to the troops at least once in every six months.

WINFIELD SCOTT.

In this interval of comparative inactivity, high army rank again came to be considered useless and burdensome. Several movements were made in the House of Representatives, to cut down Scott's long-fixed pay and emoluments, and one, quite formidable, in its inception, to abolish his office.

A previous motion to reduce his pay, etc., was defeated by a side battery, opened by the Hon. Charles J. Ingersoll, member of the House from Philadelphia.[4] There was another bill lying on the clerk's table touching the daily compensation of the members of both Houses of Congress, and Mr. Ingersoll argued that the latter should first become a law, before Congress could, with decency, cut down the pay of the army.

Both propositions affecting Scott came to a definite vote in the House of Representatives, March, 1844.

Mr. Adams (J. Q.) "felt bound to declare that he did think it a very ill reward for the great and eminent services of that officer [Scott] during a period of thirty-odd years, in which there were some as gallant exploits as our history could show, and in which he had not spared to shed his blood, as well as for more recent services of great importance in time of peace—services of great difficulty and great delicacy—now to turn him adrift at his advanced age."

In respect to the reduction of his pay, etc., Mr. Adams "could not a moment harbor in his heart the thought that General Scott, if he had received from Government thousands of dollars more than he had, would have received one dollar which he did not richly deserve at the hands of his country."—*National Intelligencer, March* 30, 1844.

"Mr. C. J. Ingersoll wished to add but a single word. Perhaps he was the only member present who could recollect the day when this same General Scott had been the first man to show that the disciplined soldiery of our own country were fully able to cope with the trained troops of a foreign nation.[5] When gentlemen were about to legislate General Scott out of office, he must be permitted to add one consideration to those which had so properly been stated by the venerable gentleman from Massachusetts (Mr. Adams), and it was this: That, while we were sitting here very coolly giving votes to legislate General Scott out of office, we ought not quite to forget that it was by virtue of his brave achievements we possessed the opportunity of voting here at all. It was easy for gentlemen to call those 'caterpillars' who, in the hour of peril, had been the 'pillars' of the public trust. He should be sorry indeed that this blow should fall upon the man who had struck the first blow in that struggle through which alone this Government had been preserved in being down to this hour. But it was obvious that neither office nor officer was in the slightest danger."—*National Intelligencer, March* 30, 1844.

Both propositions were voted down by large majorities.

It may be remarked that Mr. Adams and Mr. Ingersoll, in a common service of six years on the same floor of Congress, scarcely ever before agreed on any subject whatever. Indeed Mr. C. J. Ingersoll was an object of unusual hatred with the Whig party generally. Dr. Johnson "loved a good hater," and Mr. Ingersoll, to do him justice, fully repaid the Whigs in kind. Yet he was always to the autobiographer a valuable friend. Their acquaintance and friendship commenced early in the War of 1812, when no man, in the House of Representatives, struck more valiantly for his country than Mr. Ingersoll.

During a residence of some three years in Philadelphia, beginning in 1819, and always afterward, when on a visit to that city, Scott, perhaps never failed, a single Sunday, to be invited to Mr. Ingersoll's hospitable table, after the second church, where were met the usual guests—Judge Hopkinson, the author of *Hail Columbia;* Nicholas Biddle (two of the most accomplished and amiable men in America), Joseph Bonaparte, James Brown, Ex-Senator and Minister to France, and any stranger of eminence that might be passing through. In all these agreeable reunions, Mr. Ingersoll, a good scholar and linguist, bore his part well-giving and receiving pleasure.

CHAPTER XXV

LETTER ON SLAVERY–TRACTS ON PEACE AND WAR–MR. POLK PRESIDENT

Scott's views on the question of negro slavery are strongly alluded to, but not fully developed, in the foregoing narrative. Begging the reader to forgive a partial repetition of the same ideas and expressions, he inserts his formal letter on the subject here:[1]

WASHINGTON, February 9, 1843.

DEAR SIR:

I have been waiting for an evening's leisure to answer your letter before me, and, after an unreasonable delay, am at last obliged to reply in the midst of official occupations.

That I ever have been named in connection with the Presidency of the United States, has not, I can assure *you,* the son of an ancient neighbor and friend, been by any contrivance or desire of mine; and certainly I shall never be in the field for that high office unless placed there *by a regular nomination.* Not, then, being a candidate, and seeing no near prospect of being *made* one, I ought, perhaps, to decline troubling you or others with my humble opinions on great principles of State Rights and Federal Administration; but as I cannot plead ignorance of the partiality of a few friends, in several parts of the Union, who may, by possibility, in a certain event, succeed in bringing me within the field from which a Whig candidate is to be selected, I prefer to err on the side of frankness and candor, rather than, by silence, to allow any stranger unwittingly to commit himself to my support.

Your inquiries open the whole question of domestic slavery, which has, in different forms, for a number of years, agitated Congress and the country.

Premising that you are the first person who has interrogated me on the subject, I give you the basis of what *would* be my reply in greater detail, if time allowed and the contingency alluded to above were less remote.

In boyhood, at William and Mary College, and in common with most, if not all, my companions, I became deeply impressed with the views given by Mr. Jefferson, in his "Notes on Virginia," and by Judge Tucker, in the Appendix to his edition of Blackstone's Commentaries, in favor of a gradual emancipation of slaves.[2] That Appendix I have not seen in thirty odd years, and, in the same period, have read scarcely anything on the subject; but my early impressions are fresh and unchanged. Hence, if I had had the honor of a seat in the Virginia Legislature in the winter of 1831–'2, when a bill was brought forward to carry out those views, I should certainly have given it my hearty support.

I suppose I scarcely need say that, in my opinion, Congress has no color of authority, under the Constitution, for touching the relation of master and slave within a State.

I hold the opposite opinion in respect to the District of Columbia. Here, with the consent of the owners, or on the payment of "just compensation," Congress may legislate at its discretion. But my conviction is equally strong that, unless it be step by step with the Legislatures of Virginia and Maryland, it would be dangerous to both races in those States to touch the relation between master and slave in this District.

I have from the first been of opinion that Congress was bound by the Constitution to receive, to refer, and to report upon petitions relating to domestic slavery as in the case of all other petitions; but I have not failed to see and to regret the unavoidable irritation which the former have produced in the Southern States, with the consequent peril to the two colors, whereby the adoption of any plan of emancipation has everywhere among us been greatly retarded.

I own, myself, no slave; but never have attached blame to masters for not liberating their slaves—well knowing that liberation, without the means of sending them in comfort to some position favorable to "the pursuit of happiness," would, in most cases, be highly injurious to all around, as well as to the manumitted families themselves—unless the operation were general and under the auspices of prudent legislation. But I am persuaded that it is a high moral obligation of masters and slaveholding States to employ all means, not incompatible with the safety of both colors, to meliorate slavery even to extermination.

It is gratifying to know that general melioration has been great, and is still progressive, notwithstanding the disturbing causes alluded to above. The more direct process of emancipation may, no doubt, be earlier commenced and quickened in some communities than in others. Each, I do not question, has the right to judge for itself, both as to time and means, and I consider interference or aid from without, except on invitation from authority within, to be as hurtful to the sure progress of melioration, as it may be fatal to the lives of vast multitudes of all ages, sexes, and colors. The work of liberation cannot be *forced* without such horrid results. Christian philanthropy is ever mild and considerate. Hence all violence ought to be deprecated by the friends of religion and humanity. Their persuasions cannot fail at the right time to free the master from the slave, and the slave from the master; perhaps before the latter shall have found out and acknowledged that the relation between the parties had long been mutually prejudicial to their worldly interests.

There is no evil without, in the order of Providence, some compensating benefit. The bleeding African was torn from his savage home by his ferocious neighbors, sold into slavery, and cast upon this continent. Here, in the mild South, the race has wonderfully multiplied, compared with anything ever known in barbarous life. The descendants of a few thousands have become many millions; and all, from the first, made acquainted with the arts of civilization, and, above all, brought under the light of the Gospel.

From the promise made to Abraham, some two thousand years had elapsed before the advent of our Saviour, and the Israelites, the chosen people of God, were, for wise purposes, suffered to remain in bondage longer than Africans have been on our shore. This race has already experienced the resulting compensations alluded to; and, as the white missionary has never been able to penetrate the dark regions of Africa, or to establish himself in its interior, it may be within the scheme of Providence that the great work of spreading the Gospel over that vast continent, with all the arts and comforts of civilization, is to be finally accomplished by the black man restored from American bondage. A foothold there has already been gained for him, and in such a scheme centuries are but as seconds to Him who moves worlds as man moves a finger.

I do but *suggest* the remedies and consolations of slavery, to inspire patience, hope, and charity on all sides. The mighty subject calls for the exercise of all man's wisdom and virtue, and these may not suffice without aid from a higher source.

It is in the foregoing manner, my dear sir, that I have long been in the habit, in conversation, of expressing myself, all over our common country, on the question of negro slavery, and I must say that I have found but very few persons to differ with me, however opposite their geographical positions.

Such are the views or opinions which you seek. I cannot suppress or mutilate them, although now liable to be more generally known. Do with them what you please. I neither court nor shun publicity.

I remain, very truly, yours,
WINFIELD SCOTT.

T. P. Atkinson Esq., Danville, Virginia.

Peace and War
WASHINGTON, March 24, 1845

I have received your letter of the 21st instant, accompanied by certain proceedings of the General Peace Convention.[3]

My participation in war, as well as endeavors on several occasions to preserve peace, without sacrificing the honor and the interests of my country, are matters of public history. These antecedents, together with my sentiments on the abstract question of *peace and war,* inserted a year ago in a Peace Album, and since published, I learn, in several journals, might be offered as a sufficient reply to your communication.

I have always maintained the moral right to wage a just and necessary war, and, consequently, the wisdom and humanity, as applicable to the United States, in the present state of the world, of *defensive preparations.* If the principal nations of the earth liable to come in conflict with us in our natural growth and just pursuits, can be induced to disarm, I should be happy to see the United States follow the example. But without a general agreement to that effect, and a strong probability that it would be carried out in good faith by others, I am wholly opposed to giving up *home preparation,* and the natural and Christian right of *self-defence.*

The published sentiments alluded to may not have fallen under your observation. I enclose a copy.

I remain respectfully,
Your most obedient servant,
WINFIELD SCOTT.

J. C. Beckwith, Esq., Corresponding Secretary.

[Written in a Peace Album.]
Peace and War.

If war be the natural state of savage tribes, peace is the first want of every civilized community. Pat no doubt is, under any circumstances, a great calamity; yet submission to outrage would often be a greater calamity. Of the two parties to any war, one, at least, must be in the wrong—not unfrequently both. An error in such an issue is, on the part of chief magistrates, ministers of state, and legislators having a voice in the question, a crime of the greatest magnitude. The slaying of an individual by an individual is, in comparative guilt, but a drop of blood. Hence the highest moral obligation to treat national differences with temper, justice, and fairness; always to see that the cause of war is not only *just* but *sufficient;* to be sure that we do not *covet* our neighbor's lands, "nor any thing that is his"; that we are as ready to give as to demand explanation, apology, indemnity; in short, we should especially remember, "All things whatsoever ye would that men should do to you, do ye even so to them." This divine precept is of universal obligation it is as applicable to rulers, in their transactions with other nations, as to private individuals in their daily intercourse with each other. Power is intrusted by "the Author of peace and lover of concord," to do good and to avoid evil. Such, clearly, is the revealed will of God.

WINFIELD SCOTT.

WASHINGTON, April 26, 1844.

On the approach of the next Presidential election, it was agreed by all Whigs, the chances of success seeming favorable, to leave the field without a convention to Mr. Clay; but Mr. Polk was chosen and inaugurated March 4, 1845.

Mr. Tyler, doubtless, like several of his successors, was weaker in office than Mr. Polk, whose little strength lay in the most odious elements of the human character—*cunning and hypocrisy.*[4] It is true that these qualities, when discovered, become positive weaknesses; but they often triumph over wisdom and virtue before discovery. It may be added that a man of meaner presence is not often seen. He was, however, virtually, the nominee of General Jackson.

CHAPTER XXVI

WAR WITH MEXICO—GENERAL TAYLOR

Hostilities with Mexico, might, perhaps, have been avoided; but Texas lay between—or rather in the scale of war.

At an advanced stage of the diplomatic quarrel, Brigadier-General Taylor was ordered, with a respectable number of regular troops, to Corpus Christi, near the Mexican frontier, as a good point of observation.[1] This selection of the commander was made with the concurrence of the autobiographer, who, knowing him to be slow of thought, of hesitancy in speech, and unused to the pen, took care, about the same time, to provide him, unsolicited, with a staff officer, Captain (subsequently, Lieutenant-Colonel) Bliss, his exact complement, who superadded modest, quiet manners, which qualities could not fail to win the confidence of his peculiar commander, and on which usefulness entirely depended.[2] The whole intent was a success: the combination of the general and the chief of his staff working like a charm. Though, perhaps, somewhat in advance of chronology, a little fuller sketch of one of the most fortunate of men, may here not be out of place. The autobiographer knew him well.

General Taylor's elevation to the Presidency, the result of military successes, though a marvel, was not a curse to his country. Mr. Webster, in his strong idiomatic English, said of the nomination that it was "not *fit* to be made"; but probably he would have been equally dissatisfied with any candidate other than himself.

With a good store of common sense, General Taylor's mind had not been enlarged and refreshed by reading, or much converse with the world. Rigidity of ideas was the consequence. The frontiers and small military posts had been his home. Hence he was quite ignorant, for his rank, and quite bigoted in his ignorance. His simplicity was childlike, and with innumerable prejudices—amusing and incorrigible—well suited to the tender age. Thus if a man, however respectable, chanced to wear a coat of an unusual color, or his hat a little on one side of the head;—or an officer to leave the corner of his handkerchief dangling from an outside pocket—in any such case, this critic held the offender to be a coxcomb—perhaps, something worse, whom he would not, to use his oft-repeated phrase, "touch with a pair of tongs." Any allusion to literature much beyond good old Dilworth's Spelling Book,[3] on the part of one wearing a sword, was evidence, with the same judge, of utter unfitness for heavy marchings and combats. In short, few men have ever had a more comfortable, labor-saving contempt for learning of every kind.* {Marlborough, one of the greatest generals of any age, and the first diplomat and courtier of his own, was also without science and literature knowing nothing of history except the little he picked up at the acting of some of Shakspeare's dramas.} Yet this old soldier and neophyte statesman, had the true basis of a great character:—pure, uncorrupted morals, combined with indomitable courage. Kind-hearted, sincere, and hospitable in a plain way, he had no vice but prejudice, many friends, and left behind him not an enemy in the world, not even in the autobiographer, whom, in the blindness of his great weakness, he [Taylor], *after* being named for the Presidency, had seriously wronged.

Ought this, charitably, to be supposed an unconscious error, or placed to a different account?

"To keep the proud thy friend, see that thou do him not a service: For, behold, he will hate thee for his debt."   Prov. Philosophy.

As early as May, 1846, when it was known that the Mexicans had assumed a threatening attitude on the Rio Grande, an inclination to send Scott to that frontier was intimated. He replied, 1. That it was harsh and unusual for a senior, without reënforcements to supersede a meritorious junior; 2. That he doubted whether that was the right season, or the Rio Grande the right basis for *offensive* operations against Mexico; and suggested the plan of conquering a peace which he ultimately executed.

Leading Democrats took alarm at the appointment of a Whig to so high a trust—fearing, as they did him the honor to say—his "knack at success," and caused Mr. Polk to doubt and reject his views. Whereupon Scott intimated that without the approval of his plan of campaign, and the steady confidence and support of the Government, he would not be able to conduct any expedition to advantage; for soldiers had a far greater dread of a fire upon the rear, than of the most formidable enemy in front. The President at once caused him to be relieved from the proposed mission.[4]

At this period, Scott usually—as always in troublous times—spent from fifteen to eighteen hours a day in his office, happened, on being called upon by the Secretary of War to be found absent. In explanation, Scott hurriedly wrote a note to say that he was back in the office, having only stepped out, for the moment, to take—regular meals being out of the question—"a hasty plate of soup." This private note being maliciously thrown into party newspapers, all the witlings—forgetting their own *hasty* pudding, fastened upon it, with much glee, and also tried their clumsy wit on the phrase "conquer a peace"; but not *after* the early fact, as also on the "fire upon the rear"; but never *after* the fire of the enemy and that of the Administration, on front and rear, had been silenced by the campaign of 1847.[5]

These were no *trivialities* in their day; for, by the aid of party madness and malice they came very near destroying Scott's usefulness in the Mexican war.

Taylor's early successes on this side of the Rio Grande, so handsomely reported by Bliss, won him great favor with the country. A resolution giving him the thanks of Congress, and a sword was promptly introduced. Scott hastened to address a circular (private) note to a dozen members of the two Houses of Congress—including the Kentucky Senators, and Mr. Jefferson Davis—arguing that the gold medal ought to be substituted for the sword—being the higher honor, and eminently Taylor's due.[6] The suggestion was adopted, and further to show that Scott did not neglect the hero of the Rio Grande, he annexes the following report:

"HEADQUARTERS OF THE ARMY,
WASHINGTON, July 25, 1846.
"Hon. W. L. MARCY, Secretary of War:
[Endorsed by Major-General Scott, on the Resolution of Congress voting a medal to Major-General Taylor, which Resolution the Secretary had referred to General Scott.]

"As medals are among the surest monuments of history, as well as monuments of individual distinction, there should be given to them, besides intrinsic value and durability of material the utmost grace of design, with the highest finish in mechanical execution. All this is necessary to give the greater or adventitious value; as in the present instance, the medal is to be, at once, an historical record and a reward of distinguished merit. The credit of the donor thus becomes even more than that of the receiver interested in obtaining a perfect specimen in the fine arts.

"The within resolution prescribes *gold* as the material of the medal. The general form (circular) may be considered as equally settled by our own practice, and that of most nations, ancient and modern. There is, however, some little diversity in *diameter* and *thickness* in the medals heretofore ordered by Congress, at different periods, as may be seen in the cabinets of the War and Navy Departments. Diversity in dimensions is even greater in other countries.

"The specific character of the medal is shown by its two faces, or the *face* and the *reverse*. The within resolution directs 'appropriate devices and inscriptions thereon.'

"For the face, a bust likeness is needed, to give, with the name and the rank of the donee, *individuality*. To obtain the likeness, a first-rate miniature painter should, of course, be employed.

"The reverse receives the device, appropriate to the events commemorated. To obtain this, it is suggested that the resolutions and despatches, belonging to the subject, be transmitted to a master in the art of design—say Professor Weir, at West Point—for a drawing—including, if practicable, this inscription:[7]

PALO ALTO;
RESACA DE LA PALMA.
May 8 and 9, 1846.

"A third artist—all to be well paid—is next to be employed—a die sinker. The mint of the United States will do the coinage.

"Copies, in cheaper metal, of all our gold medals, should be given to the libraries of the Federal and State Governments, to those of colleges, etc.

"The medals voted by the Revolutionary Congress were executed—designs and dies—under the superintendence of Mr. Jefferson, in Paris, about the year 1786. Those struck in honor of victories, in our war of 1812; were all—at least so far as it respected the land service—done at home, and not one of them presented, I think, earlier than the end of Mr. Monroe's Administration (1825). The delay principally resulted from the want of good die sinkers. There was only one of mediocre merit (and he a foreigner) found for the army. What the state of this art may now be in the United States I know not. But I beg leave again to suggest that the honor of the country requires that medals, voted by Congress, should always exhibit the arts, involved, in their highest state of perfection wherever found; for letters, science, and the fine arts constitute but one republic, embracing the world. So thought our early Government, and Mr. Jefferson—a distinguished member of that general republic.

"All which is respectfully submitted to the Secretary of War."

But before his written solicitude about the medal—in May—the day on which the news of Taylor's first victories (two) arrived—a number of leading Whigs (not including Mr. Clay or Mr. Webster) in a panic, about the soup, called upon the autobiographer to inquire whether Taylor was a Whig or not, and whether he might not advantageously be Scott's substitute as their next Presidential candidate? More amused than offended at their cowardice and candor, Scott gave emphatically, all the points in the foregoing sketch of the then rising general, omitting (it is believed) any allusion to his lack of general information, and added, as a striking proof of his honesty this anecdote:

Early in the times of Jacksonism, in Kentucky, the demagogues broke the Constitution, and the supreme judges of the State, together; set up a new supreme court of their own, and a rag bank without a dollar in specie—literally to "emit bills of credit" in violation of the Constitution of the United States. Money (bills of credit) being superabundant, a wild spirit of speculation became general running into madness, soon followed by coextensive bankruptcy and ruin. Colonel Zachary Taylor chanced to visit Louisville (his home) in the height of the speculation; but though not infected himself, he was induced to endorse a heavy obligation of a friend, which, of course, in due time fell upon him. He resolutely refused to take any relief from the stop-laws of the same demagogues, or to pay in their rag currency, and although a dear lover of money, persistently paid his endorsement in specie. In continuation, Scott stated that being in Louisville, in the command of the Western Department of the army, he gave the colonel the short leave of absence that brought him there with the heavy bags which finally freed him from debt. The parting with the cash agonized him not a little, but soon he recovered, and the next moment felt happy in his double-proof integrity.

And had Scott no trial of his own? The statement, just given fixed Taylor as the next Whig candidate for the Presidency; but Scott, without murmur or petulance, did not fail to make his backsliding Whig friends feel their inferiority. Never had he been better self-poised, and to his last hour he cannot fail to point to this period of obloquy on the part of enemies and desertion of friends, as by far the most heroic of his life. Happily by the ruling of Providence, that, and other defeats in politics, have proved to him blessings in disguise. Whether, looking to subsequent events, the country has equally profited by the results, he has the vanity to doubt.

By extraordinary importunities from Washington, one object being to decry Scott's plea for adequate preparation, and his doubts as to the line of operations from the Rio Grande—aided by a letter from that man of rare abilities and every moral excellence—John J. Crittenden—written at Scott's desk, and which he read with a dissenting smile—Taylor was told to say no more of reënforcements and means of transportation; but, added Crittenden—"the public is impatient; take foot in hand and off for the Halls of Montezuma." Thus stimulated, Taylor, against his own judgment, marched under the greatest difficulties upon the little village of Monterey, which he captured (*cui bono?*) and became *planted*—as it was impracticable—no matter with what force, to reach any vital part of Mexico by that route.[8] Accordingly, Taylor remained fast at Monterey and its neighborhood, with varying numbers, down to the peace.

Reliable information reached Washington, almost daily (see Taylor's own Reports, Ex. Doc. No. 60, H. of R., 30th Con., 1st Session), that the wild volunteers as soon as beyond the Rio Grande, committed, with impunity, all sorts of atrocities on the persons and property of Mexicans, and that one of the former, from a concealed position, had oven shot a Mexican as he marched out of Monterey, under the capitulation.* {This case was one reported by Taylor, who asked for advice. And what advice does the reader suppose the Secretary to have given? To execute the brute under martial law? No! Taylor was advised to send the monster home—that is, to reward him with a discharge! See the same document. (P. 369.) I had left Washington two days earlier.} There was no legal punishment for any of those offences, for by the strange omission of Congress, American troops take with them beyond the limits of their own country, no law but the Constitution of the United States, and the rules and articles of war. These do not provide any court for the trial or punishment of murder, rape, theft, &c., &c.—no matter by whom, or on whom committed.

To suppress these disgraceful acts abroad, the autobiographer drew up an elaborate paper, in the form of an order—called, his *martial law order*—to be issued and enforced in Mexico, until Congress could be stimulated to legislate on the subject. On handing this paper to the Secretary of War (Mr. Marcy) for his approval, a *startle* at the title was the only comment he then, or ever made on the subject. It was soon silently returned, as too explosive for safe handling. A little later the Attorney-General called (at whose instance can only be guessed) and asked for a copy, and the law officer of the Government whose business it is to speak on all such matters, was stricken with legal dumbness. All the authorities were evidently alarmed at the proposition to establish martial law, even in a foreign country, occupied by American troops. Hence they touched the subject as daintily as a "terrier mumbles a hedgehog." I therefore was left in my own darkness on the subject. I sent the paper, however, to General Taylor, telling him frankly, that it had been seen by at least two members of the cabinet, but that it was not approved or disapproved by either, and for that reason it was not enjoined upon him, but left to his own responsibility to adopt it as his order or not, as he might think proper.

It is understood that Taylor on casting his eye slightly over the paper, and perceiving it contained what he termed, "a learned commentary on the military code," threw it aside—saying, "It is another of *Scott's Lessons*" or "*Novels*"—as his tactics and military institutes had been previously called by officers of a certain age (not West Point graduates) who deemed it a great hardship, late in life, to be obliged, for the first time, to study the simplest elements of their profession.

This paper will be inserted entire, in a subsequent part of this narrative: 1. On account of its history just given; 2. Because, without it, I could not have maintained the discipline and honor of the army, or have reached the capital of Mexico.[9]

The martial law order was not published until the autobiographer was fairly out of the United States—at Tampico. It was successively republished at Vera Cruz, Puebla, and the capital, so that it might be familiarly known to every man in the army, and in a translation, it was also extensively circulated among the people of the country. Under it, all offenders, Americans and Mexicans, were alike punished—with death for murder or rape, and for other crimes proportionally. It will be seen that the order did not in the least interfere with the administration of justice between Mexican and Mexican, by the ordinary courts of the country. It only provided a special American tribunal for any case to which an American might be a party. And further, it should be observed, that military commissions in applying penalties to convicted felons, were limited to "*known* punishments, in like cases, in some of the States of the United States"—the latter, as such, being; without a common law, or a common criminal code.

Notwithstanding the cowardice of certain high functionaries on the subject, there has been no pursuit of the author. On the contrary, it has been admitted by all that the order worked like a charm; that it conciliated Mexicans; intimidated the vicious of the several races, and being executed with impartial rigor, gave the highest moral deportment and discipline ever known in an invading army.

CHAPTER XXVII

SCOTT ORDERED TO MEXICO—VISITS CAMARGO—REËMBARKS FOR VERA CRUZ

SEVERAL times in the summer and autumn of 1846, I repeated to the War Department my desire to be ordered to Mexico at the head of a competent force. At length my request was acceded to.

WAR DEPARTMENT, WASHINGTON,
November 23, 1846.

SIR:

The President, several days since, communicated in person to you his orders to repair to Mexico, to take the command of the forces there assembled, and particularly to organize and set on foot an expedition to operate on the Gulf coast, if, on arriving at the theatre of action, you shall deem it to be practicable. It is not proposed to control your operations by definite and positive instructions, but you are left to prosecute them as your judgment, under a full view of all the circumstances, shall dictate. The work is before you, and the means provided, or to be provided, for accomplishing it, are committed to you, in the full confidence that you will use them to the best advantage.

The objects which it is desirable to obtain have been indicated, and it is hoped that you will have the requisite force to accomplish them.

Of this you must be the judge, when preparations are made, and the time for action arrived.

Very respectfully,
Your obedient servant,
W. L. MARCY,
SECRETARY OF WAR.

GENERAL WINFIELD SCOTT.

From an early day—it is believed, the very beginning—the Secretary of the Treasury, Mr. Walker, and Mr. Secretary Marcy, were in favor of giving me the substantial direction of the war on land—each having often done me the honor to express his fullest confidence in my zeal and capacity for the occasion.[1]

For a week prior to Mr. Marcy's letter, President Polk sent for me once or twice daily. In these interviews every expression of kindness and confidence was lavished upon me. Such was the warmth and emphasis of his professions, that he fully won my confidence. I gave him a cordial reciprocation of my personal sympathy and regard—being again and again assured that the country would be bankrupted and dishonored unless the war could be made plainly to march toward a successful conclusion, and that I only could give to it the necessary impetus and direction. Not to have been deceived by such protestations, would have been, in my judgment, unmanly suspicion and a crime. Accordingly, though oppressed with the labors of military preparation, I made time to write a circular to the leading Whigs in Congress (a few days before their meeting) to say how handsomely I had been treated by the President and Secretary of War—begging that the new regiments might be authorized with the least possible delay, &c., &c.

In the very act of embarking, at New Orleans, on the expedition, a stranger, Mr. Hodge of that city (since Assistant Secretary of the Treasury and a resident of Washington), saw me half a minute, to communicate a letter from my dear friend—Alexander Barrow—then a senator from Louisiana—saying that the President had asked for the grade of lieutenant-general, in order to place Senator Benton over me in the Army of Mexico.[2] I begged that Mr. Barrow might be thanked for his kindness, but added that he must be mistaken about Mr. Benton; for if the rank were asked for, it could only—remembering Mr. Polk's assurances of support and reward—be intended for me on the report of my first success, and I continued, a short time longer, to carry on, besides the *official,* a semi-official correspondence, with the War Department, for the President, as before.[3]

A grosser abuse of human confidence is nowhere recorded.

Mr. Polk's mode of viewing the case seems to have been this: "Scott is a Whig; therefore the Democracy is not bound to observe good faith with him. Scott is a Whig; therefore, his successes may be turned to the prejudice of the Democratic party. We must, however, profit by his military experience, and, if successful, by the force of patronage and other helps, contrive to crown Benton with the victory, and thus triumph both in the field and at the polls." This bungling treachery was planned during the precise period of my very friendly interviews with Mr. Polk! It soon became fully developed, and, in all essentials, acknowledged before Congress. The lieutenant-generalcy was, however, rejected, when Mr. Polk taxed his supporters to the utmost to procure for him authority to place a junior Major-General (Benton) over a senior (Scott), and was again ignominiously defeated—aided by the manly spirit of the same small number of Democrats.

This vile intrigue so disgusted Congress, and its defeat so depressed the zeal and influence of the Administration, that instead of authorizing the additional forces needed for the war at once, the augmentation was delayed till near the end of the session. This was the first fruit of bad faith or political blindness; for, in war, time is always a great element of success—sometimes the first.

I reached the Brazos San Jago, near the mouth of the Rio Grande, in Christmas week, and proceeded up that river to Camargo, which place or vicinage I had appointed for a meeting with Major-General Taylor by a communication that preceded me four days; but, by the gross neglect of the officer who bore it, it lost three of those days at that place. In the mean time Taylor made a strange digression, with a part of his troops, toward Tampico—for it was fully as difficult for an army to penetrate Mexico from that point, as from Monterey. But in either case, why divide his forces?

A fatality attended my communication to Taylor. It was most confidential, and so marked, outside and in—containing a sketch of my views and intentions. Yet at the volunteer headquarters, Monterey, it was opened, freely read and discussed by numbers—all not in a condition to be wise or discreet. The package being remade, it was next forwarded after Taylor by a very young officer with a few men, who was inveigled into Villa Gran and slain; his despatches taken, and received by Santa Anna before Taylor saw the duplicate.[4]

The appointed meeting with Taylor, for harmonizing operations with him, after full discussion having failed, by reason of his digression toward Tampico, and the blunders resulting in the loss of the despatches was a great disappointment to me. In them, I had said, that he should have his choice of the two armies, that is, either remain as the immediate commander in Northern Mexico, or accompany me in the command of a division, to the capital, with every assurance, in either case, of confidence and support.

I had now, without the benefit of the consultation I had sought, to detach from the army of the Rio Grande such regular troops as I deemed indispensable to lead the heavier masses of volunteers and other green regiments, promised for the descent on Vera Cruz and the conquest of the capital—leaving Taylor a sufficient defensive force to maintain the false position at Monterey, and discretion to contract his line to the Rio

Grande, with the same means of defence. This contraction, with a view to economize men and money, I certainly should have ordered at once, if Taylor had been present to support me; but as many of the wiseacres at Washington still preferred the short impracticable cut to "the Halls of Montezuma," *via* Monterey and San Luis Potosi—a blunder, concurred in at one time by Taylor,—and as I had then discovered that my friend Barrow's message by Mr. Hodge was well founded—that is instead of a friend in the President I had, in him, an enemy more to be dreaded than Santa Anna and all his hosts—I left the basis of operations or the line of defence in that quarter, in *statu quo,* but only with troops sufficient for the latter purpose.

Both Taylor and the Secretary of War had vacillated on all those points. Each for a time had inclined to a direct advance from the Rio Grande. Each had glanced at the Vera Cruz basis, an idea always mine; each had favored the defensive line of Monterey or the Sierra Madre; and Taylor, a little later, seemed to favor standing on the defensive on the banks of the Rio Grande, which he had left against his judgment. (See Executive Doc. No. 56.)

The Mexicans had never any apprehension of an effective invasion from that quarter or from Tampico. In respect to either of these routes, they might have expressed what the Russians felt when Napoleon marched upon Moscow: "Come unto us with few, and we will overwhelm you; come unto us with many, and you shall overwhelm yourselves." As to holding the line of the Sierra Madre or other line of defence, and standing fast, that would have been, the worst possible state of things—"a little war," or "a war like a peace"—a perpetual condition; for Santa Anna would have regarded it as a mere scratch on the surface.

To compel a people, singularly obstinate, to *sue for peace,* it is absolutely necessary, as the sequel in this case showed, to strike, effectively, at the vitals of the nation.

The order for the troops to descend from Monterey to the sea-coast, was issued at Camargo, Jan. 3, 1847, and I immediately returned to the Brazos San Jago.

It was this order, that, at first, caused the gentle regrets of Taylor, but soon began to sour his mind in proportion as he became more and more prominent as a candidate for the Presidency. Thus, after the peace, when coming North, and running the gauntlet of universal cheers and praise, the ovation unhinged his mind, when, in replying to a flattering address, at a Pascagoula barbecue, he made this extraordinary speech:

"You have alluded to my being stripped of my troops on the Rio Grande; and my being left, as it might seem, at the mercy of the enemy, just before the battle of Buena Vista, renders it proper, probably, that I should make a few remarks in relation to that matter. I received at Victoria, while on my march to Tampico—a movement which I had advised the War Department I should make for certain reasons—an order from the General-in-Chief of the Army (Scott) stripping me of the greater part of my command, and particularly of regular troops and volunteers well instructed. The order was received by me with much surprise, and, I must confess, produced the strongest feelings of regret, mortification and disappointment, *as I knew that Santa Anna was in striking distance of my lines, with an army of 25,000—probably the best appointed men ever collected in Mexico.*"

The harmless errors, both of fact and opinion, of a good man, ought to be treated as a nurse treats a child—a little sick and a little spoiled—gently; but if his errors, springing from vanity and self-love, wound another, the injury is the deeper in proportion to the standing of the author, and, therefore, are to be dealt with unsparingly.

1. Elated with flattery, our hero
  _____ "grew vain;
  Fought all his battles o'er again;
  And thrice be routed all his foes, and thrice he slew the slain."[5]

He calls the army of the Rio Grande "my troops!"

2. *He knew that Santa Anna, with an overwhelming force, was in striking distance.*

If so, he not only withheld the fact from the War Department and the General-in-Chief, but—I write it in sorrow—he actually, up to the last moment, gave the contrary assurance to both!

The proof:—some alarm, in front, having taken him from Monterey to Saltillo, he writes thence, February 4: "I found everything quiet in our front."

* * * * * *

"Indeed it is reported that a large portion of the troops, at San Luis, have taken the direction of Vera Cruz." Ex. Document, 56. (Santa Anna had, some time before, received the captured despatches.) Three days later, Taylor wrote again (to me) at the Brazos San Jago, to the like effect, and the same day, February 7, Document 56, p. 300, to the War Department: "There is understood to be no considerable force in our front, nor is it likely that any serious demonstration will be made in this direction. The frequent alarms" (in Worth's and Wood's camps)—always frequent in Worth's—"since the middle of December, seem to have been without foundation." Both of these letters were written at Agua Nueva, some eighteen miles in advance of Saltillo—his forces being a good deal scattered, notwithstanding my admonition, in concurrence with the War Department, to hold himself, while standing on the defensive, in a concentrated coil. One letter more of the same tenor, written (February 14), nine days before the battle of Buena Vista, which reached the Brazos, when I was many days at sea, bent on conquest. In this letter— same Document, 56, p. 308—Taylor, at Agua Nueva, says: "Everything is quiet in and about Saltillo."

* * * * * *

"Up to the 26th of January, the Mexican Congress had done nothing to supply the wants of the army, which had received nothing for January, and had but half the necessary funds for December. Rumors reach our camp, from time to time, of the projected advance of a Mexican force upon this position; but I think such a movement improbable!"

Those are sad self-contradictions! But are the uncharitable beyond the pale of Christian charity? Certainly not. Bliss wrote the despatches, about which the general knew but little, and remembered less; and not Bliss, but vanity, dictated the barbecue speech in question.

3. *He had been stripped, etc.—left at the mercy of the enemy!*

Indeed! but the facts: I left, under him, a small fraction less than seven thousand men, with a reasonable portion of regulars, including batteries of field artillery—and other regiments soon expected, with advice to stand concentrated behind the stone walls of Monterey, or to consider himself at liberty to take up, the impregnable line of the Rio Grande. The defence of Texas was now the main purpose of this army— it having been shown that even with his whole force he could make no effective impression on Mexico from that quarter. With this preface, my very sufficient defence shall again be quoted from reports under General Taylor's own signature.

After the detached troops had reached the seaboard he writes, from Monterey, January 27, 1847 (Ex. Doc. No. 56, p. 292), "the force with which I am left, in this quarter, though greatly deficient in regular troops, will, doubtless, enable me to hold the positions now occupied." Nothing more had been enjoined, nor was expected, without large reënforcements, and *penetration* had not been previously attempted, nor was attempted, the following summer, when his numbers again became formidable, although he solicited the War Department for reënforcements (in his letter of February 14, before quoted), and says he is "urging forward supplies; for, if joined by a sufficient force of new regiments,

I wish to be able to take any opportunity that may offer to make a diversion in favor of Major-General Scott's operations." (All have heard of a pavement of good intentions!) After awhile he got the regiments (and kept them from me), making his numbers eight thousand effectives—I being in Puebla at the time, with rather less than fifty-five hundred—in the heart of the enemy's country—cut loose (by the want of numbers) from the coast, and only with one other small detachment, left at Jalapa. General Taylor now quite at his ease, writes coolly and leisurely to the War Department from Monterey, June 16: "In my communication of May 28 (Ex. Doc. 56, p. 387), I had reason to present my views in relation to operations against San Luis Potosi, at least in regard to the minimum force (six thousand or eight thousand) with which I thought they could be undertaken. I shall prepare the force under my orders for service in that direction, should it be found expedient and practicable thus to operate; but[!] I may be permitted to question the utility of moving, at a very heavy expense over an extremely long line and having no communication with the main column operating from Vera Cruz[!]. If I were called upon to make a suggestion on the general subject of operations against Mexico, it would certainly be to hold, in this quarter [Monterey] a *defensive* line, and throw all the remaining troops into the other column!!" Then why the clamor about being "stripped?" why his clamor for reënforcements by which Brigadier-General Cadwallader and three regiments were diverted from me?[6] why not attempt a feint toward San Luis Potosi, even if the advance had been forced to stop at a fourth or a fifth of the distance; and, above all—why detain so long the reënforcements of Cadwallader's and other brigades I so much needed!! A farther delay was incurred waiting for the Secretary's concurrence, dated July 15, and, finally, most of those reënforcements came to me long after the war was finished, and the dictated or conquered peace, was actually in preparation for signature. And thus my rivals and enemies were, at a late day, forced to acknowledge, practically, the justness of my early plans, views, and predictions!

4. One more remark on a point in the same barbacue speech: *Santa Anna's twenty-five thousand well appointed army at Buena Vista.*

It is true that Santa Anna in summoning Taylor to surrender, gives, to intimidate (a hopeless endeavor), his strength at twenty-five thousand; but four days before the battle of Buena Vista the Mexican official return of his forces, dated at Encarnacion, puts down his total numbers at fourteen thousand and forty-eight, all told, including sick and lame (more than two thousand) and the remainder, half famished with thirst and hunger. General Taylor, too, giving his reasons for not concentrating his army at Monterey, as he was advised to do—preferring the advanced position of Agua Nueva, says it was in order "to fight the Mexican general, immediately after he had crossed the desert country [about one hundred and fifty miles in extent] which lay just in my front, and before he could have time to refresh and recruit his army." This seems not to be bad reasoning; but suppose the Americans had been concentrated within the strong walls of Monterey;—the repulse of the enemy would have been more certain and more crippling, with less loss on our part, beside saving the battle of Buena Vista, and by delaying Santa Anna, the battle of Cerro Gordo, and hastening the capture of "the Halls of Montezuma."[7] The victory of Buena Vista, was, no doubt, glorious in it self, and resounded as such all over America and Europe; but, as has been said of the barren capitulation of Monterey—*cui bono?* It did not advance the campaign an inch, nor quicken a treaty of peace an hour, as the Mexicans universally regarded it as a mere border affair.

At the Brazos San Jago, I had to wait for the descent of the troops from Monterey, and also for the means of transportation to Vera Cruz. The general embarkation was thus unavoidably delayed till about February 15. At New Orleans I fortunately heard from old shipmasters that tolerable intermediate anchorage might be found in the terrible *northers,* behind the Lobos Islands—a group a third of the distance from Tampico toward Vera Cruz. Accordingly, I appointed that group as the general rendezvous for all the troop and supply ships of the expedition—many of them being still due from New Orleans and ports farther North.

Here, at the distance of some one hundred and twenty miles from Vera Cruz, I lay a few days with the van of the expedition, till the greater part of the troops and *matériel* of war expected had come up with me. Next we sailed a little past Vera Cruz and came to anchor, March 7, at Anton Lizardo, to take time for choosing, after reconnaissance, the best point of descent, to launch our boats and then to seize the first favorable state of the surf for debarkation—there being no harbor at or near the city. Ignorant of President Santa Anna's desperate march over the desert, upon Major-General Taylor, we did not doubt meeting at our landing the most formidable struggle of the war. No precaution therefore was neglected.

CHAPTER XXVIII

SIEGE AND CAPTURE OF VERA CRUZ AND THE CASTLE OF SAN JUAN DE ULLOA

Successful as was every prediction, plan, siege, battle, and skirmish of mine in the Mexican war, I have here paused many weeks to overcome the repugnance I feel to an entrance on the narrative of the campaign it was my fortune—I had almost said—*misfortune*—to conduct, with half means, beginning at Vera Cruz, March 9, and terminating in the capital of the country, September 14, 1847, six months and five days. This feeling is occasioned by the lively recollection of: 1. The perfidy of Mr. Polk; 2. The senseless and ungrateful clamor of Taylor, which, like his other prejudices, abided with him to the end; 3. The machinations of an ex-aide-de-camp—who owed his public status mainly to my helping hand; a vain man, of weak principles, and most inordinate ambition. The change commenced on learning that I had fallen under the ban at Washington;[1] 4. The machinations of a Tennessee major-general, the special friend and partisan of Mr. Polk;—an anomaly,—without the least malignity in his nature—amiable, and possessed of some acuteness, but the only person I have ever known who was wholly indifferent in the choice between truth and falsehood, honesty and dishonesty;—ever as ready to attain an end by the one as the other, and habitually boastful of acts of cleverness at the total sacrifice of moral character. Procuring the nomination of Mr. Polk for the Presidency, he justly considered his greatest triumph in that way.[2] These conspirators—for they soon coalesced—were joined by like characters—the first in time and malignity, a smart captain of artillery, whom they got brevetted, on brevet, more for the smoke of his guns than their shots, and to whom Mr. Polk, near the end of his term, gave the substantial reward of colonel and inspector-general,—an office that happened to fall vacant just then.[3] "The ox knoweth his owner, and the ass his master's crib." And alas, poor human nature! Even the brave Colonel Riley, the hero of Contreras (for which he was made a brigadier afterward), got the brevet of major-general and the command in California, by yielding to the same weakness. (See his testimony in the Pillow investigation.) These

appointments proved an estate to Riley.[4] The certainty of such fat benefits, freely promised by the conspirators, called into activity the sordid
passions of other bribe-worthy officers. Hence the party of miscreants
became quite respectable in numbers after the conquest. Those were
not the only disgusts. The master outrage soon followed.

The offences of the two anonymous generals becoming a little too
prononcé, I arrested both, and asked that a court might be ordered by
the President for their trial. A court was ordered. I was relieved in the
command, and the wronged and the wrong-doers, with stern impartiality! placed before the tribunal!! If I had lost the campaign it would have
been difficult to heap upon me greater vexations and mortification.

May I add, that while I was before the court appointed by President
Jackson, at Frederick, Maryland, Santa Anna passed by, and paid me,
though I did not see him, an extravagant compliment? When he heard
in exile, that I was before a court at Mexico, he said to an American: "I
thank President Polk—I am revenged!"

And why refer the appointment of a court to Washington? In 1830,
Adjutant-General R. Jones was, on some slight occasion, arrested by the
General-in-Chief, Macomb.[5] The former had many friends in Congress,
who ran a bill through the two Houses enacting that, when a commanding general arrests an officer or becomes the prosecutor of one, the
court for the trial of the case shall be appointed by the President, etc.
This provision being general, has caused a rent in the Administration of
justice in the army, and ought to have been entitled *An Act to cripple generals commanding distant expeditions, and to unhinge the discipline* (subordination) *of armies.* Repeal is the only cure; but this error, it is feared,
like universal suffrage, is a bourn from which there is no return. That it
placed me, with such a President and such soldier demagogues, between
the upper and nether millstones, must be perceived by all readers!

March 9—the precise day when I had been thirty years a general
officer—the sun dawned propitiously on the expedition. There was but
little surf on the beach—a necessary condition—as we had to effect
a landing from the open sea. Every detail, providing for all contingencies, had been discussed and arranged with my staff, and published
in orders. The whole fleet of transports—some eighty vessels, in the
presence of many foreign ships of war, stood up the coast, flanked by
two naval steamers and five gunboats to cover the movement. Passing
through them in the large propeller, the Massachusetts, the shouts and
cheers from every deck gave me assurance of victory, whatever might
be the force prepared to receive us.

CHAPTER XXVIII

We anchored opposite to a point a little beyond the range of the guns of the city and castle, when some fifty-five hundred men instantly filled up the sixty-seven surf boats I had caused to be built for this special occasion—each holding from seventy to eighty men—besides a few cutters belonging to the larger war vessels. Commodore Conner also supplied steerers (officers) and sailors as oarsmen.[6] The whole, again cheering, as they passed my ship wearing the broad pennant, pulled away right for the shore, landed in the exact order prescribed, about half past five P.M., without the loss of a boat or a man, and, to the astonishment of all, without opposition other than a few whizzing shells that did no harm. Another trip or two enabled the row-boats to put ashore the whole force, rather less than twelve thousand men, though I had been promised double the number—my *minimum;* but I never had, at any one time in the campaign, more than thirteen thousand five hundred, until the fighting was over, when I was encumbered with the troops that Taylor found at last he could not use.

An article from the New Orleans *Bulletin,* of March 27, 1847, written by an intelligent pen, respecting the landing of troops, is here inserted:

"The landing of the American army at Vera Cruz has been accomplished in a manner that reflects the highest credit on all concerned; and the regularity, precision, and promptness with which it was effected, has probably not been surpassed, if it has been equalled, in modern warfare.

"The removal of a large body of troops from numerous transports into boats in an open sea—their subsequent disembarkation on the sea-beach, on an enemy's coast, through a surf, with all their arms and accoutrements, without a single error or accident, requires great exertion, skill, and sound judgment.

"The French expedition against Algiers, in 1830, was said to be the most complete armament, in every respect, that ever left Europe; it had been prepared with labor, attention, and experience, and nothing had been omitted to insure success, and particularly in the means and facilities for landing the troops. This disembarkation took place in a wide bay, which was more favorable than an open beach directly on the ocean, and (as in the present instance) without any resistance on the part of the enemy—yet, only nine thousand men were landed the first day, and from thirty to forty lives were lost by accidents, or upsetting of boats; whereas, on the present occasion, twelve thousand men were landed in one day, without, so far as we have heard, the slightest accident, or the loss of a single life."

The city of Vera Cruz, and its castle, San Juan de Ulloa, were both strongly garrisoned.[7] Santa Anna, relying upon them to hold out till the *vomito* (yellow fever) became rife, had returned to his capital, and was busy in collecting additional troops, mostly old, from every quarter of the republic, in order to crush the invasion, should it advance, at the first formidable pass in the interior.

The walls and forts of Vera Cruz, in 1847, were in good condition. Subsequent to its capture by the French under Admiral Baudin and Prince de Joinville, in 1838,[8] the castle had been greatly extended—almost rebuilt, and its armament about doubled. Besides, the French were allowed to reconnoitre the city and castle, and choose their positions of attack without the least resistance—the Mexicans deprecating war with that nation, and hence ordered not to fire the first gun. Of that injunction the French were aware. When we approached, in 1847, the castle had the capacity to sink the entire American navy.

Immediately after landing, I made, with Colonel (soon after Brigadier-General) Totten, and other staff officers, a reconnaissance of the land side of the city, having previously reconnoitred the water front.[9] This was at once followed by a close investment, so that there could be no communication between the garrisons and the interior. The blockade, by Commodore Conner, had long before been complete. Grave deliberations followed. From the first my hope had been to capture the castle under the shelter of, and through the city. This plan I had never submitted to discussion. Several Generals and Colonels—among them Major-General Patterson—an excellent second in command, notwithstanding his failure as chief on the Shenandoah in 1861—solicited the privilege of leading storming parties.[10] The applicants were thanked and applauded; but I forebore saying to them more. In my little cabinet, however, consisting of Colonel Totten, Chief Engineer, Lieutenant Colonel Hitchcock, acting Inspector-General,[11] Captain R. E. Lee, Engineer, and (yet) First Lieutenant Henry L. Scott, acting Adjutant-General—I entered fully into the question of storming parties and regular siege approaches. A death-bed discussion could hardly have been more solemn. Thus powerfully impressed—feeling Mr. Polk's halter around my neck, as I expressed myself at the time—I opened the subject substantially as follows:

"We, of course, gentlemen, must take the city and castle before the return of the *vomito*—if not by headwork, the slow, scientific process, by storming—and then escape, by pushing the conquest into the healthy interior. I am strongly inclined to attempt the former unless you can convince me that the other is preferable. Since our thorough reconnoissance, I think the suggestion practicable with a very moderate loss on our part.

"The second method, would, no doubt, be equally successful, but at the cost of an immense slaughter to both sides, including non-combatants—Mexican men, women, and children—because assaults must be made in the dark, and the assailants dare not lose time in taking and guarding prisoners without incurring the certainty of becoming captives themselves, till all the strongholds of the place are occupied. The horrors of such slaughter, with the usual terrible accompaniments, are most revolting. Besides these objections, it is necessary to take into the account the probable loss of some two thousand, perhaps, three thousand of our best men in an assault, and I have received but half the numbers promised me. How then could we hope to penetrate the interior?"

"For these reasons," I added, quoting literally—"although I know our countrymen will hardly acknowledge a victory unaccompanied by a long butcher's bill (report of killed and wounded) I am strongly inclined—policy concurring with humanity—to 'forego their loud applause and ayes vehement,' and take the city with the least possible loss of life. In this determination I know, as Dogberry says truly of himself, I 'write me down an ass.'"[12]* {When the victory of Buena Vista reached Major-General Brooke[13] (a noble old soldier) commanding at New Orleans, and a friend of Major General Taylor, he rushed, with the report in hand, through the streets to the Exchange, and threw the whole city into a frenzy of joy. By and by, came the news that the Stars and Stripes waved over Vera Cruz and its castle, and Brooke, also a friend of mine, was again eager to spread the report. Somebody in the crowd early called out: "How many men has Scott lost?" Brooke was delighted to reply—"Less than a hundred." "That won't do," was promptly rejoined. "Taylor always loses thousands. He is the man for my money." Only a few faint cheers were heard for Vera Cruz. The long butcher's bill was wanted. When I received friend Brooke's letter giving these details, I own that my poor human nature was piqued for a moment; and I said: "Never mind. Taylor is a Louisianian. We shall, in due time, hear the voice of the Middle, the Northern, and Eastern States. They will estimate victories on different principles." But I was mistaken. The keynote raised in New Orleans was taken up all over the land. Mortifications are profitable to sufferers, and I record mine to teach aspirants to fame to cultivate humility; for blessed is the map who expects little, and can gracefully submit to less.}

My decided bias in favor of proceeding by siege, far from being combated, was fully concurred in. Accordingly Colonel Totten, the able chief engineer, and his accomplished assistants, proceeded to open the trenches and establish the batteries deemed necessary, after, by a general sweep, every post and sentry of the enemy had been driven in.

All sieges are much alike, and as this is not a treatise on engineering, scientific details are here omitted. We took care, in our approaches to keep the city as a shield between us and the terrible fire of the castle; but the forts in the walls of the city were formidable spitfires. They were rarely out of blast. Yet the approaches were so adroitly conducted, that our losses in them were surprisingly small, and no serious sortie was hazarded by the garrison.

The arming of the advanced batteries had been retarded by a very protracted gale (*norther*) which cut off all communication with our vessels in the offing. Ground was, however, broken on the 18th, and by the 22d, heavy ordnance enough for a beginning being in position, the governor of the city, who was also governor of the castle, was duly summoned to surrender. The refusal was no sooner received than a fire on the walls and forts was opened. In the attempt to batter in breach, and to silence the forts, a portion of our shots and shells, in the course of the siege, unavoidably penetrated the city and set fire to many houses. By the 24th, the landing of additional heavy guns and mortars gave us all the battering power needed, and the next day, as I reported to Washington, the whole was in "awful activity." The same day there came a memorial from the foreign consuls in Vera Cruz, asking for a truce to enable them, and the women and children of the inhabitants, to withdraw in safety. They had in time been duly warned of the impending danger, and allowed to the 22d to retire, which they had sullenly neglected, and the consuls had also declined the written *safe-guards* I had pressed upon them. The season had advanced, and I was aware of several cases of yellow fever in the city and neighborhood. Detachments of the enemy too were accumulating behind us, and rumors spread, by them, that a formidable army would soon approach to raise the siege. Tenderness therefore for the women and children—in the form of delay—might, in its consequences, have led to the loss of the campaign, and, indeed to the loss of the army—two thirds by pestilence, and the remainder by surrender. Hence I promptly replied to the consuls that no truce could be allowed except on the application of the governor (General Morales), and *that* with a view to surrender. Accordingly, the next morning General Landero, who had been put in the supreme command for that purpose, offered to entertain the question of submission.[14] Commissioners were appointed on both sides, and on the 27th terms of surrender, including both the city and castle of Ulloa, agreed upon, signed and exchanged. The garrisons marched out, laying down their arms, and were sent home prisoners of war on parole.

This was better for the consuls, women, and children, as well as for the United States, than the temporary truce that I rejected—notwithstanding the ignorant censure cast on my conduct, on that occasion, by Mr. William Jay, in his book—*Review of the Causes and Consequences of the Mexican War,* pp. 202–4.[15]

The surrender of the castle of San Juan de Ulloa, was necessarily involved in the fate of the city, because the enemy, until a late moment, had expected the former would be the first object of attack, and relying upon its impregnable strength, had neglected to lay in a supply of fresh water and provisions—as these could be sent over daily from the city. The capture of the latter, therefore, placed the castle entirely at our mercy.

The economy of life, by means of head-work, to which, as has been seen, Americans were quite indifferent, was never more conspicuous than on this occasion. The city and castle; the republic's principal port of foreign commerce; five thousand prisoners, with a greater number of small arms; four hundred pieces of ordnance and large stores of ammunition, were the great results of the first twenty days after our landing, and all at the very small loss, in numbers, of sixty-four officers and men killed or wounded. Among the slain were two captains, J. R. Vinton and W. Alburtis, both of high merit—Vinton, perhaps, the most accomplished officer in the army.[16] The enemy's loss in killed and wounded was not considerable, and of other persons—citizens—not three were slain—all being in stone houses, and most of the inhabitants taking refuge in basements.

The official report of those extraordinary successes, in which due praise was bestowed on corps and officers by name, as well as on the coöperation of the navy, was taken to Washington by Colonel Totten, of the Engineers, who was duly brevetted a brigadier-general for his great services in the siege.

CHAPTER XXIX

BATTLE OF CERRO GORDO, JALAPA, PEROTE AND PUEBLA–HALTS–VISIT TO CHOLULA

Fortunately, the frequency of the gales, called *northers,* had kept off the *vomito,* as an epidemic, though a few cases had occurred in the city; but, unfortunately, the want of road-power—horses and mules—detained the body of the army at Vera Cruz from its capture, March 29, till toward the middle of April.

Some wagons and harness came first, and by the 8th, we hitched up a train sufficient to put Brigadier-General Twiggs's division, composed of brigades under Colonels Harney and Riley, with Major Talcott's light battery, all regulars, in march for the interior. Major-General Patterson, commanding a division of three volunteer brigades, under Brigadier-Generals Pillow, Quitman, and Shields, was next supplied with partial means of transportation, and followed Twiggs.[1] Draft animals and wagons continued to arrive slowly (more of the latter than the former), but never in sufficient numbers. Hence a siege train of six pieces only, four of which were heavy, was fitted for the road, and hence Worth's division of regulars was detained until the 16th. Each division and detachment of troops had instructions to take, in wagons, subsistence for men equal to six days, and oats for horses equal to three, besides the usual number of cooked rations for men in haversacks.

Those supplies were deemed indispensable to take the corps to Jalapa, a productive region, abounding in many articles of food as well as in mules, which we so much needed for the remaining wagons at Vera Cruz. Some hundreds of these animals were purchased, and sent below to bring up ammunition, medicines, hospital stores, clothing, and some bacon, there being but little in the country, and fresh beef not always to be had. But this is anticipating.

Hearing that Twiggs, supported by Patterson, found himself confronted at Plan del Rio, some fifty miles in the interior, by a strong body of the enemy, and that both divisions were desirous of my presence, I left Vera Cruz on the 12th of April, with a small escort of cavalry under Captain Philip Kearny (who fell in 1862, a distinguished major-general),[2] and hastened to the front. Major-General Patterson, though quite sick, had assumed the command on joining Twiggs, in order to prohibit any aggressive movement before my arrival, according to the universal wish of the troops. No commander was ever received with heartier cheers—the certain presage of the victories that followed.

The two advanced divisions lay in the valley of the Plan del Rio, and the body of the enemy about three miles off, on the heights of Cerro Gordo. Reconnaissances were pushed in search of some practicable route, other than the winding, zig-zag road, among the spurs of mountains, with heavy batteries at every turn. The reconnaissances were conducted with vigor under Captain Lee, at the head of a body of pioneers, and at the end of the third day, a passable way for light batteries was accomplished—without alarming the enemy—giving the possibility of turning the extreme left of his line of defences, and capturing his whole army, except the reserve that lay a mile or two higher up the road. Santa Anna said, after the event, that he had not believed a goat could have approached him in that direction. Hence the surprise and results were the greater.

The time for aggression being at hand, I—in order to insure harmony by letting all commanders know what each was expected to execute—issued this prophetic order:

GENERAL ORDERS,   HEADQUARTERS OF THE ARMY,
No. 111.   Plan Del Rio, April 17, 1847.

The enemy's whole line of intrenchments and batteries will be attacked in front, and at the same time turned, early in the day to-morrow—probably before ten o'clock A.M.

The second (Twiggs's) division of regulars is already advanced within easy turning distance toward the enemy's left. That division has instructions to move forward before daylight to-morrow, and take up position across the national road in the enemy's rear, so as to cut off a retreat toward Jalapa. It may be reënforced to-day, if unexpectedly attacked in force, by regiments—one or two—taken from Shields's brigade of volunteers. If not, the two volunteer regiments will march for that purpose at daylight to-morrow morning, under Brigadier-General Shields, who will report to Brigadier-General Twiggs on getting up with him, or to the general-in-chief, if he be in advance.

The remaining regiment of that volunteer brigade will receive instructions in the course of this day.

The first division of regulars (Worth's) will follow the movement against the enemy's left at sunrise tomorrow morning.

As already arranged, Brigadier-General Pillow's brigade will march at six o'clock to-morrow morning, along the route he has carefully reconnoitred, and stand ready, as soon as he hears the report of arms on our right, or sooner, if circumstances should favor him, to pierce the enemy's line of batteries at such point—the nearer to the river the better—as he may select. Once in the rear of that line, he will turn to the right or left, or both, and attack the batteries in reverse, or, if abandoned, he will pursue the enemy with vigor until further orders.

Wall's field battery and the cavalry will be held in reserve on the national road, a little out of view and range of the enemy's batteries.[3] They will take up that position at nine o'clock in the morning.

The enemy's batteries being carried or abandoned, all our divisions and corps will pursue with vigor.

This pursuit may be continued many miles, until stopped by darkness or fortified positions, toward Jalapa. Consequently, the body of the army will not return to this encampment; but be followed, to-morrow afternoon or early the next morning, by the baggage trains of the several corps. For this purpose, the feebler officers and men of each corps will be left to guard its camp and effects, and to load up the latter in the wagons of the corps. A commander of the present encampment will be designated in the course of this day.

As soon as it shall be known that the enemy's works have been carried, or that the general pursuit has been commenced, one wagon for each regiment and battery, and one for the cavalry, will follow the movement, to receive, under the direction of medical officers, the wounded and disabled, who will be brought back to this place for treatment in general hospital.

The surgeon-general will organize this important service, and designate that hospital as well as the medical officers to be left at it.

Every man who marches out to attack or pursue the enemy will take the usual allowance of ammunition, and subsistence for at least two days.

By command of Major-General Scott.[4]

H. L. SCOTT,
A. A.-General.

Headquarters of the Army, Plan del Rio,
Fifty miles from Vera Cruz, April 19, 1847.

SIR:

The plan of attack, sketched in General Orders No. 111, herewith, was finely executed by this gallant army before two o'clock P.M., yesterday. We are quite embarrassed with the results of victory—prisoners of war, heavy ordnance, field batteries, small arms, and accoutrements. About 3,000 men laid down their arms, with the usual proportion of field and company officers, besides five generals, several of them of great distinction—Pinson, Jarrero, La Vega, Noriega, and Obando.[5] A sixth general, Vasquez, was killed in defending the battery (tower) in the rear of the line of defence, the capture of which gave us those glorious results.

Our loss, though comparatively small in numbers, has been serious. Brigadier-General Shields, a commander of activity, zeal, and talent, is, I fear, if not dead, mortally wounded.[6] He is some five miles from me at the moment. The field of operations covered many miles, broken by mountains and deep chasms, and I have not a report as yet from any division or brigade. Twiggs's division, followed by Shields's (now Colonel Baker's)[7] brigade, are now at or near Jalapa, and Worth's division is in route thither; all pursuing, with good results, as I learn, that part of the Mexican army, perhaps six or seven thousand men, that fled before our right had carried the tower, and gained the Jalapa road. Pillow's brigade alone is near me at this depot of wounded, sick, and prisoners, and I have time only to give from him the names of First Lieutenant F. B. Nelson, and Second Lieutenant C. G. Gill, both of the 2d Tennessee Foot (Haskell's regiment), among the killed;[8] and in the brigade, one hundred and six of all ranks killed or wounded. Among the latter, the gallant Brigadier-General himself has a smart wound in the arm, but not disabled, and Major R. Farqueson, 2d Tennessee; Captain H. F. Murray, Second Lieutenant G. T. Sutherland, First Lieutenant W. P. Hale (Adjutant), all of the same regiment, severely, and First Lieutenant W. Yearwood, mortally wounded.[9] And I know, from personal observation on the ground, that First Lieutenant Ewell, of the Rifles, if not now dead, was mortally wounded in entering, sword in hand, the intrenchments around the captured tower.[10] Second Lieutenant Derby, Topographical Engineers,[11] I also saw, at the same place, severely wounded, and Captain Patten, 2d United States' Infantry, lost his right hand.[12] Major Sumner, 2d United States' Dragoons,[13] was slightly wounded the day before, and Captain Johnston, Topographical Engineers[14] (now Lieutenant-Colonel of infantry), was very severely wounded, some days earlier, while reconnoitring.

I must not omit to add that Captain Mason and Second Lieutenant Davis, both of the Rifles,[15] were among the very severely wounded in storming the same tower. I estimate our total loss in killed and wounded may be about two hundred and fifty, and that of the enemy three hundred and fifty.[16] In the pursuit toward Jalapa (twenty-five miles hence), I learn we have added much to the enemy's loss in prisoners, killed, and wounded. In fact, I suppose his retreating army to be nearly disorganized; and hence my haste to follow, in an hour or two, to profit by events.

In this hurried and imperfect report I must not omit to say that Brigadier-General Twiggs, in passing the mountain range beyond Cerro Gordo, crowned with the tower, detached from his division, as I suggested the day before, a strong force to carry that height, which commanded they Jalapa road at the foot, and could not fail, if carried, to cut off the whole or any part of the enemy's forces from a retreat in any direction A portion of the 1st Artillery, under the often distinguished Brevet Colonel Childs, the 3d Infantry, under Captain Alexander, the 7th Infantry, under Lieutenant-Colonel Plympton, and the Rifles, under Major Loring, all under the temporary command of Colonel Harney, 2d Dragoons, during the confinement to his bed of Brevet Brigadier-General P. F. Smith, composed that detachment.[17] The style of execution, which I had the pleasure to witness, was most brilliant and decisive. The brigade ascended the long and difficult slope of Cerro Gordo, without shelter, and under the tremendous fire of artillery and musketry, with the utmost steadiness, reached the breastworks, drove the enemy from them, planted the colors of the 1st Artillery, 3d and 7th Infantry— the enemy's flag still flying—and after some minutes of sharp firing, finished the conquest with the bayonet.

It is a most pleasing duty to say that the highest praise is due to Harney, Childs, Plympton, Loring, Alexander, their gallant officers and men, for this brilliant service, independent of the great results which soon followed.

Worth's division of regulars coming up at this time, he detached Brevet Lieutenant-Colonel C. F. Smith, with his light battalion, to support the assault, but not in time.[18] The general, reaching the tower a few minutes before me, and observing a white flag displayed from the nearest portion of the enemy toward the batteries below, sent out Colonels Harney and Childs to hold a parley. The surrender followed in an hour or two.

Major-General Patterson left a sickbed to share in the dangers and fatigues of the day; and after the surrender went forward to command the advanced forces toward Jalapa.

Brigadier-General Pillow and his brigade twice assaulted with great daring the enemy's line of batteries on our left; and, though without success, they contributed much to distract and dismay their immediate opponents.

President Santa Anna, with Generals Canalizo and Ampudia, and some six or eight thousand men, escaped toward Jalapa just before Cerro Gordo was carried, and before Twiggs's division reached the national road above.[19]

I have determined to parole the prisoners—officers and men—as I have not the means of feeding them here beyond to-day, and cannot afford to detach a heavy body of horse and foot, with wagons, to accompany them to Vera Cruz. Our baggage train, though increasing, is not yet half large enough to give an assured progress to this army. Besides, a greater number of prisoners would probably escape from the escort in the long and deep sandy road without subsistence—ten to one—than we shall find again out of the same body of men in the ranks opposed to us. Not one of the Vera Cruz prisoners is believed to have been in the lines of Cerro Gordo. Some six of the officers, highest in rank, refuse to give their paroles, except to go to Vera Cruz, and thence, perhaps, to the United States.

The small arms and their accoutrements, being of no value to our army here or at home, I have ordered them to be destroyed; for we have not the means of transporting them. I am also somewhat embarrassed with the pieces of artillery—all bronze—which we have captured. It would take a brigade and half the mules of this army to transport them fifty miles. A field battery I shall take for service with the army; but the heavy metal must be collected and left here for the present. We have our own siege-train and the proper carriages with us.

Being much occupied with the prisoners and all the details of a forward movement, besides looking to the supplies which are to follow from Vera Cruz, I have time to add no more—intending to be at Jalapa early to-morrow. We shall not probably again meet with serious opposition this side of Perote—certainly not, unless delayed by the want of the means of transportation.

I have the honor to remain, sir, with high respect, your most obedient servant,

WINFIELD SCOTT.

P. S.—I invite attention to the accompanying letter to President Santa Anna, taken in his carriage yesterday; also to his proclamation, issued on hearing that we had captured Vera Cruz, etc., in which he says: "If the enemy advance one step more, the national independence will be buried in the abyss of the past." We have taken that step.

W. S.

I make a second postscript, to say there is some hope, I am happy to learn, that General Shields may survive his wounds.

One of the principal motives for paroling the prisoners of war is to diminish the resistance of other garrisons in our march.

W. S.

HON. WM. L. MARCY, Secretary of War.

HEADQUARTERS OF THE ARMY, JALAPA, April 23, 1847.

Sir:

In forwarding the reports of commanders which detail the operations of their several corps against the Mexican lines at Cerro Gordo, I shall present, in continuation of my former report, but an outline of the affair, and while adopting heartily their commendations of the ardor and efficiency of individuals, I shall mention by name only those who figure prominently, or, from position, could not be included in those sub-reports.

The field sketch herewith, indicates the positions of the two armies. The *tierra caliente,* or low level,[20] terminates at *Plan del Rio,* the site of the American camp, from which the road ascends immediately in a long circuit among lofty hills, whose commanding points had all been fortified and garrisoned by the enemy. His right, intrenched, rested on a precipice overhanging an impassable ravine that forms the bed of the stream; and his intrenchments extended continuously to the road, on which was placed a formidable battery. On the other side, the lofty and difficult height of Cerro Gordo commanded the approaches in all directions. The main body of the Mexican army was encamped on level ground, with a battery of five pieces, half a mile in rear of that height toward Jalapa.

Resolving, if possible, to turn the enemy's left, and attack in rear, while menacing or engaging his front, I caused daily reconnaissances to be pushed, with the view of finding a route for a force to debouch on the Jalapa road and cut off retreat.

The reconnaissance begun by Lieutenant Beauregard, was continued by Captain Lee, Engineers, and a road made along difficult slopes and over chasms—out of the enemy's view, though reached by his fire when discovered—until, arriving at the Mexican lines, further reconnaissance became impossible without an action.[21] The desired point of debouchure, the Jalapa road, was not therefore reached, though believed to be within easy distance; and to gain that point, it now became necessary to carry the height of Cerro Gordo. The dispositions in my plan of battle—general orders No. 111, heretofore enclosed—were accordingly made.

Twiggs's division, reënforced by Shields's brigade of volunteers, was thrown into position on the 17th, and was, of necessity, drawn into action in taking up the ground for its bivouac and the opposing height for our heavy battery. It will be seen that many of our officers and men were killed or wounded in this sharp combat—handsomely commenced by a company of the 7th Infantry under Brevet First Lieutenant Gardner, who is highly praised by all his commanders for signal services.[22] Colonel Harney coming up with the rifle regiment and 1st Artillery (also parts of his brigade) brushed away the enemy and occupied the height—on which, in the night, was placed a battery of one 24-pounder and two 24-pound howitzers, under the superintendence of Captain Lee, Engineers, and Lieutenant Hagner, Ordnance.[23] These guns opened next morning, and were served with effect by Captain Steptoe and Lieutenant Brown, 3d Artillery, Lieutenant Hagner (Ordnance), and Lieutenant Seymour, 1st Artillery.[24]

The same night, with extreme toil and difficulty, under the superintendence of Lieutenant Tower, Engineer, and Lieutenant Laidley, Ordnance, an eight-inch howitzer was put in position across the river and opposite to the enemy's right battery.[25] A detachment of four companies, under Major Burnham, New York Volunteers,[26] performed this creditable service, which enabled Lieutenant Ripley, 2d Artillery,[27] in charge of the piece, to open a timely fire in that quarter.

Early on the 18th, the columns moved to the general attack, and our success was speedy and decisive. Pillow's brigade, assaulting the right of the intrenchments, although compelled to retire, had the effect I have heretofore stated. Twiggs's division, storming the strong and vital point of Cerro Gordo, pierced the centre, gained command of all of the intrenchments, and cut them off from support. As our infantry (Colonel Riley's brigade)[28] pushed on against the main body of the enemy, the guns of their own fort were rapidly turned to play on that force (under the immediate command of General Santa Anna), who fled in confusion. Shields's brigade, bravely assaulting the left, carried the rear battery (five guns) on the Jalapa road, and aided materially in completing the rout of the enemy.

The part taken by the remainder of our forces, held in reserve to support and pursue, has already been noticed.

The moment the fate of the day was decided, the cavalry, and Taylor's,[29] and Wall's field batteries were pushed on toward Jalapa in advance of the pursuing columns of infantry—Twiggs's division and the Brigade of Shields (now under Colonel Baker)—and Major-General Patterson was sent to take command of them. In the hot pursuit many Mexicans were captured or slain before our men and horses were exhausted by the heat and distance.

The rout proves to have been complete—the retreating army, except a small body of cavalry, being dispersed and utterly disorganized. The immediate consequences have been our possession of this important city, the abandonment of the works and artillery at La Hoya, the next formidable pass between Vera Cruz and the capital and the prompt occupation by Worth's division of the fortress of Perote (second only to San Juan de Ulloa), with its extensive armament of sixty-six guns and mortars, and its large supplies of *matériel*.[30] To General Worth's report, annexed, I refer for details.

I have heretofore endeavored to do justice to the skill and courage with which the attack on the height of Cerro Gordo was directed and executed, naming the regiments most distinguished, and their commanders, under the lead of Colonel Harney. Lieutenant G. W. Smith led the engineer company as part of the storming force, and is noticed with distinction.[31]

The reports of this assault make favorable mention of many in which I can well concur, having witnessed the daring advance and perfect steadiness of the whole. Beside those already named, Lieutenant Brooks, 3d Infantry; Lieutenant Macdonald, 2d Dragoons; Lieutenant Vandorn, 7th Infantry—all acting staff officers—Captain Magruder, 1st Artillery, and Lieutenant Gardner, 7th Infantry, seem to have won especial praise.[32]

Colonel Riley's brigade and Talcott's rocket and howitzer battery, were engaged on and about the heights, and bore an active part.

The brigade so gallantly led by General Shields, and, after his fall, by Colonel Baker, deserves high commendation for its fine behavior and success. Colonels Foreman and Burnett, and Major Harris, commanded the regiments; Lieutenant Hammond, 3d Artillery, and Lieutenant Davis, Illinois Volunteers, constituted the brigade staff.[33] These operations, hid from my view by intervening hills, were not fully known when my first report was hastily written.

Brigadier-General Twiggs, who was in the immediate command of all the advanced forces, has earned high credit by his judgment, spirit, and energy.

The conduct of Colonels Campbell, Haskell, and Wynkoop,[34] commanding the regiments of Pillow's brigade, is reported in terms of strong approbation by Major-General Patterson. I recommend for a commission, Quartermaster-Sergeant Henry, of the 7th Infantry (already known to the army for intrepidity on former occasions), who hauled down the national standard of the Mexican fort.[35]

In expressing my indebtedness for able assistance to Lieutenant-Colonel Hitchcock, Acting Inspector-General, to Majors Smith[36] and Turnbull,[37] the respective Chiefs of Engineers and Topographical Engineers—to their Assistants, Lieutenants Mason,[38] Beauregard, Stevens,[39] Tower,[40] G. W. Smith, McClellan,[41] Engineers, and Lieutenants Derby and Hardcastle,[42] Topographical Engineers—to Captain Allen,[43] Chief Quartermaster, and Lieutenant Blair,[44] Chief Commissary—and to Lieutenants Hagner and Laidley, Ordnance—all actively employed—I am compelled to make special mention of the services of Captain R. E. Lee, Engineer. This officer, greatly distinguished at the siege of Vera Cruz, was again indefatigable, during these operations, in reconnaissances as daring as laborious, and of the utmost value. Nor was he less conspicuous in planting batteries, and in conducting columns to their stations under the heavy fire of the enemy.

My personal staff, Lieutenants Scott,[45] Williams,[46] and Lay,[47] and Major Van Buren,[48] who volunteered for the occasion, gave me zealous and efficient assistance.

Our whole force present, in action and in reserve, was eight thousand five hundred; the enemy is estimated at twelve thousand, or more. About three thousand prisoners, four or five thousand stands of arms, and forty-three pieces of artillery were taken. By the accompanying return, I regret to find our loss more severe than at first supposed, amounting in the two days to thirty-three officers and three hundred and ninety-eight men—in all four hundred and thirty-one, of whom sixty-three were killed. The enemy's loss is computed to be from one thousand to one thousand two hundred.

I am happy in communicating strong hopes of the recovery of the gallant General Shields, who is so much improved as to have been brought to this place.

Appended to this report are the following papers:

A.—General return by name of killed and wounded.

B.—Copies of report of Lieutenant-Colonel Hitchcock, Acting Inspector-General (of prisoners taken) and accompanying papers.

C.—Report of Brigadier-General Twiggs, and sub-reports.

D.—Report of Major-General Patterson, and reports of brigade commanders.

E.—Copy of report of Brigadier-General Worth, announcing the occupation by his division of the castle and town of Perote, without opposition with an inventory of ordnance there found.

I have the honor to remain, sir, with high respect, your most obedient servant,

WINFIELD SCOTT.

Hon. Wm. L. Marcy, Secretary of War.

The terrible blow following closely on the captures of the preceding month, threw the Mexicans into consternation. Jalapa was abandoned, and I pushed Worth's division forward to tread on the heels of the fugitives and increase the panic.

Approaching Perote, its formidable castle also opened its gates without firing a gun, and the same division took quiet possession of the great city of Puebla. But here the career of conquest was arrested for a time.

I had been obliged to lessen the strength of a diminutive army by leaving respectable garrisons of regulars, in Vera Cruz and the Castle of San Juan de Ulloa. And now at Jalapa, without having received any reënforcements, it became necessary to discharge some four thousand volunteers whose respective terms of service were about to expire. They gave notice that they would continue with me to the last day, but would then certainly demand discharges and the means of transportation homeward. As any delay might throw them upon the yellow fever, at Vera Cruz, the discharges were given at once.[49]

We were delayed nearly a month at Jalapa waiting for a partial supply of necessaries from Vera Cruz by the second and third trips of our feeble trains, and with a faint hope of reënforcements. Not a company came. At length, toward the end of May, I marched, with the reserve, to join the advanced division (Worth's) at Puebla—leaving a strong garrison at Jalapa, under Colonel Childs, to keep the line of communication open with Vera Cruz as long as possible.[50] Indeed, at that time, I had not entirely lost the hope of receiving new regiments of regulars and volunteers in numbers sufficient to maintain our communications with the ocean and home throughout the campaign by means of garrisons at the National Bridge, Perote, Puebla, and Rio Frio, as well as at Vera Cruz and Jalapa.

Waiting for reënforcements, the halt, at Puebla, was protracted and irksome. The Benton intrigue had so disgusted a majority of the two houses of Congress, that the bill authorizing the ten new regiments of regulars lingered from the beginning of December down to the 11th of February—the Administration having sunk too low to hasten its passage a day in advance of the usual sluggish forms of legislation.[51]

In the mean time, the army at Puebla was not inactive. All the corps, amounting to about five thousand effective men, were daily put through their manoeuvres and evolutions. We were also kept on the alert by an army sometimes of superior numbers, hovering about us, and often assuming a menacing attitude; but always ready for flight the moment they saw that we were under arms. On these occasions it was painful to restrain the ardor of the troops. But I steadily held to the policy not to wear out patience and sole leather by running to the right or left in the pursuit of small game. I played for the big stakes. Keeping the army massed and the mind fixed upon the capital, I meant to content myself with beating whatever force that might stand directly in the way of that conquest—being morally sure that all smaller objects would soon follow that crowning event.

The city of Puebla, washed by a fine, flowing stream, is near the centre of a valley of uncommon fertility and beauty, producing, annually, two abundant crops for the subsistence of men and animals—one by rains, and the other by artificial irrigation. All the cereals—wheat, barley, maize and rye; all the grasses, including clover, lucerne, and timothy, and all the fruit-trees—the apple, peach, apricot and pear, grow here as well as in the region of Frederic, Maryland—the elevation (near seven thousand feet above the ocean) making a difference in climate, equal to eighteen or twenty degrees of latitude. Many objects within the horizon of Puebla are among the sublimest features of nature. The white peak of Orizaba, the most distant, may always be seen in bright weather. The Malinche mountain, near by, is generally capped with snow; Popocatapetl and his white sister, always, since the first snow fell after the creation.[52] The city itself, with her hundred steeples and cathedral, in majestic repose—seen from a certain elevation, is itself a magnificent object in the general landscape.

During this halt, every corps of the army in succession, made a most interesting excursion of six miles, to the ruins of the ancient city of Cholula, long, in point of civilization and art, the Etruria of this continent, and in respect to religion, the Mecca of many of the earliest tribes known to tradition. Down to the time of Cortes, a little more than three hundred years before the Americans, Cholula, containing an ingenious and peaceable population of perhaps one hundred and fifty thousand souls, impressed with a *unique* type of civilization, had fallen off, in 1847, to a miserable hamlet, its towers and dwellings of sun-baked bricks and stucco, in heaps of ruins.[53] From these melancholy wrecks are yet disinterred productions of art of great beauty and delicacy, in metals and porcelain, both for ornament and use. The same people also manufactured cloths of cotton and the fibre of the agave plant.

One grand feature, denoting the ancient grandeur of Cholula, stands but little affected by the lapse of perhaps thousands of years—a pyramid built of alternate layers of brick and clay, some two hundred feet in height, with a square basis of more than forty acres, running up to a plateau of seventy yards square. There stood in the time of Cortes, the great pagan temple of the Cholulans, with a perpetual blazing fire on its altar, seen in the night many miles around. This the Spaniards soon replaced by a *bijou* of a church, something larger than the *Casa Santa* at Loretto, with a beautiful altar and many pictures.[54] The ascent to this plateau is by a flight of some hundred and forty steps.

The prosperity of Cholula, in 1520, was already on the decline, having recently fallen under the harsh rule of the Montezumas, and it now sustained a heavy blow at the hands of Cortes, an invited guest, who, to punish a detected conspiracy, that was intended to compass the destruction of his entire army, massacred more than six thousand of the inhabitants, including most of the chiefs, besides destroying entire streets of houses.

An admirer of scenery, and curious to view the ruins of Cholula, the autobiographer, one bright morning in June, suddenly determined to overtake a fine brigade of regulars that had advanced on that excursion, half an hour before. Even escorted by a squadron of cavalry this was an enterprise not without some danger, considering that he could make no movement without causing several citizens to fly off at full speed, on fine Andalusian horses, to report the fact to detachments of cavalry lurking in the vicinity.

Coming up with the brigade marching at ease,* all intoxicated with the fine air and splendid scenery, he was, as usual, received with hearty and protracted cheers. {Troops, marching at ease, bear their arms on either shoulder or in either hand, always keeping the muzzles of their arms up, and are at liberty to talk, laugh, sing or crack their jokes to

their heart's content—only taking care not to confound their ranks.}
The group of officers who surrounded him, differed widely in the objects of their admiration—some preferring this or that snow-capped
mountain, others the city, and several the pyramid of Cholula, that was
now opening upon the view. An appeal from all was made to the general-
in-chief. He emphatically replied: "I differ from you all. My greatest delight is in this fine body of troops, without whom, we can never sleep
in the Halls of the Montezumas, or in our own homes." The word was
caught up by some of the rank and file, marching abreast, and passed
rapidly to the front and rear of the column, each platoon, in succession,
rending the air with its acclamation.

CHAPTER XXX

ADVANCE ON THE CAPITAL–HALT AT AYOTLA–RECONNAISSANCES–SAN AUGUSTIN–CONTRERAS

At length reënforcements began to approach. Lieutenant-Colonel McIntosh with some eight hundred men, escorting a large train, was checked and delayed by the enemy in the march near Jalapa; but being soon joined by Brigadier-General Cadwallader, with a portion of his brigade and a field battery, the enemy was swept away and the two detachments arrived in safety at Puebla. Major-General Pillow followed with another detachment of a thousand men, and finally came Brigadier-General Pierce (August the 6th) with a brigade of two thousand five hundred.[1]

About this time, when General Taylor had more troops than he could employ, and yet clamored for reënforcements—I was obliged, by paucity of numbers, to call up the garrison from Jalapa, under Colonel Childs, to make up my entire force at Puebla including the late reënforcements, to about fourteen thousand men, of whom two thousand five hundred were sick in hospital (mostly diarrhoea cases), and about six hundred convalescents, yet too feeble for an ordinary day's march. The latter, and an equal number of effective troops were designated as the garrison, under Colonel Childs, of the important city of Puebla—the whole route to Vera Cruz and all communications with home, being, for the time, abandoned. We had to throw away the scabbard and to advance with the naked blade in hand.

The composition of the army in its march from Puebla to Mexico was as follows:

GENERAL STAFF.
Lieutenant-Colonel Hitchcock, Assistant Inspector-General.
Captain H. L. Scott, Acting Adjutant-General.
First Lieutenant T. Williams, Aide-de-Camp.
Brevet First Lieutenant G. W. Lay, Aide-de-Camp.
Second Lieutenant Schuyler Hamilton, Aide-de-Camp.[2]
Major J. P. Gaines, Volunteer Aide-de-Camp.[3]

ENGINEER CORPS.

Major J. L. Smith, Chief.
Captain R. E. Lee.
Lieutenant P. G. T. Beauregard.
    "   Isaac I. Steven.
    "   Z. B. Tower.
    "   G. W. Smith.
    "   George B. McClellan.[4]
    "   J. G. Foster.[5]

ORDNANCE DEPARTMENT.

Captain Benjamin Huger, Chief, with Siege Train.[6]
First Lieutenant P. V. Hagner.
Second Lieutenant C. P. Stone.[7]

TOPOGRAPHICAL ENGINEERS.

Major William Turnbull, Chief.
Captain J. McClellan.
Second Lieutenant George Thom.[8]
Brevet Second Lieutenant E. L. F. Hardcastle.

QUARTERMASTERS DEPARTMENT.

Captain J. R. Irwin, Chief.[9]
    "   A. C. Myers.[10]
    "   Robert Allen.
    "   H. C. Wayne.[11]
    "   J. McKinstry.[12]
    "   G. W. F. Wood.[13]
    "   J. Daniels.[14]
    "   O'Hara.[15]
    "   S. McGowan.[16]

SUBSISTENCE DEPARTMENT.

Captain J. B. Grayson, Chief.[17]
    "   T. P. Randle.[18]

PAY DEPARTMENT.

Major E. Kirby, Chief.[19]
    "   A. Van Buren.
    "   A. G. Bennett.[20]

MEDICAL DEPARTMENT.

Surgeon-General Thomas Lawson.[21]
Surgeon B. F. Harney.[22]
"   R. S. Satterlee.[23]
"   C. S. Tripler.[24]
"   B. Randall.[25]
"   J. M. Cuyler.[26]
Assistant-Surgeon A. F. Suter.[27]
"   J. Simpson.[28]
"   D. C. DeLeon.[29]
"   H. H. Steiner.[30]
"   J. Simons.[31]
"   J. K. Barnes.[32]
"   L. H. Holden.[33]
"   C. C. Keeney.[34]
"   J. F. Head.[35]
"   J. F. Hammond.[36]
"   J. M. Steiner.[37]
"   C. P. Deyerle.[38]
"   E. Swift.[39]
Surgeon J. M. Tyler, Volunteer.
"   McMillan,   "
"   C. J. Clark,[40]   "
"   W. B. Halstead,   "

Assistant-Surgeon R. Hagan, Volunteer.[41]
"   H. L. Wheaton,   "

Surgeon R. Ritchie, 1st Volunteers.[42]
"   J. Barry,   "
"   Edwards,   "
"   L. W. Jordan,[43]   "
"   R. McSherry,[44]   "
"   Roberts,   "

CORPS.

COLONEL HARNEY'S BRIGADE.[45]

Detachment of 1st Light Dragoons, under Captain Kearny.
"   2d   "   "   Major Sumner.
"   3d   "   "   Major McReynolds.[46]

I.—BREVET MAJOR-GENERAL WORTH'S DIVISION.
    1. COLONEL GARLAND'S BRIGADE.[47]
2d Regiment of Artillery, serving as Infantry.
3d   "   "   "   "
4th   "   of Infantry.
Duncan's Field Battery.

    2. COLONEL CLARK'S BRIGADE.[48]
5th, 6th and 8th Regiments of Infantry.
A Light Battery.

II.—BREVET MAJOR-GENERAL TWIGGS'S DIVISION.
    1. BREVET BRIGADIER-GENERAL P. F. SMITH'S BRIGADE.
Rifle Regiment.
1st Regiment of Artillery, serving as Infantry.
3d Regiment of Infantry.
Taylor's Light Battery.

    2. COLONEL RILEY'S BRIGADE.
4th Regiment of Artillery, serving as Infantry.
1st Regiment of Infantry.
7th   "   "

III.—MAJOR-GENERAL PILLOW'S DIVISION.
    1. BRIGADIER-GENERAL G. CADWALLADER'S BRIGADE.
Voltigeurs.
11th and 14th Infantry.
A Light Battery.

    2. BRIGADIER-GENERAL PIERCE'S BRIGADE.[49]
9th, 12th, and 15th Infantry.

IV.—MAJOR-GENERAL QUITMAN'S DIVISION.
    1. BRIGADIER-GENERAL SHIELDS'S BRIGADE.
New York Volunteers.
South Carolina Volunteers.

    2. LIEUTENANT-COLONEL WATSON'S BRIGADE.[50]
A Detachment of 2d Pennsylvania Volunteers.
Detachment of United States' Marines.

It has been seen that the last body of recruits (Pierce's brigade) arrived August 6, 1847. The army commenced its advance, by divisions, on the 7th—Twiggs's division first, with Harney's brigade of cavalry leading, and the siege train following. The other three divisions successively followed on the 8th, 9th, and 10th—each of the four divisions making but a half day's march at the beginning. So that no division (even the leading or rearmost one) was ever separated more than seven or eight miles from support, or rather half that distance, by means of a double movement—one division advancing and the other falling back. By similar means, three divisions might easily have been united in little more than two hours, in the case of a formidable attack upon an interior division.

This concatenation of the advancing corps was deemed prudent inasmuch as President Santa Anna had now had nearly four months (since the battle of Cerro Gordo) to collect and reorganize the entire means of the Republic for a last vigorous attempt to crush the invasion. A single error on our part—a single victory on his, might have effected that great end.* {The Duke of Wellington, with whom the autobiographer was slightly acquainted, took quite an interest in the march of this army from Vera Cruz, and at every arrival caused its movements to be marked on a map. Admiring its triumphs up to the basin of Mexico, he now said to a common friend: "Scott is lost. He has been carried away by successes. He can't take the city, and he can't fall back upon his base."} His vigilance and energy were unquestionable, and his powers of creating and organizing worthy of admiration. He was also great in administrative ability, and though not deficient in personal courage, he, on the field of battle, failed in quickness of perception and rapidity of combination. Hence his, defeats.

We had confidently expected to meet him, at the latest, in the defiles of Rio Frio; but he preferred remaining in coil about the city in the midst of formidable lines of defence both natural and artificial.

August 10, the leading division, with which I marched, crossed the Rio Frio range of mountains, the highest point, in the bed of the road between the Atlantic and Pacific Oceans.

Descending the long western slope, a magnificent basin, with, near its centre, the object of all our dreams and hopes—toils and dangers;— once the gorgeous seat of the Montezumas, now the capital of a great Republic—first broke upon our enchanted view. The close surrounding lakes, sparkling under a bright sun, seemed, in the distance, pendant diamonds. The numerous steeples of great beauty and elevation, with Popocatepetl, ten thousand feet higher, apparently near enough to touch with the hand, filled the mind with religious awe. Recovering from the sublime trance, probably, not a man in the column failed to say to his neighbor or himself: *That splendid city soon shall be ours!* All were ready to suit the action to the word.

Report No. 31.
HEADQUARTERS OF THE ARMY, SAN AUGUSTIN,
ACAPULCO ROAD, NINE MILES FROM MEXICO,
August 19, 1847.

SIR:

Leaving a competent garrison in Puebla, this army advanced upon the capital, as follows: Twiggs's division, preceded by Harney's brigade of cavalry, the 7th; Quitman's division of volunteers, with a small detachment of United States' Marines, the 8th; Worth's division, the 9th, and Pillow's division, the 10th—all in this month. On the 8th, I overtook, and then continued with the leading division.

The corps were, at no time, beyond five hours, or supporting distance, apart; and on descending into the basin of the capital (seventy-five miles from Puebla) they became more closely approximated about the head of Lake Chalco, with Lake Tescuco a little in front and to the right.

On the 12th and 13th, we pushed reconnaissances upon the Peñon, an isolated mound (eight miles from Mexico) of great height, strongly fortified to the top (three tiers of works) and flooded around the base by the season of rain and sluices from the lakes.[51] This mound close to the national road, commands the principal approach to the city from the east. No doubt it might have been carried, but at a great and disproportionate loss, and I was anxious to spare the lives of this gallant army for a general battle which I knew we had to win before capturing the city, or obtaining the great object of the campaign—a just and honorable peace.

Another reconnaissance (which I also accompanied) was directed (the 13th) upon Mexicalcingo, to the left of the Peñon, a village at a fortified bridge across the outlet or canal, leading from Lake Jochimilco to the capital—five miles from the latter. It might have been easy (masking the Peñon) to force this passage; but on the other side of the bridge, we should have found ourselves four miles from this (San Augustin) road, on a narrow causeway, flanked on the right and left by water or boggy ground.

Those difficulties, closely viewed, threw me back upon the project, long entertained, of turning the strong eastern defences of the city, by passing around south of Lake Chalco and Jochimilco, at the foot of the hills and mountains, so as to reach this point (San Augustin), and hence to manoeuvre, on hard ground, though much broken, to the south and southwest of the capital, which has been more or less under our view, since the 10th instant.

Accordingly, by a sudden inversion—Worth's division, with Harney's cavalry brigade, leading—we marched on the 15th instant. Pillow's and Quitman's divisions followed closely, and then Twiggs's division, which was left till the next day at Ayotla, in order to threaten the Peñon and Mexicalcingo, and to deceive the enemy as long as practicable.

Twiggs, on the 16th, marching from Ayotla toward Chalco (six miles), met a corps of more than double his numbers—cavalry and infantry—under General Valencia.[52] Twiggs halted, deployed into line, and by a few rounds from Captain Taylor's field battery, dispersed the enemy, killing or wounding many men and horses. No other molestation has been experienced except a few random shots from guerilleros on the heights; and the march of twenty-seven miles, over a route deemed impracticable by the enemy, is now accomplished by all the corps—thanks to their indomitable zeal and physical energy.

Arriving here, the 18th, Worth's division and Harney's cavalry were pushed forward a league, to reconnoitre and to carry, or to mask, San Antonio on the direct road to the capital. This village was found strongly defended by field works, heavy guns, and a numerous garrison. It could only be turned by infantry, to the left, over a field of volcanic stones and lava; for, to our right, the ground was boggy.[53]

It was soon ascertained by the daring engineers, Captain Mason and Lieutenants Stevens and Tower, that the point could only be approached by the front, over a narrow causeway, flanked with wet ditches of great depth. Worth was ordered not to attack, but to threaten and to mask the place.

The first shot fired from San Antonio (the 18th) killed Captain S. Thornton, 2d Dragoons, a gallant officer, who was covering the operations with his company.[54]

The same day, a reconnaissance was commenced to the left of San Augustin, first over difficult grounds, and farther on, over the same field of volcanic matter which extends to the mountains, some five miles from San Antonio, toward Magdalena. This reconnaissance was continued to-day by Captain Lee, assisted by Lieutenants Beauregard and Tower, all of the Engineers; who were joined in the afternoon by Major Smith of the same corps. Other divisions coming up, Pillow's was advanced to make a practicable road for heavy artillery, and Twiggs's thrown farther in front, to cover that operation; for, by the partial reconnaissance of yesterday, Captain Lee discovered a large corps of observation in that direction, with a detachment of which his supports of cavalry and foot under Captain Kearny and Lieutenant-Colonel Graham, respectively, had a successful skirmish.[55]

By three o'clock this afternoon, the advanced divisions came to a point where the new road could only be continued under the direct fire of twenty-two pieces of the enemy's artillery (most of them of large calibre) placed in a strong intrenched camp to oppose our operations, and surrounded by every advantage of ground, besides immense bodies of cavalry and infantry hourly reënforced from the city, over an excellent road beyond the volcanic field, and consequently beyond the reach of our cavalry and artillery.

Arriving on the ground an hour later, I found that Pillow's and Twiggs's divisions had advanced to dislodge the enemy, picking their way (all officers on foot) along his front, and extending themselves toward the road Born the city and the enemy's left. Captain Magruder's field battery, of 12 and 6-pounders, and Lieutenant Callender's[56] battery of mountain howitzers and rockets, had also, with great difficulty, been advanced within range of the intrenched camp. These batteries, most gallantly served, suffered much in the course of the afternoon, from the enemy's superior weight of metal.

The battle, though mostly stationary, continued to rage with great violence until nightfall. Brevet Brigadier-General P. F. Smith's and Brevet Colonel Riley's brigades (Twiggs's division), supported by Brigadier-Generals Pierce's and Cadwallader's brigades (Pillow's division), were more than three hours under a heavy fire of artillery and musketry along the almost impassable ravine in front and to the left of the intrenched camp.

Besides the twenty-two pieces of artillery, the camp and ravine were defended closely by masses of infantry, and these again supported by clouds of cavalry at hand, hovering in view. Consequently no decided impression could be made by daylight on the enemy's most formidable position, because, independently of the difficulty of the ravine, our infantry, unaccompanied by cavalry and artillery, could not advance in column without being mowed down by the grape and canister of the batteries, nor advance in line without being ridden over by the enemy's numerous cavalry. All our corps, however, including Magruder's and Callender's light batteries, not only maintained the exposed positions

CHAPTER XXX

early gained, but all attempted charges upon them, respectively—particularly on Riley, twice closely engaged with cavalry in greatly superior numbers—were repulsed and punished.

From an eminence, soon after arriving near the scene, I observed the church and hamlet of Contreras (or Ansalda) on the road leading up from the capital through the intrenched camp to Magdalena, and seeing, at the same time, the stream of reënforcements advancing by that road from the city, I ordered (through Major-General Pillow) Colonel Morgan[57] with his regiment, the 15th, till then held in reserve by Pillow, to move forward and to occupy Contreras (or Ansalda)—being persuaded, if occupied, it would arrest the enemy's reënforcements and ultimately decide the battle.

Riley was already on the enemy's left, in advance of the hamlet. A few minutes later, Brigadier-General Shields with his volunteer brigade (New York and South Carolina regiments—Quitman's division) coming up under my orders from San Augustin, I directed Shields to follow and sustain Morgan. These corps, over the extreme difficulties of ground—partially covered with a low forest—before described, reached Contreras, and found Cadwallader's brigade in position, observing the formidable movement from the capital, and much needing the timely reënforcement.

It was already dark, and the cold rain had begun to fall in torrents upon our unsheltered troops; for the hamlet, though a strong defensive position, could only hold the wounded men, and, unfortunately, the new regiments have little or nothing to eat in their haversacks. Wet, hungry, and without the possibility of sleep; all our gallant corps, I learn, are full of confidence, and only wait for the last hour of darkness to gain the positions whence to storm and carry the enemy's works.

Of the seven officers despatched since about sundown, from my position opposite to the enemy's centre, and on this side of the volcanic field—to communicate instructions to the hamlet—not one has succeeded in getting through these difficulties increased by darkness. They have all returned. But the gallant and indefatigable Captain Lee, of the Engineers, who has been constantly with the operating forces, is (eleven o'clock P.M.) just in from Shields, Smith, Cadwallader, etc., to report as above, and to ask that a powerful diversion be made against the centre of the intrenched camp toward morning.[58]

Brigadier-General Twiggs cut off as above, from the part of his division beyond the impracticable ground, and Captain Lee are gone, under my orders, to collect the forces remaining on this side with which to make that diversion at about five o'clock in the morning.

And here I will end this report, commenced at its date, and in another, continue the narrative of the great events which now impend.

I have the honor to be, etc.,
etc.,
WINFIELD SCOTT.

Hon. WM. L. MARCY, Secretary of War.

CHAPTER XXXI

VICTORIES OF CONTRERAS— SAN ANTONIO—CHURUBUSCO

Report No. 32.
HEADQUARTERS OF THE ARMY,
TACUBAYA, AT THE GATES OF
MEXICO, August 28, 1847.

SIR:

My report, No. 31, commenced in the night of the 19th instant, closed with the operations of the army on that day.

The morning of the 20th opened with one of a series of unsurpassed achievements, all in view of the capital, and to which I shall give the general name—*Battles of Mexico.*

In the night of the 19th, Brigadier-Generals Shields, P. F. Smith, and Cadwallader, and Colonel Riley, with their brigades, and the 15th Regiment, under Colonel Morgan, detached from Brigadier-General Pierce—found themselves in and about the important position—the village, hamlet or *hacienda,* called indifferently, Contreras, Ansalda, San Geronimo—half a mile nearer to the city than the enemy's intrenched camp, on the same road, toward the factory of Magdalena.

That camp had been, unexpectedly, our formidable point of attack in the afternoon before, and we had now to take it, without the aid of cavalry or artillery, or to throw back our advanced corps upon the direct road from San Augustin to the city, and thence force a passage through San Antonio.

Accordingly, to meet contingencies, Major-General Worth was ordered to leave early in the morning of the 20th, one of his brigades to mask San Antonio, and to march with the other six miles, *via* San Augustin, upon Contreras. A like destination was given to Major-General Quitman and his remaining brigade in San Augustin—replacing, for the moment, the garrison of that important depot with Harney's brigade of cavalry, as horse could not pass over the intervening lava, etc., to reach the field of battle.

A diversion for an earlier hour (daylight) had been arranged the night before, according to the suggestion of Brigadier-General P. F. Smith, received through the Engineer, Captain Lee, who conveyed my orders to our troops remaining on the ground, opposite to the enemy's centre—the point for the diversion or a real attack, as circumstances might allow.

Guided by Captain Lee, it proved the latter, under the command of Colonel Ransom[1] of the 9th, having with him that regiment and some companies of three others—the 3d, 12th, and Rifles.

Shields, the senior officer at the hamlet, having arrived in the night, after Smith had arranged with Cadwallader and Riley the plan of attack for the morning, delicately waived interference; but reserved to himself the double task of holding the hamlet with his two regiments (South Carolina and New York Volunteers) against ten times his numbers on the side of the city, including the slopes to his left, and in case the enemy's camp in his rear should be carried, to face about and cut off the flying enemy.

At three o'clock A.M. the great movement commenced on the rear of the enemy's camp, Riley leading, followed successively by Cadwallader's and Smith's brigades, the latter temporarily under the orders of Major Dimick of the 1st Artillery[2]—the whole force being commanded by Smith, the senior in the general attack, and whose arrangements, skill, and gallantry always challenge the highest admiration.

The march was rendered tedious by the darkness, rain, and mud; but about sunrise, Riley, conducted by Lieutenant Tower, Engineer, had reached an elevation behind the enemy, whence lie precipitated his columns stormed the intrenchments, planted his several colors upon them, and carried the work—all in seventeen minutes.

Conducted by Lieutenant Beauregard, Engineer, and Lieutenant Brooks of Twiggs's Staff both of whom, like Lieutenant Tower, had, in the night, twice reconnoitred the ground—Cadwallader brought up to the general assault, two of his regiments—the Voltigeurs and the 11th; and at the appointed time Colonel Ransom, with his temporary brigade, conducted by Captain Lee, Engineer, not only made the movement in front, to divert and to distract the enemy, but, after crossing the deep ravine, advanced, and poured into the works and upon the fugitives many volleys from his destructive musketry.

In the mean time Smith's own brigade, under the temporary command of Major Dimick, following the movements of Riley and Cadwallader, discovered, opposite to, and outside of the works, a long line of Mexican cavalry, drawn up as a support. Dimick having at the head of the brigade the company of Sappers and Miners, under Lieutenant G. W. Smith, Engineer, who had conducted the march, was ordered by Brigadier-General Smith to form his line faced to the enemy, and in a charge, against a flank, routed the cavalry.

Shields, too, by the wise disposition of his brigade and gallant activity, contributed much to the general results. He held masses of cavalry and infantry, supported by artillery, in check below him, and captured hundreds, with one general (Mendoza),[3] of those who fled from above.

I doubt whether a more brilliant or decisive victory—taking into view ground, artificial defences, batteries, and the extreme disparity of numbers—without cavalry or artillery on our side—is to be found on record. Including all our corps directed against the intrenched camp, with Shields's brigade at the hamlet, we positively did not number over four thousand five hundred rank and file; and we knew by sight, and since, more certainly, by many captured documents and letters, that the enemy had actually engaged on the spot seven thousand men, with at least twelve thousand more hovering within sight and striking distance—both on the 19th and 20th. All, not killed or captured, now fled with precipitation.

Thus was the great victory of Contreras achieved; one road to the capital opened; seven hundred of the enemy killed; eight hundred and thirteen prisoners, including, among eighty-eight officers, four generals; besides many colors and standards; twenty-two pieces of brass ordnance—half of large calibre; thousands of small arms and accoutrements; an immense quantity of shot, shells, powder, and cartridges; seven hundred pack mules, many horses, etc., etc.—all in our hands.

It is highly gratifying to find that, by skillful arrangement and rapidity of execution, our loss, in killed and wounded, did not exceed, on the spot, sixty—among the former the brave Captain Charles Hanson, of the 4th Infantry—not more distinguished for gallantry than for modesty, morals, and piety. Lieutenant J. P. Johnstone, 1st Artillery, serving with Magruder's battery, a young officer of the highest promise, was killed the evening before.[4]

One of the most pleasing incidents of the victory is the recapture, in their works, by Captain Drum,[5] 4th Artillery, under Major Gardner,[6] of the two brass 6-pounders, taken from another company of the same regiment, though without the loss of honor, at the glorious battle of Buena Vista—about which guns the whole regiment had mourned for so many long months! Coming up a little later I had the happiness to join in the protracted cheers of the gallant 4th on the joyous event; and, indeed, the whole army sympathizes in its just pride and exultation.

The battle being won before the advancing brigades of Worth's and Quitman's divisions were in sight, both were ordered back to their late positions:—Worth, to attack San Antonio, in front, with his whole force, as soon as approached in the rear by Pillow's and Twiggs's divisions— moving from Contreras, through San Angel and Coyoacan. By carrying San Antonio, we knew that we should open another—a shorter and better road to the capital for our siege and other trains.

Accordingly, the two advanced divisions and Shields brigade marched from Contreras, under the immediate orders of Major-General Pillow, who was now joined by the gallant Brigadier-General Pierce of his division, personally thrown out of activity, late, the evening before, by a severe hurt received from the fall of his horse.

After giving necessary orders on the field, in the midst of prisoners and trophies, and sending instructions to Harney's brigade of cavalry (left at San Augustin) to join me, I personally followed Pillow's command.

Arriving at Coyoacan, two miles by a cross road, from the rear of San Antonio, I first detached Captain Lee, Engineer, with Captain Kearny's troop, 1st Dragoons, supported by the Rifle Regiment, under Major Loring, to reconnoitre that strong point; and next despatched Major-General Pillow, with one of his brigades (Cadwallader's), to make the attack upon it, in concert with Major-General Worth on the opposite side.

At the same time, by another road to the left, Lieutenant Stevens of the Engineers, supported by Lieutenant G. W. Smith's company of sappers and miners, of the same corps, was sent to reconnoitre the strongly fortified church or convent of San Pablo, in the hamlet of Churubusco— one mile off. Twiggs with one of his brigades (Smith's—less the Rifles) and Captain Taylor's[7] field battery, were ordered to follow and to attack the convent. Major Smith, senior Engineer, was despatched to concert with Twiggs the mode and means of attack, and Twiggs's other brigade (Riley's) I soon ordered up to support him.

Next (but all in ten minutes) I sent Pierce (just able to keep the saddle) with his brigade (Pillow's division), conducted by Captain Lee, Engineer, by a third road a little farther to our left, to attack the enemy's right and rear, in order to favor the movement upon the convent, and to cut off a retreat toward the capital. And finally, Shields, senior brigadier to Pierce, with the New York and South Carolina Volunteers (Quitman's division), was ordered to follow Pierce closely, and to take the command of our left wing. All these movements were made with the utmost alacrity by our gallant troops and commanders.

Finding myself at Coyoacan, from which so many roads conveniently branched, without escort or reserve, I had to advance for safety close upon Twiggs's rear. The battle now raged from the right to the left of our whole line.

Learning on the return of Captain Lee, that Shields in the rear of Churubusco was hard pressed, and in danger of being outflanked, if not overwhelmed, by greatly superior numbers, I immediately sent under Major Sumner, 2d Dragoons, the Rifles (Twiggs's reserve) and Captain Sibley's troop,[8] 2d Dragoons, then at hand, to support our left, guided by the same engineer.

About an hour earlier, Worth had, by skillful and daring movements upon the front and right, turned and forced San Antonio—its garrison, no doubt, much shaken by our decisive victory at Contreras.

His second brigade (Colonel Clarke's) conducted by Captain Mason, Engineer, assisted by Lieutenant Hardcastle, Topographical Engineer, turned to the left, and by a wide sweep came out upon the high road to the capital. At this point the heavy garrison (three thousand men) in retreat was, by Clarke, cut in the centre: one portion, the rear, driven upon Dolores, off to the right, and the other upon Churubusco, in the direct line of our operations. The first brigade (Colonel Garland's), same division, consisting of the 2d Artillery, under Major Galt, the 3d Artillery, under Lieutenant-Colonel Belton, and the 4th Infantry, commanded by Major F. Lee, with Lieutenant-Colonel Duncan's field battery (temporarily) followed in pursuit through the town, taking one general prisoner, the abandoned guns (five pieces), much ammunition, and other public property.

The forcing of San Antonio was the *second* brilliant event of the day.

Worth's division being soon reunited in hot pursuit, lie was joined by Major-General Pillow, who, marching from Coyoacan and discovering that San Antonio had been carried, immediately turned to the left according to my instructions and, though much impeded by ditches and swamps, hastened to the attack of Cburubusco.

The hamlet or scattered houses bearing this name, presented besides the fortified combat, a strong fieldwork (*tête de pont*) with regular bastions and curtains at the head of a bridge over which the road passes from San Antonio to the capital.

The whole remaining forces of Mexico—some twenty-seven thousand men—cavalry, artillery, and infantry, collected from every quarter—were now in, on the flanks, or within supporting distance of those works, and seemed resolved to make a last and desperate stand; for if beaten here, the feebler defences at the gates of the city—four miles off—could not, as was well known to both parties, delay the victors an hour. [?] The capital of an ancient empire, now of a great republic; or an early peace, the assailants were resolved to win. Not an American—and we were less than a third of the enemy's numbers—had a doubt as to the result.

The fortified church or convent, hotly pressed by Twiggs, had already held out about an hour, when Worth and Pillow—the latter having with him Cadwallader's brigade—began to manoeuvre closely upon the *tête de pont,* with the convent at half gunshot to their left. Garland's brigade (Worth's division), to which had been added the light battalion under Lieutenant-Colonel C. F. Smith, continued to advance in front and under the fire of a long line of infantry off on the left of the bridge; and Clarke of the same division, directed his brigade along the road or close by its side. Two of Pillow's and Cadwallader's regiments, the 11th and 14th, supported and participated in this direct movement: the other (the voltigeurs) was left in reserve. Most of these corps—particularly Clarke's brigade—advancing perpendicularly, were made to suffer much by the fire of the *tête de pont,* and they would have suffered greatly more by flank attacks from the convent, but for the pressure of Twiggs on the other side of that work.

This well-combined and daring movement at length reached the principal point of attack, and the formidable *tête de pont* was at once assaulted and carried by the bayonet. Its deep wet ditch was first gallantly crossed by the 8th and 5th Infantry, commanded respectively by Major Waite[9] and Lieutenant-Colonel Martin Scott[10]—followed closely by the 6th Infantry (same brigade), which had been so much exposed on the road—the 11th regiment, under Lieutenant-Colonel Graham, and the 14th commanded by Colonel Trousdale,[11] both of Cadwallader's brigade, Pillow's division. About the same time, the enemy in front of Garland, after a hot conflict of an hour and a half gave way, in a retreat toward the capital.

The immediate results of this *third* signal triumph of the day were three field pieces, one hundred and ninety-two prisoners, much ammunition and two colors taken at the *tête de pont.*

Lieutenant I. F. Irons,[12] 1st Artillery, aide-de-camp to Brigadier-General Cadwallader, a young officer of great merit and conspicuous in battle on several previous occasions, received in front of the work, a mortal wound. (Since dead.)

As the concurrent attack upon the convent favored, physically and morally, the assault upon the *tête de pont,* so reciprocally, no doubt, the fall of the latter contributed to the capture of the former. The two works were only some four hundred and fifty yards apart; and as soon as we were in possession of the *tête de pont,* a captured 4-pounder was turned and fired—first by Captain Larkin Smith,[13] and next by Lieutenant Snelling,[14] both of the 8th Infantry—several times upon the convent. In the same brief interval, Lieutenant-Colonel Duncan (also of Worth's division) gallantly brought two of his guns to bear at a short range from the San Antonio road, upon the principal face of the work and on the tower of the church, which in the obstinate contest, had been often re-filled with some of the best sharpshooters of the enemy.

Finally, twenty minutes after the *tête de pont* had been carried by Worth and Pillow, and at the end of a desperate conflict of two hours and a half, the church or convent—the citadel of the strong line of defence along the rivulet of Churubusco—yielded to Twiggs's division, and threw out on all sides signals of surrender. The white flags, however, were not exhibited until the moment when the 3d infantry, under Captain Alexander,[15] had cleared the way by fire and bayonet, and had entered the work. Captain I. M. Smith[16] and Lieutenant O. L. Shepherd,[17] both of that regiment, with their companies, had the glory of leading the assault. The former received the surrender, and Captain Alexander instantly hung out from the balcony the colors of the gallant 3d. Major Dimick with a part of the 1st Artillery, serving as infantry, entered nearly abreast with the leading troops.

Captain Taylor's field battery, attached to Twiggs's division, opened its effective fire at an early moment upon the outworks of the convent and the tower of its church. Exposed to the severest fire of the enemy, the captain, his officers and men, won universal admiration; but at length much disabled in men and horses, the battery was by superior orders withdrawn from the action, thirty minutes before the surrender of the convent.

Those corps, excepting Taylor's battery, belonged to the brigade of Brigadier-General P. F. Smith, who closely directed the whole attack in front with his habitual coolness and ability; while Riley's brigade—the 2d and 7th Infantry, under Captain T. Morris[18] and Lieutenant Colonel Plympton respectively—vigorously engaged the right of the work and part of its rear. At the moment the Rifles, belonging to Smith's, were detached in support of Brigadier-General Shields's on our extreme left, and the 4th Artillery, acting as infantry, under Major Gardner, belonging to Riley's brigade, had been left in charge of the camp, trophies, etc., at Contreras. Twiggs's division at Churubusco had thus been deprived of the services of two of its most gallant and effective regiments.

The immediate results of this victory were:—the capture of seven field pieces, some ammunition, one color, three generals, and one thousand two hundred and sixty-one prisoners, including other officers.

Captains E. A. Capron and M. I. Burke, and Lieutenant S. Hoffman, all of the 1st Artillery, and Captain J. W. Anderson and Lieutenant Thomas Easley, both of the 2d Infantry—five officers of great merit—fell gallantly before this work.[19]

The capture of the enemy's citadel was the *fourth* great achievement of our arms in the same day.

It has been stated that some two hours and a half before, Pierce's, followed closely by the volunteer brigade—both under the command of Brigadier-General Shields—had been despatched to our left to turn the enemy's works;—to prevent the escape of the garrisons and to oppose the extension of the enemy's numerous corps from the rear upon and around our left.

Considering the inferior numbers of the two brigades, the objects of the movement were difficult to accomplish. Hence the reënforcement (the Rifles, etc.) sent forward a little later.

In a winding march of a mile around to the right, this temporary division found itself on the edge of an open wet meadow, near the road from San Antonio to the capital, and in the presence of some four thousand of the enemy's infantry, a little in rear of Churubusco, on that road. Establishing the right at a strong building, Shields extended his left parallel to the road, to outflank the enemy toward the capital. But the enemy extending his right supported by three thousand cavalry more rapidly (being favored by better ground), in the same direction, Shields concentrated the division about a hamlet and determined to attack in front. The battle was long, hot and varied; but ultimately, success crowned the zeal and gallantry of our troops, ably directed by their distinguished commander, Brigadier-General Shields. The 9th, 12th, and 15th Regiments, under Colonel Ransom, Captain Wood,[20] and Colonel Morgan respectively, of Pierce's brigade (Pillow's division), and the New York and South Carolina Volunteers, under Colonels Burnett and Butler,[21] respectively, of Shields's own brigade (Quitman's division), together with the mountain howitzer battery, now under Lieutenant Reno of the Ordnance Corps,[22] all shared in the glory of this action—our *fifth* victory in the same day.

Brigadier-General Pierce, from the hurt of the evening before—under pain and exhaustion—fainted in the action. Several other changes in command occurred on this field. Thus Colonel Morgan being severely wounded, the command of the 15th Infantry devolved on Lieutenant-Colonel Howard;[23] Colonel Burnett receiving a like wound, the command of the New York Volunteers fell to Lieutenant-Colonel Baxter;[24] and, on the fall of the lamented Colonel P. M. Butler—earlier badly wounded, but continuing to lead nobly in the hottest part of the battle—the command of the South Carolina Volunteers devolved—first, on Lieutenant-Colonel Dickinson, who being severely wounded (as before in the siege of Vera Cruz), the regiment ultimately fell under the orders of Major Gladden.[25]

Lieutenants David Adams and W. R. Williams of the same corps;[26] Captain Augustus Quarles and Lieutenant J. B. Goodman of the 15th,[27] and Lieutenant. E. Chandler,[28] New York Volunteers—all gallant officers, nobly fell in the same action.

Shields took three hundred and eighty prisoners, including officers; and it cannot be doubted that the rage of the conflict between him and the enemy, just in the rear of the *tête de pont* and the convent, had some influence on the surrender of those formidable defences.

As soon as the *tête de pont* was carried, the greater part of Worth's and Pillow's forces passed that bridge in rapid pursuit of the flying enemy. These distinguished generals, coming up with Brigadier-General Shields, now also victorious, the three continued to press upon the fugitives to within a mile and a half of the capital. Here, Colonel Harney, with a small part of his brigade of cavalry, rapidly passed to the front, and charged the enemy up to the nearest gate.

The cavalry charge was headed by Captain Kearny, of the 1st Dragoons, having in squadron with his own troop, that of Captain McReynolds of the 3d—making the usual escort to general headquarters; but, being early in the day detached for general service, was now under Colonel Harney's orders. The gallant captain not hearing the *recall,* that had been sounded, dashed up to the San Antonio gate, sabring in his way all who resisted. Of the seven officers of the squadron, Kearny lost his left arm; McReynolds and Lieutenant Lorimer Graham[29] were both severely wounded, and Lieutenant R. S. Ewell,[30] who succeeded to the command of the escort, had two horses killed under him. Major F. D. Mills,[31] of the 15th infantry, a volunteer in this charge, was killed at the gate.

So terminated the series of events which I have but feebly presented. My thanks were freely poured out on the different fields—to the abilities and science of generals and other officers—to the zeal and prowess of all—the rank and file included. But a reward infinitely higher—the applause of a grateful country and Government—will, I cannot doubt, be accorded, in due time, to so much merit of every sort, displayed by this glorious army, which has now overcome all difficulties—distance, climate, ground, fortifications, numbers.

It has in a single day, in many battles, as often defeated thirty-two thousand men;[32] made about three thousand prisoners, including eight generals (two of them ex-presidents) and two hundred and five other officers; killed or wounded four thousand of all ranks—besides entire corps dispersed and dissolved; captured thirty-seven pieces of ordnance—more than trebling our siege train and field batteries—with a large number of small arms, a full supply of ammunition of every kind, etc., etc.

These great results have overwhelmed the enemy. Our loss amounts to one thousand and fifty-three—*killed,* one hundred and thirty-nine, including sixteen officers; *wounded,* eight hundred and seventy-six, with sixty officers. The greater number of the dead and disabled were of the highest worth. Those under treatment, thanks to our very able medical officers, are generally doing well.

I regret having been obliged, on the 20th, to leave Major-General Quitman, an able commander, with a part of his division—the fine 2d Pennsylvania Volunteers, and the veteran detachment of United States' Marines—at our important depot, San Augustin. It was there that I had placed our sick and wounded; the siege, supply, and baggage trains. If these had been lost, the army would have been driven almost to despair; and considering the enemy's very great excess of numbers, and the many approaches to the depot, it might well have become, emphatically, *the post of honor.*

After so many victories, we might, with but little additional loss, have occupied the capital the same evening.[?] But Mr. Trist,[33] commissioner, etc., as well as myself, had been admonished by the best friends of peace—intelligent neutrals and some American residents—against precipitation; lest, by wantonly driving away the government and others—dishonored—we might scatter the elements of peace, excite a spirit of national desperation, and thus indefinitely postpone the hope of accommodation.* {There were other reasons such as are alluded to in my report of the capture of Vera Cruz. If we had proceeded to assault the city by daylight our loss would have been dangerously great, and if a little later in the night, the slain, on the other side, including men, women, and children, would have been frightful, because if the assailants stopped to make prisoners before occupying all the strongholds, they would soon become prisoners themselves. Other atrocities, by the victors, are, in such cases, inevitable. Pillage always follows, and seems authorized by the usage of war. Hence I promised (September 13), at the gates of Mexico, a contribution in lieu of pillage, in order to avoid the horrors in question, and the consequent loss of discipline and efficiency.}[34]

Deeply impressed with this danger, and remembering our mission—*to conquer a peace*—the army very cheerfully sacrificed to patriotism—to the great wish and want of our country—the *éclat*[35] that would have followed an entrance—sword in hand—into a great capital. Willing to leave something to this republic—of no immediate value to us—on which to rest her pride, and to recover temper—I halted our victorious corps at the gates of the city (at least for a time), and have them now cantoned in the neighboring villages, where they are well sheltered and supplied with all necessaries.

On the morning of the 21st, being about to take up battering or assaulting positions, to authorize me to summon the city to surrender, or to sign an armistice with a pledge to enter at once into negotiations for peace—a mission came out to propose a truce. Rejecting its terms, I despatched my contemplated note to President Santa Anna—omitting the summons.[36] The 22d, commissioners were appointed by the commanders of the two armies; the armistice was signed the 23d, and ratifications exchanged the 24th.

All matters in dispute between the two governments, have been thus happily turned over to their plenipotentiaries, who have now had several conferences, and with, I think, some hope of signing a treaty of peace.

There will be transmitted to the Adjutant-General reports from divisions, brigades, etc., on the foregoing operations, to which I must refer, with my hearty concurrence in the just applause bestowed on corps and individuals by their respective commanders. I have been able—this report being necessarily a summary—to bring out, comparatively, but little of individual merit not lying directly in the way of the narrative. Thus I doubt whether I have, in express terms, given my approbation and applause to the commanders of divisions and independent brigades; but left their fame upon higher grounds—the simple record of their great deeds and the brilliant results.* {*Litera scripta manet.*[37] In this edition of my reports of battles, etc., I, of course, expunge none of the praises therein bestowed on certain division and brigade commanders; but as a caution to future generals-in-chief I must say I soon had abundant reason to know, that I had in haste too confidently relied upon the partial statements of several of those commanders respecting their individual skill and prowess, and the merits of a few of their favorites—subordinates. I except from this remark, Generals Quitman, Shields, P. F. Smith, N. S. Clarke, Riley, and Cadwallader.}

To the staff, both general and personal, attached to general headquarters, I was again under high obligations for services in the field, as always in the bureaux. I add their names, etc.: Lieutenant-Colonel Hitchcock, Acting Inspector-General; Major J. L. Smith, Captain R. E. Lee (as distinguished for felicitous execution as for science and daring), Captain Mason, Lieutenants Stevens, Beauregard, Tower, G. W. Smith, George B. McClellan, and Foster—all of the Engineers; Major Turnbull, Captain J. McClellan, and Lieutenant Hardcastle, Topographical Engineers; Captain Huger and Lieutenant Hagner, of the Ordnance; Captains Irwin and Wayne, of the Quartermaster's Department; Captain Grayson, of the Commissariat; Surgeon-General Lawson, in his particular department; Captain H. L. Scott, Acting Adjutant-General; Lieutenant T. Williams, Aide-de-Camp, and Lieutenant Lay, Military Secretary.

Lieutenant Schuyler Hamilton,* another aide-de-camp, had a week before been thrown out of activity by a severe wound received in a successful charge of cavalry against cavalry, and four times his numbers; but on the 20th, I had the valuable services, as volunteer aids, of Majors Kirby and Van Buren, of the Pay Department, always eager for activity and distinction, and of a third, the gallant Major J. P. Gaines, of the Kentucky Volunteers.

> I have the honor to be, etc.,
> etc.,
> WINFIELD SCOTT.

Hon. WM. L. MARCY, Secretary of War.

{This gallant, intelligent officer being sent with a detachment of cavalry from Chalco to an iron foundery, some fifteen miles off, beyond Mira Flores, to make contingent arrangements for shots and shells—we having brought up but few of either, from the want of road power—returning, fell into an ambuscade, and though he cut his way through, was, while slaying one man in his front, pierced through the body with a lance, by another, and thus thrown *hors de combat*[38] for the remainder of the campaign. In 1861, he, as a private, was in one of the first regiments of volunteers that hastened to the defence of Washington; again became one of my aides-de-camp, and, in succession, a distinguished brigadier and major-general of volunteers in the Southwest.}

CHAPTER XXXII

ARMISTICE–NEGOTIATIONS–HOSTILITIES RENEWED–BATTLE OF MOLINOS DEL REY– CAPTURE OF CHAPULTEPEC AND MEXICO

Report No. 33.
HEADQUARTERS OF THE ARMY,
TACUBAYA, NEAR MEXICO,
September 11, 1847.

SIR:

I have heretofore reported that I had, August 24, concluded an armistice with President Santa Anna, which was promptly followed by meetings between Mr. Trist and Mexican commissioners appointed to treat of peace.

Negotiations were actively continued with, as was understood, some prospect of a successful result up to the 2d instant, when our commissioner handed in his *ultimatum* (on boundaries), and the negotiators adjourned to meet again on the 6th.

Some infractions of the truce in respect to our supplies from the city, were earlier committed, followed by apologies on the part of the enemy.[1] These vexations I was willing to put down to the imbecility of the government, and waived any pointed demands of reparation while any hope remained of a satisfactory termination of the war. But on the 5th, and more fully on the 6th, I learned that as soon as the *ultimatum* had been considered in a grand council of ministers and others, President Santa Anna on the 4th or 5th, without giving me the slightest notice, actively recommended strengthening the military defences of the city, in gross violation of the 3d article of the armistice.

On that information, which has since received the fullest verification, I addressed to him my note of the 6th. His reply, dated the same day, received the next morning, was absolutely and notoriously false, both in recrimination and explanation. I enclose copies of both papers, and have had no subsequent correspondence with the enemy.

Being delayed by the terms of the armistice more than two weeks, we had now, late on the 7th, to begin to reconnoitre the different approaches to the city, within our reach, before I could lay down any definitive plan of attack.

The same afternoon a large body of the enemy was discovered hovering about the *Molinos del Rey,* within a mile and a third of this village, where I am quartered with the general staff and Worth's division.

It might have been supposed that an attack upon us was intended; but knowing the great value to the enemy of those mills (*Molinos del Rey*), containing a cannon foundery, with a large deposite of powder in *Casa Mata* near them; and having heard two days before that many church bells had been sent out to be cast into guns, the enemy's movement was easily understood, and I resolved at once to drive him early the next morning, to seize the powder, and to destroy the foundery.

Another motive for this decision—leaving the general plan of attack upon the city for full reconnaissance—was, that we knew our recent captures had left the enemy not a fourth of the guns necessary to arm, all at the same time, the strong works at each of the eight city gates; and we could not cut the communication between the foundry and the capital without first taking the formidable castle on the heights of Chapultepec, which overlooked both and stood between.

For this difficult operation we were not entirely ready, and moreover we might altogether neglect the castle, if, as we then hoped, our reconnaissances should prove that the distant southern approaches to the city were more eligible than this southwestern one.

Hence the decision promptly taken, the execution of which was assigned to Brevet Major-General Worth, whose division was reënforced with Cadwallader's brigade of Pillow's division, three squadrons of dragoons under Major Sumner, and some heavy guns of the siege train under Captain Huger of the Ordnance, and Captain Drum of the 4th Artillery—two officers of the highest merit.

For the decisive and brilliant results, I beg to refer to the report of the immediate commander, Major-General Worth, in whose commendations of the gallant officers and men—dead and living—I heartily concur; having witnessed, but with little interference, their noble devotion to fame and to country.

The enemy having several times reënforced his line, and the action soon becoming much more general than I had expected, I called up, from the distance of three miles, first Major-General Pillow, with his remaining brigade (Pierce's), and next Riley's brigade of Twiggs's division—leaving his other brigade (Smith's) in observation at San Angel. Those corps approached with zeal and rapidity; but the battle was won just as Brigadier-General Pierce reached the ground, and had interposed his corps between Garland's brigade (Worth's division) and the retreating enemy.[2]

The accompanying report mentions, with just commendation, two of my volunteer aids—Major Kirby, Paymaster, and Major Gaines, of the Kentucky Volunteers. I also had the valuable services, on the same field, of several other officers of my staff, general and personal: Lieutenant-Colonel Hitchcock, Acting Inspector-General; Captain R. E. Lee, Engineer; Captain Irwin, Chief Quartermaster; Captain Grayson, Chief Commissary; Captain H. L. Scott, Acting Adjutant General; Lieutenant Williams, Aide-de-Camp; and Lieutenant Lay, Military Secretary.

I have the honor to be, etc.,
etc.,
WINFIELD SCOTT.

Hon. WM. L. Marcy, Secretary of War.

Report No. 34
HEADQUARTERS OF THE ARMY,
NATIONAL PALACE OF MEXICO,
September 18, 1847.

SIR:

At the end of another series of arduous and brilliant operations, of more than forty-eight hours' continuance, this glorious army hoisted, on the morning of the 14th, the colors of the United States on the walls of this palace.

The victory of the 8th, at the Molinos del Rey, was followed by daring reconnaissances on the part of our distinguished engineers—Captain Lee, Lieutenants Beauregard, Stevens and Tower—Major Smith, senior, being sick, and Captain Mason, third in rank, wounded. Their operations were directed principally to the south—toward the gates of the Piedad, San Angel, (Niño Perdido), San Antonio, and the Paseo de la Viga.[3]

This city stands on a slight swell of ground, near the centre of an irregular basin, and is girdled with a ditch in its greater extent—a navigable canal of great breadth and depth—very difficult to bridge in the presence of an enemy, and serving at once for drainage, custom-house purposes, and military defence; leaving eight entrances or gates, over arches—each of which we found defended by a system of strong works, that seemed to require nothing but some men and guns to be impregnable.

Outside and within the cross-fires of those gates, we found to the south other obstacles but little less formidable. All the approaches near the city are over elevated causeways, cut in many places (to oppose us), and flanked on both sides by ditches, also of unusual dimensions. The numerous cross-roads are flanked in like manner, having bridges at the intersections, recently broken. The meadows thus checkered, are, moreover, in many spots, under water or marshy; for, it will be remembered, we were in the midst of the wet season, though with less rain than usual, and we could not wait for the fall of the neighboring lakes and the consequent drainage of the wet grounds at the edge of the city—the lowest in the whole basin.

After a close personal survey of the southern gates, covered by Pillow's division and Riley's brigade of Twiggs's—with four times our numbers concentrated in our immediate front—I determined, on the 11th, to avoid that network of obstacle, and to seek, by a sudden inversion to the southwest and west, less unfavorable approaches.

To economize the lives of our gallant officers and men, as well as to insure success, it became indispensable that this resolution should be long masked from the enemy; and again, that the new movement when discovered, should be mistaken for a feint, and the old as indicating our true and ultimate point of attack.

Accordingly, on the spot, the 11th, I ordered Quitman's division from Coyoacan, to join Pillow *by daylight* before the southern gates, and then that the two major-generals with their divisions, should *by night* proceed (two miles) to join me at Tacubaya, where I was quartered with Worth's division. Twiggs, with Riley's brigade and Captains Taylor's and Steptoe's field batteries[4]—the latter of 12-pounders—was left in front of those gates to manoeuvre, to threaten, or to make false attacks, in order to occupy and deceive the enemy. Twiggs's other brigade (Smith's) was left at supporting distance in the rear at San Angel, till the morning of the 13th, and also to support our general depot at Mixcoac. The stratagem against the south was admirably executed throughout the 12th and down to the afternoon of the 13th, when it was too late for the enemy to recover from the effects of his delusion.

The first step in the new movement was to carry Chapultepec, a natural and isolated mound of great elevation, strongly fortified at its base, on its acclivities and heights. Besides a numerous garrison, here was the military college of the republic, with a large number of sub-lieutenants and other students. Those works were within direct gunshot of the village of Tacubaya, and, until carried, we could not approach the city on the west without making a circuit too wide and too hazardous.

In the course of the same night (that of the 11th), heavy batteries within easy ranges were established. No. 1, on our right, under the command of Captain Drum, 4th Artillery (relieved the next day for some hours by Lieutenant Andrews[5] of the 3d), and No. 2, commanded by Lieutenant Hagner, Ordnance—both supported by Quitman's division. Nos. 3 and 4, on the opposite side, supported by Pillow's division, were commanded, the former by Captain Brooks[6] and Lieutenant S. S. Anderson,[7] 2d Artillery, alternately, and the latter by Lieutenant Stone, Ordnance. The batteries were traced by Captain Huger, Ordnance, and Captain Lee, Engineer, and constructed by them with the able assistance of the young officers of those corps and of the artillery.

To prepare for an assault, it was foreseen that the play of the batteries might run into the second day; but recent captures had not only trebled our siege pieces, but also our ammunition; and we knew that we should greatly augment both by carrying the place. I was, therefore, in no haste in ordering an assault before the works were well crippled by our missiles.

The bombardment and cannonade, under the direction of Captain Huger, were commenced early in the morning of the 12th. Before nightfall, which necessarily stopped our batteries, we had perceived that a good impression had been made on the castle and its outworks, and that a large body of the enemy had remained outside, toward the city, from an early hour, to avoid our fire, but to be at hand on its cessation in order to reënforce the garrison against an assault. The same outside force was discovered the next morning after our batteries had reopened upon the castle, by which we again reduced its garrison to the minimum needed for the guns.

Pillow and Quitman had been in position since early in the night of the 11th. Major-General Worth was now ordered to hold his division in reserve, near the foundery, to support Pillow; and Brigadier-General Smith, of Twiggs's division, had just arrived with his brigade from Piedad (two miles), to support Quitman. Twiggs's guns before the southern gates, again reminded us, as the day before, that he, with Riley's brigade and Taylor's and Steptoe's batteries, was in activity threatening the southern gates, and thus holding a great part of the Mexican army on the defensive.

Worth's division furnished Pillow's attack with an assaulting party of some two hundred and fifty volunteer officers and men, under Captain McKenzie,[8] of the 2d Artillery; and Twiggs's division supplied a similar one, commanded by Captain Casey,[9] 2d Infantry, to Quitman. Each of these little columns was furnished with scaling ladders.

The signal I had appointed for the attack was the momentary cessation of fire on the part of our heavy batteries. About eight o'clock in the morning of the 13th, judging that the time had arrived, by the effect of the missiles we had thrown, I sent an aide-de-camp to Pillow, and another to Quitman, with notice that the concerted signal was about to be given. Both columns now advanced with an alacrity that gave assurance of prompt success. The batteries, seizing opportunities, threw shots and shells upon the enemy over the heads of our men with good effect, particularly at every attempt to reënforce the works from without to meet our assault.

Major-General Pillow's approach on the west side, lay through an open grove filled with sharpshooters, who were speedily dislodged: when, being up with the front of the attack, and emerging into open space at the foot of a rocky acclivity, that gallant leader was struck down by an agonizing wound. The immediate command devolved to Brigadier-General Cadwallader, in the absence of the senior brigadier (Pierce) of the same division—an invalid since the events of August 19. On a previous call of Pillow, Worth had just sent him a reënforcement— Colonel Clarke's brigade.

The broken acclivity was still to be ascended, and a strong redoubt, midway, to be carried, before reaching the castle on the heights. The advance of our brave men, led by brave officers, though necessarily slow, was unwavering, over rocks, chasms, and mines, and under the hottest fire of cannon and musketry. The redoubt now yielded to resistless valor, and the shouts that followed announced to the castle the fate that impended. The enemy were steadily driven from shelter to shelter. The retreat allowed not time to fire a single mine, without the certainty of blowing up friend and foe. Those who, at a distance, attempted to apply matches to the long trains, were shot down by our men. There was death below, as well as above ground. At length the ditch and wall of the main work were reached; the scaling ladders were brought up and planted by the storming parties; some of the daring spirits, first in the assault, were cast down—killed or wounded; but a lodgment was soon made; streams of heroes followed; all opposition was overcome, and several of our regimental colors flung' out from the upper walls, amidst long-continued shouts and cheers, which sent dismay into the capital. No scene could have been more animating or glorious.

Major-General Quitman, nobly supported by Brigadier-Generals Shields and Smith (P. F.), his other officers and men, was up with the part assigned him. Simultaneously with the movement on the west, he had gallantly approached the southeast of the same works over a causeway with cuts and batteries, and defended by an army strongly posted outside, to the east of the works. Those formidable obstacles Quitman had to face, with but little shelter for his troops or space for manoeu-vring. Deep ditches, flanking the causeway, made it difficult to cross on either side into the adjoining meadows, and these again were inter-sected by other ditches. Smith and his brigade had been early thrown out to make a sweep to the right, in order to present a front against the enemy's line (outside), and to turn two intervening batteries, near the foot of Chapultepec.

This movement was also intended to support Quitman's storming parties, both on the causeway. The first of these, furnished by Twiggs's division, was commanded in succession by Captain Casey, 2d Infantry, and Captain Paul,[10] 7th Infantry, after Casey had been severely wounded; and the second, originally under the gallant Major Twiggs,[11] Marine Corps, killed, and then Captain Miller,[12] 2d Pennsylvania Volunteers. The storming party, now commanded by Captain Paul, seconded by Captain Roberts[13] of the Rifles, Lieutenant Stewart,[14] and others of the same reg-iment, Smith's brigade, carried the two batteries in the road, took some guns, with many prisoners, and drove the enemy posted behind in sup-port. The New York and South Carolina Volunteers (Shields's brigade), and the 2d Pennsylvania Volunteers, all on the left of Quitman's line, together with portions of his storming parties, crossed the meadows in front under a heavy fire, and entered the outer enclosure of Chapultepec just in time to join in the final assault from the west.

Besides Major-Generals Pillow and Quitman, Brigadier-Generals Shields, Smith, and Cadwallader, the following are the officers and corps most distinguished in those brilliant operations: The Voltigeur regiment, in two detachments, commanded respectively by Colonel Andrews[15] and Lieutenant-Colonel Joseph Johnston—the latter mostly in the lead, accompanied by Major Caldwell;[16] Captains Barnard[17] and C. J. Biddle,[18] of the same regiment—the former the first to plant a reg-imental color, and the latter among the first in the assault;—the storm-ing party of Worth's division, under Captain McKenzie, 2d Artillery, with Lieutenant Selden,[19] 8th Infantry, early on the ladder and badly wounded; Lieutenant Armistead,[20] 6th Infantry, the first to leap into the ditch to plant a ladder; Lieutenant Rogers, of the 4th, and J. P. Smith, of the 5th Infantry—both mortally wounded;[21] the 9th Infantry, under Colonel Ransom, who was killed while gallantly leading that gallant reg-iment; the 15th Infantry, under Lieutenant-Colonel Howard and Major Woods,[22] with Captain Chase,[23] whose company gallantly carried the re-doubt, midway up the acclivity;—Colonel Clarke's brigade (Worth's divi-sion), consisting of the 5th, 8th, and part of the 6th regiments of infantry, commanded respectively by Captain Chapman, Major Montgomery, and Lieutenant Edward Johnson[24]—the latter specially noticed—with Lieutenants Longstreet (badly wounded, advancing, colors in hand), Pickett, and Merchant—the last three of the 8th Infantry;[25]—portions of the United States' Marines, New York, South Carolina, and 2d Pennsylvania Volunteers, which, delayed with their division (Quitman's) by the hot engagement below, arrived just in time to participate in the assault of the heights; particularly a detachment, under Lieutenant Reed,[26] New York Volunteers, consisting of a company of the same, with one of marines; and another detachment, a portion of the storming party (Twiggs's division, serving with Quitman), under Lieutenant Steele,[27] 2d Infantry, after the fall of Lieutenant Gantt,[28] 7th Infantry.

In this connection, it is but just to recall the decisive effect of the heavy batteries, Nos. 1, 2, 3, and 4, commanded by those excellent officers, Captain Drum, 4th Artillery, assisted by Lieutenants Benjamin[29] and Porter[30] of his own company; Captain Brooks and Lieutenant Anderson, 2d Artillery, assisted by Lieutenant Russell,[31] 4th Infantry, a volunteer; Lieutenants Hagner and Stone, of the Ordnance, and Lieutenant Andrews, 3d Artillery—the whole superintended by Captain Huger, Chief of Ordnance with this army, an officer distinguished by every kind of merit. The Mountain Howitzer Battery, under Lieutenant Reno, of the Ordnance, deserves also to be particularly mentioned. Attached to the Voltigeurs, it followed the movements of that regiment, and again won applause.

In adding to the list of individuals of conspicuous merit, I must limit myself to a few of the many names which might be enumerated:—Captain Hooker,[32] Assistant Adjutant-General, who won special applause, successively, in the staff of Pillow and Cadwallader; Lieutenant Lovell,[33] 4th Artillery (wounded), chief of Quitman's staff; Captain Page,[34] Assistant Adjutant-General (wounded), and Lieutenant Hammond, 3d Artillery, both of Shields's staff, and Lieutenant Van Dorn (7th Infantry), Aide-de-Camp to Brigadier-General Smith.

Those operations all occurred on the west, southeast, and heights of Chapultepec. To the north, and at the base of the mound, inaccessible on that side, the 11th Infantry, under Lieutenant-Colonel Hebert,[35] the 14th, under Colonel Trousdale, and Captain Magruder's field battery, 1st Artillery, one section advanced under Lieutenant Jackson,[36] all of Pillow's division, had, at the same time, some spirited affairs against superior numbers, driving the enemy from a battery in the road, and capturing a gun. In these, the officers and corps named gained merited praise. Colonel Trousdale, the commander, though twice wounded, continued on duty until the heights were carried.

Early in the morning of the 13th, I repeated the orders of the night before to Major-General Worth, to be with his division at hand to support the movement of Major-General Pillow from our left. The latter seems soon to have called for that entire division, standing momentarily in reserve, and Worth sent him Colonel Clarke's brigade. The call, if not unnecessary, was at least, from the circumstances, unknown to me at the time; for, soon observing that the very large body of the enemy, in the road in front of Major-General Quitman's right, was receiving reënforcements from the city—less than a mile and a half to the east—I sent instructions to Worth, on our opposite flank, to turn Chapultepec with his division, and to proceed cautiously by the road at its, northern base, in order, if not met by very superior numbers, to threaten or to attack in rear that body of the enemy. The movement it was also believed could not fail to distract and to intimidate the enemy generally.

Worth promptly advanced with his remaining brigade—Colonel Garland's—Lieutenant- Colonel C. F. Smith's light battalion, Lieutenant-Colonel Duncan's field battery—all of his division—and three squadrons of dragoons, under Major Sumner, which I had just ordered up to join in the movement.

Having turned the forest on the west, and arriving opposite to the north centre of Chapultepec, Worth came up with the troops in the road, under Colonel Trousdale, and aided, by a flank movement of a part of Garland's brigade, in taking the one-gun breastwork, then under the fire of Lieutenant Jackson's section of Captain Magruder's field battery. Continuing to advance, this division passed Chapultepec, attacking the right of the enemy's line, resting on that road, about the moment of the general retreat consequent upon the capture of the formidable castle and its outworks.

Arriving some minutes later, and mounting to the top of the castle, the whole field to the east lay plainly under my view.

There are two routes from Chapultepec to the capital—the one on the right entering the same gate, Belén, with the road from the south, *via* Piedad; and the other obliquing to the left, to intersect the great western, or San Cosme road, in a suburb outside of the gate of San Cosme.

Each of these routes (an elevated causeway) presents a double roadway on the sides of an aqueduct of strong masonry, and great height, resting oft open arches and massive pillars, which, together, afford fine points both for attack and defence. The sideways of both aqueducts were, moreover, defended by many strong breastworks at the gates, and before reaching them. As we had expected, we found the four tracks unusually dry and solid for the season.

Worth and Quitman were prompt in pursuing the retreating enemy—the former by the San Cosme aqueduct, and the latter along that of Belén.[37] Each had now advanced some hundred yards.

Deeming it all-important to profit by our successes, and the consequent dismay of the enemy, which could not be otherwise than general, I hastened to despatch from Chapultepec, first Clarke's brigade, and then Cadwallader's, to the support of Worth, and gave orders that the necessary heavy guns should follow. Pierce's brigade was, at the same time, sent to Quitman, and in the course of the afternoon I caused some additional siege pieces to be added to his train. Then after designating the 15th Infantry, under Lieutenant-Colonel Howard—Morgan, the colonel, had been disabled by a wound at Churubusco—as the garrison of Chapultepec, and giving directions for the care of the prisoners of war, the captured ordnance and ordnance stores, I proceeded to join the advance of Worth, within the suburb, and beyond the turn at the junction of the aqueduct with the great highway from the west to the gate of San Cosme.

At this junction of roads, we first passed one of those formidable systems of city defences, spoken of above, and it had not a gun!—a strong proof, 1. That the enemy had expected us to fail in the attack upon Chapultepec, even if we meant anything more than a feint; 2. That in either case, we designed, in his belief, to return and double our forces against the southern gates, a delusion kept up by the active demonstrations of Twiggs with the forces posted on that side; and 3. That advancing rapidly from the reduction of Chapultepec, the enemy had not time to shift guns—our previous captures had left him, comparatively, but few—from the southern gates.

Within those disgarnished works, I found our troops engaged in a street fight against the enemy posted in gardens, at windows and on housetops—all flat, with parapets. Worth ordered forward the mountain howitzers of Cadwallader's brigade, preceded by skirmishers and pioneers, with pick-axes and crow-bars, to force windows and doors, or to burrow through walls. The assailants were soon on an equality of position fatal to the enemy. By eight o'clock in the evening, Worth had carried two batteries in this suburb. According to my instructions, he here posted guards and sentinels, and placed his troops under shelter for the night, *within* the San Cosme gate (custom-house).

I had gone back to the foot of Chapultepec, the point from which the two aqueducts begin to diverge, some hours earlier, in order to be near that new dépôt, and in easy communication with Quitman and Twiggs, as well as with Worth.

From this point I ordered all detachments and stragglers to their respective corps, then in advance; sent to Quitman additional siege guns, ammunition, intrenching tools; directed Twiggs's remaining brigade (Riley's) from Piedad, to support Worth; and Captain Steptoe's field battery, also at Piedad, to rejoin Quitman's division.

I had been, from the first, well aware that the western or San Cosme, was the less difficult route to the centre and conquest of the capital; and therefore intended that Quitman should only manoeuvre and threaten the Belén or southwestern gate, in order to favor the main attack by Worth—knowing that the strong defences at the Belén were directly under the guns of the much stronger fortress, called *the citadel,* just within. Both of these defences of the enemy were also within easy supporting distance from the San Angel (or Niño Perdido) and San Antonio gates. Hence the greater support, in numbers, given to Worth's movement as the main attack.

Those views I repeatedly, in the course of the day, communicated to Major-General Quitman; but being in hot pursuit, gallant himself, and ably supported by Brigadier-Generals Shields and Smith—Shields badly wounded before Chapultepec and refusing to retire—as well as by all the officers and men of the column, Quitman continued to press forward, under flank and direct fires, carried an intermediate battery of two guns, and then the gate, before two o'clock in the afternoon, but not without proportionate loss, increased by his steady maintenance of that position.

Here, of the heavy battery—4th Artillery—Captain Drum and Lieutenant Benjamin were mortally wounded,[38] and Lieutenant Porter, its third in rank, slightly. The loss of these two most distinguished officers the army will long mourn. Lieutenants I. B. Moragne and William Canty, of the South Carolina Volunteers,[39] also of high merit, fell on the same occasion—besides many of our bravest non-commissioned officers and men, particularly in Captain Drum's veteran company. I cannot in this place, give names or numbers; but full returns of the killed and wounded of all corps, in their recent operations, will accompany this report.

Quitman, within the city, adding several new defences to the position he had won, and sheltering his corps as well as practicable, now awaited the return of daylight under the guns of the formidable citadel, yet to be subdued.

At about four o'clock next morning (September 14), a deputation of the *ayuntamiento* (city council) waited upon me to report that the Federal Government and the army of Mexico had fled from the capital some three hours before, and to demand terms of capitulation in favor of the church, the citizens, and the municipal authorities. I promptly replied, that I would sign no capitulation; that the city had been virtually in our possession from the time of the lodgments effected by Worth and Quitman the day before; that I regretted the silent escape of the Mexican army; that I should levy upon the city a moderate contribution, for special purposes; and that the American army should come under no terms, not *self*-imposed—such only as its own honor, the dignity of the United States, and the spirit of the age, should, in my opinion, imperiously demand and impose.

For the terms so imposed, I refer the department to subsequent general orders, Nos. 287 and 289 (paragraphs 7, 8, and 9, of the latter), copies of which are herewith enclosed.

At the termination of the interview with the city deputation, I communicated, about daylight, orders to Worth and Quitman to advance slowly and cautiously (to guard against treachery) toward the heart of the city, and to occupy its stronger and more commanding points. Quitman proceeded to the great *plaza* or square, planted guards, and hoisted the colors of the United States on the national palace—containing the Halls of Congress and Executive apartments of Federal Mexico. In this grateful service, Quitman might have been anticipated by Worth, but for my express orders, halting the latter at the head of the *Alameda* (a green park), within three squares of that goal of general ambition.

The capital, however, was not taken by any one or two corps, but by the talent, the science, the gallantry, the vigor of this entire army. In the glorious conquest, all had contributed—early and powerfully—the killed, the wounded, and *the fit for duty*—at Vera Cruz, Cerro Gordo, Contreras, San Antonio, Churubusco (three battles), the Molinos del Rey, and Chapultepec—as much as those who fought at the gates of Belén and San Cosme.

Soon after we had entered, and were in the act of occupying the city, a fire was opened upon us from the flat roofs of the houses, from windows and corners of streets, by some two thousand convicts, liberated the night before, by the flying Government—joined by, perhaps, as many Mexican soldiers, who had disbanded themselves and thrown off their uniforms. This unlawful war lasted more than twenty-four hours, in spite of the exertions of the municipal authorities, and was not put down till we had lost many men, including several officers, killed or wounded, and had punished the miscreants. Their objects were to gratify national hatred; and, in the general alarm and confusion, to plunder the wealthy inhabitants—particularly the deserted houses. But families are now generally returning; business of every kind has been resumed, and the city is already tranquil and cheerful, under the admirable conduct (with exceptions very few and trifling) of our gallant troops.

This army has been more disgusted than surprised that, by some sinister process on the part of certain individuals at home, its numbers have been, generally, almost trebled in our public papers—beginning at Washington.

Leaving, as we all feared, inadequate garrisons at Vera Cruz, Perote, and Puebla—with much larger hospitals; and being obliged, most reluctantly, from the same cause (general paucity of numbers) to abandon Jalapa, we marched [August 7–10] from Puebla with only ten thousand seven hundred and thirty-eight rank and file. This number includes the garrison of Jalapa, and the two thousand four hundred and twenty-nine men brought up by Brigadier-General Pierce, August 6.

At Contreras, Churubusco, etc. [August 20], we had but eight thousand four hundred and ninety-seven men engaged—after deducting the garrison of San Augustin (our general dépôt), the intermediate sick and the dead; at the Molinos del Rey (September 8), but three brigades, with some cavalry and artillery-making in all three thousand two hundred and fifty-one men—were in the battle; in the two days—September 12 and 13 our whole operating force, after deducting again the recent killed, wounded, and sick, together with the garrison of Mixcoac (the then general dépôt) and that of Tacubaya, was but seven thousand one hundred and eighty; and, finally, after deducting the new garrison of Chapultepec, with the killed and wounded of the two days, we took possession (September 14) of this great capital with less than six thousand men! And I reassert, upon accumulated and unquestionable evidence, that, in not one of these conflicts, was this army opposed by fewer than three and a half times its numbers—in several of them, by a yet greater excess.[40]

I recapitulate our losses since we arrived in the basin of Mexico:

August 19, 20: *Killed,* 137, including 14 officers. *Wounded,* 877, including 62 officers. *Missing* (probably killed), 38 rank and file. *Total,* 1,052.

September 8: *Killed,* 116, including 9 officers. *Wounded,* 665, including 49 officers. *Missing,* 18 rank and file. *Total,* 789.

September 12, 13, 14: *Killed,* 130, including 10 officers. *Wounded,* 703, including 68 officers. *Missing,* 29 rank and file. *Total,* 862.

Grand total of losses, 2,703, including 383 officers.

On the other hand, this small force has beaten on the same occasions, in view of their capital, the whole Mexican army, of (at the beginning) thirty-odd thousand men—posted, always, in chosen positions, behind intrenchments, or more formidable defences of nature and art; killed or wounded, of that number, more than seven thousand officers and men; taken 3,730 prisoners, one-seventh officers, including thirteen generals, of whom three had been presidents of this republic; captured more than twenty colors and standards, seventy-five pieces of ordnance, besides fifty-seven wall pieces, twenty thousand small arms,* an immense quantity of shots, shells, powder, etc., etc. {Besides those in the hands of prisoners. The twenty thousand new muskets (British manufacture) found in the citadel, were used in a novel way. Iron being scarce in the interior, the barrels made excellent shoes for our horses and mules, and the brass cuffs or bands were worked up into spear heads for the color-staffs, and spurs for the cavalry and all mounted officers.}

Of that enemy, once so formidable in numbers, appointments, artillery, etc., twenty-odd thousand have disbanded themselves in despair, leaving, as is known, not more than three fragments—the largest about two thousand five hundred—now wandering in different directions, without magazines or a military chest, and living *at free quarters* upon their own people.

General Santa Anna, himself a fugitive, is believed to be on the point of resigning the chief magistracy, and escaping to neutral Guatemala. A new President, no doubt, will soon be declared, and the Federal Congress is expected to reassemble at Queretaro, one hundred and twenty-five miles north of this, on the Zacatecas road, some time in October. I have seen and given safe conduct through this city to several of its members. The Government will find itself without resources; no army, no arsenals, no magazines, and but little revenue, internal or external. Still such is the obstinacy, or rather infatuation, of this people, that it is very doubtful whether the new authorities will dare to sue for peace on the terms which, in the recent negotiations, were made known by our minister.

****

In conclusion, I beg to enumerate, once more, with due commendation and thanks, the distinguished staff officers, general and personal, who, in our last operations in front of the enemy accompanied me, and communicated orders to every point and through every danger. Lieutenant—Colonel Hitchcock, Acting Inspector-General; Major Turnbull and Lieutenant Hardcastle, Topographical Engineers; Major Kirby, Chief Paymaster; Captain Irwin, Chief Quartermaster; Captain Grayson, Chief Commissary; Captain H. L. Scott, Chief in the Adjutant-General's Department; Lieutenant Williams, Aide-de-Camp; Lieutenant Lay, Military Secretary, and Major J. P. Gaines, Kentucky Cavalry, Volunteer Aide-de-Camp. Captain Lee, Engineer, so constantly distinguished, also bore important orders from me (September 13) until he fainted from a wound and the loss of two nights' sleep at the batteries. Lieutenants Beauregard, Stevens, and Tower, all wounded, were employed with the divisions, and Lieutenants G. W. Smith, and G. B. McClellan, with the company of Sappers and Miners. Those five lieutenants of engineers, like their captain, won the admiration of all about them. The Ordnance officers, Captain Huger, Lieutenants Hagner, Stone, and Reno, were highly effective, and distinguished at the several batteries; and I may add that Captain McKinstry, Assistant Quartermaster, at the close of the operations, executed several important commissions for me as a special volunteer.

Surgeon-General Lawson, and the medical staff generally, were skilful and untiring in and out of fire, in ministering to the numerous wounded.

To illustrate the operations in this basin, I enclose two beautiful drawings, prepared under the directions of Major Turnbull, mostly from actual survey.

> I have the honor to be, etc.,
> etc.,
> WINFIELD SCOTT.

Hon. Wm. L. MARCY, Secretary of War.
The foregoing reports are taken from Ex. Doc. 60 (H. of R. April 28, 1848), beginning at p. 1046.

The aides-de-camp engaged in copying the original sheets as they were written, said to me several times: "Why, General! you have understated the general result." I replied: "Mum! If our countrymen believe what is given, we may be content; whereas if I tell the whole truth, they may say—'It is all a romance.'"

Under a brilliant sun, I entered the city at the head of the cavalry, cheered by Worth's division of regulars drawn up in the order of battle in the Alameda, and by Quitman's division of volunteers in the grand plaza between the National Palace and the Cathedral—all the bands playing, in succession, *Hail Columbia, Washington's March, Yankee Doodle, Hail to the Chief,* etc. Even the inhabitants, catching the enthusiasm of the moment, filled the windows and lined the parapets, cheering the cavalcade as it passed at the gallop.

On entering the Palace, the following order was early published to the army:

GENERAL ORDERS. HEADQUARTERS OF THE ARMY,
No. 286. NATIONAL PALACE OF MEXICO,
September, 1847.

The General-in-Chief calls upon his brethren in arms to return, both in public and private worship, thanks and gratitude to God for the signal triumphs which they have recently achieved for their country.

Beginning with the 19th of August, and ending the 14th instant, this army has gallantly fought its way through the fields and forts of Contreras, San Antonio, Churubusco, Molino del Rey, Chapultepec, and the gates of San Cosme and Tacubaya or Belén, into the capital of Mexico.

When the very limited numbers who have performed those brilliant deeds shall have become known, the world will be astonished, and our own countrymen filled with joy and admiration.

But all is not yet done. The enemy, though scattered and dismayed, has still many fragments of his late army hovering about us, and, aided by an exasperated population, he may again reunite in treble our numbers, and fall upon us to advantage if we rest inactive on the security of past victories.

Compactness, vigilance, and discipline are, therefore, our only securities. Let every good officer and man look to those cautions and enjoin them upon all others.

By command of Major-General Scott.

H. L. SCOTT,
A. A.-General.

The day after entering the capital the British consul-general called to ask for an escort of cavalry, and a written passport in behalf of the young and beautiful wife of President Santa Anna, to enable her to follow her husband. Both were, of course, promised; but, finally, she only accepted the passport, deeming that a sufficient protection.

At first, I said to the consul I would do myself the honor to make my respects to the fair lady in person; but reflecting a moment, I gave up the visit, as, under the circumstances, it might by others be regarded as a vaunt on my part.

CHAPTER XXXIII

BRILLIANT ALLUSION TO THE CAMPAIGN–RETALIATORY MEASURES–MARTIAL LAW–SAFEGUARDS–PROCLAMATION–DEFENCE OF PUEBLA

So ended the second conquest of Mexico, which has been beautifully, though extravagantly alluded to by a distinguished person—Sir Henry Bulwer, sometime British Minister accredited to this country.[1] At the celebration of St. Andrew's Day, New York, November 30, 1850, Sir Henry being called up, brought into parallelism two British subjects with two Americans—thus:

"All [present] were children of St. Andrew, or to say the least, nephews of St. George. All were birds of the same feather, though they might roost on different trees; members of the same family, though they might be adopted by different lands. Even their national history was individualized by the same names. Who was the first martyr to religious liberty in Scotland? One PATRICK HAMILTON (if he did not mistake), who was burnt in front of the College of St. Salvador, in Edinburgh, by an archbishop of St. Andrew's.[2] Who was the foremost amongst the wisest, because the most moderate of the early champions of civil liberty in America? ALEXANDER HAMILTON, who perished beneath the cliffs of Weehawken, also a victim to a barbarous custom and the courage with which he vindicated his opinions. Nor was this all. Passing from the royal house of Hamilton to the princely house of Buccleuch, might he not say, in later and more recent times, that if Waverley and Guy Mannering had made the name of Scott immortal, on one side of the Atlantic, Cerro Gordo and Churubusco had equally immortalized it on the other.[3] If the novelist had given the garb of truth to fiction, had not the warrior given to truth the air of romance?"—*National Intelligencer,* December 4, 1850.

No doubt the conquest so splendidly alluded to by the orator, was mainly due to the science and prowess of the army. But valor and professional science could not alone have dictated a treaty of peace with double our numbers, in double the time, and with double the loss of life, without the measures of conciliation perseveringly adhered to, the perfect discipline and order maintained in the army. Those measures heretofore alluded to are here recorded:

The *martial law order,* often alluded to above, page 200, etc., was first published at Tampico, February 19, 1847. The second edition was reprinted at Vera Cruz, the third at Puebla, and the last as follows:

GENERAL ORDERS,   HEADQUARTERS OF TILE ARMY,
No. 287.   NATIONAL PALACE OF MEXICO,
                              September 17, 1847.

The General-in-Chief republishes, with important additions, the General Orders, No. 20, of February 19, 1847 (declaring MARTIAL LAW*), to govern all who may be concerned.*

1. It is still to be apprehended that many grave offences, not provided for in the Act of Congress "establishing rules and articles for the government of the armies of the United States," approved April 10, 1806, may again be committed—by, or upon, individuals of those armies, in Mexico, pending the existing war between the two Republics. Allusion is here made to offences, any one of which, if committed within the United States or their organized Territories, would, of course, be tried and severely punished by the ordinary or civil courts of the land.

2. Assassination, murder, poisoning, rape, or the attempt to commit either; malicious stabbing or maiming; malicious assault and battery, robbery, theft; the wanton desecration of churches, cemeteries or other religious edifices and fixtures; the interruption of religious ceremonies, and the destruction, except by order of a superior officer, of public or private property; are such offences.

3. The good of the service, the honor of the United States and the interests of humanity, imperiously demand that every crime, enumerated above, should be severely punished.

4. But the written code, as above, commonly called the *rules and articles of war,* does not provide for the punishment of any one of those crimes, even when committed by individuals of the army upon the persons or property of other individuals of the same, except in the very restricted case in the 9th of those articles; nor for like outrages, committed by the same class of individuals, upon the persons or property of a hostile country, except very partially, in the 51st, 52d, and 55th

articles; and the same code is absolutely silent as to all injuries which may be inflicted upon individuals of the army, or their property, against the laws of war, by individuals of a hostile country.

5. It is evident that the 99th article, independent of any reference to the restriction in the 87th, is wholly nugatory in reaching any one of those high crimes.

6. For all the offences, therefore, enumerated in the second paragraph above, which may be committed abroad—in, by, or upon the army, a supplemental code is absolutely needed.

7. That *unwritten* code is *Martial Law,* as an addition to the written military code, prescribed by Congress in the rules and articles of war, and which unwritten code, all armies, in hostile countries, are forced to adopt—not only for their own safety, but for the protection of the un-offending inhabitants and their property, about the theatres of military operations, against injuries, on the part of the army, contrary to the laws of war.

8. From the same supreme necessity, martial law is hereby declared as a supplemental code in, and about, all cities, towns, camps, posts, hospitals, and other places which may be occupied by any part of the forces of the United States, in Mexico, and in, and about, all columns, escorts, convoys, guards, and detachments, of the said forces, while engaged in prosecuting the existing war in, and against the said republic, and while remaining within the same.

9. Accordingly, every crime, enumerated in paragraph No. 2, above, whether committed—1. By any inhabitant of Mexico, sojourner or traveller therein, upon the person or property of any individual of the United States forces, retainer or follower of the same; 2. By any individual of the said forces, retainer or follower of the same, upon the person or property of any inhabitant of Mexico, sojourner or traveller therein; or 3. By any individual of the said forces, retainer or follower of the same, upon the person or property of any other individual of the said forces, retainer or follower of the same—shall be duly tried and punished under the said supplemental code.

10. For this purpose it is ordered, that all offenders, in the matters aforesaid, shall be promptly seized, confined, and reported for trial, before *military commissions,* to be duly appointed as follows:

11. Every military commission, under this order, will be appointed, governed, and limited, as nearly as practicable, as prescribed by the 65th, 66th, 67th, and 97th, of the said rules and articles of war, and the proceedings of such commissions will be duly recorded, in writing,

reviewed, revised, disapproved or approved, and the sentences executed—all, as near as may be, as in the cases of the proceedings and sentences of courts martial, *provided,* that no military commission shall try any case clearly cognizable by any court martial, and *provided,* also, that no sentence of a military commission shall be put in execution against any individual belonging to this army, which may not be, according to the nature and degree of the offence, as established by evidence, in conformity with known punishments, in like cases, in some one of the States of the United States of America.

12. The sale, waste or loss of ammunition, horses, arms, clothing or accoutrements, by soldiers, is punishable under the 37th and 38th articles of war. Any Mexican or resident or traveller, in Mexico, who shall purchase of. any American soldier, either horse, horse equipments, arms, ammunition, accoutrements or clothing, shall be tried and severely punished, by a military commission, as above.

13. The administration of justice, both in civil and criminal matters, through the ordinary courts of the country, shall nowhere and in no degree, be interrupted by any officer or soldier of the American forces, except, 1. In cases to which an officer, soldier, agent, servant, or follower of the American army may be a party; and 2. In *political* cases—that is, prosecutions against other individuals on the allegations that they have given friendly information, aid or assistance to the American forces.

14. For the ease and safety of both parties, in all cities and towns occupied by the American army, a Mexican police shall be established and duly harmonized with the military police of the said forces.

15. This splendid capital—its churches and religious worship; its convents and monasteries; its inhabitants and property are, moreover, placed under the special safeguard of the faith and honor of the American army.

16. In consideration of the foregoing protection, a contribution of $150,000 is imposed on this capital, to be paid in four weekly instalments of thirty-seven thousand five hundred dollars ($37,500) each, beginning on Monday next, the 20th instant, and terminating on Monday, the 11th of October.

17. The Ayuntamiento, or corporate authority of the city, is specially charged with the collection and payment of the several instalments.

18. Of the whole contributions to be paid over to this army, twenty thousand dollars shall be appropriated to the purchase of *extra* comforts for the wounded and sick in hospital; ninety thousand dollars ($90,000) to the purchase of blankets and shoes for gratuitous distri-

bution among the rank and file of the army, and forty thousand dollars ($40,000) reserved for other necessary military purposes.

19. This order will be read at the head of every company of the United States' forces, serving in Mexico, and translated into Spanish for the information of Mexicans.

By command of Major-General Scott.

H. L. SCOTT,

A. A.-General.

The following printed regulations, among others, were in the hands of the whole army, and are here extracted as subsidiary to the martial law order:

As a *special* security, any general-in-chief, general of an army corps, or division, is authorized to give *safeguards* to hospitals, public establishments of instruction, of religion, or of charity, also to mills, post offices, and the like. They may, further, give them to individuals whom it is the particular interest of the army to protect.

"Whosoever, belonging to the armies of the United States, employed in foreign parts, shall force a safeguard, shall suffer death" (54th article of war).

A safeguard may consist of one or more men of fidelity and firmness, generally non-effective sergeants or corporals, furnished with a printed or written paper, purporting the character and object of the guard, or it may consist of such paper only, delivered to the inhabitant of the country, whose house, etc., it is designed to protect. Disrespect to such a paper, when produced, constitutes the offence, and incurs the penalty mentioned in the article, etc., above cited.

The men left with a safeguard may require of the persons for whose benefit they are so left, reasonable subsistence and lodging; and the neighboring inhabitants will be held responsible, by the army, for any violence done them.

The bearers of a safeguard left by one corps, may be replaced by the corps that follows; and if the country be evacuated, they will be recalled; or they may be instructed to wait for the arrival of the enemy, and demand of him a safe conduct to the outposts of the army.

The following form will be used:

SAFEGUARD.

BY AUTHORITY OF MAJOR-GEN. —— (Or Brigadier-Gen. ——).

The person, the property, and the family of —— (or such a college, and the persons and things belonging to it; such a mill, etc.), *are placed under the safeguard of the United States. To offer any violence or injury to them is expressly forbidden; on the contrary, it is ordered that safety and protection be given to him, or them, in case of need.*

Done at the Headquarters of ——, this —— day of ——, 18——.

Forms of safeguards ought to be printed in blank, headed by the article of war relative thereto, and held ready to be filled up, as occasions may offer. A duplicate, etc., in each case, might be affixed to the houses, or edifices, to which they relate.

But the crowning act of conciliation was the proclamation that I issued at Jalapa, May 11, 1847, indignantly denying the "calumnies put forth by the [Mexican] press in order to excite hostility against us," and confidently appealing to "the clergy, civil authorities, and inhabitants of all the places we have occupied." "The army of the United States," I continued, "respects, and will ever respect private property and persons, and the property of the Mexican Church. Woe to him who does not, where we are!"—*Ex. Doc. No. 60, H. of R., 30th Congress, let Session.* Brevet Major General Worth, though hostile to me, wrote from the advanced position, Puebla—"It was most fortunate that I got hold of one copy of your proclamation. I had a third edition struck off, and am now with hardly a copy on hand. It takes admirably and my doors are crowded for it."

"It has produced more decided effects than all the blows from Palo Alto to Cerro Gordo."—*Ibid.,* p. 967.

Retiring from the capital, Santa Anna collected several fragments of his late army and laid siege to Puebla—the garrison of which being considerably less than was intended; for, although, on advancing from that city I gave the strictest orders that all convalescents as well as the sick should be left behind, about six hundred of the former imposed themselves upon their medical and company officers as entirely restored to health. For stationary or garrison duty they would have been fully qualified, but proved a burden to the advancing columns; for they soon began to break down and to creep into the subsistence wagons faster than these were lightened by the consumption of the troops.

The siege was prosecuted with considerable vigor for twenty-eight days, and nobly repulsed by our able and distinguished commander, Colonel Childs, with his gallant but feeble garrison, at all points and at every assault. During those arduous and protracted operations, the glory of our arms was nobly supported by officers and men. Colonel Childs specially commends by name—and no doubt justly—the skill, zeal, and prowess of Lieutenant-Colonel Black and Captain Small, both of the Pennsylvania Volunteers;[4] the highly accomplished Captain [now Professor] Kendrick, United States 4th Artillery,[5] chief of that arm, and Captain Miller, of the same regiment;[6] Lieutenant Laidley, of the Ordnance; Captain Rowe of the 9th Infantry,[7] and Lieutenant T. G. Rhett, A.C.S.[8] Captain W. C. De Hart (Artillery),[9] and Lieutenant-Governor of Puebla, though in feeble heath, conducted a sortie with success, and was otherwise distinguished. Death soon after deprived the service of this accomplished officer.

CHAPTER XXXIV

QUESTION OF FREE QUARTERS—SYSTEM OF FINANCE—SPREAD OF THE TROOPS

EARLY in the campaign I began to receive letters from Washington, urging me to support the army by forced contributions. Under the circumstances, this was an impossibility. The population was sparse. We had no party in the country, and had to encounter the hostility of both religion and race. All Mexicans, at first, regarded us as infidels and robbers. Hence there was not among them a farmer, a miller, or dealer in subsistence, who would not have destroyed whatever property he could not remove beyond our reach sooner than allow it to be seized without compensation. For the first day or two we might, perhaps, have seized current subsistence within five miles of our route; but by the end of a week the whole army must have been broken up into detachments and scattered far and wide over the country, skirmishing with *rancheros* and regular troops, for the means of satisfying the hunger of the day. Could invaders, so occupied, have conquered Mexico?

The war being virtually over, I now gave attention to a system of finance for the support of the army and to stimulate overtures of peace. The subject required extensive inquiries and careful elaboration. My intention was to raise the first year about twelve millions of dollars, with the least possible pressure on the industry and wealth of the country, with an increase to fifteen millions in subsequent years. The plan is given at large, in seven papers (four reports and three orders). See *Ex. Doc. No. 60, H. of R., 30th Congress, 1st Session,* p. 1046, and following. The orders are here omitted and the finance details, contained in the four reports, also.

Report No. 40
HEADQUARTERS OF THE ARMY,
Mexico, December 17, 1847.

SIR:

The troop of Louisiana horse, under Captain Fairchild, that so handsomely escorted up from Vera Cruz Mr. Doyle, the British Chargé d'Affaires, being about to return to its station, I avail myself of the opportunity to write to the department.[1]

I invite attention to my order, No. 376, and particularly to its seventh paragraph—import and export duties. Since its publication, I have seen in a slip, cut from a Vera Cruz newspaper (received here by a merchant), what purports to be a letter, dated the 17th ultimo, from the department to me on the same subject.

****

Major-General Butler's[2] and Lieutenant-Colonel Johnston's columns will lie here to-day, to-morrow, and the next day; and in a week I propose to despatch one column to San Luis de Potosi. When, or whether, I shall have a sufficient independent force for Zacatecas, is yet, to me, quite uncertain. The San Luis column, with a view to Tampico, and in part to Zacatecas, is the more important, and may be enlarged to, perhaps, seven thousand men.

The following distances from the Mexican official itineraries may be useful: From the capital to Queretaro, is 57 leagues, or 142 miles; thence to Zacatecas, 282 miles—the two distances making 424. From the capital to San Luis, is 113 leagues, or 382 miles (Queretaro may be avoided), and, in continuance by that route, 260 miles to Tampico, or 134 to Zacatecas. Thus, from Mexico, *via* San Luis, to Tampico, is 642 miles, and to Zacatecas, 516; whereas, the distance from Zacatecas to Tampico is but 398. Zacatecas, therefore, may be advantageously reached, or its trade opened with Tampico, *via* San Luis. The difficulty is, to occupy the state capitals of Guanajuato, etc., without passing through and including Queretaro, the temporary capital of the Federal Government; and I am reluctant to disturb that Government whilst it continues intent on a peace with us, without further knowledge of the views at Washington on the subject. That information I hope soon to receive; and, if in favor of covering the country, to hear of the approach of reënforcements behind the column of Brigadier-General Marshall, now I suppose, as far advanced as Jalapa.[3]

> I have the honor to be, etc.,
> etc.,
> WINFIELD SCOTT.

HON. SECRETARY OF WAR.

Report No. 41.
HEADQUARTERS OF THE ARMY, MEXICO, December 25, 1847.

Sir:

As I had apprehended (in Report No. 37), Lieutenant-Colonel Johnston's train has returned without one blanket, coat, jacket, or pair of pantaloons, the small depot at Vera Cruz having been exhausted by the troops under Generals Patterson, Butler, and Marshall, respectively, all fresh from home or the Brazos, and, as in the case of other arrivals, since June, without clothing! The regiments that came with me must, therefore, remain naked, or be supplied with very inferior garments, of every color and at high prices, as we may possibly be able to find the poor materials, and cause them to be made up here. This disappointment may delay any distant expedition for many weeks; for some of the new volunteers are already calling for essential articles of clothing.

Referring again to former letters on the subject, I beg leave to add that every old regiment forwarded, more than a twelvemonth ago, its usual annual requisition for clothing, which has never arrived, or it has been issued as above. With excessive labor I had brought the old regiments—volunteers as well as regulars—favored by our long and necessary halts at Vera Cruz, Jalapa, and Puebla, to respectable degrees of discipline, instruction, conduct, and economy. The same intolerable work, at general headquarters, is to be perpetually renewed, or all the credit heretofore acquired by this army for moral conduct, as well as skill and prowess in the field, will be utterly lost by new arrivals, and there is now no hope of bringing up to the proper standard distant posts and detachments. These cannot be governed by any written code of orders or instructions, sent from a distance. I do not mean to accuse the reënforcements, generally, of deficiency in valor, patriotism, or moral character. Far from it; but among all new levies, of whatever denomination, there are always a few miscreants in every hundred, enough, without *discipline,* to disgrace the entire mass, and what is infinitely worse—the *country* that employs them. My daily distresses under this head weigh me to the earth.

I am about to send a detachment, the 9th Infantry, under Colonel Withers, to Pachuca, near the great mines of Real del Monte, some fifty miles to the northeast.[4] There is an assay office at Pachuca, to which a large amount of silver bullion is soon to be brought, and if we have not troops present, the Federal officers of Mexico will seize the assay duties to our loss. I shall send another detachment in a few days to occupy Toluca, the capital of this State, with the general object of securing the contribution claimed for our military chest.—See General Orders, No. 376, paragraph 5. I am nearly ready to publish the details promised in the tenth paragraph of that order. I have found them very difficult to obtain and to methodize.

There will, I apprehend, be no difficulty in collecting at the assay offices and mints within our reach the ordinary internal dues on the precious metals. As to other internal dues and taxes (not abolished by my order, No. 376), I propose to find the net amount paid, to the Federal Government, for example, by the State of Vera Cruz, for 1843, and to assess that sum, in mass, upon the State, to be paid into our military chest, a twelfth at the end of every month, by the State Government, and so of the other States which are or may be occupied by our troops. Each State will be required to collect the amount claimed, according to the Federal assessment for the year 1843, under certain penalties, which may be the seizure, without payment, of the supplies needed for the support of the occupation, and particularly the property of the State functionaries, Legislative and Executive, with the imprisonment of their persons, etc., etc., etc. The fear is, those functionaries may abdicate, and leave the States without Governments. In such event, the like penalties will be, so far as practicable, enforced.

The success of the system—on the details of which I am now, with ample materials, employed—depends on our powers of conciliation. With steady troops I should not doubt the result; but the great danger lies in the want of that quality on the part of the new reënforcements, including the recruits of the old regiments. The average number of disorders and crimes, always committed by undisciplined men, with inexperienced officers, may destroy the best-concerted plans, by exasperating the inhabitants, and rendering the war, on their part, national, interminable, and desperate.

It will be perceived that I do not propose to seize the ordinary State or city revenues; as that would, in my humble judgment, be to make war on civilization; as no community can escape absolute anarchy without civil government, and all government must have some revenue for its support. I shall take care, however, to see that the means collected within any particular State or city for that purpose are moderate and reasonable.

It cannot be doubted that there is a considerable party in this country in favor of annexing it entire to the United States. How far that desire may be reciprocated at home, I know not, and it would be impertinent in a soldier to inquire. I am here (whilst I remain) to execute the military orders of my Government. But, as a soldier, I suppose it to be my duty to offer a suggestion on the subject, founded on professional and local knowledge, that may not occur to the minds of statesmen generally.

Annexation and military occupation would be, if we maintain the annexation, one and the same thing, as to the amount of force to be employed by us; for if, after the formal act, by treaty or otherwise, we should withdraw our troops, it cannot be doubted that all Mexico, or rather the active part thereof, would again relapse into a permanent state of revolution, beginning with one *against* annexation. The great mass of this people have always been passive under every form of government that has prevailed in the country, and the turbulent minority, divided into *ins* and *outs,* particularly the military demagogues, are equally incapable of self-government, and delight in nothing but getting power by revolution, and abusing that power when obtained.

I still entertain the belief that propositions, looking to a peace, will be submitted by the incoming Government here, in all the next month; but that any concession of boundaries, satisfactory to the United States, would, on the withdrawment of our forces, create a revolt, or the overthrow of that Government, with a nullification of the treaty, I hold to be events more than probable. In the mean time it would be highly advantageous to me, officially, to have an early intimation of the views of our Government as to the terms of a treaty that would now be satisfactory, only to prevent a wrong distribution of the troops in respect to those unknown views.

I have received no acknowledged communication from the Department. The letter of the 17th ultimo, published, as I have heretofore mentioned, in a Vera Cruz newspaper, has not come to hand, but I am daily expecting a mail up from that city.

> I have the honor to be, etc.,
> etc.,
> WINFIELD SCOTT.

HON. SECRETARY OF WAR.

> Report No. 42.
> HEADQUARTERS OF THE ARMY,
> Mexico, January 6, 1848.

Sir:

Nothing of interest has occurred since my report of the 26th ultimo; not even the arrival of a mail; but a private conveyance brought up yesterday a letter from Brigadier-General Marshall, representing that he was at Jalapa the 22d ultimo, with a column of troops (number not given), one half of whom were on the sick report, with measles and diarrhœa, and that he had sent back his train to Vera Cruz for medicines and other supplies. He gave no day for the recommencement of his march.

The number on the sick report, in this basin, is also great. In a total of 14,964, we have only 11,162 "for duty." The measles are rife among the new volunteers.

Colonel Withers, with the 9th Infantry, occupied Pachuca, quietly, more than a week ago. Brigadier General Cadwallader, with the remainder of his brigade, will march for Lerma and Toluca (State capital, thirty-eight miles off, in a direction opposite to Pachuca) to-day. The general object in occupying the three cities is to commence levying the assessments for the last month, and, through them, to enforce peace. Please see copies of General Orders, Nos. 395–8, herewith. (Giving the finance details promised in Order, No. 376.)

The tobacco monopoly I have thought it necessary to abolish. It would be worthless without a prohibition of the plant at the custom houses, and I doubted whether our Government, considering the interests of some five of our own tobacco-growing States, would prohibit the importation. Again, to protect the monopoly, including licenses to cultivators, would require a host of excise men. Probably a reasonable duty on importation will give larger net receipts for a year or two than could be derived in that time from any monopoly however strictly enforced.

Like difficulties in management caused me to relinquish to the Mexican States, respectively, the stamped-paper and playing-card monopolies. More than a substitute will be found in the quadrupling of the direct assessments on the States.

From the want of sufficient numbers to send, at once, columns of five thousand men each to Zacatecas and San Luis de Potosi, respectively, I next proposed to despatch to the latter place a force of seven thousand, which would be sufficient to open the channel of commerce between Tampico and Zacatecas, a distance of three hundred and ninety-four miles, and, by the operation, double, perhaps, the receipts at that seaport, as well as the interior dues on the precious metals. The commercial wealth of Durango would soon fall into the same channel. But assuming seven thousand men as the minimum force for this neighborhood, including the capital, Chapultepec, Pachuca, Lerma, and Toluca, I am obliged to wait for further reënforcements to make up the one column for San Luis. The delay of Brigadier-General Marshall, who had been expected daily for nearly a week, is, therefore, quite a vexatious disappointment. Possibly before his arrival (should the measles here have earlier subsided), I may risk a column of five thousand men, leaving, for a time, two intermediate posts vacant, and instruct the commander (Major-General Butler) to take into his sphere of operation a part of the forces belonging to the base of the Rio Grande. A detachment moving upon Tula, and, perhaps, leaving Victoria to the left, might coöperate very advantageously with the forces at the new centre, San Luis, and without endangering the line of Monterey, in which direction, it is supposed, the Mexicans cannot have any formidable number of organized troops. To concert the double movement, by correspondence, would be the principal difficulty; but ample discretion would be allowed in my general instructions.

Many of the States of this republic, on account of their remoteness from the common centre, sparseness of population, and inability to pay more than a trifle in the way of contributions, are not worth being occupied. Their influence on the question of peace or war is, proportionally, inconsiderable. As reënforcements arrive, I shall therefore endeavor to occupy only the more populous and wealthy States.

Most of the mints (all but two, I learn) have been farmed by foreigners for terms of years (unexpired), on the payment of large sums in advance. The principal mint (here) is in hands of the British Consul-General, who paid down about $200,000 in February last for the term of ten years, and contracted to pay, currently, one *per centum* on the amount of coinage. I suppose myself bound to respect such contracts until otherwise instructed. Other mints pay, I am informed, one and a half *per centum* on the money turned out. Hence a direction in General Orders, No. 395, to examine the contracts between the Mexican Government and the several mints. Those not under contract will be assessed as heretofore.

By two conveyances I am expecting mails up from Vera Cruz in two and four days. I am anxious to receive the views of the Department on several points of importance to me in this command.

The new Federal Executive and Congress are, as yet, not installed. Both, it is believed, will be strongly inclined to a peace.

I have the honor, etc., etc.,
WINFIELD SCOTT.

HON. SECRETARY OF WAR

HEADQUARTERS OF THE ARMY,
Mexico, January 13, 1848.

SIR:

I have not had a line from any public office at Washington of a date later than October 26.

The spy company has returned from Vera Cruz;[5] but it seems that despatches for me had been intrusted to a special messenger (I suppose from Washington), who, after a delay of many days at Perote, came up with the company to Puebla, where he again stopped and retained all my letters.

Brigadier-General Cadwallader has quietly occupied Toluca and Lerma. As was known, the State Government had retired (thirteen leagues) to Sultepec. The general has invited that Government to provide for the payment of the assessment upon the State; but there has not been yet time to receive a reply.

Some days since, Colonel Wynkoop, of the 1st Pennsylvania Volunteers, tendered his services to go, with a few men, to seize the guerilla priest, Jarauta, at the head of a small band that has long been the terror of all peaceable Mexicans within his reach, and who has frequently had skirmishes with our detachments.[6] The colonel having missed that object, heard that General Valencia and staff were at a distant hacienda, and by hard riding in the night, succeeded in capturing that general and a colonel of his staff. I consider this handsome service worthy of being recorded.

Colonel Hays, with a detachment of Texan Rangers, returned last night from a distant expedition in search of the robber priest.[7] In a skirmish, without loss on his part, he killed some eight of Jarauta's men, and thinks that the priest was carried off among the many wounded.

The spy company, coming up from Vera Cruz, had also a very successful affair with a large party of the enemy, and captured some forty prisoners, including three generals.

The second train, now out from Vera Cruz eleven days, was, as I learn by the enclosed correspondence, attacked by a numerous body of the enemy, and suffered a loss that looks like a disaster—the first that we have sustained; but further details are needed.

I have the honor, etc., etc.,
WINFIELD SCOTT,

HON. SECRETARY OF WAR.

Report No. 44.
HEADQUARTERS OF THE ARMY,
Mexico, February 2, 1848.

SIR:

Since my last report (January 13), I have received from the War Office letters dated November 8 and 17, and December 14.

My orders, Nos. 362, 376, and 395 of the last year, and 15 of the present (heretofore forwarded), will exhibit the system of finance I have established for the parts of the country occupied by this army.

It will be seen that the export duties on coins, and the prohibition of the export of bars, varies materially from your instructions of November 17, acknowledged above. I hope, for the reasons suggested in my report, No. 40 (December 17), the President may be induced to adopt my views in respect to the precious metals.

I am without reports from commanders of departments below, on the progress made in collecting the direct assessments under my orders and circulars. The *ayuntamiento* (city council) of the capital has charged itself with the payment, on account of the Federal district, of $400,000, of the $668,332 per year, imposed on the State of Mexico, and arrangements are in progress to meet that engagement. Two months are now due. Brigadier-General Cadwallader, at Toluca, hopes soon to begin to collect, through the *ayuntamiento* of that city, a large part of the remainder of the monthly assessments, and I have sent Colonel Clarke with a small brigade to Cueruavaca (some forty-three miles south, on the Acapulco road), to complete the same collection.

The *war of masses* having ended with the capture of this city, the *war of detail,* including the occupation of the country, and the collection of revenue, requires a large additional force, as I suggested in my despatch, No. 34.

I see that I am, at Washington, supposed to have at my command more than thirty thousand men. Including the forces at Tampico, Vera Cruz, on the line thence, and in this neighborhood, our total does not exceed twenty-four thousand eight hundred and sixteen. Deducting the indispensable garrisons and the sick, I have not left a disposable force for distant expeditions of more than four thousand five hundred men, and I do not hear of the approach of any considerable reënforcement. Seven thousand men I deem the *minimum* number necessary to open the important line from Durango, through Zacatecas and San Luis, to Tampico. Premising that I find it impossible to obtain from the volunteers, at a distance, regular returns, I send an approximate estimate of all the forces under my immediate orders. The numbers, among the volunteers, afflicted with the measles and mumps, in this vicinity, continue to be very great, and the erysipelas is common among all the corps.

I write in haste by the express who carries *the project* of a treaty that Mr. Trist has, at the moment, signed with Mexican commissioners. If accepted, I hope to receive, as early as practicable, instructions respecting the evacuation of this country; the disposition to be made of wagons, teams, cavalry, and artillery horses; the points in the United States to which I shall direct the troops respectively, etc., etc. (I have not yet read the treaty, except in small part.) In the same contingency, if not earlier recalled (and I understand my recall has been demanded by two of my juniors!!), I hope to receive instructions to allow me to return to the United States, as soon as I may deem the public service will permit, charging some other general officer with completing the evacuation, which ought, if practicable, to be finished before the return of the vomito; say early in May.

In about forty days I may receive an acknowledgment of this report. By that time, if the treaty be not accepted, I hope to be sufficiently reënforced to open the commercial line between Zacatecas and Tampico. The occupation of Queretaro, Guanajuato, and Guadalajura would be the next in importance, and some of the ports of the Pacific, the third. Meanwhile, the collection of internal dues on the precious metals, and the direct assessments, shall be continued.

I enclose a letter from Commodore Shubrick, and have the honor to remain, etc., etc.,[8]

WINFIELD SCOTT.

HON. SECRETARY OF WAR.

Report No. 45.
HEADQUARTERS OF THE ARMY,
Mexico, February 9, 1848.

SIR:

I have received no communication from the War Department, or the Adjutant-General's Office, since my last report (No. 44), dated the 2d instant; but slips from newspapers and letters from Washington have come to interested parties here, representing, I learn, that the President has determined to place me before a court, for daring to enforce necessary discipline in this army against certain of its high officers! I make only a passing comment upon these unofficial announcements; learning with pleasure, through the same sources, that I am to be superseded by Major-General Butler. Perhaps, after trial, I may be permitted to return to the United States. My poor services with this most gallant army are at length to be requited as I have long been led to expect they would be.

I have the honor, etc., etc.,

WINFIELD SCOTT.

HON. SECRETARY OF WAR.

CHAPTER XXXV

SUPPRESSION OF OUTLAWS—PEACE COMMISSIONER—TREATY SIGNED—MEXICAN OVERTURES—COURT OF INQUIRY

A CENSURE of Mr. Jay, on my conduct at Vera Cruz, is noticed above, at page 217. Another occurs in his book (*Review of the Mexican War*), page 207. Considering the gravity of his character, this censure also demands a passing notice.[1]

Some three months after entering the capital of Mexico I issued an order declaring:

"The highways used, or about to be used, by the American troops, being still infested in many parts by those atrocious bands called *guerillas* or *rancheros,* who, under instructions from the late Mexican authorities, continue to violate every rule of warfare observed by civilized nations, it has become necessary to announce to all the views and instructions of general headquarters on the subject." And it was added: "No quarter will be given to known murderers or robbers, whether guerillas or rancheros, and whether serving under [obsolete] commissions or not. Offenders of this character, accidentally falling into the hands of American troops [that is, without knowing their character], will be momentarily held as prisoners, that is, not put to death without due solemnity," meaning (and it was so prescribed) a trial by a council of three officers. This order Mr. Jay denounces as harsh or cruel.

Now in charity, Mr. Jay must be supposed to have been ignorant of what was universally known in Mexico, that the outlaws, denounced in the order, never made a prisoner, but invariably put to death every accidental American straggler, wounded or sick man, that fell into their hands—whether he was left by accident, in hospital or in charge of a Mexican family. And Mr. Jay, no doubt, must have known that it is a universal right of war, not to give quarter to an enemy that puts to death all who fall into his hands.

Some time before the date of that order, Mr. Trist, our peace commissioner, long my guest, reopened negotiations at the instance of the

Mexican Government, in the hope of terminating hostilities; but early in the negotiations he was recalled.[2] I encouraged him, nevertheless, to finish the good work he had begun. The Mexican commissioners, knowing of the recall, hesitated. On application, I encouraged them also, giving it as my confident belief that any treaty Mr. Trist might sign would be duly ratified at Washington.

Mr. Trist approached me at Jalapa under circumstances quite adverse to harmony. We had known each other very slightly at Washington, with, from accident, evident feelings of mutual dislike. With his arrival I received the most reliable information from Washington, that his well-known prejudice against me had had much weight in his appointment; and I remembered that, on taking leave of the President, he told me he intended or hoped to send to reside at headquarters with me, the very eminent statesman, Silas Wright,[3] as peace commissioner, with an associate—leaving me half at liberty to believe, I might, myself, be the other commissioner. What could have been more natural? Writing to the Secretary of War on this subject, May 20, 1847, from Jalapa, I said:

"The Hon. Mr. Benton has publicly declared, that if the law had passed making him General-in-Chief of the United States armies in Mexico, either as lieutenant-general or as junior major-general over seniors, the power would have been given him not only of agreeing to an armistice (which would, of course, have appertained to his position), but the much higher one of concluding a treaty of peace; and it will be remembered also, that in my letter to Major-General Taylor, dated June 12, 1846, written at your instance [etc.], his power to agree to an armistice was merely adverted to in order to place upon it certain limitations. I understand your letter to me of the 14th ultimo, as not only taking from me, the commander of an army, under the most critical circumstances, all voice or advice in agreeing to a truce with the enemy, but as an attempt to place me under the military command of Mr. Trist; for you tell me that 'should he make known to you in writing, that the contingency had occurred in consequence of which the President is willing that further active military operations should cease, you will regard such notice as a direction from the President to suspend them until further orders from this Department.' That is, I am required to respect the judgment of Mr. Trist, here, on passing events, purely military, as the judgment of the President, who is some two thousand miles off!

"I suppose this to be the second attempt of the kind ever made to dishonor a General-in-Chief in the field before or since the time of the French Convention. That other instance occurred in your absence from

Washington in June, 1845, when Mr. Bancroft, Acting Secretary of War,[4] instructed General Taylor in certain matters to obey the orders of Mr. Donaldson, Chargé d'Affaires in Texas;[5] and you may remember the letter I wrote to General Taylor, with the permission of both Mr. Bancroft and yourself, to correct that blunder."

****

"Whenever it may please the President to instruct me directly, or through any authorized channel, to propose or to agree to an armistice with the enemy, on the happening of any given contingency, or to do any other military act, I shall most promptly and cheerfully obey him; but I entreat to be spared the personal dishonor of being again required to obey the orders of the chief clerk of the State Department."

****

"To Mr. Trist as a functionary of my Government, I have caused to be shown since his arrival here every proper attention. I sent the chief quartermaster and an aide-de-camp to show him the rooms I had ordered for him. I have caused him to be tendered a sentinel to be placed, etc. I shall, from time to time, send him word of my personal movements, and shall continue to show him all other attentions necessary to the discharge of any diplomatic function with which he may be entrusted."

The coolness between Mr. Trist and myself was much aggravated by accident. He fell ill at Vera Cruz, and was obliged to take much morphine to save life. Hence the offensive tone of certain letters. He several times relapsed. At Puebla, he was again dangerously ill, and I placed him under the special care of his and my friend, General Persifer F. Smith, at whose instance I visited his charge. My sympathy became deeply interested in his recovery, when he became my guest for more than six months. I never had a more amiable, quiet, or gentlemanly companion. He was highly respected by the Mexican authorities, and foreign diplomats residing in Mexico. The United States could not have had a better representative. I am sorry to add that, poor and retaining all his good habits and talents, he has been strangely neglected by his Government up to this moment.

In occupying the capital and other cities, strict orders were given that no officer or man should be billeted, without consent, upon any inhabitant; that troops should only be quartered in the established barracks and such other public buildings as had been used for that purpose by the Mexican Government. Under this limitation, several large convents or monasteries, with but a few monks each, furnished ample quarters for many Americans, and, in every instance, the parties lived together in the most friendly manner, as was attested by the mutual tears shed by many, at the separation. Good order, or the protection of religion, persons, property, and industry were coextensive with the American rule. The highways, also, were comparatively freed from those old pests, robbers, or (the same thing) *rancheros,* who pillage, murder (often) all within their power, including their own priests. Everything consumed or used by our troops was as regularly paid for as if they had been at home. Hence Mexicans had never before known equal prosperity; for even the spirit of revolution, the chronic disease of the country, had been cured for the time.

Intelligent Mexicans, and, indeed, the great body of the people, felt and acknowledged the happy change. Hence, as soon as it was known that a treaty had been signed, political overtures from certain leaders were made to the General-in-Chief.

Of course, it was generally understood that, on the ratification of peace, about seven tenths of the whole rank and file of our regulars and all volunteers would stand, *ipso facto,* discharged from their enlistments, and also that all officers are always at liberty to resign their commissions after the execution of the last order. With the addition of ten or twenty *per centum* to the American pay, it would certainly have been easy to organize in Mexico an army of select American officers and men, say of fifteen thousand (to be kept up to that figure by recruits from home), to serve as a nucleus, which, with an equal native force, would suffice to hold the Republic in tranquillity and prosperity, under a new Government. The plan contemplated a *pronunciamento,* in which Scott should declare himself dictator of the Republic for a term of six or four years,—to give time to politicians and agitators to recover pacific habits, and to learn to govern themselves. Being already in possession of the principal forts, arsenals, founderies, mines, ports of entry and cities, with nearly all the arms of the country, it was not doubted that a very general acquiescence would soon have followed.

The plan was ultimately declined by Scott, though, to him, highly seductive both as to power and fortune, on two grounds: 1. It was required that he should pledge himself to slide, if possible, the Republic of Mexico into the Republic of the United States, which he deemed a measure, if successful, fraught with, extreme peril to the free institutions of his country, and, 2. Because, although Scott had, in his official Report, No. 41 (December 25, 1847, page 282, above), suggested the question of annexation, President Polk's Government carefully withheld its wishes from him thereon.

The following sums of money came into the hands of the General-in-Chief in Mexico. About $12,000 captured at Cerro Gordo; $150,000 levied at the capital, in lieu of pillage; $50,000 (nearly) produced by the sale of captured Government tobacco, and two or three smaller sums for licenses, etc.,—making a total of about $220,000. The following disposition was made of this fund. A little more than $63,000 for extra blankets and shoes, distributed gratis among the rank and file; a considerable amount given to wounded men ($10 each) on leaving hospital; about $118,000 remitted to Washington to constitute a basis for an Army Asylum—for disabled men, not officers, and the remainder turned over, with the command, to Major-General Butler.

The treaty of peace was signed, February 2, 1848, and, in time, duly ratified at Washington, as I had in advance assured the Mexican authorities that it would be. On the 18th of the same month I received the President's instructions to turn over the command of the army in Mexico to Major-General William O. Butler (which I instantly did, in complimentary terms), and to submit myself to a court of inquiry—and such a court!—Towson, Cushing, and Belknap!*[6]—on its arrival at Mexico. {Brevet Brigadier-General Towson, president of the court, was duly brevetted a major-general, and Colonel Belknap brevetted a brigadier general for their acceptable services in shielding Pillow and brow-beating Scott. The other member, General Cushing, in his pride as a lawyer and scholar, covered up his opinions in nice disquisitions and subtleties not always comprehended by his associates.} The same mail brought orders restoring (from arrests) the three factious officers—Major-Generals Worth and Pillow, with Lieutenant-Colonel Duncan*—to their former commands and honors. {These three officers were not strictly confined to their respective quarters, as by law they must have been but for Scott's special indulgence in extending the limits of each, from the beginning of the arrest, to the city and its environs.}Thus a series of the greatest wrongs ever heaped on a successful commander was consummated—in continuation of the Jackson persecution.

After a session of some weeks in Mexico, and some progress made in Pillow's case, the court was adjourned to meet next at Frederick, Maryland. Here the sessions were continued long enough to finish the whitewashing of Pillow by the means alluded to. The charges against Scott had been withdrawn under his open defiance of power and its minions, when the court was finally adjourned and dissolved.

CHAPTER XXXVI

RECEPTIONS AT NEW YORK AND ELIZABETH—OTHERS DECLINED—BAD HEALTH—THANKS OF CONGRESS, ETC.

A RRIVING at Vera Cruz, on my way home, I had a right to select the best steamer for my conveyance, and there were several at anchor off the castle in the service of the army. But the same reason that induced me to select non-effectives for oarsmen, the morning after the battle of Lundy's Lane, and, on the same occasion, to take a broken-down surgeon to attend me toward Philadelphia, now caused me to leave the steamers at Vera Cruz for the benefit of the corps soon to follow. Accordingly, I embarked in a small sailing brig, loaded down with guns, mortars, and ordnance stores.

Sunday morning, May 20, we were, at daylight, boarded by the health officer at the Narrows, and I engaged a rowboat to take me to my family at Elizabeth. Having the Mexican disease upon me, I was in great want of repose and good nursing. I was, however, overpowered by deputations from New York; visited the city, and was honored with a most magnificent reception both civic and military.

At the instance of Scott, and in compliment to Taylor, then the regular nominee of the Whigs for the Presidency, Scott was limited to the command of the Eastern Department of the army, headquarters, New York; and the command of the Western Department was assigned to the other Major-General, Taylor, as in the time of the two Major-Generals, Brown and Jackson, in 1815, who commanded, down to 1821, the "*Division*" of the North and the South respectively.

Joint Resolution expressive of the Thanks of Congress to Major-General Winfield Scott, aid the Troops under his command, for their distinguished Gallantry and good Conduct in the Campaign of eighteen hundred and forty-seven.

SEC. 1. *Resolved, unanimously, by the Senate and House of Representatives of the United States of America, in Congress assembled,* That the thanks of Congress be, and they are hereby, presented to Winfield Scott, Major-General commanding in Chief the army in Mexico, and through him, to the officers and men of the regular and volunteer corps under him, for their uniform gallantry and good conduct, conspicuously displayed at the siege and capture of the City of Vera Cruz and castle of San Juan de Ulloa, March twenty-ninth, eighteen hundred and forty-seven; and in the successive battles of Cerro Gordo, April eighteenth; Contreras, San Antonio, and Churubusco, August nineteenth and twentieth; and for the victories achieved in front of the City of Mexico, September eighth, eleventh, twelfth, and thirteenth, and the capture of the metropolis, September fourteenth, eighteen hundred and forty-seven, in which the Mexican troops, greatly superior in numbers, and with every advantage of position, were in every conflict signally defeated by the American arms.

SEC. 2. *Resolved,* That the President of the United States be, and he is hereby, requested to cause to be struck a gold medal, with devices emblematical of the series of brilliant victories achieved by the army, and presented to Major-General Winfield Scott, as a testimony of the high sense entertained by Congress of his valor, skill, and judicious conduct in the memorable campaign of eighteen hundred and forty-seven.

SEC. 3. *Resolved,* That the President of the United States be requested to cause the foregoing resolutions to be communicated to Major-General Scott, in such terms as he may deem best calculated to give effect to the objects thereof.

Approved, March 9, 1848.

It was enacted in 1798, that a lieutenant-general should be appointed, and General Washington accepted the office. The next year the grade of full general was provided for, and the law declared that on filling the latter, the former should stand repealed. On the next meeting of Congress, President Adams being a little dilatory in nominating to the new place, the Father of his country died a lieutenant-general, and, consequently, the act providing for that appointment was never repealed.

IN SENATE.

February 24, 1849, Hon. Mr. Fitzgerald "asked and obtained leave to bring in a joint resolution to confer upon Major-General Winfield Scott the brevet rank of lieutenant-general, which was read and passed to a second reading."

A motion to read the resolution a third time the same day being objected to by a single Senator, the subject went over for the want of time, Congress being within a week of dissolution.

July 29, 1850, Hon. Mr. Clemens submitted the following:[1]

"*Resolved,* That the Committee on Military Affairs be instructed to inquire into the expediency of conferring by law the brevet rank of lieutenant-general on Major-General Winfield Scott, with such additional pay and allowances as may be deemed proper, in consideration of the distinguished services rendered to the Republic by that officer during the late war with Mexico."

Eight days later that resolution was referred to the Senate's Military Committee.

On the last day of the session (September 30, 1850), Hon. Jefferson Davis, Chairman, reported the following resolution on the same subject:

"*Resolved,* That the President of the United States be, and he is hereby, requested to refer to an army board of officers, to be designated by him, the following questions, viz.:

"Is it expedient or necessary to provide for additional grades of commissioned officers in the army of the United States; and, if so, what grades, in addition to the present organization, should be created?"

This was an ingenious fetch of Mr. Davis, not doubting that jealousies in the service would give a quietus to the lieutenant-generalcy; but when the report came in, though in reply to his own call, he dropped it as repugnant to his cherished hatred. See original ground of his hostility, page 79 (note), above. Mr. Davis, moreover, was the heir to his father-in-law's prejudices (—General Taylor's), who, for a long time, spurned him.

In pursuance of this request, the President of the United States appointed a board of officers—Generals Jesup (President), Wool, Gibson, Totten, Talcott, Hitchcock, and Colonel Crane—who reported *unanimously,* as follows:[2]

"Under the first inquiry referred to it, the Board is of opinion that it is expedient to create by law for the army the additional grade of lieutenant-general, and that when, in the opinion of the President and Senate, it shall be deemed proper to acknowledge eminent services of officers of the army, and in the mode already provided for in subordinate grades, it is expedient and proper that the grade of lieutenant-general may be conferred by brevet."

December 17, 1850, that report was laid before the Senate, and referred to the Committee on Military Affairs, etc.

January 25, 1851, Hon. Mr. Shields reported a joint resolution in conformity with the recommendation of the Military Board.[3]

February 13, 1851, the joint resolution passed the Senate by 31 votes to 16, several of its friends (among them the Hon. Mr. Clemens) being absent.

HOUSE OF REPRESENTATIVES.

March 3, 1851, an attempt was made by the Hon. A. H. Stephens[4] to call up, out of turn, the joint resolution (about the ninetieth of the bills, etc., on the Speaker's table), when the yeas were 112, to 72 nays; several of the friends of the measure—among them the Hon. Mr. Gorman[5]—happening to be out of their seats. The same motion was repeated the same evening, by the Hon. Mr. Toombs, with a like result.[6] A change of some eight or ten votes would have made a two-thirds majority.

IN SENATE.

December 8, 1851, Hon. Mr. Clemens asked and obtained leave to bring in a joint resolution, "authorizing the President of the United States to confer the title of lieutenant-general by brevet for eminent services; which was read the first and second time, by unanimous consent, and referred to the Committee on Military Affairs." (This joint resolution is similar to the one on the same subject passed by the Senate at the preceding session.)

December 23, 1851, the joint resolution was reported back to the Senate without amendment, and slept the remainder of the session.

December 7, 1852, (the second day of the new session) lion. Mr. Clemens again brought up the same resolution in the Senate, and it passed that body on the 21st, by a vote of 34 to 12.

The resolution having been again passed by the Senate was taken up in the House by the resolute Judge Bailey, and passed through all the forms of legislation before resuming his seat.

Mr. Jefferson Davis, soon in the Cabinet, allowed of no intermission in his hostility. The rank could not be withheld; but he next resolved it should carry no additional compensation, however clearly embraced. Yet he permitted the question of compensation to go to the Attorney-General;[7] but coupled the reference with a volunteer argument of fourteen pages—against the claim—he, himself, being profoundly ignorant of law—for the benefit of the law officer of the Government! It is true he informed me that he had made the reference; but I was purely indebted to accident for my knowledge of his *legal* argument.

To overcome this deadly enemy, my friends in the two Houses of Congress, including quite a roll of Democrats, had again to push through all the forms of legislation a *declaratory* provision that gave me what might reasonably be claimed under the first enactment. I regret being unable to insert all the names of these noble Democrats; but Shields led in the Senate, and Clingham in the House, most triumphantly.[8]

But I was not even yet out of the hands of Mr. Davis. The declaratory resolution standing alone, he would certainly have caused it to be vetoed. The danger was perceived by all my friends, and their next step was to embody it in the Military Appropriation Bill. Another triumph. It was the last hour of the administration. The President and his whole Cabinet were, as is usual, in a drawing-room adjoining the Senate chamber, and the Secretaries much on the floor of the latter. My friends appointed several of their number to keep an eye on the engrossing clerk, lest, in copying a great number of amendments, he might not *accidentally* leave out my resolution. And thus it might be said (with due extravagance) of another old soldier—

"Thrice he routed all his foes and thrice he slew the slain."

On the inauguration of President Taylor, Scott, though again assuming the command of the whole army, continued his headquarters at New York, not being called to Washington on account of the personal hostility of the President; but on the succession of President Fillmore (in 1850) the headquarters of the General-in-Chief were reestablished at Washington, and there continued till the accession of President Pierce, when by request of Scott, there was another change back to New York. Here his office remained down to his retirement from command, in 1861, though his last ten months on duty—hard, disabling service—were spent in Washington.

Among the incidents of this period, the autobiographer's third and greatest humiliation in politics must not be omitted. The first (but slight) happened in the Whig Convention at Harrisburg, in 1839; the second at the Philadelphia Convention in 1848, that nominated Taylor. (Certain Whigs—several still living—may thank me that I do not here expose their vile tricks on that occasion; but I have long forgiven them.)

In June, 1852, the Whig Convention that met at Baltimore, to choose candidates to be run in the following November, for President and Vice-President, after a great number of ballots finally put the autobiographer in nomination for the Presidency. His competitors, before that body, were the actual President, Mr. Fillmore, and Mr. Webster, Secretary of State. William A. Graham, the Secretary of the Navy, was chosen as the candidate for the Vice-Presidency on the same ticket, and General Pierce had, some time before, been made the Democratic candidate for the higher office.

It is very generally held that the leaders of a party are bound to support its regular nominations, particularly such leaders as sought the honor of nomination by the body appointed to select candidates. Mr. Fillmore, who was ambitious of another executive term, disregarded this obligation. He, with several of his Cabinet, in a huff, openly eschewed the nomination. Mr. Webster, already *moribond* (he died before the election), acted on the occasion as if he had been cheated out of a rightful inheritance, and stimulated his son and several leading friends to take an active part on the side of his resentment. He failed, however, to influence the vote of his noble State.

At the election, Scott was signally defeated—receiving only the votes of Massachusetts, Vermont, Kentucky, and Tennessee. Virginia, his dear mother State, utterly repudiated him—her wiseacres preferring a succession or two more of pliant administrations to pave the way for rebellion and ruin.[9]

The mortification of the defeated candidate was, however, nearly lost in the following reflections:

1. In the nomination and election of high functionaries, since the days of "modern degeneracy" (*Jacksonism*), the virtue and wisdom of candidates have had but little if any weight, either in primary movements or at the polls. It would, therefore, be illogical to ascribe Scott's defeat in the election of 1852, exclusively to his demerits—positive or comparative.

2. Scott was a Whig. The conflicts, however, between Mr. Clay and President Tyler, combined with the ambiguous position of Mr. Webster ("Where am I to go?"), had pretty well run the party *under ground;* for Taylor, though nominated on the same basis, and throwing out in the canvass side glances at the other party, was, nevertheless, a minority President. The outsiders—Whig office-seekers—it is true, worked like beavers for him; but the split in the Democratic ranks—running two candidates—Cass and Van Buren—decided the election.

3. In 1852, Scott had not one of those adventitious helps. The Democrats were thoroughly united. Their famished office-*seekers,* remembering their long enjoyment of the flesh-pots of Government, were desperately bent on the recovery of their old livings; whereas, now there was nothing left for the outsiders, the universal Whig office-holders, "a careless herd full of the pasture,"—"fat and greasy citizens"—were

happy to follow the example of Mr. Fillmore and abstain from any inter-ference in the election—in accordance, also, with the known principles and wishes of Scott. Hence the issue went against him as if *by default.*

For his political defeats, the autobiographer cannot too often return thanks to God. As he has said before, they proved benefits to him. Have they been such to his country? This is a point that may, perhaps, here-after be doubted by calm inquirers.

The following extracts present a subject that needs no explanation:

"Kansas and Scott.

"Mr. Crittenden's resolution, in relation to sending General Scott to Kansas, to take command of the United States troops there, was taken up in the Senate, yesterday, and warmly discussed. The resolution was ably advocated by Senators Crittenden, Bell, Clayton, and Seward, and opposed by Messrs. Brown, of Mississippi, Toucey, Mallory, and Mason.[10] The Senate adjourned without any decision on the subject. The prop-osition to send General Scott to Kansas, with power to settle the diffi-culties existing there according to his own judgment, appears to have occurred to several persons simultaneously. It was suggested by the Albany *Evening Journal;* and Hon. Robert C. Winthrop, in a letter writ-ten early last week, in reference to the Kansas meeting in Faneuil Hall, says:[11]

"'I cannot help thinking that, if the gallant veteran, who ought at this moment to have been at the head of the nation, and who is still at the head of its army—whose presence has almost as often been the pledge of peace, in scenes of strife, as it has been of victory on the field of bat-tle—could be sent at once to Kansas, with full powers to command and enforce a cessation of lawless violence and conflict, and to put down the reign of terror in that region, the dangers which now threaten the peace of the whole country might still be averted.'

"But the administration Senators profess to believe that the Kansas difficulty is 'not much of a shower,' and the only thing they recommend is to stop agitating the matter, when the difficulties will settle them-selves of their own accord. But the greatest difficulty of all they will find will be to stop the agitation. It must be agitated until the cause of the agitation shall have been removed."—*New York Times,* June 12, 1856.

"If General Scott could be sent to Kansas with instructions to re-store and maintain peace and order, and with a liberal discretion as to the means to be employed to effect that object, we should feel a moral certainty of his triumphant and glorious success. But to send him there to obey the instructions of Jeff. Davis and enforce the acts of the tyrannical bogus Legislature would be to lacerate his feelings, tarnish his proud fame, and probably hasten his descent to the tomb. As the mere instrument of Davis and Shannon, Marshal Donaldson, and 'Sheriff' Jones, we do not see how he could do better than Colonel Sumner has done, while the employment would be entirely beneath his position and alien to his character.[12] If such be the work contemplated, we trust a fitter instrument will be selected."—*New York Tribune,* June 12, 1856.

During the thirteen years following the peace with Mexico, but few incidents of historical interest to the autobiographer occurred.

As belonging to the history of the times, the subjoined letter may be here inserted.

On the occasion of a threatened renewal of political agitations in the Canadas, the autobiographer being interrogated on the subject by an eminent citizen and a friend, replied:

To John C. Hamilton, Esquire.[13]

WEST POINT, June 29, 1849.

MY DEAR SIR:

The news from the Parliament of Great Britain this morning must, I think, increase the discontents of our neighbors on the other side of the St. Lawrence and the lakes not a little; and that those discontents may in a few years lead to a separation of the Canadas, New Brunswick, etc., etc., from England seems equally probable.

Will those Provinces form themselves into an independent nation, or seek a connection with our Union? I think the probability is greatly in favor of the latter. In my judgment the interests of both sides would be much promoted by annexation—the several Provinces coming into the Union on equal terms with our present thirty States. The free navigation of the St. Lawrence is already of immense importance to, perhaps, a third of our present population, and would be of great value to the remainder.

After annexation, two revenue cutters below Quebec would give us a better security against smuggling than thirty thousand custom-house *employés* strung along the line that separates us from the British possessions on our continent. I am well acquainted with that line, and know a great deal about the interests and character of the Provincials. Though opposed to incorporating with us any district densely peopled with the *Mexican* race, I should be most happy to fraternize with our northern and northeastern neighbors.

What may be the views of our Executive Government on the subject, I know absolutely nothing; but I think I cannot err in saying that two thirds of our people would rejoice at the incorporation, and the other third soon perceive its benefits.

Of course I am opposed to any underhanded measures on our part, in favor of the measure, or any other act of bad faith toward Great Britain. Her good will, in my view of the matter, is only second to that of the Provincials themselves, and that the former would soon follow the latter—considering the present temper and condition of Christendom—cannot be doubted.

The foregoing views I have long been in the habit of expressing in conversation. I give them to you for what they may be worth.

Faithfully yours,
WINFIELD SCOTT.

J. C. HAMILTON, ESQ.

Mr. Hamilton, a pious son—a large contributor to our early history—in the Life and Times of his father,* and also as the editor of a recent and most accurate edition of the *Federalist*—with a splendid introduction and valuable notes—has had the kindness to refer the autobiographer to the following interesting facts in regard to the Canadas. {The exact title of this able work is—*History of the Republic of the United States, as traced in the Writings of Alexander Hamilton and of his Contemporaries*, 7 vols. 8vo.}

In the Articles of Confederation (the 11th) it was provided: "Canada acceding to this Confederation, and joining in the measures of the United States, shall be admitted into and entitled to all the advantages of this Union; but no other colony shall be admitted into the same, unless such admission be agreed to by *nine* States."

Several attempts were made to bring those Provinces (Upper and Lower Canada) into the Union, down to 1797; but from various causes they failed, though a favorite object with a large portion of the Union.

The expedition set on foot by Mr. Secretary Floyd, in 1857, against the Mormons and Indians about Salt Lake was, beyond a doubt, to give occasion for large contracts and expenditures, that is, to open a wide field for frauds and peculation.[14] This purpose was not comprehended nor scarcely suspected in, perhaps, a year; but, observing the desperate characters who frequented the Secretary, some of whom had desks near him, suspicion was at length excited. Scott protested against the expedition on the general ground of inexpediency, and specially because the season was too late for the troops to reach their destination in comfort or even in safety. Particular facts, observed by different officers, if united, would prove the imputation. The Governor of the Territory, Mr. Cumming; the commander of the troops, Brigadier-General A. S. Johnston, and our officers, stood above all suspicion of complicity.

An incident occurred in 1859 on the Pacific coast which the President regarded as endangering not little our peaceful relations with Great Britain. At the moment when commissioners were engaged in running the boundary line between the two countries, but differing as to which party the San Juan Island, in Puget's Sound, should be assigned, the question of course reverted to the two paramount Governments. Brigadier-General Harney, who commanded our forces in that quarter, was a great favorite with the five Democratic Presidents. Full of blind admiration for his patrons, he had before, in Florida, hung several Indians, under the most doubtful circumstances, in imitation of a like act on the part of General Jackson, in the same quarter, and now, as that popular hero gained much applause by wrenching Pensacola and all Middle Florida from Spain, in time of peace, Harney probably thought he might make himself President too, by cutting short all diplomacy and taking forcible possession of the disputed island! Imitations on the part of certain people always begin by copying defects. President Buchanan, however, well knowing the difference in power between Spain and Great Britain, kindly inquired of the autobiographer (now recently a cripple from a fall) whether, without injury, he could go on a mission to Puget's Sound? The voyage, *via* Panama, was promptly undertaken, and Scott sailed from New York, September 20, 1859, in *The Star of the West.* Arriving in the Sound, near the British Governor at Victoria, a few courteous notes restored the island to its late neutral condition—the joint possession of the two parties. It is not known that the *protegé,* Harney, was even reprimanded for his rashness. He certainly was not recalled, although the measure was suggested by the writer.[15]

Perhaps but few readers will complain of the insertion, in this narrative, of the following poem, written by Mrs. Scott, then in Paris, to cheer her husband on in his mission of peace. An English lady, a friend of the authoress, begged permission to copy the poem, which she sent to the London *Ladies' Magazine.*

> Oh, Star of the West! throw thy radiance benign,
> Unchanging and strong, on the warrior's way!
> May the waves that surround him, by favor divine,
> Be as lustrous and calm as thine own cheering ray.

"The hero of many a battle" goes now
More joyfully forth on a mission of peace:
oh! Star of the West! be the prototype thou
of success, whose pure blessings shall never surcease.

God prosper the barque that hath borrowed thy name!
Supplications, heartborn, to his throne are address'd
For the good, and the brave, and the pious, who claim
our devotion—our prayers—in the "Star of the West."

They go, all unarm'd—save, with holiest views
The ills of ambition and strife to arrest;
And the spirit of St. John (loved Apostle) imbues
Hearts, approaching his Isle, in the "Star of the West."

Unarm'd they will land! 'mid contention and wrath;
But, on high, tis decreed that "Peacemakers be blest."
They will follow, once more, their long, long ocean path,
And regain their own shores, with the "Star of the West."

Sail on, gallant Scott! true disciple of virtue!
Whose justice and faith every danger will breast
Nor swerve in the conflict. Heaven will not desert you,
There are angels on guard 'round the "Star of the West."
Paris, October 6, 1859

Of my many persevering efforts to improve the condition of the army, and, consequently, its efficiency, several proofs have been embodied in this narrative. The General Order reproduced at page 184, had in view, mainly, the protection of the rank and file against the abuses of commissioned and non-commissioned officers. I shall here add two other measures which greatly improved the comforts and usefulness of commissioned officers generally. 1. I claim credit for a long and active correspondence with military committees in the two Houses of Congress, resulting in the law that has given, since 1834, the cumulative rations to our medical officers, that has prevented many of the most valuable from resigning on obtaining high professional skill by experience. 2. And I claim also a special agency in procuring the provision giving, since 1838, to "every commissioned officer of the line or staff, *exclusive of general officers*," "one additional ration per diem, for every five years he may have served, or shall serve, in the army of the United

States." For several years in succession I had written and pressed upon the two military committees of Congress a section to that effect. Passing through Washington to the Cherokee country, in 1838, the Hon. Gouverneur Kemble,[16] an intelligent friend of the army and member of the House Committee, called upon me on the part of the body to say that, although they could report the bill, and might carry it in the House against all opposition; yet if the chairman of the committee (McKay) and another radical member (Walter Coles) should speak against the measure in the House, its passage would be doubtful.[17] Hence the desire that I should meet the committee.

I found the chairman gruff and immovable. At length he grumbled out—"Have you not pay enough?" I rejoined: "Leave me out; leave out the generals." He added, "Agreed," and thence the service ration.

By that suggestion, it may be that I have lost, up to the present time (twenty-six years), the current receipts from five hundred to a thousand dollars a year, which would have been a great comfort to the declining years of an old soldier, as the bill might, in a year or two more, if not in 1838, have been passed—nothing being more reasonable—without excluding the general officers.

But an increase of physical infirmities admonishes me to bring this narrative to a close. Happily but little remains to be added.

In the Presidential canvass of 1860, it was plainly seen that a disruption of the Union was imminent. Deeply impressed with the danger, I addressed a memorial to President Buchanan on the subject, of which the following are extracts:

"OCTOBER 29, 1860.

"The excitement that threatens secession is caused by the near prospect of a Republican's election to the Presidency. From a sense of propriety, as a soldier, I have taken no part in the pending canvass, and, as always heretofore, mean to stay away from the polls. My sympathies, however, are with the Bell and Everett ticket. With Mr. Lincoln I have had no communication whatever, direct or indirect, and have no recollection of ever having seen his person; but cannot believe any unconstitutional violence or breach of law, is to be apprehended from his administration of the Federal Government.

"From a knowledge of our Southern population it is my solemn conviction that there is some danger of an early act of rashness preliminary to secession, viz., the seizure of some or all of the following posts: Forts Jackson and St. Philip, on the Mississippi, below New Orleans, both without garrisons; Fort Morgan, below Mobile, without a garrison; Forts Pickens and McRee, Pensacola Harbor, with an insufficient garrison for one; Fort Pulaski, below Savannah, without a garrison; Forts Moultrie and Sumter, Charleston Harbor, the former with an insufficient garrison, and the latter without any; and Fort Monroe, Hampton Roads, without a sufficient garrison. In my opinion all these works should be immediately so garrisoned as to make any attempt to take any one of them, by surprise or *coup de main,* ridiculous.

"With the army faithful to its allegiance, and the navy probably equally so, and with a Federal Executive, for the next twelve months, of firmness and moderation, which the country has a right to expect—*moderation* being an element of power not less than *firmness*—there is good reason to hope that the danger of secession may be made to pass away without one conflict of arms, one execution, or one arrest for treason. In the mean time it is suggested that exports might be left perfectly free—and to avoid conflicts all duties on imports be collected outside of the cities, in forts or ships of war."

The inauguration of President Lincoln was, perhaps, the most critical and hazardous event with which I have ever been connected. In the preceding two months I had received more than fifty letters, many from points distant from each other—some earnestly dissuading me from being present at the event, and others distinctly threatening assassination if I dared to protect the ceremony by a military force. The election having been entirely regular, I resolved that the Constitution should not be overturned by violence if I could possibly prevent it. Accordingly, I caused to be organized the *élite* of the Washington Volunteers, and called from a distance two batteries of horse artillery, with small detachments of cavalry and infantry, all regulars.

In concert with Congressional Committees of arrangements, the President was escorted to and from the Capitol by volunteers—the regulars, with whom I marched, flanking the movement in parallel streets,—only I claimed the place immediately in front of the President for the fine company of Sappers and Miners under Captain Duane of the Engineers.[18] To this choice body of men it was only necessary to say: *The honor of our country is in your hands.*

With a view to freedom of movement, I remained just outside of the Capitol Square with the light batteries. The procession returned to the President's mansion in the same order, and happily the Government was saved.

To show the new Administration that it was from no neglect of mine that several of our Southern forts had fallen into the hands of the rebels, I drew up and submitted the following defensive statement in March, 1861:

Southern Forts.

October 29, 1860.—I emphatically, as has been seen, called the attention of the President to the necessity of strong garrisons in all the forts below the principal commercial cities of the Southern States, including, by name, the forts in Pensacola Harbor, etc.

October 31.—I suggested to the Secretary of War that a circular should be sent at once to such of those forts as had garrisons, to be on the alert against surprises and sudden assaults.* {Permission not granted.}

After a long confinement to my bed, in New York, I came to this city (Washington), December 12. Next day I personally urged upon the Secretary of War the same views, viz.: strong garrisons in the Southern forts—those of Charleston and Pensacola Harbors, at once; those on Mobile Bay and the Mississippi, below New Orleans, next, etc., etc. I again pointed out the organized companies and the recruits at the principal depots available for the purpose. The Secretary did not concur in one of my views, when I begged him to procure for me an early interview with the President, that I might make one effort more to save the forts and the Union.

By appointment, the Secretary accompanied me to the President, December 15, when the same topics, secessionism, etc., were again pretty fully discussed. There being, at the moment, in the opinion of the President, no danger of an early secession, beyond South Carolina, the President, in reply to my arguments for immediately reinforcing Fort Moultrie, and sending a garrison to Fort Sumter, said, in substance, the time had not arrived for doing so; that he would wait the action of the Convention of South Carolina, in the expectation that a commission would be appointed and sent to negotiate with him and Congress, respecting the secession of the State and the property of the United States held within its limits; and that, if Congress should decide against the secession, then he would send a reënforcements, and telegraph the commanding officer (Major Anderson)[19] of Fort Moultrie, to hold the forts (Moultrie and Sumter) against attack.

And the Secretary, with animation, added: "We have a vessel of war (the Brooklyn) held in readiness at Norfolk, and he would then send three hundred men, in her, from Fort Monroe, to Charleston." To which I replied, first, "That so many men could not be withdrawn from that garrison, but could be taken from New York. Next, that it would then be too late, as the South Carolina Commissioners would have the game in their hands—by first using, and then cutting the wires; that, as there was not a soldier in Fort Sumter, any handful of armed secessionists might seize and occupy it," etc., etc.

Here the remark may be permitted, that, if the Secretary's three hundred men had then (or some time later) been sent to Forts Moultrie and Sumter, both would now have been in the possession of the United States, and not a battery, below them, could have been erected by the Secessionists. Consequently, the access to those forts from the sea would now (the end of March, 1861) be unobstructed and *free.*

"The plan invented by General Scott to stop secession was, like all campaigns devised by him, very able in its details and nearly certain of general success. The Southern States are full of arsenals and forts, commanding their rivers and strategic points. General Scott desired to transfer the army of the United States to these forts as speedily and as quietly as possible. The Southern States could not cut off communication between the Government and the fortresses without a great fleet, which they cannot build for years—or take them by land without one hundred thousand men, many hundred millions of dollars, several campaigns, and many a bloody siege. Had Scott been able to have got these forts in the condition he desired them to be, the Southern Confederacy would not now exist."—*Part of the Eulogy pronounced on Secretary Floyd, by the Richmond Examiner, on his reception at that city.*

The same day, December 15, I wrote the following note:

"Lieutenant-General Scott begs the President to pardon him for supplying, in this note, what he omitted to say this morning, at the interview with which he was honored by the President. 1. Long *prior* to the *Force Bill* (March 2, 1833), prior to the issue of his proclamation, and, in part, *prior* to the passage of the ordinance of nullification—President Jackson, under the act of March 3, 1807—'authorizing the employment of the land and naval forces'—caused reënforcements to be sent to Fort Moultrie, and a sloop-of-war (the Natchez), with two revenue cutters, to be sent to Charleston Harbor [all under Scott], in order to prevent the seizure of that fort by the nullifiers, and 2. To insure the execution of the revenue laws, General Scott himself arrived at Charleston the day after the passage of the ordinance of nullification, and many of the additional companies were then in route for the same destination.

"President Jackson familiarly said at the time: 'That, by the assemblage of those forces, for lawful purposes, he was not making war upon South Carolina; but that if South Carolina attacked them, it would be South Carolina that made war upon the United States.'

"General Scott, who received his first instructions (oral) from the President, Jackson, in the temporary absence of the Secretary of War (General Cass), remembers those expressions well.

"*Saturday night, December 16, 1860.*"

December 28.—Again, after Major Anderson had gallantly and wisely thrown his handful of men from Fort Moultrie into Fort Sumter—learning that, on demand of South Carolina, there was great danger he might be ordered by the Secretary back to the less tenable work, or *out* of the harbor, I wrote this note to the Secretary of War:

"Lieutenant-General Scott (who has had a bad night, and can scarcely hold up his head this morning) begs to express the hope to the Secretary of War—1. That orders may not be given for the evacuation of Fort Sumter; 2. That one hundred and fifty recruits may instantly be sent from Governor's Island to reënforce that garrison, with ample supplies of ammunition and subsistence, including fresh vegetables, as potatoes, onions, turnips, etc; 3. That one or two armed vessels be sent to support the said fort.

"Lieutenant-General Scott avails himself of this opportunity also to express the hope that the recommendation heretofore made by him to the Secretary of War, respecting Forts Jackson, St. Philip, Morgan, and Pulaski, and particularly in respect to Forts Pickens and McRee, and the Pensacola Navy Yard, in connection with the last two named works, may be reconsidered by the Secretary.

"Lieutenant-General Scott will further ask the attention of the Secretary to Forts Jefferson (Tortugas), and Taylor (Key West), which are wholly national—being of far greater value even to the most distant points of the Atlantic Coast and the people on the upper waters of the Missouri, Mississippi, and Ohio Rivers, than to the State of Florida. There is only a feeble company at Key West for the defence of Fort Taylor, and not a soldier in Fort Jefferson to resist a handful of fillibusters or a rowboat of pirates; and the Gulf, soon after the beginning of secession or revolutionary troubles in the adjacent States, will swami with such nuisances."

December 30.—I addressed the President again, as follows:

"Lieutenant-General Scott begs the President of the United States to pardon the irregularity of this communication. It is Sunday, the weather is bad, and General Scott is not well enough even to go to church.

"But matters of the highest national importance seem to forbid a moment's delay, and, if misled by zeal, he hopes for the President's forgiveness.

"Will the President permit General Scott, without reference to the War Department,* and, otherwise, as secretly as possible, to send two hundred and fifty recruits, from New York Harbor, to reënforce Fort Sumter, together with some extra muskets or rifles, ammunition, and subsistence. {The Secretary was already suspected.}

"It is hoped that a sloop-of-war and cutter may be ordered, for the same purpose, as early as to-morrow.

"General Scott will wait upon the President at any moment he may be called for."

The South Carolina Commissioners had already been many days in Washington, and no movement of defence (on the part of the United States) was permitted.

I will here close my notice of Fort Sumter by quoting from some of my previous reports.

It would have been easy to reënforce this fort down to about the 12th of February. In this long delay Fort Moultrie had been rearmed and greatly strengthened, in every way, by the rebels. Many powerful new land batteries (besides a formidable raft) had been constructed. Hulks, too, were sunk in the principal channel, so as to render access to Fort Sumter from the sea impracticable, without first carrying all the lower batteries of the Secessionists. The difficulty of reënforcing had thus been increased ten or twelve fold. First, the late President refused to allow any attempt to be made, because he was holding negotiations with the South Carolina Commissioners; afterward, Secretary Holt and myself endeavored, in vain, to obtain a ship of war for the purpose, and were finally obliged to employ the passenger steamer the *Star of the West*.[20] That vessel, but for the hesitation of the master, might, as is generally believed, have delivered at the fort the men and subsistence on board. This attempt at succor failing, I next verbally submitted to the late Cabinet, either that succor be sent by ships of war, fighting their way by the batteries (increasing in strength daily), or that Major Anderson should be left to ameliorate his condition by the muzzles of his guns; that is, enforcing supplies by bombardment, and by *bringing to* merchant vessels, helping himself (giving orders for payment), or, finally, be allowed to evacuate the fort, which, in that case, would be inevitable.

But before any resolution was taken—the late Secretary of the Navy making difficulties about the want of suitable war vessels—another Commissioner from South Carolina arrived, causing further delay. When this had passed away, Secretaries Holt and Toucey, Captain Ward of the Navy and myself[21]—with the knowledge of the President (Buchanan)—

settled upon the employment, under the Captain (who was eager for the expedition), of three or four small steamers, belonging to the Coast Survey. At that time (late in January), I have but little doubt, Captain Ward would have reached Fort Sumter, with all his vessels. But he was kept back by something like a truce or armistice made (here), embracing Charleston and Pensacola Harbors, agreed upon between the late President and certain principal seceders of South Carolina, Florida, Louisiana, etc., and this truce lasted to the end of that administration.

******

It was not till January 3 (when the first Commissioners from South Carolina withdrew) that the permission I had solicited, October 31, was obtained—to admonish commanders of the few Southern forts (with garrisons) to be on the alert against surprises and sudden assaults. (Major Anderson was not among the admonished, being already straitly beleaguered.)

January 3.—To Lieutenant Slemmer, Commanding in Pensacola Harbor:[22]

"The General-in-Chief directs that you take measures to do the utmost in your power to prevent the seizure of either of the forts in Pensacola Harbor, by surprise or assault—consulting first with the Commander of the Navy Yard, who will, probably, have received instructions to coöperate with you." (This order was signed by Aide-de-Camp Lay.)[23]

It was just before the surrender of the Pensacola Navy Yard (January 12) that Lieutenant Slemmer, calling upon Commodore Armstrong,[24] obtained the aid of some thirty common seamen or laborers (but no marines), which, added to his forty-six soldiers, made up his numbers to seventy-six men, with whom this meritorious officer has since held Fort Pickens, and performed (working night and day) an immense amount of labor in mounting guns, keeping up a strong guard, etc., etc.

Early in January I renewed (as has been seen) my solicitations to be allowed to reënforce Fort Pickens; but a good deal of time was lost in vacillations. First, the President "thought, if no movement is made by the United States, Fort McRee will probably not be occupied, nor Fort Pickens attacked. In case of movement by the United States, which will doubtless be made known by the wires, there will be corresponding local movements, and the attempt to reënforce will be useless." (Quotation from a note made by Aide-de-Camp Lay, about January 12, of the President's reply to a message from me.) Next, it was doubted whether it would be safe to send reënforcements in an unarmed steamer, and the want, *as usual,* of a suitable naval vessel—the Brooklyn being long held in reserve at Norfolk for some purpose unknown to me. Finally, after I had kept a body of three hundred recruits in New York Harbor ready for some time—(and they would have been sufficient to reënforce, temporarily, Fort Pickens, and to occupy Fort McRee also)—the President, about January 18, directed that the sloop-of-war Brooklyn should take a single company (ninety men from Fort Monroe, Hampton Roads), and reënforce Lieutenant Slemmer, in Fort Pickens, but without a surplus man for the neighboring fort, McRee!

The Brooklyn, with Captain Vogdes' Company alone,[25] left the Chesapeake, for Fort Pickens, about January 22, and on the 29th, President Buchanan, having entered into a *quasi* armistice with certain leading seceders at Pensacola and elsewhere, caused Secretaries Holt and Toucey to instruct, in a joint note, the commanders of the war vessels off Pensacola and Lieutenant Slemmer, commanding Fort Pickens, to commit no act of hostility, and not to land Captain Vogdes' Company unless that fort should be attacked!

******

It was known at the Navy Department that the Brooklyn, with Captain Vogdes on board, would be obliged in open sea to stand off and on Fort Pickens, and, in rough weather, might sometimes be fifty miles off. Indeed, if so at sea, the fort might have been attacked and easily carried before the reënforcement could have reached the beach (in open sea), where alone it could land.

Respectfully submitted,
WINFIELD SCOTT.

HEADQUARTERS OF THE ARMY,
WASHINGTON, March 30, 1861.

WASHINGTON, March 3, 1861.

DEAR SIR:

Hoping that in a day or two the new President will have happily passed through all personal danger, and find himself installed an honored successor of the great Washington, with you as the chief of his Cabinet—I beg leave to repeat in writing what I have before said to you orally—this Supplement to my printed "Views" (dated in October last) on the highly disordered condition of our (so late) happy and glorious Union.

To meet the extraordinary exigencies of the times, it seems to me that I am guilty of no arrogance in limiting the President's field of selection to one of the four plans of procedure subjoined:

I. Throw off the *old* and assume a *new* designation—the *Union Party;* adopt the conciliatory measures proposed by Mr. Crittenden or the Peace Convention, and, my life upon it, we shall have no new case of Secession; but on the contrary, an early return of many, if not of all the States which have already broken off from the Union. Without some equally benign measure, the remaining slaveholding States will probably join the Montgomery Confederacy in less than sixty days—when this city, being included in a foreign country, would require a permanent garrison of at least thirty-five thousand troops, to protect the Government within it.

II. Collect the duties on foreign goods outside the ports of which this Government has lost the command, or close such ports by act of Congress, and blockade them.

III. Conquer the seceded States by invading armies. No doubt this might be done in two or three years, by a young and able general—a Wolfe—a Desaix, or a Hoche,[26] with three hundred thousand disciplined men [kept up to that number], estimating a third for garrisons, and the loss of a yet greater number by skirmishes, sieges, battles, and Southern fevers. The destruction of life and property on the other side would be frightful—however perfect the moral discipline of the invaders. The conquest completed, at that enormous waste of human life to the North and Northwest, with at least $250,000,000 added thereto, and *Cui bono?*[27] Fifteen devastated Provinces! not to be brought into harmony with their conquerors; but to be held for generations by heavy garrisons, at an expense quadruple the net duties or taxes which it would be possible to extort from them, followed by a Protector or an Emperor.

IV. Say to the seceded States—*Wayward Sisters, depart in peace!*

In haste, I remain,
Very truly yours,
WINFIELD SCOTT.

HON. WILLIAM H. SEWARD.

But few contemporaries have been more highly complimented with literary distinctions and testimonials of public esteem than the autobiographer. A designation of some of those precious muniments he cannot deny himself the pleasure of citing in this narrative

Nassau Hall, Princeton, conferred the honorary degree of *Master of Arts* in September, 1814, and the year before I had been elected a member of the Whig Society of the same college.

Columbia College, New York, in 1850, conferred on me the honorary degree of LL.D.

And in 1861, a like distinction was superadded by Harvard College, Massachusetts.

A cripple, unable to walk without assistance for three years, Scott, on retiring from all military duty, October 31, 1861—being broken down by recent official labors of from nine to seventeen hours a day, with a decided tendency to vertigo and dropsy, I had the honor to be waited on by President Lincoln, at the head of his Cabinet, who, in a neat and affecting address, took leave of the worn-out soldier.

Testimonials followed from several States, Governors, and Cities, the Legislature of New Jersey, Rahway, and Elizabeth; two from Philadelphia—one headed by the Hon. Horace Binney, and the other by the Hon. Joseph R. Ingersoll[28]—each signed by hundreds of the most substantial citizens. A similar compliment was received from St. Louis, very numerously signed. The City of New York, in no ordinary terms, heaped upon the retired soldier her distinguished approbation. The *Chamber of Commerce* and *The Union Defence Committee,* each passed highly complimentary resolutions—the first presented by its venerable President, the late Peletiah Perit, at the head of a Committee, and the second by the eloquent Judge Edwards Pierrepont, on the part of the Committee of Defence, headed by Governor Hamilton Fish, Chairman.[29]

I deeply regret the want of space for all of those beautiful and honorable addresses, and it would be invidious to embody a part only.

In his first Annual Message to Congress (December, 1861), President Lincoln, prompted by his own kind and friendly nature, thus presented the autobiographer to the two Houses of Congress:

"Since your last adjournment, Lieutenant-General Scott has retired from the head of the army. During his long life the nation has not been unmindful of his merits; yet in calling to mind how faithfully and ably and brilliantly he has served his country, from a time far back in our history, when few now living had been born, and thenceforward continually—I cannot but think we are still his debtors. I submit, therefore, for your consideration what further mark of consideration is due to him and to ourselves as a grateful people."

THE END.

APPENDIX

Officers in Winfield Scott's Army in Mexico Who Later Became Civil War Generals

Northern Generals	Southern Generals
Robert Allen	James J. Archer
Lewis G. Arnold	Lewis Armistead
Robert Anderson	P. G. T. Beauregard
Joseph K. Barnes	Barnard Bee
John M. Brannan	Milledge L. Bonham
William Brooks	Simon B. Buckner
Robert Buchanan	James Cantey
Don Carlos Buell	Benjamin F. Cheatham
George Cadwalader	George B. Crittenden
Edward Canby	Arnold Elzey
Silas Casey	Richard S. Ewell
Napoleon Jackson Tecumseh Dana	Daniel Frost
Frederick T. Dent	Birkett Fry
Gustavus Adolphus DeRussy	Franklin Gardner
John Gray Foster	William Gardner
William French	John B. Grayson
John W. Geary	William Hardee
George W. Getty	James Hawes
Alfred Gibbs	Daniel Harvey Hill
Charles Gilbert	Paul O. Hebert
George H. Gordon	Benjamin Huger
Lawrance Graham	Thomas J. Jackson
Gordon Granger	Edward Johnson
Ulysses S. Grant	Joseph E. Johnston
Charles S. Hamilton	Davis R. Jones

Northern Generals	Southern Generals
Schuyler Hamilton	Robert E. Lee
Winfield Scott Hancock	James Longstreet
William S. Harney	William W. Loring
Joseph A. Haskin	Mansfield Lovell
John Porter Hatch	William W. Mackall
William Hays	John Magruder
Charles Heckman	George Maney
Ethan Allen Hitchcock	Arthur M. Manigault
Joseph Hooker	James Martin
Henry J. Hunt	Dabney Maury
Henry M. Judah	Samuel B. Maxey
Philip Kearny	John P. McCown
Michael K. Lawler	Abraham C. Myers
Nathaniel Lyon	John Pemberton
Jasper A. Maltby	George Pickett
George McClellan	Gideon Pillow
Justus McKinstry	Roswell Ripley
William R. Montgomery	Daniel Ruggles
George W. Morgan	Henry H. Sibley
James Scott Negley	James E. Slaughter
William Nelson	Edmund Kirby Smith
Innis N. Palmer	Gustavus W. Smith
Robert Patterson	William Duncan Smith
Gabriel René Paul	William Steele
John J. Peck	Alexander Steen
John W. Phelps	David E. Twiggs
Thomas G. Pitcher	Earl Van Dorn
Andrew Porter	John G. Walker
Fitz John Porter	William Walker
Henry Prince	Henry C. Wayne
Jesse Lee Reno	Cadmus M. Wilcox
Israel Richardson	John H. Winder

Northern Generals

Benjamin S. Roberts

David A. Russell

John Sedgwick

Truman Seymour

James Shields

Charles Smith

Frederick Steele

Isaac Ingalls Stevens

Charles P. Stone

Edwin V. Sumner

Thomas W. Sweeny

George Sykes

Joseph G. Totten

Zealous B. Tower

Stewart Van Vliet

Thomas Welsh

Henry Wessells

Seth Williams

Thomas Williams

George Wright

EDITOR'S NOTES

Introduction

1. Edmund Ludlow (1617–1692) served as an officer in the Parliamentarian forces in the English Civil War. He fought against King Charles I's Royalists at the Battles of Worcester, Edgehill, and Newbury and later led forces in Ireland. He was a member of the Long Parliament and Rump Parliament and was one of the fifty-nine judges who signed King Charles I's death sentence in 1649.

2. Sir Bulstrode Whitelocke (1605–1675) was a member of the Long Parliament and a supporter of Oliver Cromwell, but he was sympathetic to the monarchy and took no part in Charles I's trial and execution.

3. Edward Hyde, 1st Earl of Clarendon (1609–1674) was a member of the Short Parliament and Long Parliament as well as chancellor of the exchequer under Charles I. He was a strong supporter of the Church of England. After the restoration of the monarchy, Hyde served as minister for Charles II. He is perhaps best known as the author of *History of the Rebellion and Civil Wars of England*. He was also the grandfather of two British monarchs, Mary II and Queen Ann. Hyde is buried in Westminster Abbey.

4. Gilbert Burnet, bishop of Salisbury (1643–1715) was, in addition to being a Scottish theologian, an author and historian who wrote about church history.

5. Sir William Temple (1628–1699) was a British diplomat and statesman who negotiated the marriage of William and Mary, and for a time he employed Jonathan Swift (1667–1745), dean of St. Patrick's (Dublin) and author of *Gulliver's Travels* as well as *An Argument Against Abolishing Christianity*.

6. Both Tory Parliamentarians, Henry St. John, Viscount Bolingbroke (ca. 1678–1751) and Robert Harley, 1st Earl of Oxford (1661–1724) served Queen Anne and were the chief architects of the Treaty of Utrecht in 1713.

7. Dr. Samuel Johnson (1709–1784) was a journalist, essayist, biographer, and author of the *Dictionary of the English Language,* which was published in 1755. His popularity as a writer brought him celebrity status.

8. Sidney Godolphin, 1st Earl of Godolphin (1645–1712) was in Parliament for half a century. He served as first lord of the treasury and was later chief advisor to Queen Anne. In 1707 he played a role in helping to engineer the Act of Union with Scotland.

9. Lord Somers was John Somers, 1st Baron of Somers (1651–1716). He was solicitor general, became a chief advisor to William III, and in 1697 became lord chancellor.

10. John Churchill, 1st Duke of Marlborough (1650–1752) was an English statesman and soldier who won the Battle of Blenheim in 1704.

11. In the second paragraph of his introduction, Scott continued what he started in the first by mentioning the great soldiers and statesmen who have left their autobiographies and memoirs in the service of history (*pour servir à l'histoire*). Some of the names in this paragraph, such as Frederick the Great, Napoleon, and Talleyrand, are readily identifiable to the educated reader, but others—the Roman military leaders Marcus Porcius Cato and Lucius Cornelius Sulla, the second-century Greek historian Polybius, the sixteenth- to seventeenth-century French soldier and finance minister Sully, or the seventeenth-century president of the Parlement of Paris Jacques Auguste de Thou—are perhaps not. Interestingly, many of the men on Scott's list distinguished themselves as both soldiers and statesmen, mirroring Scott's own accomplishments in both fields. Xenophon (ca. 430–ca. 355 B.C.), whose name appears early in the paragraph, was a soldier and historian who was among the Greek mercenaries who accompanied Cyrus the Younger on his military expedition in Persia (401 B.C.). In his work, *The Anabasis*, Xenophon relates his role after the battle in leading the Greek "Ten Thousand" from deep in enemy territory to the Black Sea. The Greek term *anabasis* literally refers to a trip from the coast to the interior, reminiscent of Scott's 250-mile march from Veracruz to Mexico City during the war with Mexico.

    Scott saw himself as one of the "eminent men" of history worthy of being added to this lofty list. He wanted the reader to know at the outset of his *Memoirs* that he was erudite and well read. Through much of his introduction, Scott continued to mention the names of great men of history, both to illustrate for the reader his extensive knowledge and to underscore the historical value of recording great deeds.

12. Conyers Middleton (1683–1750) was both an author and clergyman. His *Life of Cicero* appeared in 1741.

13. Lucius Sergius Catiline (108–62 B.C.) was a controversial figure who is believed to have conspired to murder senators and overthrow the Roman Republic.

14. Publius Cornelius Tacitus (A.D. 56–117) was a Roman senator and historian who wrote extensively on the Roman Empire.

15. Thomas Babington Macaulay (1800–1859) was a British poet, historian, and politician.

16. The Bodleian Library is at the University of Oxford.

17. Here Scott referred to his successful Mexico City Campaign in 1847, which was followed by his removal from command and his appearance before a court of inquiry. The episode was an embarrassment rendered by President James K. Polk, who hoped to injure Scott's political chances in 1848.

18. Pelion and Ossa are two mountains in Greece. Scott was referring to an ancient saying, "Heap Pelion upon Ossa," which refers to a futile attempt to reach extreme heights.

Chapter I
Birth—Parentage—School—College

1. Scott's grandfather was James Scott, a Scottish clansman who fought with other Jacobites against the English army in a failed attempt to restore the Stuarts to the throne of England. The Pretender is Charles Edward Stuart (1720–1788). The last battle of this Jacobite uprising was at Culloden on April 16, 1746. James Scott was among the many clan members who fled Scotland after their decisive defeat. The Scotts of Buccleuch were lowlanders.

2. Homer was the ancient Greek poet and supposed author of the *Illiad,* the *Odyssey,* and other classics.

3. Horace, Quintus Horatius Flaccus (65–8 B.C.), was a Roman citizen and soldier. He is widely believed to be one of the most accomplished poets who wrote in Latin.

4. Gaius Plinius Secundas (A.D. 23–79), more commonly known as Pliny the Elder, was a first-century Roman official and naval officer who is most noted for writing his famous thirty-seven-volume *Natural History,* and thus Scott's reference to him as Pliny the naturalist.

5. François Rabelais (1494–1553) was a French Renaissance writer.

6. Famous for writing the Divine Comedy, Durante degli Alighieri (Dante) (1265–1321) was a prominent Italian poet who lived during the Middle Ages.

7. Carl Linnaeus (1707–1778) is regarded as the father of modern taxonomy and was a noted Swedish zoologist and botanist.

8. Reverend James Madison (1749–1812) was a bishop in the Episcopal Church and president of the College of William and Mary from 1777 to 1812. He was the cousin of the more famous James Madison, fourth president of the United States.

9. These men were all Enlightenment philosophers and writers whose deist and atheist views would have been viewed as dangerous by Bishop Madison.

Chapter II
Law Studies—The Bar—Trial of Burr

1. In December 1860, as several southern states began to consider secession, Congress feverishly worked on compromise proposals to prevent the

fracturing of the Union. Kentucky senator John J. Crittenden (1787–1863) proposed constitutional amendments designed to secure slavery and the Union, but his efforts failed. In February 1861, as representatives from the seven seceded states met in Montgomery, Alabama, to forge a new government, peace delegates from other slave states as well as northern free states met in Washington in what was known as the Washington Peace Convention. It convened in the Willard Hotel with former president and Virginia delegate John Tyler presiding. After working for three weeks, the group was unable to produce much other than a recycled version of Crittenden's earlier compromise proposals.

2. Antonio Canova (1757–1822) was an Italian sculptor famous for his neo-classical marble sculptures.

3. Scott was incorrect: Luther Martin (1748–1826) from Maryland was not a signer of the Declaration of Independence. However, he had been a del-egate at the Constitutional Convention in 1787, and as an anti-Federalist he opposed ratification of the new framework for government because it took too much power away from the states. He opposed slavery and fought against ratification of the Constitution. A brilliant defense attorney, Thomas Jefferson called him the "bulldog of Federalism." Martin and John Wickham (1763–1839), a New York loyalist during the Revolution and later a capable Virginia attorney, successfully defended Aaron Burr of the charge of treason. Before his death in 1826, Martin, in his capacity as attorney general of Maryland, argued his state's case before the Supreme Court in *McCullough v. Maryland* (1819).

4. At age thirty-one, Benjamin Botts (1776–1811) was the youngest of Burr's attorneys. Four years later, in 1811, Botts, his wife, Virginia governor George W. Smith (1762–1811), and sixty-nine others perished in the Rich-mond Theater fire. See also Scott's additional note on Botts's death.

5. Edward Irving (1792–1834) was a Scottish clergyman and founder of the Catholic Apostolic Church.

6. William Wirt (1772–1834) was a Virginia attorney who led the prosecu-tion of Jefferson's nemesis, Burr, in 1807. Later Wirt served as the ninth attorney general of the United States during the administrations of James Monroe and John Quincy Adams and still has the longest tenure in that office (1817–29). He also argued before the U.S. Supreme Court on behalf of the Cherokee Indians in *Worcester v. Georgia* (1832).

7. George Hay (1765–1830) was a Virginia Republican who had written in de-fense of the First Amendment and in opposition to the Sedition Act during John Adams's administration. In 1803 Jefferson appointed him U.S. district attorney.

8. Commodore Thomas Truxtun (1755–1822) was a privateer during the American Revolution and a successful naval commander during the Quasi War with France in 1798–1800. His most noted accomplishments in the

Quasi War were his capture of the French frigate *Insurgente* (1799) and his defeat of the *Vengence* (1800). Truxtun testified during Burr's trial that Burr had approached him to engage his participation in a military expedition against Spanish Mexico.

9. A native of Connecticut, William Eaton (1764–1811) served in the Continental army and captured the Tripolitan town of Derna in April 1805 during the war with Tripoli. Because Burr had tried to engage his services in his western land scheme, Eaton testified for the prosecution.

10. Andrew Jackson had met with Burr several times in Nashville in 1805 and 1806 and nearly had been unwittingly brought into the conspiracy. Jackson later became suspicious of Burr's true intentions and was a prosecution witness at Burr's grand jury. Scott later came to view Jackson and other Democrats as arch villains.

11. Later famous for writing "The Legend of Sleepy Hollow" and "Rip Van Winkle," a young Washington Irving (1783–1859) was not yet a famous author. He later became one of the first prominent American writers to be recognized in Europe.

12. Distinguished indeed were all the Virginians that Scott mentioned here. They were all senators at various times, and three of the four were congressmen. Two served as governors of the state (Giles, a Democrat, 1827–30, and Tazewell, a Whig, 1834–36) and two (Randolph and Taylor) were prominent in that offshoot of the Republicans called the Quids. Randolph, who was foreman of the grand jury, concluded that Gen. James Wilkinson (1757–1825) was just as guilty as Burr.

13. John Marshall (1755–1835) was a Revolutionary War veteran, a prominent Federalist, and a member of the American delegation to France during the famous XYZ Affair. He served as chief justice of the U.S. Supreme Court from 1801 to 1835 and did more than anyone else to write into constitutional law the concept of nationalism.

14. The latter two are references to John C. Calhoun (1782–1850) of South Carolina, Andrew Jackson's vice president and the architect of nullification, and John C. Breckinridge (1768–1851) of Kentucky, James Buchanan's vice president and a Confederate general.

Chapter III
Change of Profession—Adventure as a Volunteer— Returns to the Bar—Enters the Army

1. On June 22, 1807, the British ship HMS *Leopard* stopped the frigate USS *Chesapeake* near Norfolk, Virginia, requesting to search the American vessel. When Commodore James Barron (1768–1851) denied permission, the *Leopard* fired a broadside into the *Chesapeake,* killing three and wounding another eighteen, including Barron. The British then sent a boarding

party onto the *Chesapeake* and as a culminating insult impressed four Americans into service. Impressment had been a problem for years, but this was the first time that Americans had been impressed off a naval vessel. Technically an act of war, the episode outraged the public and brought a stern response from the Thomas Jefferson administration.

2. Sir Thomas Hardy (1769–1839) had commanded Admiral Lord Horatio Nelson's flagship *Victory* at the Battle of Trafalgar two years earlier.

3. The phrase "for the nonce" means for the time being or temporary.

4. William Lowndes (1782–1822) served in the South Carolina state legislature and the U.S. Congress. He was the son-in-law of Thomas Pinckney (1750–1828). At the time of his unexpected death in 1822, he was being mentioned as a possible presidential candidate in the upcoming 1824 election.

5. Langdon Cheves (1776–1857) was one of the "war hawks" elected to Congress in 1810 who would help lead the way to a declaration of war against England in 1812. Later Cheves served as president of the Second Bank of the United States.

6. William Drayton (1776–1846) from South Carolina served as a colonel in both the Tenth and Eighteenth Infantry Regiments. He was a congressman, proslavery author, and a president of the Second Bank of the United States. His two sons, Thomas and Percival, fought on different sides in the Civil War. Scott will refer to him again in chapter VIII as a colonel during the War of 1812.

7. Scott may have been referring to Thomas Lowndes, brother of William. Both men were congressmen. The Deases were probably William Allen Deas and James Sutherland Deas, both South Carolina politicians.

8. This is a reference to Judge Samuel Wilds (1775–1810).

9. Dr. Mitchell was Samuel Latham Mitchell (1764–1831), a senator from New York. Some sources spell the name Mitchill.

10. New York congressman Barent Gardenier (1762–1822) ardently opposed the Embargo Act and spoke out repeatedly against it and the administration. So heated were Gardenier's words on the floor of Congress against administration supporter and Tennessee congressman George W. Campbell (1769–1848) that the latter challenged the former to a duel in which Gardenier was seriously but not mortally wounded.

11. Cesare, Marquis of Beccaria (1738–1794), an Italian politician, opposed the harsh treatment of criminals, especially capital punishment. His best known work in which he outlined his benevolent views was *On Crimes and Punishments,* which was published in 1764.

Chapter IV
Four Years' Vacillation Between Peace and War—The Bar and the Sword

1. Between the *Chesapeake-Leopard* Affair in 1807 and the declaration of war in 1812, the tension between the United States and England rose and subsided periodically, and with it the prospects for war. New Orleans, because it controlled access to the Mississippi River and the hundreds of miles of navigable waterways in the heartland of the country, had to be defended. Louisiana had been purchased only five years earlier, and in the waning months of his presidency, Thomas Jefferson sent an army of about two thousand to New Orleans to protect the vulnerable area.

2. Fort Bowyer was an earthen fort built in 1813 and located near present-day Mobile, Alabama, and was the site of fighting during the War of 1812. It was later replaced by Fort Morgan.

3. For a few officers in this list, Scott provided adequate identifying information. However, for some, first names are needed and for others their exceptional service warrants more. Alexander Macomb (1782–1841) was commissioned a second lieutenant of infantry in 1801 and a first lieutenant in the U.S. Army Corps of Engineers in 1802. He would be Scott's chief rival for command of the army when Jacob Brown died in 1828. Joseph G. Swift (1783–1865) was the first graduate of West Point and chief of engineers during the War of 1812. He played a prominent role in army engineering projects after the war but resigned his commission in 1818. He and Scott remained lifelong friends. William McRee (1788–1833) was commissioned second lieutenant in the Corps of Engineers in 1805 after graduating West Point. He served with distinction in the War of 1812, resigned from the army in 1819, and died in 1833. Eleazer Derby Wood (1783–1814), Joseph G. Totten (1788–1864), and Sylvanus Thayer (1785–1872) all served capably in the War of 1812. Wood was killed late in the war (September 17, 1814), Totten was chief engineer of the army for two and a half decades before dying of pneumonia during the Civil War, and Thayer became known as the "Father of West Point" because of his capable superintendency of the academy. The remaining officers for whom Scott gave only last names were Henry Burbeck (1754–1848), James House (d. 1834), George Bomford (1780–1848), Julius Frederick Heileman (d. 1836), Zebulon M. Pike (1779–1813), Henry Dearborn (1759–1829), and Edmund P. Gaines (1777–1849).

4. The term "booby" was a common insult used in the eighteenth and nineteenth centuries to refer to someone considered dim witted or ignorant. Around the turn of the twentieth century the "y" was dropped, but the word continued to be a reference to a dunce. By the mid-twentieth century it began to take on a sexual connotation.

5. James Wilkinson (1757–1825) had served in the army since the Revolutionary War, but his career was racked with scandals. He was implicated in

Aaron Burr's conspiracy case but was not charged because he agreed to testify against Burr. For years Wilkinson was on the payroll of Spanish authorities, and he benefitted financially by contracting with corrupt agents for army supplies while stationed in New Orleans.

6. Wade Hampton (1754–1835) was a South Carolinian, a Revolutionary War veteran, and congressman. He rejoined the army in 1808 in anticipation of war with England and served in various capacities, ending the conflict with Andrew Jackson's army in New Orleans. He was the grandfather of the famous Confederate cavalry general of the same name.

7. Scott's rash actions and imprudent statements about his superior officer made him more culpable than his sanitized version suggests. Furthermore, the irregularities that characterized his handling of monthly pay allotments were not the only incidents of questionable financial dealings during his time in New Orleans. When Scott began his initial trip to New Orleans in 1808, a man named Daniel Bedinger asked him to deliver a slave boy to a man named Sheppard in the Creole City. When his ship got lodged on a sandbar near the mouth of the Mississippi River, Scott and the ship's captain became worried because the slave boy had not been entered on the ship's manifest. The slave was thus being illegally transported, and if discovered, the ship's owner could have been charged. So as an expedient, Scott sold the slave for $500 to a visitor who boarded the ship and supposedly mailed the money to Bedinger. However, the details of the story are murky and there is no evidence that Bedinger ever received his money.

8. Benjamin Hawkins (1754–1816) was a North Carolina delegate to the Continental Congress and later served in the Continental army. He served for a time on George Washington's staff. After a term as senator, President Washington appointed Hawkins superintendent of Indian Affairs in 1796, a post he filled until his death.

9. This was the trial of Col. Thomas H. Cushing, who was court-martialed for "disobedience of orders."

10. Jean Domat (seventeenth century) and Robert Joseph Pothier (eighteenth century) were notable French legal scholars and jurists. Their works contributed to the French Code Civil and were influential in both England and the United States. The Napoleonic Code drew heavily from their writings.

11. Scott's reference here is unclear. William Murray, 1st Lord of Mansfield, was a famous eighteenth-century British jurist who died in 1793. The British minister plenipotentiary to the United States at the time of the declaration of war was Sir Augustus John Foster (1780–1848).

Chapter V
War Declared—Double Promotion—March to Canada

1. Thomas Sumter (1734–1832) and Francis Marion (1732–1795), both South Carolinians, fought against the British in the Revolution. Their guerrilla tactics in the Carolina backcountry won them the nicknames "Carolina Gamecock" and "Swamp Fox" respectively. The Battle of Eutaw Springs on September 8, 1781, was the last battle in the campaign to win control of the Carolinas.

2. William Eustis (1753–1825) from Massachusetts served the Continental army as a physician during the Revolution. He filled the post of secretary of war (1809–1813) during James Madison's presidency and later served as minister to Holland and congressman from Massachusetts.

3. The two South Carolinians alluded to were David Rogerson Williams (1776–1830), who was a congressman and governor, and Paul Hamilton (1762–1816), who served as governor and secretary of the navy.

4. William Cowper (1731–1800) was a famous eighteenth-century English poet. Here Scott quoted from Cowper's poem "Slavery." The third line in its entirety is "Where rumor of oppression and deceit."

Chapter VI
Niagara Frontier—Capture of War Vessels—Battle of Queenstown—A Prisoner of War—Paroled

1. Jesse Duncan Elliott (1782–1845) was a naval officer who played a prominent but controversial role in the Battle of Lake Erie in September 1813.

2. Capt. Oliver Hazard Perry (1785–1819) defeated a British fleet at the Battle of Lake Erie on September 10, 1813. The public hailed both Perry and Elliott as heroes until a controversy arose questioning Elliott's actions during the battle.

3. Nathan Towson (1784–1854) from Maryland served with distinction as an artillery officer, especially at the Battle of Chippewa in 1814. Isaac Roach (1786–1848) was an artillery officer who would be wounded (Battle of Queenston Heights) and captured before the war ended. In 1838 he was elected mayor of Philadelphia.

4. In August 1812, Gen. William Hull (1753–1825), a Revolutionary War veteran, surrendered his army at Detroit in an abortive effort to invade Canada. At that time the USS *Adams* fell into British hands and was renamed the HMS *Detroit*. Later in the chapter, while narrating the Battle of Queenston Heights, Scott referred to this humiliating surrender to a smaller British force at Detroit, for which Hull was later court-martialed.

5. Stephen Van Rensselaer (1764–1839) was a wealthy landowner and politician in New York and the founder of Rensselaer Polytechnic Institute.

He was a state legislator, lieutenant governor of the state, and an officer in the state militia, which resulted in his War of 1812 command. He was a disappointment in field command.

6. The three lieutenant colonels were John R. Fenwick (1780–1842), John Christie (d. 1813), and Irish immigrant James Robert Mullany (1780–1846), who served as quartermaster general of the Northern Division of the U.S. Army.

7. This was Solomon Van Rensselaer (1774–1852), who was the cousin of the older Stephen Van Rensselaer. Solomon was the son of a Revolutionary War hero, and in the Niagara offensive under examination in Scott's *Memoirs,* he served as his cousin's chief of staff.

8. James N. Barker (1784–1858) was a Philadelphia native and briefly mayor of the city. He was also a playwright.

9. The full names of those in the list not previously identified are John Machesnesy from New Jersey; John E. Wool (1784–1869), a future general from New York; Henry B. Armstrong (1791–1884), a New Yorker and son of Secretary of War John Armstrong; Peter Ogilvie from New York; and Richard Montgomery Malcolm (1776–1823) from New York.

10. Joseph Gilbert Totten (1788–1864) from Connecticut was the tenth graduate of West Point in the 1805 class of three. He had a long and distinguished career as an engineer in the army, serving with distinction in the War of 1812 and as Scott's chief of engineers in the Mexican War. He went on to serve as a general in the Union army. Totten died of pneumonia in Washington in 1864, just days after his seventy-sixth birthday.

11. Maj. Gen. Sir Isaac Brock (1769–1812) was killed while leading an attack against American forces at Queenston, and his successor, Lt. Col. John Macdonell (1785–1812), was also mortally wounded.

12. Maj. Gen. Sir Roger Hale Sheaffe (1763–1851) was born in Boston, Massachusetts, to a loyalist family. After attending military school in England, he was commissioned an officer in the Fifth Regiment of Foot in 1778. Sheaffe replaced Brock as lieutenant governor of Upper Canada. For successfully leading British/Canadian troops to victory at Queenston, he was subsequently made a baronet.

13. Scott's reference is to Brig. Gen. William Wadsworth (1765–1833) of the New York Militia, who declined to pull rank on Scott and Lt. Col. Farrand Stranahan (1778–1807), another New York native.

14. Young Brant's father was Joseph Brant (1743–1807), the Mohawk Indian who allied himself with the British during the Revolutionary War.

15. A gorget is a metal or leather collar worn to protect the neck in combat.

Chapter VII
Kingston—Prescott—Montreal—Quebec—Sailed for Home—Gut of Canso—Washington

1. Lt. Col. Thomas Pearson (d. 1847) was a veteran of the Napoleonic Wars, most recently the Peninsular War in Spain.
2. These British officers were Col. Robert Lethbridge (b. 1760) and Maj. Gen. George Glasgow (d. 1820).
3. Prevost was repulsed when he tried to capture Sacket's Harbor in May 1813. The following year, in September, Prevost was again defeated at Plattsburgh on Lake Champlain, where his conduct was called into question. He demanded a court-martial to clear his name but died before the court convened.
4. Several editions of Edward D. Mansfield's panegyric biography appeared during Scott's lifetime. They were usually used as promotional material when Scott was maneuvering for the presidency.
5. Alexander Selkirk (1676–1721) was a Scottish sailor who was stranded on an island off the coast of Chile in South America from 1704 to 1709. He was rescued by English pirate and explorer William Dampier, and published accounts of Selkirk's time as a castaway made him famous. Daniel Defoe's novel *Robinson Crusoe* was based on Selkirk's adventure.
6. "Finny prey" is a reference to fish or animals that have fins.

Chapter VIII
Colonel and Adjutant-General—Fort George—Ogdensburg—Hoop-Pole Creek—French Mills

1. This 1813 French military manual was written by Paul Charles François Adrien Henri Dieudonné Thiébault (1769–1846).
2. Samuel B. Archer (1783–1825) from Virginia was a captain in the Second Artillery.
3. Lt. Col. George McFeely (1781–1854) was from Pennsylvania.
4. Col. Moses Porter (1756–1822) from Massachusetts had already served as an artillery officer for over thirty-five years and in September 1813 would be promoted to brigadier general. John Parker Boyd (1764–1830), John Chandler (1762–1841), and William H. Winder (1775–1824) were all brigadier generals. For more on Winder, see chapter XII, note 9.
5. Commodore Isaac Chauncey (1779–1840) was born in Connecticut and had served during the Quasi War with France and the Barbary War. In 1813 he rendered valuable services as commander of American naval forces on Lake Ontario. Gen. John Vincent (1764–1848) commanded British forces at Fort George.

6. See chapter VI, note 2.

7. Col. James Miller (1776–1851) from New Hampshire went on to command the Twenty-first Infantry with valor at the Battle of Lundy's Lane on July 25, 1814. He left the army in 1819, served as the first governor of the Arkansas Territory, and died in 1851.

8. Capt. Jacob Hindman (1789–1827) was a Maryland native, and Capt. Thomas Stockton (1781–1846) was a future governor of Delaware.

9. Col. James Burns, Second Dragoons, hailed from South Carolina.

10. Gen. Morgan Lewis (1754–1844) had previously served in the Revolution then became a lawyer. He served in the New York state legislature and defeated Aaron Burr for governor of New York in 1804. His order to halt the pursuit of British troops revealed timidity.

11. Col. Charles G. Boerstler (1778–1817) from Maryland commanded the Fourteenth Infantry Regiment.

12. Maj. Gen. Francis de Rottenburg was of Swiss origin but became an officer in the British army. He was the commander of Upper Canada in 1813.

13. Red Jacket (1750–1830) was a Seneca chief and in his sixties by the time of the War of 1812. While fighting against the colonists during the Revolution, he had been given a red jacket by the British, who dubbed him Red Jacket. The Mohawk leader Joseph Brant (1743–1807) was his enemy and rival. Red Jacket was known for his oratory, and his opposition to missionaries among his people positioned him as the leader of the more traditional branch of Seneca.

14. The branch of the Seneca that fell under the influence of missionaries came to be known as the Christian Party, and it was led by a chief called Captain Pollard.

15. Farmer's Brother was another Seneca warrior chief.

16. This is not the same Swift who was mentioned in chapter IV (note 3). That reference was to Joseph Gardner Swift. Here and in chapter XII, Scott was referring to Joseph's brother John Swift (1761–1814), who commanded New York Militia.

17. "Voltigeur" was a French term that usually referred to light infantry acting as skirmishers for the rest of the army.

18. Gen. George McClure was an officer in the New York Militia.

19. John G. Camp was from Virginia, but despite Scott's reference to him as a colonel, his rank apparently never exceeded major prior to his discharge in 1815.

20. The captains from the First Artillery were Nathaniel Leonard (1765–1844) from Vermont and probably James Read (d. 1813) from Pennsylvania. The lieutenant colonels were all of the New York Militia: George Fleming (d. 1822), Henry Bloom (1767–1818), and likely Hugh W. Dobbins.

21. Jacob Hindman was mentioned previously in note 8. He was a native of Maryland and an artillery officer who entered the army in 1808, was promoted to major in June 1813, and transferred to the artillery in May 1814. He fought with distinction as chief of Gen. Jacob Brown's artillery along the Niagara in 1814. Hindman died in 1827.

22. The Congreve rocket was a new weapon named for Englishman William Congreve (1772–1828). The rocket made a loud whistling sound and had a bright tail of fire that trailed it. It was this rocket's red glare that Francis Scott Key witnessed during the bombardment of Fort McHenry in 1814.

23. The skirmish of Hoople Creek on November 10, 1813, was one of several setbacks suffered by American troops in their push up the St. Lawrence River. Lieutenant Colonel Dennis is British brevet major James Dennis of the Forty-ninth Regiment of Foot. Scott's account of Gen. James Wilkinson's 1813 campaign tends to put a positive spin on what was actually a disappointing failure.

24. The artillery officer was Capt. Robert Hector Macpherson (1784–1817).

25. The American defeat at the Battle of Crysler's Farm on November 11, 1813, ended Wilkinson's ill-fated attempt to capture Montreal. The battle was fought on the farm of John Crysler near present-day Morrisburg, Ontario.

Chapter IX
Reflections on Past Disasters—Called to Washington—Buffalo—Camp of Instruction—Campaign of 1814 Opened

1. Scott's references are to Brig. Gen. William Hull's surrender at Detroit on August 16, 1812, Brig. Gen. John Chandler's defeat and capture at the Battle of Stoney Creek on June 5, 1813, Col. Charles Boerstler's command, which was surprised and captured by a smaller British and Native American force while marching to Beaver Dams, and Brig. Gen. George McClure's disgraceful burning of the town of Newark as he abandoned Fort George on December 10, 1813.

2. Gulian C. Verplanck (1786–1870) was a theology professor, member of the New York State Assembly, mayor of New York City, and a Democratic congressman. He left the Democrat Party and joined the Whigs when Andrew Jackson began his attacks on the National Bank.

3. Isaac Chauncey (1779–1840) commanded American naval forces on Lake Ontario. On May 29, 1813, he repulsed an attack on Sacket's Harbor by a British fleet under Capt. James Lucas Yeo (1781–1818). They fought a series of hit-and-run naval battles with the fleets that had been built on Lake Ontario.

4. John Armstrong (1758–1843) was James Madison's secretary of war (1813–14). He was criticized and held responsible for the British capture

and burning of Washington in 1814. In chapter XXI, Scott referred to him as "Minister at Paris." He was the U.S. minister to France during the Jefferson administration, 1804–10.

5. John Nicholas (1764–1819) of Williamsburg, Virginia, served in Congress from 1793 to 1801. He moved to Geneva, New York, in 1803 and was elected to the state legislature.

6. Phineas Riall (1775–1850) commanded British troops in Upper Canada in 1813 and 1814. In December 1813, Riall's force crossed over to the American side of the Niagara River and for more than a week marched through western New York burning towns and villages in retaliation for the burning of Newark earlier in the month. He would be defeated by an American force in Scott's command at Chippewa in July 1814.

7. George Bomford (1780–1848) was a West Point graduate who served in the Corps of Engineers. He was the chief designer of the columbiad, a heavy gun that was used for many years for U.S. coastal defense. Despite Scott's reference to him as a colonel, Bomford was not promoted to lieutenant colonel until February 1815.

8. Daniel Tompkins (1774–1825) served as the fourth governor of New York and would later be vice president during James Monroe's presidency. Financial and alcohol problems led to an early death. Judges Spencer and Thompson are probably John C. Spencer (1788–1855) and William A. Thompson.

9. Elisha Jenkins (1772–1849) and Francis Bloodgood (1768–1840) were New York politicians who both served as mayor of Albany. In 1807 Bloodgood famously engaged in a street fight with Solomon Van Rensselaer, who played a role in the Battle of Queenston Heights in October 1812.

10. Spencer Roane (1762–1822) was one of the preeminent jurists of his day who would have perhaps been appointed chief justice of the Supreme Court instead of John Marshall if Thomas Jefferson and not John Adams had made the nomination. Roane was a Virginian and Patrick Henry's son-in-law. A staunch advocate of states' rights, he was one of the intellectual architects of the state compact theory and nullification.

11. At age twenty-seven, Scott was the youngest general in the army. He would go on to serve as a general officer for forty-seven years, the last twenty of which (1841–61) he was a major general and commanding general of the United States Army.

12. Jacob J. Brown (1775–1828) was born in Pennsylvania and raised a Quaker. When the War of 1812 started, he held the rank of brigadier general in the New York Militia, and despite having no formal military training, he rose through the ranks and received a regular army commission because of his competence on the battlefield. In 1814 he was a major general, Scott's superior officer, and commander on the Niagara River front.

13. Eleazar W. Ripley (1782–1839) was a Massachusetts lawyer and 1800 graduate of Dartmouth College. He had fought with distinction earlier in the war, even in Gen. James Wilkinson's ill-fated Montreal Campaign in 1813. In 1814 he was among the new young generals in the army. He commanded a brigade in Gen. Jacob Brown's army along the Niagara River but ran afoul of the commanding general after the Battle of Lundy's Lane on July 25, 1814.

14. This is a reference to Scott's training camp, which was wisely located on well-drained Flint Hill outside of Buffalo. For ten weeks Scott oversaw training and drill for a sizable portion of Jacob Brown's army, which would fight along the Niagara River that summer. However, slightly less than half the army was in the camp the entire time. Some regiments came and went after brief stays. It was here that Scott began to turn the poorly trained army into a more disciplined fighting force.

15. Scott's reference is probably to the 1791 French system of tactics published as *Règlement Concernant l'Exercise et les Manoeuvres de l'Infanterie,* and the "bad translation" may have referred to Alexander Smyth's 1812 adaptation.

16. When General Brown brought the army together to initiate action in the summer of 1814, it was organized as follows: Maj. Jacob Hindman (see chapter VIII, note 20) commanded the artillery; Scott commanded the First Brigade, made up of the Ninth, Eleventh, Twenty-second, and Twenty-fifth Regiments; and Brig. Gen. Eleazar Ripley commanded the Second Brigade, comprised of the First, Twenty-first, and Twenty-third Regiments. Peter Buel Porter (1773–1844), a politician/soldier and a major general in the New York Militia, commanded Pennsylvania and New York volunteers. Porter was a war hawk in Congress before the war and later served as John Quincy Adams's secretary of war.

17. Fort Erie was located at the southern end of the Niagara River.

18. All three lieutenants were from New York and served as aides to Scott. Gerard D. Smith (1790–1835) stayed in the army until 1819 and died in 1835. William Jenkins Worth (1794–1849) was raised in a Quaker family but rejected its pacifism. The young officer became a longtime friend of Scott, but in 1847 their friendship fractured while Worth served as a division commander in Scott's army during the war with Mexico. George Watts (d. 1819) also served with distinction during the campaign and left the army in 1816. All three officers received brevet promotions for their conspicuous gallantry in 1814.

19. Thomas Sidney Jesup (1788–1860) had a long and distinguished career in the army. He entered the army in the same year as Scott, 1808, and served until his death in 1860. He is best known for his work in building and heading the Quartermaster Department. He served with distinction in Scott's brigade along the Niagara River in 1814, but the longtime friends crossed swords after Scott failed campaign against the Creek Indians (chapter XX).

Chapter X
Running Fight—Chippewa

1. Henry Leavenworth (1783–1834) was born in Connecticut and grew up in New York. He was a lawyer and major in the state militia when he received a commission in the regular army in 1812. His competence and bravery were on display at both Chippewa and Lundy's Lane in July 1814. After the war Leavenworth served for many years on the western plains and eventually achieved the rank of brigadier general before his death in 1834. Fort Leavenworth in Kansas was named for him.

2. John McNeil Jr. (1784–1850) was from New Hampshire and he was a brigadier general at the time of his resignation in 1830. He was the son-in-law of prominent Revolutionary War hero Gen. Benjamin Pierce, whose influence helped him secure the job of supervisor of the Port of Boston, which McNeil held for the last twenty years of his life.

3. Samuel D. Harris from Massachusetts commanded a regiment of mounted troops and served in the army until the reduction of 1821. Afterward he worked in the Boston Fire Department.

4. Thomas Biddle (1790–1831) was a native of Philadelphia, Pennsylvania, and was brevetted a major for his distinguished service in 1814. His brother was Nicholas Biddle, who became the president of the Second Bank of the United States. Thomas was killed in a duel with a Missouri congressman.

5. George Hay (1787–1876) from Scotland was the eighth Marquess of Tweeddale.

6. For William McRee and Eleazer Derby Wood, see chapter IV, note 3.

7. This is a reference to Fort Schlosser, New York.

8. The military academy at West Point adopted gray after the War of 1812 and continues that tradition today. However, despite Scott's embellishment, it was not because of the gray-clad militia at the Battle of Chippewa. Rather, it was because gray cloth was abundant and cheap.

9. The reference is to Horatio Nelson (1758–1805), the famous British naval officer, who blockaded and captured the French towns of Bastia and Calvi in 1794 during the wars of the French Revolution.

10. This is French general Jean Victor Marie Moreau (1763–1813).

11. "Rencounter" refers to a chance meeting on a battlefield.

12. The Hartford Convention was a meeting of New England Federalists, who came together in December 1814 to express their dissatisfaction with the war and with the James Madison administration in general. The secret meeting in Hartford, Connecticut, resulted in a set of resolutions that were states' rights in nature, but when the meeting became publicly known, its unpopularity contributed to the demise of the Federalist Party.

Chapter XI
Investment of Forts—Battle of Niagara or Lundy's Lane

1. Translated, the phrase means "Man proposes and God disposes."

2. The name of the homeowner was James Forsyth.

3. Sir Gordon Drummond (1772–1854) was a Canadian-born officer and colonial administrator. He reinforced Riall's force, was wounded at Lundy's Lane, and failed the following month to capture Fort Erie.

4. Hugh Brady (1768–1851) from Pennsylvania entered the army in 1792 and was a veteran of Gen. "Mad" Anthony Wayne's Battle of Fallen Timbers in 1794. Brady left the service in 1800 but was commissioned a colonel when the War of 1812 began. After the war he served at various posts, including Fort Snelling, Minnesota, and Detroit, Michigan. He attained the rank of major general in 1848 and died in a carriage accident in 1851.

5. Scott's shoulder wound was serious, and he felt the effects of it for the rest of his life. In chapter XII Scott recounts his convalescence.

6. Having assumed command of the American army after Brown's and Scott's wounds, General Ripley ordered the battlefield abandoned, including the hotly contested British guns that the Americans had captured. Ripley's decision to give up the field of battle became a controversy.

Chapter XII
Hors de Combat—Princeton College— Philadelphia—Baltimore—Washington

1. In order to expand credit in the state, the Mississippi legislature chartered numerous banks during the economic boom of the 1830s. Among the banks thus chartered was the Mississippi Union Bank, which was to be financed in part by the state's sale of $5 million in bonds. These are the bonds in which Wilson had invested. When the economic panic of the late 1830s hit, numerous Mississippi Democrats wanted to repudiate the debt and refuse to repay the bonds. Many of the Union Bank Bonds had been purchased by investors outside the state, and some Mississippians did not want to see hard-earned and hard-to-come-by Mississippi dollars leave the state to pay bondholders. So the state repudiated the debt, leaving investors like the Englishman Wilson holding worthless bonds. The controversy over repudiation became the great overriding issue in Mississippi for years, and when Jefferson Davis first ran for Congress in the 1840s, he came down on the side of repudiation. It is with perhaps some exaggeration that Scott contended that it was his writing on behalf of the bondholders that produced the ill will between himself and Davis when the latter became secretary of war in 1853.

2. This is a reference to James Brisbane (1776–1851) and his sister Margaret Eleanor Brisbane, who married Trumbull Carey. James was the grandfather of Arthur Brisbane, the famous newspaper editor.

3. Dr. Philip Syng Physick (1768–1837) was known as the father of American surgery. He studied at the University of Pennsylvania, London's Royal College of Surgeons, and the University of Edinburgh. He was an innovative and talented surgeon and was his generation's foremost teacher of surgical techniques.

4. Despite his early death, Dr. John Syng Dorsey (1783–1818), Physick's nephew, was a talented surgeon in his own right and wrote the first textbook on surgery in America, *The Elements of Surgery,* in 1813.

5. William Gibson (1788–1868) studied under Physick in Philadelphia and at the University of Edinburgh.

6. William Lowndes (1782–1822) was a South Carolina congressman.

7. "Rasselas" is short for *The History of Rasselas, Prince of Abissinia,* an essay published in book form by Samuel Johnson in 1759. It is an allegorical story about human suffering and the source of true happiness.

8. William Cumming (1788–1863) was a Georgia lawyer and planter as well as an army officer and Princeton graduate.

9. William H. Winder (1775–1824) from Maryland was responsible for the defense of Washington. He was defeated at the Battle of Blandensburg on August 24, 1814, and when the capital subsequently fell into British hands, they burned the city. Winder was court-martialed but was acquitted of all charges.

Chapter XIII
Reduction of the Army—Visit to Europe—England—France

1. Alexander James Dallas (1759–1817) was born in Jamaica and lived in Scotland and England before marrying and later settling in Pennsylvania, where he became a lawyer of note.

2. William H. Crawford (1772–1834) was from Georgia. A congressman and senator, Crawford was a presidential candidate in 1824.

3. The Prussian king to whom Scott referred was Frederick William III.

4. Gebhard Leberecht von Blücher was a Prussian field marshal during the Napoleonic Wars. As punishment for the French army's depredations against the Prussians, Blücher wanted to destroy the beautiful Jena Bridge in Paris.

5. Alexander von Humboldt (1769–1859) was a famous German scientist who worked extensively in Latin America.

6. Thomas Bolling Robertson (1779–1828) was from a prominent Virginia family. The William and Mary graduate and Petersburg attorney emigrated to the Louisiana Territory soon after its purchase from France. He was the first congressman elected after Louisiana became a state and later served as its third governor before becoming a federal judge. His mother, Elizabeth Bolling, was supposedly a descendant of Pocahontas.

7. Thaddeus Kosciusko (1746–1817) was a Pole and a graduate of Poland's Royal Military School in Warsaw. He traveled to America in 1776 and received a commission in the Continental army. His skills as an army engineer were evident at Saratoga and West Point, New York. After the American Revolution, Kosciusko returned to Poland and fought for Polish independence in the 1790s. After Poland's partitioning, he lived the rest of his life in exile.

8. Louis Philippe, comte de Ségur (1753–1830) was a French diplomat and historian who had served under comte de Rochambeau, the commander of French forces in the American Revolution.

9. François Barbé-Marbois (1745–1837) was secretary in the French legation to the United States during the American Revolution and later chargé d'affaires. He married Elizabeth Moore, the daughter of a Pennsylvania governor. After his return to France, he helped negotiate the Louisiana Purchase in 1803.

10. Étienne Maurice Gérard (1773–1852) rose to prominence as a French general during the Napoleonic Wars and served briefly as prime minister of France in the 1830s.

11. The Englishman Admiral Sir George Cockburn (1772–1853) had made a name for himself in the Napoleonic Wars and, by the time of the War of 1812, had developed a reputation as a plunderer who took full economic advantage of seized enemy areas. He sailed up and down the coast along the Chesapeake Bay during the War of 1812 wreaking havoc on American shipping, and in August 1814 he was chiefly responsible for the burning of Washington, D.C. He enjoyed a long naval career and later served in Parliament.

12. After leading troops against the French in Spain, Gen. Robert Ross (1766–1814) was ordered to North America to participate in invasion of the Chesapeake in 1814. Ross's troops defeated the American force under Gen. William H. Winder at Blandensburg, captured Washington, D.C., and burned the public buildings. In September 1814, while marching against Baltimore, a sniper shot and killed Ross.

13. Cumberland Island is one of Georgia's barrier islands. After the Revolutionary War, American general Nathaniel Greene bought over ten thousand acres on the island and moved there. After his untimely death in 1786, his widow, Catherine, built the four-story mansion known as Dungeness. The

USS *Constitution* was built with wood from Cumberland Island. When Cockburn occupied the island, he freed 149 slaves owned by Louisa Greene Shaw, the daughter of Nathaniel Greene and widow of James Shaw. During a visit to Cumberland Island in 1818, "Lighthorse" Harry Lee died there. Lee's gravesite was visited by his son, Robert E. Lee, but not until 1913 were Harry's remains moved to Lexington, Virginia. Dungeness burned in 1866. For the past 130 years family descendants of Andrew Carnegie have owned and lived on the island.

14. Mikhail Semenovich Vorontsov (1782–1856) was a general in the Russian army, a participant of the Battle of Borodino, and commander of Russian occupation forces in France from 1815 to 1818. His father, Semyon Romanovich Vorontsov, was a Russian diplomat who spent a large part of his adult life in England. "Woronzow" is the English spelling of the surname.

15. The officers mentioned were William Drayton (chapter III, note 6), William McRee (chapter IV, note 3), Sylvanus Thayer (chapter IV, note 3), and Samuel B. Archer (chapter VIII, note 2).

16. The chargé was Henry Jackson (1778–1840).

Chapter XIV
England—London—Bath

1. Henry Richard Vassall Fox, 3rd Baron of Holland (1773–1840), was a Whig politician who was instrumental in outlawing the slave trade in the British Empire. His uncle, Charles James Fox, was a member of the House of Lords whose limited monarchical views were well known.

2. Sir James Mackintosh (1765–1832) was a jurist, politician, professor, and doctor from Scotland.

3. Sir Samuel Romilly (1757–1818) was a lawyer, a member of the House of Commons, and a reformer of English criminal law.

4. The Earl of Lauderdale to whom Scott referred was either James Maitland (9th Earl of Lauderdale) or Anthony Maitland (10th Earl of Lauderdale). The relative with whom Scott had a brusk exchange was Sir Frederick Lewis Maitland (1777–1839), captain of the British ship of the line HMS *Bellerophon*. After Napoleon Bonaparte's defeat at Waterloo in June 1815, he tried to escape the Continent in a French frigate with hopes of making it to America. However, on July 15, Captain Maitland positioned the seventy-four-gun *Bellerophon* to block his escape and subsequently took Napoleon into custody and sailed him to England. The topic under dispute at Scott's and Maitland's dinner table had to do with the American practice of mounting forty-four guns on their frigates rather than thirty-two to thirty-six guns, which was standard for ships rated in the frigate category.

5. The Treaty of Campo Formio in 1797 gave France control of present-day Belgium and central Italy.

6. Rebecca Franks (1760–1823) was a loyalist in Philadelphia during the American Revolution. Near the end of the war she married Lt. Col. Henry Johnson, a British army officer who rose to the rank of general. Johnson (1748–1835) was captured by the Americans at Stony Point, New York, in 1779, and after his exchange he was captured again at Yorktown in 1781 while under Charles Cornwallis's command. At the time of Scott's visit to England, Henry and wife Rebecca lived in his hometown of Bath, England.

Chapter XV
Reflections on Peace and War—The Canker
Abolitionism—State Rights—Nullification—Rebellion

1. Aristides the Just was a fifth-century Greek aristocrat, statesman, and general. Militarily, he was known for strengthening the Athenian navy and driving the Persians from Greece. He pursued a life of integrity, put the good of the state before personal considerations, and was disinterested in accumulating wealth. His sense of justice and right caused him to stand above the rest, which created envy among the masses, who then voted to banish him from Athens.

2. This is a quote for the seventeenth-century English poet John Milton. "Ammiral" is an obsolete spelling of admiral.

3. A character in Shakespeare's play *The Tempest*, Caliban, a slave, attempted to rape his master's daughter, Miranda.

4. Charles XII (1682–1718) was king of Sweden during the Great Northern War, which saw the rise of Russia and the demise of Sweden in the eastern European power play.

5. William Murray, 1st Earl of Mansfield, was an eighteenth-century lawyer (1705–1793), politician, and judge; William Blake (1757–1827) was a poet and painter; and the Duke of Marlborough, John Churchill (1650–1722), was a general and skilled strategist. All three were Englishmen.

6. Secretary of War John C. Calhoun urged President James Monroe to take harsh action against Gen. Andrew Jackson after Jackson invaded Spanish Florida in 1817 in what came to be known as the First Seminole War. The brief incursion violated Spain's sovereignty and a dozen years later would contribute to the break between then-president Jackson and Vice President Calhoun. Jackson's military foray into Florida coincided with negotiations that were underway at that time between Secretary of State John Quincy Adams and the Spanish minister to the United States, Don Louis de Onís, which culminated in the Adams-Onís Treaty in 1819, by which Spain ceded Florida to the United States.

7. The reference is to a letter Scott wrote to attorney T. P. Atkinson of Danville, Virginia, on February 9, 1843, in which he explained his views on slavery. In that letter Scott wrote "that it is a high moral obligation of

masters and slave-holding States, to employ all means, not incompatible with the safety of both colors, to meliorate slavery, even to extermination." Essentially, Scott believed slavery to be evil but did not believe the federal government had the authority to abolish it. See Charles Winslow Elliott, *Winfield Scott: The Soldier and the Man* (New York: Macmillan, 1937), 409.

8. A native of Connecticut, Edward Deering Mansfield (1801–1880) was a West Point graduate (1819) and a Princeton graduate (1822). He taught constitutional law in Cincinnati and became an author, writing a biography of Scott (*The Life and Services of General Winfield Scott*) that went through several editions. See also chapter VII, note 4.

9. This was a famous quotation by Swedish chancellor and army general Axel Oxenstierna (1583–1654) to his son: "Do you not know, my son, with how little sense this world is run?"

10. *King Lear* is a Shakespearian tragedy in which the king unwisely judged how to divide his empire among his three daughters based on the level of cajolery they directed toward him.

11. Born in Maine, Rufus King (1755–1827) attended the Constitutional Convention in Philadelphia. He practiced law in Massachusetts, served as a senator from New York, and was an opponent of slavery. In addition to being a Federalist politician, King was twice minister to Great Britain.

12. Charles Sumner (1811–1874) was a senator from Massachusetts.

Chapter XVI

Marriage—Reception of Swords and Medal

1. Maria DeHart Mayo (1789–1862) married Winfield Scott on March 11, 1817. She was the daughter of the politically and socially connected John Mayo, who was once mayor of Richmond, Virginia. Winfield and Maria had seven children—Maria, John, Virginia, Edward, Cornelia, Marcella, and Adeline—of which only three daughters lived to adulthood. Maria spent extended periods of time in Europe during her marriage to Scott, and she died in Rome, Italy, in 1862.

2. James Pleasants Jr. (1769–1836) was governor of Virginia from 1822 to 1825.

3. Daniel D. Tompkins (1774–1825) was a congressman, governor of New York (1807–1817), and vice president under James Monroe.

4. Among his numerous biographies, James Parton wrote one of Andrew Jackson in 1859–1860.

5. George Graham (1772–1830) was acting secretary of war at this time.

6. DeWitt Clinton (1769–1828) preceded Pleasants as governor of New York (1817–1822).

7. Erostratus burned the Temple of Diana simply in the hopes of making a name for himself.

8. After giving his version of his dispute and near duel (in reality, Scott was intimidated by Jackson and happy to avoid a head-on collision) with Andrew Jackson, he mentioned "a postponement of revenge," which refers to President Jackson's order to investigate Scott's failure in Florida during the Second Seminole War.

Chapter XVII
Temperance Movement—Military Institutes—Tactics—Death of General Brown—Macomb Promoted—Animated Correspondence

1. Robert Walsh (1785–1859) from Baltimore was editor of the *National Gazette and Literary Examiner,* which first appeared in 1820. Scott goes on to assert that his temperance writing caused temperance societies to spring up—another of Scott's exaggerations.

2. This maxim is taken from one of the most influential military works prior to the eighteenth century, *De Re Militari* (Concerning Military Matters) by Flavius Vegetius Renatus, who lived in the fourth century.

3. Scott's work essentially adapted France's *Législation Militaire* and England's *General Regulations and Orders for the Army,* for it drew heavily from both works. His *General Regulations for the Army; or, Military Institutes* was the first comprehensive, systematic set of military bylaws that set standards for every aspect of the soldier's life. He began work on the project in 1818 and finally finished it in 1821. The War Department granted him a leave from his duties to work on it, but family illnesses and other difficulties unexpectedly delayed its completion. The "cursed book . . . has given me so much trouble," he wrote to a friend. Scott also wrote tactical manuals, and for his 1835 *Infantry Tactics,* he received $5,000 from the War Department along with an agreed-to royalty of sixty-eight cents per copy purchased for the army. Scott was unhappy when junior officers were allowed to write their own tactical manuals, thereby encroaching upon Scott's hegemony in the field. See also chapter XX, note 1.

4. Thomas Cadwalader (1779–1841) was a successful Philadelphia lawyer and trustee of the Bank of the United States. When the War of 1812 began, he served on Philadelphia's Committee of Defense, and briefly in 1815 he commanded U.S. forces in eastern Pennsylvania, Delaware, and parts of New Jersey and Maryland. Thomas was the father of George Cadwalader, who served in Scott's army in Mexico.

5. William H. Sumner (1780–1861) from Boston was the son of a Massachusetts governor. He was an attorney and for ten years (1809–1819) a

member of the state legislature. He was appointed adjutant general of Massachusetts. He worked to make improvements to Boston Harbor and wrote *History of East Boston.*

6. The remaining members of the board were Maj. Zachary Taylor (1784–1850), Col. Enos Cutler (1781–1860), Col. Abram Eustis (1786–1843), Capt. Charles J. Nourse (1786–1851), and Daniel Beverly.

7. The Army Reduction Act of 1821 left Jacob Brown as the only major general, and he thus became the first commanding general of the army under the Monroe administration's new military organization. Scott and Edmund Pendleton Gaines (1777–1849) were the two brigadier generals, and since both had been promoted to general in 1814, a dispute erupted concerning who would succeed Brown as the army's highest ranking officer. The famous Scott-Gaines feud lasted for decades. It became so rancorous following Brown's 1828 death that President John Quincy Adams finally decided to pass over both of the antagonists and promote Alexander Macomb (1782–1841) to the post. In 1814 Macomb had actually been promoted to brigadier general prior to both Scott's and Gaines's attainment of that rank, but the latter two generals had subsequently been brevetted as major generals. When Scott and Gaines were reduced to their regular rank of brigadier general in 1821, Macomb took a reduction back to colonel. Scott based his argument of seniority on being the first of the three to reach major general, although by brevet, while Macomb's seniority was based on the fact that he reached the regular rank of brigadier general first. After Macomb's ascension to army commander in 1828, Scott continued to insist that he was the senior officer and consequently refused to obey Macomb's orders.

8. Anacosta Island is now Theodore Roosevelt Island Park.

9. Anna Maria Murray Mason and Catherine Eliza Murray Rush were the women said to have visited First Lady Louisa Catherine Johnson Adams. Mrs. Mason was the mother of Sarah Maria Mason Cooper, who was married to Samuel Cooper (1798–1876). Cooper was a West Point graduate (1815) whose military career included various staff assignments during the Second Seminole War and Mexican War. He was promoted to adjutant general of the army in 1852 and during the Civil War served as adjutant general and inspector general of the Confederate army. Cooper always denied Scott's story about the alleged role his mother-in-law played in his assignment to Macomb's staff in 1828. Cooper's authorship of a tactical manual (1836) and his service on Scott's court of inquiry (1837) guaranteed Scott's less than favorable opinion of the junior officer.

10. Madame de Maintenon (1635–1719) was the second wife of Louis XIV, king of France. Madame de Pompadour (1721–1764), as Louis XV's mistress, was said to have great influence over many of his decisions.

11. Henry Clay (1777–1852), secretary of state; Samuel L. Southard (1787–1842), secretary of the navy; William Wirt (1772–1834), attorney general; Richard Rush (1780–1859), secretary of the treasury.

12. The senator mentioned is probably Henry Johnson (1783–1864), congressman, senator, and governor of Louisiana. His wife, Elizabeth Key, was related to Francis Scott Key.

13. Salic Law (Lex Salica) originated with the Franks in Europe during the sixth century. It excluded women from royal succession to the throne.

14. Roger ap Catesby Jones (1789–1852) was adjutant general of the United States Army from 1825 to 1852.

Chapter XVIII
Black Hawk War—Cholera in the Army—
Indian Treaties—Romantic Tale

1. Henry Atkinson (1782–1842) was born in North Carolina and fought in the War of 1812. Promoted to brigadier general in 1820, he was reduced to colonel as a result of the army's reduction and reorganization in 1821. He later received a brigadier generalship by brevet. Atkinson served many years on the frontier, and Fort Atkinson near present-day Omaha, Nebraska, was named for him. Atkinson played a prominent role in the so-called Black Hawk War (1832).

2. Thomas Gardner Mower (1790–1853) was an army surgeon.

3. Known as the Black Hawk War, this episode began when the Sac warrior Black Hawk (1767–1838) led a coalition of Sac, Fox, and other Indians across the Mississippi River into Illinois in a brief and futile attempt to reclaim land ceded to the United States by treaty in 1804. The ultimate Indian defeat came at the Battle of Bad Axe on August 2, 1832.

4. Keokuk (1767–1848) was a moderate Sac leader who did not actively oppose the westward expansion of white settlers. His temperate approach put him at odds with Black Hawk.

5. Here Scott quoted from Lord Byron's *Childe Harold's Pilgrimage:* "There were his young barbarians all at play, / There was their Dacian mother— he their sire, / Butchered to make a Roman holiday." George Gordon Byron, *The Works of Lord Byron* (Frankfort: H. L. Brœnner, 1837), 44.

6. John Reynolds (1788–1865) was a jurist, state legislator, congressman, and governor of Illinois.

7. Scott and Reynolds negotiated (dictated) a series of treaties with the various tribes, resulting in the Indians signing over most of their land to the United States.

8. The phrase is translated "not easily surprised."

9. Emilia Bigottini (1784–1858) was a famous mime and ballet dancer who dominated the French opera during the first two decades of the nineteenth century.

10. Lewis Cass (1782–1866) was born in New Hampshire and fought in the War of 1812, after which President Madison appointed him territorial governor of Michigan. An expansionist, at the time of the Black Hawk War, Cass was secretary of war under President Jackson.

11. Richard Bache Jr. (1784–1848) was a native of Philadelphia and graduate of the University of Pennsylvania. He served in the War of 1812 as an artillery officer. In 1832 he abandoned his family and moved to Texas and participated in the Texas Revolution in 1836. He was Benjamin Franklin's grandson.

Chapter XIX
Rejoins His Family—Ordered to Charleston— Nullification—Incidents—Peace Restored

1. Daniel Drake (1785–1852) was a physician, author, and professor who was born in New Jersey but raised in Kentucky. He founded a medical journal as well as the Medical College of Ohio in the 1820s. His first article for a medical journal was on epidemic diseases, and he wrote extensively on diseases in the western part of the country.

2. Nathaniel Chapman (1780–1853) was another famous Philadelphia physician who attended the University of Edinburgh and studied under Dr. Benjamin Rush. For Dr. William Gibson, see chapter VII, note 5.

3. The original Delmonico's Restaurant was located on William Street in New York City. Scott spent much of his adult life in that city and was a frequent and loyal customer. Scott became friends with Lorenzo Delmonico, a member of the restaurant's founding family, and the two often shared a table at the famous restaurant.

4. Fort Moultrie, Castle Pinckney, and Fort Sumter were series of fortifications built to protect Charleston Harbor. Fort Moultrie dates from the Revolutionary War period, Castle Pinckney was built just before the War of 1812, and construction on Fort Sumter began in the late 1820s, although it would not be completed until the 1860s.

5. *Faubourg* was the French term for "suburb." Hamburg was founded in the 1820s just across the Savannah River from Augusta, Georgia, and was thus a suburb of Augusta. Both Augusta and Hamburg saw their share of cotton barges in the mid-nineteenth century. In fact, there was intense economic competition between the two communities, which were connected by the Augusta bridge.

6. The knowledgeable reader will immediately recognize this as the Nullification Crisis of 1832, wherein the state of South Carolina, in protest to

the Tariff of 1828, called a convention which declared the tariff null and void. The act of nullification, championed by John C. Calhoun, exacerbated a rift between Calhoun and President Andrew Jackson, resulting in his resignation from the vice presidency in 1832. South Carolina's actions brought the threat of federal intervention until a compromise tariff was passed by Congress.

7. This French phrase means "vigilant" or "on the alert."

8. William Campbell Preston (1794–1860) was born in Philadelphia and studied in Virginia and South Carolina as well as at the University of Edinburgh before beginning his law practice. He moved to Columbia, South Carolina in 1824 and within a few years became one of the state's most ardent nullifiers. Preston served in the U.S. Senate from 1833 to 1842. His wife (his second) was Louise Penelope Davis.

9. Preston's grandfather, Col. William Campbell, was a Revolutionary War hero, and his father, Francis Preston (1765–1836), was a congressman from Virginia in the 1790s.

10. Fort Johnson was an eighteenth-century fort on the Charleston coastline that served as the location from which the first Confederate shots were fired on Fort Sumter in 1861. Very little of Fort Johnson has been preserved.

11. The Pettigrew family had an illustrious history in Virginia, North Carolina, and South Carolina. John Louis Petigru (1789–1863) used the old French spelling of the last name. He was a lawyer, state legislator, and attorney general of South Carolina. A Unionist, Petigru opposed both nullification and later secession. Another Unionist, Joel Roberts Poinsett (1779–1851), was from Charleston. He served as congressman and secretary of war, and while the U.S. minister to Mexico in the 1830s he sent home specimens of what was called the "Christmas eve flower" but which is now known by the diplomat's name, poinsettia. Daniel E. Huger (1779–1854) was a state representative and a judge who opposed Calhoun's sectional politics. Other pro-Union South Carolinians were Benjamin F. Perry (1805–1886) and William Drayton (1776–1846).

12. James Bankhead (1783–1856) from Virginia was a lieutenant colonel of artillery in 1832.

13. Probably Gen. William H. Broadnax (1786–1834), a slave owner from Dinwiddie County, Virginia, who was involved in the Colonization Society of Virginia. He also played a role in rounding up conspirators after the Nat Turner slave revolt in 1832.

14. Robert B. Gilchrist (1796–1856) from Charleston was appointed district attorney in 1831.

15. As was his tendency, Scott overemphasized his role in resolving the Nullification Crisis. Although his effort was not insignificant, the difficult task of political compromise was done in Washington.

16. James Hamilton Jr. (1786–1857) was governor of South Carolina from 1830 to 1832. He moved to Texas in the 1850s and drowned in the Gulf of Mexico in 1857.

17. Julius Frederick Heileman was in one of the first graduating classes at West Point (1803). He died of heat exhaustion following the Battle of Micanopy (1836) during the Second Seminole War in Florida. The mayor of Charleston was Henry Laurens Pinckney (1794–1863), a states' rights Democrat and founder of the *Charleston Mercury.*

18. Samuel Ringgold (1796–1846) graduated fifth in the 1818 class at West Point. He was the inventor of the Ringgold saddle and the author of an artillery manual. Ringgold was largely responsible for innovations in speed and mobility in the way artillery units fought. He would be the first American officer to be killed (May 1846) in the war with Mexico.

19. John Lyde Wilson (1784–1848) was governor of South Carolina from 1822 to 1824.

Chapter XX
Tactics—General Regulations—Florida War—Creek War—Jackson's War upon Scott—Court of Inquiry

1. The "present adjutant-general of the Confederate army" was Samuel Cooper, who while serving on the staff of the commanding general of the army, Alexander Macomb, wrote a manual known as *A Concise System of Instruction and Regulations for the Militia and Volunteers of the United States,* which appeared in 1836. The "division commander in the Confederate army" was William Hardee, whose *Rifle and Light Infantry Tactics* was published in 1855, and the other Davis pet who commanded volunteers was William Gilham, who wrote *Manual of Instruction for the Volunteers and Militia of the United States* in 1861. Other officers also got into the act. For example, Samuel Ringgold wrote a manual for field artillery (1845), and George McClellan wrote (translated from the French) a manual for bayonet tactics (1852).

2. Maj. Francis Dade (d. 1835) and his column of 107 men were ambushed by Seminole Indians on December 28, 1835, near present-day Tampa, Florida. Only one American soldier survived to tell the story. The Seminoles suffered only eight killed and wounded. This event was the catalyst for the Second Seminole War, which lasted seven years.

3. Duncan L. Clinch (1787–1849) was a career officer and the father-in-law of Robert Anderson (1805–1871), another army officer (artillery) who later commanded Union forces at Fort Sumter. Clinch served one term as a Whig congressman from Georgia in the 1840s. See also chapter XXII, note 10.

4. Edmund Gaines appears previously in Scott's *Memoirs.* Their seniority dispute had been ongoing for a decade when the Second Seminole War broke

out. In 1836 the two generals clashed again when Scott accused Gaines of interfering with his operations in Florida. The longevity and level of Scott's animosity toward Gaines is evident in the tone he used thirty years later as he wrote these *Memoirs.*

5. William Lindsay was commissioned a major of artillery in 1812 and promoted to colonel in 1832. He died in 1838.

6. On Christmas Day 1837, Col. Zachary Taylor commanded a force of about a thousand men who defeated the Seminoles at the Battle of Lake Okeechobee. However, four more years of guerrilla fighting continued.

7. Gen. Walker Keith Armistead (1785–1845) was an 1803 West Point graduate who finished first in his class. He served in the Corps of Engineers and was promoted to general in 1828. Armistead assumed command of the Second Seminole War in the spring of 1840. His brother George (1780–1818) commanded Fort McHenry during the British bombardment in 1814, and his son Lewis was a Confederate general who was killed at Gettysburg in 1863.

8. Scott had worked for twenty years to bring professionalism and conventional expertise to the United States Army, and the war with Mexico a decade later would demonstrate the fruits of his labors. However, the Second Seminole War in Florida demonstrated just how unprepared the army was for unconventional guerrilla fighting against Native Americans. For seven frustrating years the army slogged through the swamps and everglades in an attempt to track down its elusive foe. The war proved to be a revolving door for army commanders. William Worth was the commander in 1842 when some of the final Seminole surrenders took place. Sam Jones and Billy Bowlegs were Seminole chiefs who tried to keep the peace with Americans, but continued white encroachments on their lands led to a final episode of sporadic fighting in the 1850s.

9. This is a reference to the controversy surrounding the marriage of Andrew Jackson and Rachel Donelson Robards in 1791, before Rachel's divorce from Lewis Robards. The incident generated heated and juicy gossip for years, and a remark about it made by Charles Dickinson led to a duel in 1806 in which Jackson killed the marksman Dickinson.

10. This event occurred during Jackson's controversial declaration of martial law in New Orleans in 1814–15. When Louis Louaillier, a member of the Louisiana legislature, wrote an article critical of Jackson's abuse of power, Jackson had him arrested. When the prisoner appealed to the courts, Judge Dominick A. Hall (1765–1820) upheld the appeal and sent a writ of habeas corpus to Jackson. The Tennessean then forced Hall off the bench and out of the city for participating in a mutiny against his (Jackson's) authority. Scott deals with the martial law issue at length in the next chapter.

11. John Eaton (1790–1856) was a senator from Tennessee and longtime friend of Jackson who had married Peggy O'Neal Timberlake (1799–1879) after her husband committed suicide. John and Peggy allegedly had already

been involved in an intimate relationship. Upon becoming president, Jackson appointed Eaton his secretary of war, and the resulting controversy eventually forced the president to remake his entire cabinet.

12. Ali Pasha Tepelenë (1744–1822) became the provincial governor of Janina in 1788, and over the years he ruthlessly extended his control of an ever-growing portion of the Ottoman Empire. The poet George Byron, accompanied by his friend John Hobhouse, first visited the Pasha in 1809.

13. For his failure in Florida, acrimony with Gaines, and failure in Alabama, President Jackson ordered Scott to stand before a court of inquiry to investigate his actions.

14. Here Scott is getting slightly ahead of the story. When the court rendered its decision in January 1837, it acquitted Scott of any wrongdoing, a verdict that greatly displeased the president. Jackson told the court to revisit the issue and revise its findings. After some weeks of delay, General Macomb submitted a slightly revised version a few days after Martin Van Buren's inauguration and the issue died.

15. A doge in the Middle Ages was the ruler of what is today northern Italy. Imperialo Lescaro was the doge during the reign of Louis XIV.

Chapter XXI
Honors Tendered—Biddle Family—Speech of R. Biddle, M.C., Vindicating Scott— Jackson's Martial Law—His Death

1. Scott is referring to the Panic of 1837, which was a major economic recession following President Andrew Jackson's removal of federal deposits from the Bank of the United States.

2. Cornelius Wyck Lawrence (1791–1861) was a New York attorney, congressman, and, at the time of the proposed dinner honoring Scott in 1837, mayor of New York City.

3. Richard Biddle (1796–1847) was a congressman from Pennsylvania as well as the brother of Nicholas Biddle, president of the Bank of the United States.

4. Samuel Smith Nicholas (1797–1869) was elected to the Kentucky Court of Appeals in Frankfort, Kentucky, in 1831.

5. Sir Robert Filmer (1588–1653) and Thomas Hobbes (1588–1679) were English philosophers and political theorists who both believed in the absolute power of the king and the ensuant notion of complete obedience to the monarchy.

6. In addition to being appointed judge advocate in 1790, Alexander Fraser Tytler, Lord Woodhouselee (1747–1813), was a history professor at the University of Edinburgh.

7. This was Alexander Wedderburn (1733–1805).

8. Trinity Term refers to a session of the high courts in England.

9. Sir Matthew Hale (1609–1676) was an English attorney, jurist, and author who wrote extensively about English law. He also served in Parliament.

10. Sir William Blackstone (1723–1780) was a jurist whose four-volume *Commentaries on the Laws of England* provide a thorough explanation of English law. Blackstone's influence is also evident in the legal system and legal education of the United States.

11. A collection of Italian mercenaries called Mamertines occupied then used Messina, Sicily, as a raiding base for their pirate operations.

12. *Inter arma silent leges* means "In times of war, the law falls silent."

13. After Sulla became ruler of the Roman Republic in about 83 B.C., he sent Pompey to exert control over Sicily and Africa, campaigns that facilitated Pompey's rise to military glory. Three decades later a civil war erupted pitting Julius Caesar and his forces against Pompey, who had been appointed consul by the Roman senate. At the Battle of Pharsalia (48 B.C.), Caesar defeated his adversary but was later assassinated. These events coincide with Rome's transition from a republic to an empire.

14. Gaius Verres was a first-century B.C. Roman magistrate who was known for abuse of powers, political corruption, and denying Roman citizens their rights.

15. The superintendent was Richard Delafield (1798–1873).

Chapter XXII
President Van Buren—Fine Temper—Canadian Agitations—Burning of the Caroline—Scott Sent to the Frontier—The Turmoil Quieted— Scott Sent to Remove the Cherokees

1. David Hume (1711–1776) was a Scottish philosopher.

2 Cato the Elder and Cato the Younger (grandfather and grandson) were political figures of the Roman Republic. Roland might be a reference to Jean-Marie Roland, the eighteenth-century French scientist and political leader. John Hampden (1594–1643) was a leader in Parliament.

3. For William Crawford, see chapter XIII, note 2.

4. Various associations of American filibustering groups, sometimes called Hunters' Lodges, were organized along the Canadian border in the 1830s, and they sometimes cooperated with Canadian rebels who together wanted to "liberate" portions of Canada from the British orbit.

5. A *mauvais sujet* is a bad person.

6. Col. Rensselaer Van Rensselaer (1802–1850) was the son of War of 1812 hero Solomon Van Rensselaer and a member of the famous and wealthy

Rensselaer family of Albany, New York. In addition, the younger Rensselaer owned the *Albany Evening Advertiser.* A sympathizer of the Canadian independence movement, he accepted command of a rebel army that had gathered on Navy Island on the Canadian side of the Niagara River. An international incident occurred when someone on Navy Island hired the American-owned steamer *Caroline* to transport military supplies from New York to the rebel army on the island. Subsequently, forty-five members of the Canadian militia, including their commander, Col. Allan MacNab, and a British soldier named Alexander McLeod, crossed over to Schlosser, New York, where the *Caroline* was docked on December 29. After a scuffle that left one American, Amos Durfree, dead, the militia set the steamer ablaze and turned it loose to glide with the current to the falls a mile away. The so-called *Caroline* Affair compounded already tense relations between the Martin Van Buren administration and the British government.

7. William L. Marcy (1786–1857), a New York Democrat, served as a United States senator, secretary of war and secretary of state, as well as governor of the state.

8. Hugh Brady (chapter XI, note 4), John E. Wool (chapter VI, note 9), and Abram Eustis (chapter XVII, note 6) have appeared in previous notes. William J. Worth (1794–1849) received a passing reference earlier (chapter XX, note 8), but his long relationship with Scott warrants elaboration. Worth was commissioned a lieutenant in 1813 and served as a staff officer under Scott along the Niagara River in 1814. His close relationship with Scott prompted him to name his son Winfield Scott Worth. Later Worth fought Seminoles in Florida and commanded troops in Zachary Taylor's army in Mexico before becoming one of Scott's division commanders in the Mexico City Campaign in 1847. During that operation, friction between Scott and Worth escalated into a feud over which officer should receive credit for the decision to flank Mexico City by taking the southern approach.

9. Matthew Mountjoy Payne was seriously wounded at Resaca de la Palma (May 9, 1846) while serving in the Fourth Artillery. He was promoted to colonel for distinguished service at Palo Alto and Resaca de la Palma and resigned from the service in 1861. Some sources give his birth year as 1784 and some as 1787. He died on August 1, 1862.

10. Robert Anderson (1805–1871) was a Kentucky native and West Point graduate. He assisted Scott along the Canadian border, served in the Second Seminole War in Florida, and was on Gen. Winfield Scott's staff in the Mexican War. At the Battle of Molino del Rey on September 8, 1847, Anderson was wounded in the right shoulder and left arm. In 1861 he commanded the Union force that surrendered at Fort Sumter. In his published letters, *An Artillery Officer in Mexico, 1846–7,* Anderson wrote that "Scott has his

battle-fields well reconniottred, and avails himself of all the advantages which science or skill may suggest."

11. Erasmus Darwin Keyes (1810–1895) from Massachusetts graduated tenth in his class at West Point. He was an aide to Scott from 1837 to 1841 and later served as an instructor at West Point. He had a lackluster Civil War career as a Union corps commander. After the war he moved to San Francisco, where he became a successful businessman before his death in France.

12. Francis Taylor (d. 1858) was an 1825 West Point graduate and was once Thomas J. Jackson's commanding officer. Taylor was an artillery officer who fought with distinction at the Battle of Churubusco during the war with Mexico. He received brevet promotions for his conduct at Cerro Gordo and Churubusco.

13. Capt. John Page (1793–1846) died from wounds received at the Battle of Palo Alto in May 1846, and Capt. Abner Riviere Hetzel (1805–1847), a Pennsylvanian, died in Louisville, Kentucky.

14. Henry Lee Scott (1814–1886) was a North Carolina native and West Point graduate. He fought in the Second Seminole War before his duties during Indian removal. During the Mexican War, Scott served as Gen. Winfield Scott's aide-de-camp, and soon after, in 1849, Henry married the general's third daughter, Cornelia. Winfield Scott had no sons who survived to adulthood, so any Scotts who are direct descendants of the general are through Cornelia and Henry. Prior to his October 1861 resignation from the army, there were rumors that Henry's southern sympathies led him to engage in suspicious activities.

15. Ichabod Bennet Crane (1787–1857) from New Jersey joined the Marine Corps in 1809 and later resigned to accept a commission in the army. He was a veteran of the War of 1812 as well as the Second Seminole War. Ichabod met Washington Irving in 1814, and some speculate that this is where Irving got the name Ichabod Crane for his character in "The Legend of Sleepy Hollow." Ichabod's son, Dr. Charles Crane, was one of the physicians who attended to Abraham Lincoln after he was shot at Ford's Theater.

Chapter XXIII
Scott Ordered Back to British Frontiers—
Turmoil Renewed—Maine Boundary

1. The boundary between the United States (Maine) and Canada (New Brunswick) had been disputed since the Revolutionary War. In 1838–39 the longstanding disagreement came to a head when lumberjacks and hunters from both countries ventured into the disputed Aroostook region. The result was the bloodless Aroostook War.

2. Edward Everett (1794–1865) was, in addition to governor of Massachusetts, a senator, diplomat, and president of Harvard. He was also the keynote speaker at the ceremony dedicating the Gettysburg cemetery in 1863.

3. Robert C. Winthrop (1809–1894) from Boston was congressman and Speaker of the House from 1848 to 1849.

4. "In petto" means to keep something close to ones breast or in secrecy.

5. Maine's Democrat governor was John Fairfield (1797–1847), and the lieutenant governor of New Brunswick was Sir John Harvey (1778–1852).

6. Following is the so-called Fox-Forsyth memorandum, which was drafted in a way so as to allow both countries to stand down while saving face. It did not have the desired effect.

7. Jeremiah Goodwin from the town of Alfred was treasurer of the state of Maine in 1839.

8. George Evans (1797–1867) was a lawyer, congressman, and senator from Gardiner, Maine.

9. Dr. William Ellery Channing (1780–1842) was the grandson of a signer of the Declaration of Independence. He attended Harvard and became a prominent Unitarian minister and vocal opponent of slavery and poverty. He was a friend of Ralph Waldo Emerson and a leader in the peace movement.

Chapter XXIV
Politics—General-in-Chief—Stops Unlawful Punishments—Attempts to Abolish His Rank and to Reduce His Pay—Mr. Adams and Mr. C. J. Ingersoll

1. Benjamin Watkins Leigh (1781–1849) was a lawyer and politician from Scott's hometown of Petersburg, Virginia.

2. Scott evidently never comprehended that Thurlow Weed (1797–1882), a New York newspaperman and political operative, and others had been using Scott's potential nomination as a ploy to prevent Clay from winning it.

3. John Tyler (1790–1862) was the first vice president to ascend to the presidency as a result of the death of the chief executive. He was a states' rights politician from Virginia who served in the state legislature, the U.S. Congress, and as governor before being placed on the ticket with Harrison in 1840. Tyler was former Jacksonian Democrat who broke with the party in the 1830s because of President Jackson's heavy-handedness. However, many Whigs feared that he was a Whig in name only, and their fears were realized because once Tyler became president, he vetoed key Whig legislation. Thus Scott's low opinion of him as president.

4. Charles J. Ingersoll (1782–1862) was the son of a member of the Continental Congress. He was a Democrat who served in Congress for a total of ten years in two separate tenures.

5. This is a reminder of Scott's victory over the British at the Battle of Chippewa on July 5, 1814.

Chapter XXV
Letter on Slavery—Tracts on Peace and War—Mr. Polk President

1. Slavery being the dominant political and social issue of the day, Scott obviously felt compelled to offer an official position on the topic. He did so by reprinting his letter to an attorney friend, T. P. Atkinson, in 1843. He never owned slaves but did not fault those who did, and while he expressed the desire to see slavery ended, he believed the best solution was colonization of Africa with Christian former slaves who could then proselytize the continent.

2. William Blackstone's famous *Commentaries* on English law were published in the 1760s. In 1803 William and Mary law professor St. George Tucker (1752–1827) published an edition with reference notes to U.S. law and the U.S. Constitution.

3. Like his slavery letter, Scott obviously wanted to include in his *Memoirs* his position on war, which was essentially to advocate the "just war" theory.

4. The relationship between James K. Polk (1795–1849) and Scott during the war with Mexico was characterized by a lack of trust. Polk succeeded in humiliating Scott publicly at the beginning and end of the war. At the beginning of the war in 1846, the administration made fun of the general's "hasty plate of soup" letter, which will be mentioned in the next chapter. When the war ended, the president put Scott before a court of inquiry to investigate his conduct, thus damaging his chances in the 1848 presidential election. From Scott's perspective, Polk was, next to Andrew Jackson, the great villain of his life.

Chapter XXVI
War with Mexico—General Taylor

1. Soon after the annexation of Texas was completed, the Polk administration ordered Gen. Zachary Taylor to move into the area between the Neuces River and Rio Grande with a force of about three thousand men. Taylor's "Army of Observation" was intended to serve as a show of force to protect American claims during a border dispute with Mexico.

2. William Wallace Smith Bliss (1815–1853) graduated ninth in his West Point class. Because he was efficient, had an eye for detail, and possessed clear

and accurate writing ability, he acquired the nickname "Perfect" Bliss. It was his reputation for exact penmanship that caused Scott to appoint him to Taylor's staff to make up for deficiencies in the latter. Bliss married Taylor's daughter after the war before dying of yellow fever.

3. Thomas Dilworth was an eighteenth-century clergyman who wrote a famous book, *A New Guide to the English Tongue,* in 1761 that was widely used by schoolchildren.

4. In the 1840s the army was top heavy with Whig officers. The prospects of a triumphant Whig general heroically returning home from war to be elected president troubled Polk and his Democrat political colleagues. Because Scott was known to be a political general with presidential aspirations, his relationship with the administration was rocky from the beginning. Scott's rather benign reference to "a fire upon the rear" actually pertained to a caustic exchange that occurred in the first month of the war. When the president inquired as to why Scott was still in Washington a week after his May 13 appointment to assume command of Taylor's army, a distrustful Scott responded with his famous May 21 letter to Secretary of War William Marcy. In it he explained that extensive preparations were necessary, and, he went on, "I do not desire to place myself in the most perilous of all positions:—a fire upon my rear from Washington and the fire, in front, from the Mexicans." This explosive comment caused the president to rescind Scott's appointment to combat command.

5. When Scott learned that his appointment to field command had been canceled and that he had been out of his office when Secretary Marcy came to inform him, he wrote a note to explain that he had stepped out of his office for "a hasty plate of soup." The correspondence was publicized by the administration and was published in the press, and the "hasty plate of soup" reference became the subject of many jokes around Washington. The episode succeeded in its intention of embarrassing Scott.

6. Kentucky's senators in 1846 were James T. Morehead (1797–1854) and John J. Crittenden (1787–1863).

7. Robert W. Weir (1803–1889) taught drawing at West Point from 1834 to 1876, and the inscription was a reference to the opening battles of the war fought on the American side of the Rio Grande. One of Weir's paintings, *The Embarkation of the Pilgrims,* hangs in the rotunda of the Capitol in Washington, D.C.

8. Taylor advanced into northern Mexico in summer 1846 and in September fought an intense battle that resulted in his capture of Monterrey. The old adage *Cui bono* literally means "To whose benefit" or "To what purpose." The phrase was sometimes used to suggest that personal gain might have been the motivation for actions taken.

9. Until recently Scott's use of martial law was a forgotten aspect of his Mexico City Campaign. It was an ingenious way to hold American soldiers

accountable while in a foreign country and out of reach of American laws. Strict discipline of his own troops and paying for all provisions taken from Mexicans constituted a shrewd pacification plan that was central to the success of his 1847 campaign from Veracruz to Mexico City. Its primary purpose was to prevent a popular uprising and guerrilla war.

Chapter XXVII
Scott Ordered to Mexico—Visits Camargo—
Reëmbarks for Vera Cruz

1. Robert J. Walker (1801–1869) was an attorney from Pennsylvania who moved to Mississippi, from whence he was elected to the U.S. Senate before becoming the treasury secretary.

2. Alexander Barrow (1801–1846) was a native of Nashville, Tennessee, where he practiced law. In the 1820s he moved to Louisiana, where he practiced law until becoming involved in politics. Barrow was elected to the U.S. Senate in 1841 but died in December 1846, a short time after writing the letter to which Scott alluded.

3. President Polk had indeed been in conversation with Missouri senator Thomas Hart Benton (1782–1858) about reviving the rank of lieutenant general, which had not been held since George Washington. As Scott would learn, the purpose was to bestow that rank on someone other than Scott—presumably Benton himself—so as to supersede Scott as the highest ranking officer in the army.

4. Lt. John A. Richey from Ohio was an 1845 West Point graduate and the dispatch carrier who was ambushed and killed on January 13, 1847.

5. This is a verse from English poet John Dryden's "Alexander's Feast." Where Scott inserted a blank line, Dryden wrote "the king."

6. George Cadwalader (1806–1879) was a lawyer from Philadelphia and active in the Pennsylvania state militia. He commanded reinforcements intended for Scott but diverted to the Rio Grande to support Taylor. Cadwalader's troops reached Veracruz on June 1 and proceeded to Puebla, where Scott's army was bivouacked.

7. Knowing that Taylor's army had been reduced in numbers to augment Scott's force, which was about to land at Veracruz, Santa Anna force marched his army north, where he attacked Taylor on February 23, 1847. Although outnumbered, Taylor beat back repeated Mexican attacks, winning the Battle of Buena Vista. Two months later and over three hundred miles to the south, Santa Anna tried to block Scott's advance inland from Veracruz, leading to the Battle of Cerro Gordo on April 17–18, perhaps the most decisive American victory of the war.

Chapter XXVIII
Siege and Capture of Vera Cruz and
the Castle of San Juan de Ulloa

1. This is a reference to Gen. William Worth, who served on Scott's staff in the War of 1812 and who, thirty-five years later, gave Scott so much trouble during the Mexican War. As a division commander in Scott's army in Mexico, Worth always wanted his command to play the most prominent role in battles, and he became disgruntled when he did not. While the army occupied Puebla, the simmering unease between the two generals reached a boiling point. After the occupation of Mexico City, he, along with Gideon Pillow and James Duncan, became embroiled in a dispute with Scott when they attempted to win credit in the American press for the campaign's success.

2. Here Scott is referring to Gen. Gideon Pillow, an attorney and planter from Columbia, Tennessee. Pillow played a key role in helping his friend and fellow Columbia resident, James K. Polk, attain the Democratic nomination in 1844. Polk then appointed Pillow brigadier general of volunteers in 1846 and later promoted him to major general. Despite his intelligence and organizational skills, Pillow demonstrated his military incompetence first in Zachary Taylor's army then in Scott's. However, Scott was beholden to the president for giving him field command so he tolerated Pillow, whom he knew to be Polk's eyes and ears in the army. Pillow, Worth, and Duncan were arrested at the end of the campaign for unscrupulous actions, but the tables turned when the president ordered their release and an investigation of Scott instead.

3. James Duncan is the man Scott referred to as being promoted to inspector general. Duncan, an 1834 West Point graduate, had been brevetted for meritorious conduct after the Battles of Palo Alto and Resaca de la Palma in 1846. As an artillery officer in Worth's division, he fought in the Mexico City Campaign then placed himself in the middle of the feud involving Worth, Pillow, and Scott when he wrote a letter critical of the commanding general. The letter found its way into U.S. newspapers, and Duncan found himself arrested at the same time as Worth and Pillow, only to be exonerated by order of President Polk. Duncan died in 1849.

4. Bennet C. Riley (1787–1853), a brigade commander in Scott's army, led a decisive flank attack at the Battle of Contreras (August 20, 1847) and served admirably on other battlefields as well. He was provincial governor of California after the war and helped prepare it for statehood in 1850. Fort Riley, Kansas, was named for him.

5. Roger Jones (1789–1852) served as adjutant general of the United States Army from 1825 to 1852.

6. From their anchorage south of the city near Sacrificios Island, Scott launched his beach landing at a point called Collado Beach, two miles

from the city's defenses. David Connor (1792–1856), a native of Pennsylvania, saw action as a midshipman in the War of 1812. Commodore Connor commanded the Home Squadron in the Gulf of Mexico and performed valuable service in the early stage of Scott's Mexico City Campaign. Due to ill health he was soon replace by Matthew C. Perry (1794–1858).

7. Mexico's Gen. Juan Morales commanded approximately four thousand defenders in the port city of Veracruz. A fortified, artillery-studded wall surrounded the city, and the most formidable aspect of the defenses was the Castle San Juan de Ulúa, which stood a thousand yards out in the harbor and mounted over a hundred cannon. It was a sixteenth-century Spanish fortress that also had served as a prison. Because of Veracruz's location on the coast, it was prone to yellow fever (*vomito*) outbreaks in the summers, so Scott's challenge was to capture the city and move the army inland to higher ground before the arrival of disease-carrying mosquitoes.

8. In 1838 France invaded Mexico, ostensibly to protect the lives and property of Frenchmen living in Mexico. The invasion is known as the Pastry War because the Frenchman who made the greatest demand of reparations against the Mexican government (60,000 pesos) was Monsieur Remontel, the owner of a pastry shop in Tacubaya. The French navy's blockade of Veracruz in 1838 was followed by a bombardment and attack on the port city. The French expedition was commanded by Adm. Charles Baudin and Lt. (later Adm.) François d'Orléans, prince de Joinville. Outnumbered ten to one, Mexican forces could not prevent the occupation of the city, which the French evacuated in March 1839 after an arbitrated agreement. The only major engagement in the Pastry War was the Battle of Veracruz, and it was during that battle that Santa Anna received a wound that resulted in having his leg amputated.

9. For Joseph G. Totten, see chapter VI, note 10.

10. Robert Patterson (1792–1891) was born in Ireland and moved with his family to the United States in 1799. He served in the War of 1812 then became a Pennsylvania banker and politician. He was commissioned a major general at the outbreak of the war with Mexico and later saw his military career end when he allowed himself to be outmaneuvered in the Shenandoah Valley during the Battle of First Bull Run.

11. A native of Vermont, Ethan Allen Hitchcock (1798–1870) was the grandson of Ethan Allen, the popular Revolutionary War hero. He graduated from West Point in 1817, saw frontier duty, fought in the Second Seminole War, and in 1841 uncovered graft and corruption among Indian Affairs personnel. He was Scott's inspector general in Mexico. After resigning from the army and moving to St. Louis in 1855, he reentered the military, serving as a Union general.

12. Dogberry was a character in, and the quote is taken from, Shakespeare's play *Much Ado About Nothing*.

13. Probably a reference to George Mercer Brooke from Virginia, who entered the army in 1808, fought in the War of 1812 and was promoted to major general in 1848. He died in 1851.

14. Not wanting to be the one who surrendered to the Americans and thus face Santa Anna's wrath, Gen. Juan Morales turned that task over to Gen. José Landero.

15. William Jay (1789–1858) was the son of John Jay, who, in addition to being chief justice of the Supreme Court, was also cofounder of the American Bible Society and a devoted abolitionist. In William's 1849 book, he criticized Scott for not halting the bombardment on March 25 long enough for the women and children of the city to evacuate. Jay wrote that the killing of women and children during the bombardment was unnecessary.

16. Capt. John R. Vinton from Rhode Island was commanding one of the siege batteries when he was struck by an enemy cannon ball. Capt. William Alburtis (1811–1847), from Virginia, was decapitated by a cannon ball. Both men were West Point graduates and highly respected in the army. Estimates for Mexican losses vary widely; killed and wounded for both soldiers and civilians may have approached one thousand, with perhaps four hundred of that number being civilian dead.

Chapter XXIX
Battle of Cerro Gordo, Jalapa, Perote and Puebla—Halts—Visit to Cholula

1. The officers in the paragraph who have not yet been identified were the sometimes harsh William S. Harney (1800–1889), who commanded cavalry (see chapter XXX, note 45); George Talcott (1786–1862), who commanded artillery and rockets; John A Quitman (1798–1858), who was a future filibuster and governor of Mississippi; James Shields (1810–1879), who was born in Ireland and served on the Illinois Supreme Court; and David E. Twiggs (1790–1862), who later briefly held a commission as a general in the Confederate army.

2. Philip Kearny (1815–1862) came from a wealthy New York family, graduated from Columbia University in 1833, and attended the French Cavalry School. Before and after the war with Mexico, Kearny fought with the French army, first in Algiers (1840) and later in Italy (1859). He was killed at Chantilly during the Second Bull Run Campaign in 1862.

3. William Wall from Pennsylvania finished thirteenth in the 1832 class at West Point. He fought in the Black Hawk and Seminole Wars and was a respected officer in the Third Artillery. He died in Puebla, Mexico, on August 13, 1847.

4. On the evening Scott wrote this attack order, April 17, 1847, the opening phase of the Battle of Cerro Gordo had already concluded. Having come

upon fortified Mexican positions in a mountain pass near the village of Cerro Gordo, Scott decided on a classic Napoleonic move: an assault on the main enemy line to divert attention from an attack in the flank and rear. Earlier that day the men of Gen. David Twiggs's division had come in contact with enemy troops while getting into position on the extreme Mexican left flank. To compliment this action on the Mexican flank, four volunteer regiments (First and Second Tennessee and First and Second Pennsylvania) under Gen. Gideon Pillow would attack a strong enemy position two miles away and at the other end of a line of fortified Mexican locations. Although Pillow's attack did not go smoothly, the battle as a whole unfolded remarkably like Scott indicated it would in his attack order the previous evening. Cerro Gordo was perhaps the most impressive American victories of the war.

5. José María Jarero, Rómulo Díaz de la Vega, and Luiz Pinzón were trapped on the Mexican right after the successful turning movement against their left flank. Ciriaco Vásquez was mortally wounded in the head during the fighting on El Telégrafo and a memorial stone still stands on the spot where he fell. Other Mexican generals mentioned in this paragraph were Louis Noriega and José María Obando.

6. Gen. James Shields was seriously wounded by grapeshot in the chest as he led his men on an attack on the Mexican rear near the Jalapa road. Most observers believed his wound to be mortal, but Shields survived and recovered in time to participate in the latter phase of the campaign. He went on to have a mediocre Civil War career as a Union general.

7. Edward D. Baker (1811–1861) was a lawyer and politician from Illinois as well as a friend of Abraham Lincoln. After the Mexican War, he moved to Oregon and was elected senator from that state. He was later killed at the Battle of Ball's Bluff on October 21, 1861, while serving as a colonel in the Union army.

8. William T. Haskell (1818–1859) was a lawyer from Murfreesboro, Tennessee, who served in the state legislature and the U.S. Congress. Also mentioned as killed are Lt. Frederick B. Nelson of Company D and Lt. Charles G. Gill of Company E (both companies were raised in Memphis, Tennessee).

9. Pillow went home to Tennessee, recovered from his arm wound, was promoted to major general by his friend President Polk, and returned to fight in the battles around Mexico City. Scott was probably referring to Maj. Robert Farquharson (1814–1869) from Lincoln County, Tennessee, who was actually in the First Tennessee Volunteer Regiment and fifteen years later was captured at Fort Donelson while serving as colonel in the Forty-first Tennessee, CSA. Also mentioned were Capt. Henry F. Murray, 2nd Lt. George Sutherland, Lt. Wiley P. Hale, and Lt. William Yearwood, who died on April 24.

10. This was Lt. Thomas Ewell, the brother of the famous Confederate general Richard Ewell and grandson of the first U.S. secretary of the navy, Benjamin Stoddert. Thomas lived several hours after being wounded, dying peacefully during the night. Brother Richard was a lieutenant in the First Dragoons and spent the last few hours with his dying brother on the Cerro Gordo battlefield.

11. George H. Derby (1823–1861) was born in Massachusetts but also lived in California and New York. He graduated seventh in his West Point class and was friends with fellow cadet Ulysses S. Grant. Derby was a prankster who, in his free time, wrote jokes and humorous stories using the pseudonym "Squibob." However, he was a talented engineer and surveyor for the army. He later helped open the Arizona Territory with his exploration of the Colorado River. He died of a brain tumor.

12. George Waynefleet Patten (1808–1882) was from Rhode Island. He spent much of his career in service on the western frontier, and he had a reputation as an accomplished poet. He rose to the rank of lieutenant colonel during the Civil War.

13. Edwin V. Sumner (1797–1863) from Massachusetts would later gain fame as a Union general in the Civil War. He was a veteran of the Black Hawk War in 1832. It was at the Battle of Cerro Gordo that Sumner acquired the nickname "Bull Head" or "Old Bull" because a Mexican musket ball supposedly bounced off his head. Actually, a spent musket ball hit the star on his cap, slowing its momentum before striking his forehead. The wound, to which Scott referred, was not life threatening.

14. This was Joseph E. Johnston (1807–1891), the future Confederate general. While leading a reconnaissance on April 12, as the vanguard of the army approached Cerro Gordo, a skirmish broke out in which Lt. Col. Johnston was wounded in the arm and hip.

15. Capt. Stevens Thomson Mason Jr. from Virginia lost a leg in the battle and died on May 15. Sec. Lt. Thomas Davis also died of his Cerro Gordo wounds on April 20.

16. American casualties were 63 killed and 368 wounded. Mexican casualty figures are more difficult to determine because Mexico's army was so scattered and disorganized afterward. Including those who fell during the fighting retreat west, there were probably over 1,000 killed and wounded. The Americans also captured over 3,000 prisoners.

17. The officers mentioned and not yet identified in a previous note were Thomas Childs (1796–1853) from Massachusetts, Edmund B. Alexander (1803–1888) from Virginia, Joseph Plympton (d. 1860) from Massachusetts, William W. Loring (1818–1886) from North Carolina, and Persifor F. Smith (1798–1858), a Pennsylvanian by birth who served as military governor of California before it became a state. Smith's son, Howard Smith, and stepson, Frank Crawford Armstrong, both served in the Confederate army.

18. Charles Ferguson Smith (1807–1862) was a native Pennsylvanian and West Point graduate who served meritoriously later in the campaign at Contreras and Churubusco. He later commanded volunteers in the Union army at Fort Donelson and Shiloh before dying of dysentery and a leg infection.

19. The Mexican officers were Valentín Canalizo (1794–1850) and Pedro de Ampudia (1803–1868).

20. The Tierra Caliente is the hot lowland region close to the coast and where yellow fever was most prevalent.

21. Scouting the obscure path that the U.S. Army used in its Cerro Gordo flank attack were two of the future Confederacy's most prominent generals. Capt. Robert E. Lee got credit for locating the trail, but it was actually found by lieutenant and future Confederate general P. G. T. Beauregard (1818–1893) in an early reconnaissance mission. Lee later oversaw the widening of the trail to prepare it for troop movements.

22. Franklin Gardner (1823–1873) was born in New York and graduated four spots (seventeenth) ahead of Ulysses S. Grant in the 1843 West Point class. His wife was from a prominent slaveholding family in Louisiana, and when the Civil War started, he sided with the South, serving as a Confederate general.

23. Peter V. Hagner (1815–1893) was born in Washington, D.C., and served as an ordnance officer for most of his forty-year army career.

24. Truman Seymour (1824–1891) from Vermont served with distinction in the battles around Mexico City. He later served as a Union general and was known for his watercolor paintings.

25. Theodore T. S. Laidley (1822–1886) was a native Virginian who graduated from West Point in 1842. He was brevetted a captain for his conduct at Cerro Gordo. He spent his forty year career as an ordnance officer.

26. James C. Burnham (1814–1866) was from New York City. In the 1850s he had some sketchy involvement with the "Worth Legion," a New York filibustering group that offered its services to William Walker. Burnham later became marshal of New York City.

27. Born in Ohio, Lt. Roswell S. Ripley (1823–1887) graduated from West Point in 1843. He and three companies of New York volunteers spent twelve hours pulling a heavy howitzer over hills and through gullies to position it so as to enfilade the Mexican right flank. Because he believed that General Scott's battle report did not give him proper credit, he developed a dislike for the commanding general and after the war wrote a hefty, two-volume history of the conflict that was often critical of Scott. Ripley became a publisher and businessman in the South, and after helping direct the firing on Fort Sumter, he became a Confederate general opposite his uncle, James Wolfe Ripley, who was an ordnance officer in the Union army.

28. For Bennet C. Riley, see chapter XXVIII, note 4.

29. For Francis Taylor, see chapter XXII, note 12.

30. Perote sits thirty-five miles west of Jalapa and almost a hundred miles inland from Veracruz. The famous Perote Castle was built by the Spaniards in the eighteenth century, and its sixty-foot walls and twenty-foot-deep moat made it an impregnable fortress. Made of dark lava rocks, the ominous fort was built to defend the important trade route inland from Veracruz. The Americans arrived to find that the Mexican army had abandoned the city along with the castle and its sixty guns.

31. Gustavus W. Smith (1821–1896) was a native of Kentucky and a West Point graduate. He also taught engineering at West Point. In Mexico he was twice brevetted for gallantry and meritorious conduct (Cerro Gordo and Contreras). Smith took command of Company A of the engineers upon the illness and subsequent death of Alexander Swift at the beginning of the campaign. He left the army and served as streets commissioner in New York City in the late 1850s before becoming a Confederate general in the Army of Northern Virginia.

32. William Thomas Harbaugh Brooks (1821–1870) fought in all the major battles of the war, from Palo Alto to Churubusco, and was brevetted twice for gallantry. After Churubusco he became a member of Gen. David Twiggs's staff. He was from Ohio and he served as a brigade and division commander in the Army of the Potomac during the Civil War before retiring to a farm in Huntsville, Alabama. Philip W. MacDonald (d. 1851) was a Pennsylvania native who was brevetted three times during the war and fought in all of the major engagements. Mississippian Earl Van Dorn (1840–1863) served admirably throughout the war and was wounded in the fighting at Mexico City. He received several wounds while fighting Indians on the frontier in the 1850s. As a Confederate general, he met his end in Spring Hill, Tennessee, in 1863 when he was shot and killed by a jealous husband who was angry about his wife's affair with Van Dorn. Brevetted twice during the war, the Virginian John Magruder (1807–1871) had already fought in the Second Seminole War before going to Mexico. He served capably in the Mexican War but later had an unimpressive career as a Confederate general. He fought for Maximilian's army in Mexico after the Civil War. All of the above officers were West Point graduates.

33. The names mentioned in this paragraph were Ferris Foreman (1808–1901), Third Illinois; Ward B. Burnett (d. 1884), Second New York; Thomas Harris (1816–1858), Fourth Illinois; Richard Pendell Hammond (d. 1891), Third Artillery; and George T. M. Davis (1808–1888), First Illinois.

34. These Tennesseans were William Bohen Campbell (1807–1867), First Tennessee; Francis M. Wynkoop (d. 1857), First Pennsylvania; and William T. Haskell, identified in note 8 above.

35. Thomas Henry from New York was credited with pulling down the Mexican flag when American troops took possession of El Telégrafo hill. The

"Mexican fort" is a reference to a small concrete signal station on the hill that was no more than twelve feet by twelve feet. Its remains were still visible when the editor visited the site in 1999.

36. The commander of Scott's engineers was John Lind Smith (d. 1858), a South Carolinian who had been in the army since 1813. According to the *Army and Navy Chronicle,* Smith was the first one to demonstrate (in 1834) the use of the Archimedean screw as a replacement for the paddle wheel on steamships. Promoted to major in 1839, Smith was twice promoted for gallantry and meritorious conduct in Mexico.

37. William Turnbull (1800–1857) graduated from West Point in 1819. Entering the war as a major, he was brevetted a lieutenant colonel for his conduct at the Battles of Contreras and Churubusco (August 19–20, 1847) and brevetted again to colonel for his actions at Chapultepec (September 13, 1847).

38. James Louis Mason (1817–1853) was a native of Rhode Island. An 1836 West Point graduate (second in his class), Mason served on Scott's staff with distinction, receiving a brevet promotion from captain to major for his conduct at Contreras and Churubusco. He was brevetted again to lieutenant colonel after Molino del Rey (September 8, 1847), where he received a serious wound that incapacitated him for three years and contributed to his death in 1853 at the age of thirty-six.

39. A Massachusetts native and first in his 1839 West Point class, Isaac I. Stevens (1818–1862) was brevetted twice in the war. He resigned from the army in 1853 to become the first territorial governor of Washington. He later served as a general in the Union army until his death at Chantilly on September 1, 1862.

40. Zealous Bates Tower (1819–1900) of Massachusetts finished at the top of his 1841 West Point class. He received brevet promotions three times in Mexico (Cerro Gordo, Contreras and Churubusco, and Chapultepec). In the 1850s he oversaw the construction of Fort Alcatraz in San Francisco. Tower was part of the Fort Pickens garrison in Florida at the beginning of the Civil War, and he served the Union army with distinction, finishing that war as a major general.

41. This was not the famous Union general but was John McClellan (d. 1854), who finished sixth in the 1826 West Point class. He served meritoriously throughout the Mexico City Campaign.

42. Edmund La Fayette Hardcastle (1824–1899) was from Maryland. He was commissioned a second lieutenant in the topographical engineers immediately upon his graduation from West Point in 1846. He served in all of the major battles of the Mexico City Campaign and was brevetted twice. After resigning from the army in 1856, he lived the remainder of his years on his Maryland farm, working at times for railroad companies.

43. Robert Allen (1811–1886) was an 1836 graduate of West Point. He rose to the rank of major general during the Civil War and retired from the service in 1878.

44. A native of Kentucky, Francis P. Blair Jr. (1821–1875) was the son of the more famous Francis P. Blair Sr., the journalist and Andrew Jackson confidant, and the brother of Montgomery Blair, Abraham Lincoln's postmaster general. Francis Jr. graduated from Princeton University and was elected to Congress during the Civil War.

45. For Henry Lee Scott, see chapter XXII, note 14.

46. Thomas Williams (1815–1862) grew up in Albany, New York, graduated from West Point in 1837, and served as General Scott's aide-de-camp from 1844 to 1850. He was brevetted to captain during the Mexican War. As a Union brigade commander, he was killed by a musket ball to the chest at Baton Rouge, Louisiana, on August 5, 1862.

47. George W. Lay (d. 1867), a Virginian, graduated from West Point in 1842 and was twice brevetted for gallantry and meritorious conduct in Mexico. He fought for the Confederacy, serving briefly in 1863 on Robert E. Lee's staff.

48. Abraham Van Buren (1807–1873) was the son of President Martin Van Buren. Abraham's gallantry and meritorious conduct at Contreras and Churubusco was recognized by a brevet promotion to lieutenant colonel.

49. On May 6, seven volunteer regiments from Alabama, Georgia, Illinois, and Tennessee, their twelve-month enlistments near expiration, left the army to begin the trip home. For the time being, that left the army with four volunteer regiments (two from Pennsylvania and one each from New York and South Carolina) and a total of only seventy-one hundred men.

50. Scott appointed Thomas Childs (identified in note 17 above) military governor of Jalapa, and later, as the army began its final push to Mexico City, the commanding general appointed him military governor of the city of Puebla.

51. "The Benton intrigue" refers to the attempt to get a bill passed to reinstate the rank of lieutenant general to enable the administration to appoint a Democrat to the post so as to supersede the Whig General Scott. Attention to that effort had, in Scott's opinion, caused a delay in Congress's passage of a bill to raise ten regiments of reinforcements.

52. On a clear day, Mount Orizaba, which reached an altitude of 18,700 feet, was visible from the Gulf of Mexico a hundred miles away. It is also known as Citlaltepetl (Star Mountain) and is the tallest mountain in Mexico. The second tallest mountain in the country is Mount Popocatepetl, which is twenty-five miles west of Puebla and reaches 17,800 feet.

53. Cholula is the site of an ancient temple mound built by the Aztecs and where Cortez slaughtered thousands of the native inhabitants. Etruia was a region in central Italy where the Etruscans lived.

54. This a reference to a famous basilica in Loreto, Italy.

Chapter XXX
Advance on the Capital—Halt at Ayotla—
Reconnaissances—San Augustin—Contreras

1. Scott's army was in Puebla for ten weeks awaiting reinforcements. On June 1, Col. James Simmons McIntosh (1784–1847) began the inland march from Veracruz with over seven hundred men, 130 wagons, and five hundred pack mules. McIntosh was from Georgia and had fought with distinction on the Niagara front during the War of 1812. Soon stymied by guerrillas that swarmed the countryside, the column was quickly augmented by another five hundred men under Brig. Gen. George Cadwalader from Philadelphia. Despite sporadic skirmishes with hostile partisans, the Americans pressed on to Perote some ninety-five miles inland but still eighty miles away from Scott's army at Puebla. While at Perote, two thousand additional American troops under Gideon Pillow caught up, bringing the total to thirty-two hundred men. Pillow had returned to his home in Tennessee to recuperate from a wound suffered at Cerro Gordo and soon found himself promoted from brigadier to major general and from commanding volunteers to regulars. The joint McIntosh, Cadwalader, and Pillow column reached Puebla on July 8. Brig. Gen. Franklin Pierce left Veracruz with another twenty-five hundred men on July 15 and marched into Puebla on August 6.

2. Schuyler Hamilton (1822–1903) was the grandson of Alexander Hamilton. He graduated from West Point in 1841, received brevet promotions twice in Mexico, was Scott's military secretary at the time of Scott's retirement in 1861, and saw action as a Union general in the Western Theater of the Civil War.

3. John P. Gaines (1795–1858) was a veteran of the War of 1812 who had served in the Kentucky state legislature before joining other Kentuckians in volunteering for the Mexican War. After the war he was elected to Congress as a Whig, and in the early 1850s President Millard Fillmore appointed him territorial governor of Oregon.

4. Well known for his role in the Civil War, Lt. George Briton McClellan (1826–1885) was a member of the noted 1846 West Point class. He served Scott's army admirably throughout the campaign.

5. New Hampshire native John Gray Foster (1823–1874) graduated from West Point the year the war started and received two brevet promotions for gallantry at Contreras and Churubusco on August 20 and on September 8 at Molino del Rey, where he was seriously wounded. He was chief engineer at Fort Sumter during the bombardment that commenced the Civil War. In service to the Union cause, his duty assignments included the Department of North Carolina, the Department of the South, and the Department of Florida.

6. South Carolinian Benjamin Huger (1805–1877) graduated eighth in the West Point class of 1825. He served on the Ordnance Board and was chief of several United States arsenals before the war with Mexico. As Scott's chief of ordnance in Mexico, he was brevetted three times. As a Confederate general he performed poorly in field command, but when later serving as inspector of Confederate artillery and ordnance in the Trans-Mississippi, he provided excellent service.

7. Charles Pomeroy Stone (1824–1887) was a descendant of Massachusetts Puritans. An 1845 West Point graduate, he won brevets at the Battles of Molino del Rey and Chapultepec. After resigning from the army in 1856, he worked as a surveyor for the Mexican government. He reentered the army in 1861 as a colonel of volunteers, and Commanding General Winfield Scott made him inspector general of Washington, D.C., with primary responsibility for the security of the capital. He ran afoul of Radical Republicans in Congress on the slavery issue, was falsely imprisoned for six months in 1862, and, after duty along the Gulf Coast, resigned from the army in 1864. After the war he went overseas and for thirteen years served as chief of staff of the army of the khedive of Egypt. Coming back to the United States in the 1880s, he worked as chief engineer for the construction of the concrete foundation for the Statue of Liberty.

8. George Thom (1819–1891) from New Hampshire graduated seventh in his West Point class. He later served as an engineer in the Union army.

9. James R. Irwin (1800–1848) graduated from West Point in 1825 and fought in the Second Seminole War in Florida. He survived all the battles of the Mexico City Campaign only to die of pneumonia in January 1848 during the occupation of the Mexican capital.

10. South Carolinian and 1833 West Point graduate Abraham C. Myers (1811–1889) was brevetted twice during the Mexican War; once while serving in Taylor's army and once in Scott's. His father-in-law, David Twiggs, was one of the army's division commanders, and it was Twiggs who named a fort on the Florida coast after Myers. Later Myers was one of about ten thousand Jews who fought for the Confederacy, being named in March 1861 the first quartermaster general of the Confederate army.

11. Henry Constantine Wayne (1810–1883) was an 1838 West Point graduate from Georgia. He received a brevet promotion for gallantry at Contreras and Churubusco and later served as a general in the Confederate army. Wayne was also the officer who headed the expedition to Europe and the Middle East in the 1850s to purchase camels for the War Department's experiment with an army camel corps in the American desert.

12. Justus McKinstry (1814–1897) was from Michigan, and for his bravery at Contreras and Churubusco he won brevet promotion. When the Civil War began, he was appointed brigadier general of volunteers and chief quartermaster of the Union Department of the West. After only a few months

he was arrested for accepting bribes and payoffs from government contractors and was dismissed from the army (January 1863). McKinstry went on to be a stock broker in New York and a land agent in Missouri.

13. Pennsylvanian George W. F. Wood (d. 1854) was commissioned a second lieutenant in 1838 and received brevet promotion following Contreras and Churubusco.

14. Joseph Daniels (1809–1886) was a native of Massachusetts who moved to Texas, where he eventually became aide-de-camp to Governor Sam Houston in 1844. When the Mexican War began, he received a commission as captain in the army. He served in the Quartermaster Department and on Gen. John Quitman's staff. He was brevetted for gallantry, and after the war he left the army and moved to San Francisco, where he lived until his death four decades later.

15. Theodore O'Hara (1820–1867) was a Kentucky lawyer before being commissioned a captain to go fight in Mexico. He was promoted to major by brevet for gallantry at Contreras and Churubusco. After O'Hara's discharge in 1848, he became heavily involved in filibustering activities in Cuba. Rejoining the military in 1855 with an officer's commission in the Second Cavalry, he was soon forced to resign by Col. Robert E. Lee because of drunkenness. He later joined the Confederacy and served as a colonel in the Western Theater. He is most famous for his poem "Bivouac of the Dead."

16. Samuel McGowan (1819–1897) was a South Carolina lawyer and state legislator. He enlisted in the Palmetto Regiment of South Carolina volunteers in 1846 and rose to the rank of captain. Later, as a general in the Confederate Army of Northern Virginia, he served with distinction and was wounded four times. After the Civil War, he served for fourteen years as a justice on the South Carolina Supreme Court.

17. Kentuckian John Breckinridge Grayson (1806–1861) graduated from West Point in 1825 and served as an officer of artillery and commissaries prior to 1846. In Mexico he served as Scott's chief of commissariat and was brevetted twice for bravery in battle. He died of disease in the first year of the Civil War while serving as a general in the Confederate army.

18. Thomas P. Randle served on Quitman's staff. He was honorably discharged in July 1848.

19. Connecticut native Edmund Kirby (1794–1849) entered the army in 1812 in order the fight the British. He also served in the Black Hawk War and Second Seminole War before rendering honorable service in Mexico, where he was twice brevetted for gallantry. He contracted a disease in Mexico (probably dysentery or yellow fever) and died of the illness in New York after the war ended.

20. Albert Gallatin Bennett (d. 1857) was brevetted for gallantry during action at the National Bridge near Jalapa on June 11, 1847.

21. Thomas Lawson (1789–1861) from Virginia entered the navy in 1809 as a surgeon's mate then joined the army as a surgeon's mate in 1811 before qualifying as surgeon two years later. He was president of the board of medical examiners, a board that tested the fitness of recruits. In 1836 President Andrew Jackson promoted him to surgeon general of the army. He accompanied his longtime friend, Winfield Scott, to Mexico but only in an advisory role.

22. Benjamin Franklin Harney (1788–1858), born in Delaware, had been a surgeon in the army since 1814.

23. Richard Sherwood Satterlee (1796–1880) began his medical practice in 1818, and after moving from New York to Detroit, Michigan, he began to provide medical services part time to the troops stationed at Detroit Barracks. He subsequently gained a permanent appointment in the U.S. Army Medical Corps. In Mexico he was assigned to Gen. William Worth's division. During the Civil War he was on duty in New York City.

24. New Yorker Charles Stuart Tripler (1806–1866) completed his study of medicine in 1827 and obtained the station of surgeon in the army in 1838. In Mexico he was assigned to Gen. David Twiggs's division. After the war he received assignments in Michigan and California. Sensing the coming of the Civil War, in 1858 he wrote *Manual of the Medical Officer of the Army of the United States,* which focused on the physical requirements of recruits, which deficiency he blamed on Mexican War soldiers' susceptibility to disease a decade earlier. He became renowned in the U.S. Army Medical Corps, and Tripler Army Medical Center in Hawaii was named for him.

25. Burton Randall (d. 1886) was from Maryland, and he was appointed assistant surgeon in the army in 1832. He provided capable service for thirty-six years with assignments in Florida during the Second Seminole War as well as in Mexico. During the Civil War he was put in charge of the General Hospital in Annapolis, Maryland. He contracted a disease in Florida from which he reportedly never fully recovered. He retired from the army in 1868 and ten years later was admitted to the Government Hospital for the Insane in Washington. He died there in 1886.

26. John Meck Cuyler (1810–1884) was a surgeon in the army from 1834 to 1882. In 1847 he was a major, but he eventually attained the brevet rank of brigadier general in 1865. Despite being a native of Savannah, Georgia, he remained loyal to the United States in the Civil War.

27. Alexander F. Suter was appointed assistant surgeon in the army in 1835. He died of unknown causes in Mexico City in December 1847.

28. Josiah Simpson (d. 1874) was a surgeon assigned to the Sixth Infantry in Mexico. A Pennsylvanian, he served thirty-seven years in the U.S. Army Medical Corps, including during the Second Seminole War and Civil War. He was promoted to brevet colonel in 1865, and he died in Baltimore.

29. David Camden DeLeon (1818–1872) was from South Carolina, and he was appointed assistant surgeon in the army in 1838. Living in Washington when the Civil War began, he resigned his major's commission and in May 1861 was appointed the first surgeon general of the Confederacy. His competence and his ability to hold his liquor were both suspect, and he resigned two months after his appointment. He served briefly as medical director of the Army of Northern Virginia. After the war he practiced medicine in Santa Fe, New Mexico, which is where he died.

30. Maryland native Henry Hegner Steiner (1816–1892) studied medicine at the University of Pennsylvania before receiving his appointment as assistant army surgeon in 1839. He served in the Second Seminole War and in the early 1840s was assigned to a post in Augusta, Georgia. After the war with Mexico he resigned from the army (1851) and settled in Augusta. Steiner was noted for his ability to diagnose unknown illnesses as well as an unparalleled skill as a surgeon.

31. James Simons (1816–1885) from South Carolina entered the army as an assistant surgeon in 1839. He was wounded at Molino del Rey, was dismissed from the army in 1856 for abandoning his frontier post during a cholera epidemic, and reentered the Medical Corps and served the Union cause faithfully in the Civil War before dying in 1885.

32. Joseph K. Barnes (1817–1883) from Philadelphia studied medicine at the University of Pennsylvania before his appointment as assistant surgeon in the army in 1840. He served in the Second Seminole War and was with Zachary Taylor's army in 1846 before joining Scott's army in 1847. During the Civil War he rendered medical service in Washington, where he was designated in 1864 to replace Dr. William Hamilton as surgeon general. Barnes became the first medical officer to be promoted to the rank of major general. He attended to two mortally wounded presidents during his career, Abraham Lincoln and James A. Garfield.

33. Rhode Islander Levi H. Holder began his twenty-eight years of service in the Medical Corps in 1840. He died in 1874.

34. Charles Carter Keeney was from New York. He entered the Medical Corps in July 1842 and was honorably discharged for unknown reasons two months later. He reentered the service in 1845 and later became medical inspector during the Civil War. Keeney died in 1883.

35. John Frazier Head (1821–1908) from Massachusetts was appointed to the Medical Corps in 1846 and served as an army surgeon until 1885. He was brevetted a lieutenant colonel in 1865 for his meritorious service.

36. South Carolinian John Fox Hammond was a surgeon in the Medical Corps from 1847 to 1884. He remained loyal to the Union in the Civil War and died in 1886.

37. Josephus M. Steiner (1823–1873) from Maryland was assistant surgeon in the Medical Corps from 1847 until he was dropped from the army rolls in 1856. He died in 1873.

38. Charles P. Deyerle (1820–1853) was a Virginian who graduated from Virginia Military Institute in 1842 and was appointed assistant army surgeon in 1847. He never married and died in California in 1853 while still in the service.

39. Ebenezer Swift (1817–1885) from Massachusetts entered the Medical Corps in 1847 and retired in 1883. He was promoted by brevet to lieutenant colonel and colonel in 1865 for meritorious service in the Civil War and again promoted, this time to brigadier general, in 1867 for exemplary service at Fort Harker, Kansas, during an 1867 cholera outbreak. Swift died in 1885.

40. Courtney J. Clark (b. 1816) was born in South Carolina but served as surgeon with Alabama volunteers. He later served as a regimental surgeon of the Tenth Alabama during the Civil War. Information on the surgeons of volunteer units in the remainder of Scott's list is sketchy and sometimes nonexistent.

41. Robert Hagan was born in Ireland but lived in Louisiana when he was appointed to serve as assistant surgeon of volunteers and the Fourteenth Infantry.

42. Robert Ruffin Ritchie was a Virginia surgeon who was honorably discharged in July 1848.

43. L. W. Jordan was probably Lewis W. Jordan from Tennessee.

44. Richard McSherry from Virginia retired from the Medical Corps in 1851 and died in 1885.

45. William S. Harney (1800–1889), first mentioned in chapter XXIX, entered the army in 1818 and served under Andrew Jackson. He was a veteran of the Black Hawk War and Second Seminole War, where his vulgarity and brutality were well known. He was a fearless dragoon leader in Mexico but was sometimes insubordinate. Harney distinguished himself at Cerro Gordo and received brevet promotion as a result. He worked in administrative jobs in Washington early in the Civil War and retired in 1863.

46. Andrew Thomas McReynolds (1808–1898) was born in Ireland but immigrated to Michigan. He was brevetted for gallantry at Churubusco, left the service after the war, became a politician, and later served the Union cause as a cavalry colonel.

47. Virginian John Garland (1792–1861) received a lieutenant's commission in 1813 and served in the War of 1812 and the Second Seminole War. His bravery at Palo Alto and Resaca de la Palma while fighting in Zachary Taylor's army was rewarded with a brevet promotion to colonel in 1846. The following year he again received a brevet promotion to brigadier general for

gallantry at Contreras and Churubusco. Garland was seriously wounded at Mexico City. Future Confederate general James Longstreet was his son-in-law. Garland died in 1861, one year after his wife, Harriet, died and one year before his son, Samuel Garland, was killed while serving as a general in the Confederate army.

48. Newman S. Clarke from Connecticut was a veteran of the War of 1812 and a brigade commander in Mexico. He commanded capably in every battle of the Mexico City Campaign except Molino del Rey and was brevetted once following the siege of Veracruz. He died in San Francisco, California, in 1860.

49. Franklin Pierce (1804–1869) was a former U.S. senator from New Hampshire when he volunteered to fight in Mexico. He received a commission as colonel and was quickly promoted to brigadier general. He led reinforcements that augmented Scott's army at Puebla and participated in the final stage of the campaign: Contreras, Churubusco, Chapultepec. He went on to be elected the fourteenth president of the United States in 1852, defeating Winfield Scott, who had been his commander in Mexico.

50. Samuel E. Watson and a contingent of marines arrived with reinforcements in Puebla and was with Scott's army for the final leg of the campaign. His service was mediocre and he died of disease soon after the capture of Mexico City.

51. El Peñon rose up out of Lake Texcoco and was heavily fortified with artillery and over a thousand Mexican troops. Its location adjacent to the main eastern approach to the capital made entering the city from that direction a deadly proposition. After extensive reconnaissance by Capt. Robert E. Lee, Capt. James L. Mason, and Lt. Isaac Stevens, Scott determined to swing his army around the south side of Mexico City.

52. Gabriel Valencia (1799–1848) briefly served as interim president of Mexico just prior to the outbreak of the war. He died in American-occupied Mexico City soon after the signing of the peace treaty.

53. A large field of jagged volcanic rock that stretched for about three miles and with a circumference of perhaps nine miles covered much of the terrain south of the capital. Most accounts refer to this lava bed as the Pedregal.

54. Capt. Seth Barton Thornton (1815–1847) from Virginia entered the army in 1836. He was the commander of a dragoon patrol along the Rio Grande that came under attack by Mexican lancers on April 25, 1846, precipitating the declaration of war by Congress the following month. He was killed on the outskirts of Mexico City in August 1847.

55. William Montrose Graham (1798–1847) was a native of Virginia and an 1817 West Point graduate (fourth in his class). He was promoted to major in 1835 for gallantry in the Second Seminole War. In Mexico he commanded the Eleventh Infantry Regiment and was killed on September 8

at the Battle of Molino del Rey. The Union artillery officer named William Montrose Graham Jr. was his nephew.

56. Franklin Dyer Callender (1817–1882) from New York entered the army in 1839 after his graduation from West Point. He was cited for gallantry at Contreras and Churubusco. After the Mexican War he went on to serve the Union cause in the Western Theater, rising to the brevet rank of brigadier general.

57. George Washington Morgan (1820–1893) was born in Pennsylvania, but as a teenager he as his brother traveled to Texas, where he enlisted and fought in Sam Houston's army during the Texas Revolution. He soon returned to the United States and attended West Point for two years before settling into a law practice in Ohio. He first commanded volunteers in Mexico then received a colonel's commission to command the Fifteenth Infantry Regiment. He received a brevet promotion to brigadier general for his meritorious conduct at Contreras and Churubusco. He served as a Union general until his resignation in 1863, after which he served in Congress.

58. The hamlet Scott referred to as Contreras was actually Padierna, which the Americans mistook for the nearby village of Contreras. Virtually all accounts, both contemporary and modern day, refer to the village and the battle that occurred there as Contreras. Scott's army had marched around to the south side of Mexico City, and while negotiating the difficult terrain south of the lava bed called Pedregal had encountered Mexican troops under Gen. Gabriel Valencia at the village covering the road running north into the capital. After a sharp fight on August 19, Scott approved the detachment of over a third of his army to a position between the Mexican force and the capital. That isolated portion of Scott's army found a path to the rear of the enemy and decided to reposition itself during the night so as to attack Valencia from behind. Captain Lee, with great physical exertion, had worked his way through the Pedregal at night to inform Scott of the plan and ask for a strong demonstration in Valencia's front the next morning. The plan worked brilliantly and the American attack from the rear routed the Mexican force in less than twenty minutes.

Chapter XXXI
Victories of Contreras—San Antonio—Churubusco

1. Trueman Bishop Ransom (1802–1847) from Vermont graduated from Norwich University, which had been founded by former West Point superintendent Alden Partridge in 1819 under the name American Literary, Scientific, and Military Academy. Ransom briefly served as president of the institution before volunteering for the Mexican War and receiving a commission to command the Ninth Infantry. He was killed at the Battle of Chapultepec on September 13.

2. Justin Dimick (1800–1871) was born in Connecticut and graduated from West Point in 1819. A veteran of the Second Seminole War, Dimick fought first under Taylor before commanding the First Artillery in Scott's army. He was twice brevetted for gallantry in Mexico and later commanded the Fort Warren Military Prison in Massachusetts during the Civil War.

3. This reference is to Mexican general Nicolas Mendoza.

4. Scott's losses in killed and wounded were more than the sixty he reported but were far less than the number suffered by the Mexicans. Charles Hanson was from Washington, D.C., and had entered the service as a second lieutenant in 1838. Lt. John Preston Johnston had been mortally wounded in the previous day's fighting and had died during the night. He was the orphaned nephew of Joseph E. Johnston, who had been a father figure for Preston.

5. Pennsylvanian Simon H. Drum (1807–1847) graduated from West Point in 1830. He served in Florida during the Second Seminole War and proved himself to be an exceptional artillery officer in Mexico. He was later killed in the final assault on Mexico City on September 13.

6. John Lane Gardner (1793–1869) grew up in Massachusetts and fought in the War of 1812 and the Second Seminole War before going to Mexico as commander of the Fourth Artillery. He was brevetted for meritorious conduct at Cerro Gordo and Contreras.

7. For Francis Taylor, see chapter XXII, note 12.

8. Louisiana native Henry Hopkins Sibley (1816–1886) was an 1838 West Point graduate and veteran of the Second Seminole War. He received a brevet promotion for actions during the siege of Veracruz. He later served the Confederacy in the Trans-Mississippi Theater and had a reputation with the bottle. After the war he spent four years as a general in the Egyptian army.

9. Carlos Adolphus Waite (d. 1866) was a New York native. He was commissioned a second lieutenant in the army in 1820, and in Mexico he received brevet recognition for gallantry and meritorious service at Contreras and Churubusco and again for Molino del Rey.

10. Martin Scott from Vermont entered the army in 1814. He fought with distinction during the war's first year in northern Mexico, being brevetted for Palo Alto and Resaca de la Palma and again for Monterey. Two weeks after Churubusco, during the bloody Battle of Molino del Rey, he assumed command of the Fifth Infantry when Col. James McIntosh was mortally wounded. Scott was then killed and replaced by Maj. Carlos Waite, who was also wounded.

11. William Trousdale (1790–1872) was born in North Carolina, but his parents moved to Tennessee when he was six years old. He was with a volunteer company that fought with Andrew Jackson in the War of 1812, and he later became a major general in the Tennessee State Militia while

nurturing a law practice in Gallatin. He received an appointment to the Fourteenth Infantry in the regular army in 1847. He fought with distinction at Churubusco and Molino del Rey and was later brevetted for gallantry at Chapultepec. Trousdale, a Democrat, had failed in numerous runs for Congress prior to the war, but after it he returned home a war hero and was elected governor of Tennessee in 1849. He failed in his attempt at reelection and was appointed minister to Brazil during the Franklin Pierce administration.

12. This was Joseph Finley Irons from Pennsylvania, who had entered West Point in 1837. He died six days later from his wound at Churubusco.

13. Larkin Smith (d. 1884) from Virginia graduated from West Point in 1835 and fought in the Second Seminole War before seeing duty in Mexico. He was brevetted for Contreras and Churubusco on August 20 and later wounded in the fighting at Molino del Rey. He resigned from the army in 1861 and served as a colonel in the Confederate Quartermaster Department.

14. James G. Soulard Snelling (1822–1855) from Minnesota was the son of Josiah Snelling. He graduated from West Point in 1845 and received brevet promotions for the Contreras and Churubusco action as well as Molino del Rey.

15. For Edmund Alexander, see chapter XXIX, note 17.

16. This is probably a reference to James Madison Smith, as no I. M. Smith is listed in Francis Heitman's *Historical Register and Dictionary of the United States Army*. Both Heitman and William Hugh Robarts (*Mexican War Veterans*) list a James Madison Smith who appears to have died in Jalapa in December 1847.

17. Oliver Lathrop Shepherd (d. 1894) from New York graduated from West Point in 1840. In Mexico he distinguished himself at Contreras and Churubusco and again at Chapultepec, where he received two brevet promotions. He was a Union colonel in the Civil War fighting in the Western Theater.

18. Thompson Morris (d. 1870) from Ohio graduated from West Point in 1821 and had been a captain in the Second Infantry for ten years when the war began. He received two brevet promotions in Mexico: Cerro Gordo and action at Contreras/Churubusco.

19. Erastus A. Capron (1810–1847) from Connecticut was an 1833 West Point graduate. Burke is probably Martin John Burke, a West Point graduate from New York who was killed at Churubusco. Saterlee Hoffman was from Michigan. James Willoughby Anderson (b. 1812) was from Virginia and graduated from West Point in 1833. He was brevetted for gallantry against Seminole Indians in Florida and died two days after being wounded at Churubusco. Thomas H. Easley from Virginia graduated from West Point in 1846.

20. Allen Wood helped recruit Arkansans for the Twelfth Infantry Regiment and was commissioned a captain in the regiment. On the march from Veracruz to Mexico City, he was actually in command of two Arkansas companies.

21. Pierce M. Butler (1798–1847) from South Carolina was commissioned a second lieutenant in the Fourth Infantry in 1819 but resigned from the army in 1829 having attained the rank of captain. He served one term as governor of South Carolina (1836–1838). During the Mexican War he returned to the army as a colonel of South Carolina volunteers—the Palmetto Regiment. Butler was leading his men on the American left flank when he was wounded, but he remained in command until he was killed by a shot in the head. His brother was Andrew Pickens Butler, the famous states' rights Democratic senator.

22. Jesse Lee Reno (1823–1862) entered West Point from Pennsylvania and graduated the year the war started. His classmates included George McClellan, Thomas Jackson, and George Pickett. An ordnance officer, Reno received brevet promotions for his conduct at Cerro Gordo and Chapultepec. As a major general and corps commander in the Union army, he was killed at South Mountain in September 1862.

23. Joshua Howard (d. 1868) from Massachusetts and Michigan entered the army in 1813. His meritorious conduct at Chapultepec won him a brevet promotion. He left the service in 1848 but returned during the Civil War and served as a Union paymaster of volunteers.

24. Charles Baxter of the New York volunteers would be mortally wounded on September 13 in an attack on the south wall of the Chapultepec fortress.

25. James P. Dickinson's wound was mortal. Adley Hogan Gladden (1810–1862) was a cotton broker from Columbia and was appointed postmaster of Columbia by President John Tyler. He fought against the Seminoles in Florida before volunteering in the Palmetto Regiment. Gladden was wounded at the Belén Gate at the southwest corner of Mexico City on September 13. Returning from Mexico, he settled in New Orleans. As a brigade commander in the Confederate army, Brigadier General Gladden fought at Shiloh, where he was mortally wounded on April 6, 1862.

26. David Adams of Company D and Wilson Roberts Williams of Company K were both in the South Carolina regiment.

27. Augustus Quarles had volunteered from Wisconsin and was commissioned a captain. He died at Churubusco five months after entering the service. John B. Goodman, also in the Fifteenth Infantry, hailed from Michigan and, like Quarles, died in the fifth month of his service.

28. Edgar Chandler died on September 21, the day after receiving his wound.

29. Lt. Lorimer Graham from New York was assigned to the Tenth Infantry Regiment but was detached and serving with the First Dragoons. He resigned from the army in 1853.

30. Richard Stoddert Ewell (1817–1872), West Point class of 1840, grew up in northern Virginia. He was with his brother, Thomas, when he died at Cerro Gordo. Richard received a brevet promotion to captain for his actions at Churubusco. He became a prominent Confederate general during the Civil War, lost a leg in the Second Bull Run Campaign, and was one of the scapegoats for Lee's defeat at Gettysburg. After the Civil War he settled on a farm in Spring Hill, Tennessee. His extant farm house is privately owned.

31. Frederick D. Mills was a Connecticut lawyer when he volunteered and was commissioned in the Fifteenth Infantry Regiment. After the Mexican army broke and retreated toward the capital, Mills watched as the dragoons galloped by in pursuit. Despite comrades' efforts to dissuade him, he mounted his horse and joined them. An inexperienced horseman, he ultimately rode right into the Mexican works after the other mounted Americans halted. His rashness resulted in his death.

32. The number of Mexican soldiers engaged in the various fights around the Pedregal on August 20 (Contreras, San Antonio, Churubusco) was closer to twenty-five thousand.

33. Nicholas Trist (1800–1874) was married to Virginia Randolph, Thomas Jefferson's granddaughter. In 1833 Trist was named consul to Havana, Cuba, and in 1845 he was appointed to a post in the State Department. He was fluent in Spanish and was sent to Mexico by President Polk to negotiate a treaty when the time came. Trist and Scott did not get along when the former first joined the army in Mexico, but they eventually cooperated in bringing about the postwar settlement.

34. Scott later levied a $150,000 "contribution" against Mexican officials to help defray the cost of the occupation.

35. Scott's meaning is "brilliant success."

36. By omitting the "summons" to surrender the city, Scott gave Santa Anna the opportunity to claim that Scott asked for the cease-fire, leaving the impression that the Americans were unable to press the fight forward. In actuality, Scott agreed to permit a cease-fire with the understanding that peace negotiations would follow.

37. The literal translation is "The written word remains."

38. The meaning is "unable to fight."

Chapter XXXII
Armistice—Negotiations—Hostilities Renewed—Battle of Molinos del Rey—Capture of Chapultepec and Mexico

1. When the armistice went into effect, Scott's army had only two days of rations on hand, and the terms of the cease-fire permitted Americans to go into Mexico City to gather and purchase supplies. When the first wagons went into the city, angry Mexicans attack the wagons and teamsters.

2. The attack on Molino del Rey was a significant mistake in an otherwise brilliant military operation. American casualties were heavy (116 killed, 673 wounded), and the main assault force, Gen. William Worth's, suffered a 25 percent loss. All this to discover that the Molino del Rey was not being used as a foundry.

3. Mexico City was surrounded largely by lakes and low-lying marshes. Approaches to the capital were along several raised causeways that entered the city on the south and west through the fortified gates that Scott mentioned here.

4. Edward Jenner Steptoe (1815–1865), a West Point graduate from Virginia, fought Seminoles in Florida and served with distinction in Mexico. As an officer in the Third Artillery, he was brevetted twice: Cerro Gordo and Chapultepec. Bad health forced his 1861 retirement and he died four years later.

5. George Pearce Andrews (1821–1887) from Connecticut graduated from West Point in 1845. Brevetted at Molino de Rey and again at Chapultepec, he went on to serve as a Union officer in the Civil War, retiring from the army in 1885. He died at Fort Winfield Scott in California in 1887.

6. Horace Brooks (1814–1894) entered West Point from Massachusetts in 1831. His forty-two-year career included exceptional service in the Second Seminole War, citations for gallantry and meritorious conduct in Mexico, and Civil War assignments in Florida then in the recruiting service and defense of Washington, D.C.

7. Virginian Samuel Anderson (1819–1901) graduated from West Point in 1841 and was brevetted for gallantry at Molino del Rey and Chapultepec. He served as a colonel in the Confederate army.

8. Samuel MacKenzie (d. 1847) of the Second Artillery was from North Carolina and was an 1818 West Point graduate. He fought in all the battles in which Zachary Taylor's army was engaged in 1846, then, transferring with his unit to Scott's army, he fought in all the engagements in the Mexico City Campaign, leading one of the storming parties at Chapultepec. He died of unknown causes in the enemy capital one month after it fell into American hands.

9. Silas Casey (d. 1882) was from Rhode Island and graduated from West Point in 1826. He saw extensive action in the Second Seminole War in Florida and in Mexico was twice brevetted for gallantry. His second brevet was for Chapultepec, where he led a storming party and was seriously wounded. Casey was assigned duty in the Northwest in the 1850s, served as a general officer in the Civil War commanding a division in the Peninsula Campaign, and later wrote a book on infantry tactics for "colored troops." He was reported to be a modest gentleman and astute mathematician.

10. Gabriel René Paul (1813–1886) from Missouri was a descendant of a French officer in Napoleon's army. After graduating from West Point in

1834, he was posted to southwestern forts before fighting in the Second Seminole War in Florida. He was brevetted a major for the storming of Chapultepec. Paul was an officer in the Union army, serving in the Trans-Mississippi Theater until he was promoted to general and given command of a brigade in the Army of the Potomac. On the first day of the Battle of Gettysburg, a musket ball entered his temple and exited through his left eye, which rendered him blind. He partially recovered but was unable to return to duty. He retired in February 1865, lived until 1886, and is buried in Arlington National Cemetery.

11. Levi Twiggs (1793–1847) was commissioned a second lieutenant in the Marine Corps in 1813 and served on the frigate USS *President*. He led a storming party of 120 volunteers at Chapultepec and was killed by a shot in the chest during the assault.

12. Born in Ireland, James Miller (1823–1862) commanded Company K of the Second Pennsylvania. He received a serious wound in the attack at Chapultepec, and fifteen years later, while serving as a Union colonel, he was killed at the Battle of Fair Oaks in Virginia.

13. Vermonter Benjamin S. Roberts (1810–1875) was a railroad engineer after graduating from West Point (1835) and serving briefly in the army. He worked for railroad companies in New York and Russia, where he helped build the line from St. Petersburg to Moscow. He returned to the United States, studied law, and began a legal practice in Iowa before returning to the army in 1846. He received brevet promotion to major after the Battle of Chapultepec and another to lieutenant colonel for actions against Mexican guerrillas at Matamoras and Gualaxara. Roberts served on the frontier after the Mexican War then rose to the rank of brigadier general in the Union army. He was a professor at Yale in the post–Civil War years.

14. This is James Stuart, an 1846 West Point graduate from South Carolina. Brevetted for actions at Contreras and Chapultepec, he was killed fighting Indians at Rogue River, Oregon, in 1851.

15. Timothy Patrick Andrews (d. 1868) from Ireland and Washington, D.C., was a colonel in the Voltigeurs and received a brevet for gallantry at Chapultepec. He later served as a colonel in the Union Paymaster Department before retiring in 1864.

16. George A. Caldwell (d. 1886) from Kentucky was promoted to lieutenant colonel by brevet for his actions at Chapultepec, where he was wounded. He was mustered out of the service in August 1848.

17. Moses J. Barnard from Pennsylvania commanded Company H of the Voltigeurs. He was wounded in the Chapultepec action and brevetted to major. He was mustered out of the service in August 1848.

18. Charles John Biddle (d. 1873) from Pennsylvania was brevetted for gallantry at Chapultepec, mustered out of the service in August 1848, and

reentered for a six-month period as colonel of the Thirteenth Pennsylvania in 1861.

19. Virginia native Joseph Selden entered the service in 1838 and was brevetted for gallantry and meritorious conduct twice in Mexico. He resigned from the army in April 1861 and served as assistant inspector general in the Confederate army.

20. Lewis Addison Armistead (1817–1863) was from Virginia. He entered West Point in 1834 but left the academy because of academic problems and following a fight with fellow cadet Jubal Early. However, family connections secured him a commission as second lieutenant in 1839. Armistead was brevetted for gallantry at Contreras and Churubusco and again brevetted at Molino del Rey. As a Confederate general, he was mortally wounded and captured while leading a brigade in Pickett's Charge at Gettysburg.

21. Alexander Perry Rodgers from New York graduated from West Point in 1846 and was killed fourteen months later in the Chapultepec assault on September 13, 1847. Joseph P. Smith was a second lieutenant, a New Hampshire native, and an 1844 West Point graduate.

22. Samuel Woods (d. 1887), from Indiana, was an 1837 West Point graduate. He was brevetted for his bravery at Chapultepec and later served as a colonel in the Union army.

23. Daniel Chase (d. 1877) was from Connecticut and Ohio, and he received a commission in the Fifteenth Infantry in 1847 when it was raised for one year of service in Mexico. Prior to Chapultepec, Chase had been brevetted for gallantry at Contreras and Churubusco. He later served as a major in the Union army.

24. William Chapman (d. 1887) from Maryland graduated with the West Point class of 1831 and was brevetted twice in Mexico. As a Union colonel, he was brevetted for gallantry at First Bull Run in 1861. William Reading Montgomery (1801–1871) from New Jersey graduated from West Point in 1825 and saw duty during the Canadian border disputes and in the Second Seminole War. He was brevetted while serving in Zachary Taylor's army in northern Mexico and again at Molino del Rey after the Eighth was transferred to Scott's army. As a Union general he served mostly in administrative posts prior to his April 1864 resignation. Edward Johnson, nicknamed "Old Allegheny" (1816–1873), was from Virginia and was in the 1826 West Point class. He was brevetted for gallantry at Molino del Rey and Chapultepec. As a Confederate general, he was wounded while fighting in the Shenandoah Valley Campaign in 1862, and he later was captured while fighting at the Bloody Angle at Spotsylvania. After his release, he was captured again at the Battle of Nashville.

25. During the assault on the Chapultepec castle, future Confederate general James Longstreet (1821–1904) received a musket ball in the thigh. As he

fell to the ground, he handed the regimental colors to fellow lieutenant George Pickett (1825–1875), who also rose to become a prominent Confederate general. Charles George Merchant (d. 1855) was an 1833 West Point graduate from New Hampshire.

26. The adventurous Thomas Mayne Reid (1818–1883) was Irish by birth. At age twenty-one he traveled to the United States, where he spent time in New York, Tennessee, and Louisiana. He commanded the Grenadier Company of the Second New York Volunteers along with a detachment of marines that was assigned to his command at Chapultepec. Under orders to guard an American battery south of the castle, Reid requested that his men be allowed to join the assault already underway, and permission was granted. Reid shouted, "Men! if we don't take Chapultepec the American army is lost!" During the assault, he was seriously wounded in the thigh. Records indicate that he was a lieutenant, but he later claimed to have been promoted to captain, and for the rest of his life he called himself Captain Reid. After the war he became a well-known novelist, writing such books as *The Rifle Rangers, The Boy Hunters,* and *The Headless Horseman.* In his mid-thirties, he married Elizabeth Hyde, the fifteen-year-old daughter of his publisher.

27. Descended from one of the founders of Hartford, Connecticut, but a New York native, Frederick Steele (1819–1868) graduated with the West Point class of 1843. He received brevets for gallantry at Contreras and Chapultepec. During the Civil War, he rose to the rank of major general while serving in the Western Theater. He remained in the U.S. Army until 1868, when he died in a buggy accident.

28. Levi Gantt from Washington, D.C., graduated from West Point in 1841. He was shot in the chest in the attack on Chapultepec and died on the field.

29. Calvin Benjamin from New York and Indiana graduated tenth in the 1842 West Point class.

30. Fitz John Porter (1822–1901) was born in Massachusetts into a family of naval officers. He graduated eighth in the 1845 West Point class. His bravery was noted with brevet promotions at Molino del Rey and Chapultepec. He participated in the Utah Expedition under Albert Sidney Johnston in 1857 and rose to the rank of major general in the Union army. He was convicted by court-martial of disobeying orders at Second Bull Run in 1862 and spent years trying to vindicate his name. He was exonerated fifteen years later.

31. David Allen Russell (1820–1864) from New York graduated with the West Point class of 1845. He was brevetted for action against Mexican guerrillas at the National Bridge and Cerro Gordo. As a Union general he fought at Fredericksburg and Gettysburg and was killed at Winchester, Virginia, on September 19, 1864.

32. This reference is to Joseph Hooker (1814–1879), the famous Union general in the Civil War. The Massachusetts native graduated from West Point in 1837, fought in the Second Seminole War, and served in Mexico, where he won three brevets: Monterrey, National Bridge, and Chapultepec. He resigned from the army in 1853 but returned to serve as a competent Union general except for a brief, unsuccessful tenure as commander of the Army of the Potomac in 1863.

33. Mansfield Lovell (1822–1884) was the grandson of a Massachusetts delegate to the Continental Congress. In 1842 he graduated from West Point, having been appointed to the academy from Washington, D.C. He was brevetted at Chapultepec, where later in the day, at the Belén Gate, he was wounded. As a Confederate general, Lovell surrendered the city of New Orleans to Union forces in 1862. After the Civil War he lived in New York until his death.

34. Francis Nelson Page (d. 1860), 1841 West Point graduate, had fought in Zachary Taylor's army along the Rio Grande in 1846. He won two brevet promotions in Mexico, one under Taylor and another under Scott for gallantry at Contreras and Churubusco.

35. Paul Octave Hébert (1818–1880) was born in Louisiana and graduated first in the 1840 West Point class. He resigned from the army in 1845 but received a commission as lieutenant colonel in the Fourteenth Infantry Regiment two years later. He was brevetted for gallantry at Molino del Rey, left the army again in 1848, and was elected governor of Louisiana in 1852. He was a brigadier general in the Confederate army.

36. Thomas Jonathan Jackson (1824–1863) from Virginia was an 1846 West Point graduate. He received brevet promotions at Contreras and Churubusco and again for working his battery at Chapultepec. Jackson resigned in 1852 and accepted a faculty position at the Virginia Military Institute. Subsequently, he went on to become the famous Confederate general, "Stonewall" Jackson.

37. Scott had originally planned to use Quitman's division in a feint toward the Belén Gate at the city's southwest corner, while Worth used his division to actually force entrance into the capital at the northwestern gate, called San Cosmé. However, after the castle fell, Quitman attacked at the Belén Gate, intending to be the first to enter the city. After Quitman's refusal to obey Scott's order to halt, the commanding general ordered Worth to advance, thus creating unintended but simultaneous attacks on both fortified gates on Mexico City's west side.

38. Capt. Simon Drum of the Fourth Artillery had pulled his guns along the aqueduct causeway and right into the thick of the fight outside the Belén Gate. When he ran out of ammunition, he and his fellow gunners abandoned their cannon and turned a captured Mexican 8-pounder around

to continue firing. During this heroic and bloody affair on the southwest edge of the city, Drum and Lt. Calvin Benjamin were mortally wounded. In addition, one other lieutenant was wounded, and among the noncommissioned officers, one was killed and all the rest, except one, were wounded.

39. Scott's reference is to 1st Lt. John B. Moragne and 2nd Lt. James W. Cantey Jr.

40. This is an exaggeration. The Mexican army around Mexico City during this last series of battles was probably about two and a half times the size of Scott's army.

Chapter XXXIII
Brilliant Allusion to the Campaign—Retaliatory Measures—Martial Law—Safeguards— Proclamation—Defence of Puebla

1. Henry Lytton Bulwer (1801–1872) served in the British army before joining the diplomatic service. As ambassador to the United States (1849–52), he negotiated the Clayton-Bulwer Treaty in 1850, which dealt with Anglo-American issues in Latin America.

2. Patrick Hamilton was a sixteenth-century Scottish religious reformer who was burned at the stake by Archbishop James Beaton for being a heretic.

3. The Scott clan from which Winfield Scott was descended came from the Duke of Buccleuch and Duchess Ann Scott. *Waverly* and *Guy Mannering* were both popular novels written by Sir Walter Scott in the early nineteenth century. With *Waverly* (1814), Scott is thought to have been the first to write a historical novel.

4. Samuel Watson Black (1816–1862) was a Pittsburgh attorney who volunteered and was elected lieutenant colonel on the First Pennsylvania Volunteer Regiment. In the summer of 1862, Black was killed at Gaines' Mill while fighting for the North. William F. Small (1819–1877) commanded Company C of the First Pennsylvania. He occasionally wrote articles and sent them back home for publication in newspapers. Small published *Guadaloupe: A Tale of Love and War* in 1860 and saw brief service in the Union army as a colonel.

5. Henry Lane Kendrick (1811–1891) from New Hampshire graduated from West Point in 1835. He fought at Cerro Gordo and Amozoc and was brevetted for bravery in the defense of Puebla. "Old Hanks," as he was called, was a professor of chemistry, mineralogy, and geology at West Point from 1857 to 1880.

6. John H. Miller (d. 1850) from Pennsylvania was an 1833 West Point graduate who was brevetted to major for his role in the defense of Puebla.

7. Theodore F. Rowe (d. 1868) was a New Hampshire native who volunteered and received a captain's commission in February 1847, serving until August 1848. As were others whom Scott mentioned, Rowe was brevetted for his role in the Puebla defense.

8. South Carolinian Thomas Grimké Rhett (1821–1878) was a nephew of the famous South Carolina senator Robert Barnwell Rhett. He graduated sixth in the 1845 West Point class. He later served as an officer in the Confederate army and was on the staff of P. G. T. Beauregard and Joseph E. Johnston. After the Civil War, Rhett left the country and became a colonel in the Egyptian army.

9. This was probably William Chetwood DeHart (d. 1848) from New York, who graduated from West Point in 1820.

Chapter XXXIV
Question of Free Quarters—System of Finance—Spread of the Troops

1. Hiram Fairfield was the captain of a mounted Louisiana volunteer unit that escorted Percy W. Doyle to Mexico City in December 1847.

2. William Orlando Butler (1791–1880) was a Kentucky Democrat and veteran of the War of 1812 who had been brevetted for gallantry at the Battle of New Orleans. A graduate of Transylvania University, Butler practiced law after 1815 and served as a member of Congress from Kentucky. Reentering the army in 1846 as a major general of volunteers, he served as second in command in Zachary Taylor's army in northern Mexico. Interested in superseding Whig general Scott, Polk tapped Butler to take command of Scott's army in February 1848. Butler was Lewis Cass's running mate on the 1848 Democratic ticket for president.

3. Thomas Marshall (1793–1853) was a member of the Kentucky state legislature, a nephew of Chief Justice John Marshall, and a brigadier general of volunteers in Mexico. He commanded reinforcements that arrived in Mexico City in January 1848 to participate in the occupation of the country.

4. Jones Mitchell Withers (1814–1890) from Alabama was an 1835 West Point graduate who immediately upon graduation resigned from the army to practice law and transact cotton in Tuscaloosa and Mobile. He reentered the army as a lieutenant colonel to fight in Mexico and was colonel of the Ninth Infantry during the occupation period. When the Civil War began, Withers was mayor of Mobile. As a general in the Confederate army, he fought at Shiloh, Perryville, and Stones River. After the war he was a cotton broker and again mayor of Mobile.

5. The "spy company" is a reference to a band of Mexicans who, under the command of Manuel Dominguez, hired out their services to the Americans

during the war. Some were common criminals and highwaymen, while others were simply mercenaries. Yet others were, for various reasons, disaffected with the Mexican government and willing to contribute to its defeat. Scott relied on this band as scouts, couriers, spies, and guides.

6. Father Caledonio Jarauta was a Catholic priest who emerged as a leader of guerrilla forces in central Mexico during Scott's campaign. His guerrilla bands were a constant on roads between the capital and the coast during the occupation phase.

7. John Coffee Hays (1817–1883), a native Tennessean, was a nephew of Andrew Jackson. He left home as a teenager and became a land surveyor in Mississippi before moving on to Texas, where family connections with Sam Houston secured for him a place as a Texas Ranger. During the war with Mexico, "Jack" Hays served as colonel of the First Texas Mounted Riflemen, who fought at the Battle of Monterrey in September 1846. In the fall of 1847, the War Department ordered Hays and his Rangers to Veracruz to help keep open the guerrilla-infested road from the coast to Scott's army in Mexico City. He arrived at Veracruz in October and over the subsequent months led numerous patrols along the road to Mexico City. The expedition Scott refers to here may have been to Otumba and San Juan Teotihuacán, where Jarauta was believed to be holed up in January 1847.

8. South Carolinian William Branford Shubrick (1790–1874) attended Harvard before becoming a midshipman in the navy in 1806. He was a veteran of the War of 1812, and during the war with Mexico, Shubrick commanded blockading vessels on the Pacific Coast of Mexico.

Chapter XXXV

Suppression of Outlaws—Peace Commissioner—Treaty Signed—Mexican Overtures—Court of Inquiry

1. See chapter XXVIII, note 15, for William Jay's criticism of Scott for not halting the bombardment of Veracruz long enough for the evacuation of women and children. This reference is to Jay's criticism of the harsh measures Scott employed to keep Mexican roads open and free of guerrillas. Jay called the order "sanguinary" and referred to it as unpatriotic, unjust, and inhumane.

2. In October 1847, President Polk, impatient and angry with Nicholas Trist for waffling on the Rio Grande boundary demand, issued an order through Secretary of State James Buchanan for Trist to end his negotiations and return to Washington. Trist's disobedience of the recall order infuriated the president.

3. Silas Wright (1795–1847) was a governor, congressman, and senator from the state of New York. He was a Martin Van Buren supporter at the

Democratic nominating convention in 1844 and refused to join Polk on the ticket as the vice presidential nominee. He had opposed the annexation of Texas, and his firm stand on principle won him the nickname "Cato of the Senate."

4. George Bancroft (1800–1891) was from Massachusetts. He attended Harvard, served as secretary of the navy, and was a historian and author. During the Polk administration, he served for a month as acting secretary of war.

5. Andrew J. Donelson (1799–1871) was briefly chargé d'affaires to the Republic of Texas in 1844.

6. Brig. Gen. Nathan Towson, Brig. Gen. Caleb Cushing, and Col. William Goldsmith Belknap were appointed to serve on a court to inquire into Winfield Scott's actions. Scott had been approached with the idea of ending the war in July 1847 by bribing Mexican officials to open peace talks in exchange for a million dollars. He discussed the proposal with some of his subordinate officers and even made an initial $10,000 payment, but the scheme went no further. The Polk administration wanted that plan investigated along with Scott's arrest of Gideon Pillow, William Worth, and James Duncan, all officers who had had accounts of the campaign published in U.S. newspapers against regulations. President Polk ordered their release before ordering the court of inquiry for Scott.

Chapter XXXVI

Receptions at New York and Elizabeth—Others Declined—Bad Health—Thanks of Congress, etc.

1. Jeremiah Clemens (1814–1865) was a senator from Alabama and a cousin of Mark Twain's.

2. All have been previously identified, including Ichabod Bennet Crane, who was identified in chapter XXII, note 15.

3. James Shields, formerly a general in Scott's army, was a senator from Illinois. Shields is also mentioned in chapter XXIX, notes 1 and 6.

4. Alexander H. Stephens (1812–1883) was a Georgia congressman and governor as well as vice president of the Confederacy.

5. Willis Arnold Gorman (1816–1876) volunteered to fight in Mexico after having served in the Indiana state legislature. At the time the "Lieutenant-General Bill" was being debated in Congress, Gorman was a congressman and later became territorial governor of Minnesota.

6. Robert Toombs (1810–1885) from Georgia was also a congressman at the time and later a senator. During the Civil War, he was Confederate secretary of state as well as a general in the Southern army.

7. Caleb Cushing was attorney general at the time, and the amount of back pay that Scott claimed was $29,661. He ending up receiving $10,465.

8. Thomas Lanier Clingman (1812–1897) was from North Carolina and later served as a Confederate general.

9. Scott won only four states and garnered 42 electoral votes while Pierce carried twenty-seven states and claimed 254 electoral votes.

10. The turmoil following the passage of the Kansas-Nebraska Act led to clashes between proslavery and antislavery advocates in Kansas. During "Bleeding Kansas," Kentucky Senator John J. Crittenden proposed, in June 1856, that the federal government send Scott to the troubled territory to restore order. Democrats generally opposed the measure and it was never seriously considered. In addition to Crittenden, Scott mentioned the following senators in his list: John Bell (Tennessee), John Clayton (Delaware), William Seward (New York), Albert G. Brown, Isaac Toucey (Connecticut), Stephen Mallory (Florida), and James M. Mason (Virginia).

11. Robert Charles Winthrop (1809–1894) was a Harvard-educated lawyer and former Speaker of the House of Representatives during the Polk administration. He was from Massachusetts, and Faneuil Hall was the famous meeting hall in Boston.

12. Scott's references are to Secretary of War Jefferson Davis and Kansas Territorial Governor Wilson Shannon. In April 1856, Douglas County Sheriff Samuel J. Jones was shot while trying to execute arrest warrants on several antislavery residents in Lawrence, Kansas, an episode that brought U.S. Marshal J. B. Donaldson into the fray. These events were precursors to Jones and a "posse" of over seven hundred sacking Lawrence in May 1856. All of these men were proslavery Democrats. Col. Edwin V. Sumner, who had served in Scott's army in Mexico, was commander of Fort Leavenworth, Kansas, at the time.

13. John Church Hamilton (1792–1882) was a veteran of the War of 1812 and the son of Alexander Hamilton.

14. President James Buchanan's secretary of war was Virginian John B. Floyd (1806–1863), and in 1857 he ordered U.S. troops under Gen. Albert Sidney Johnston to Utah (the Utah Expedition) to put down an anticipated rebellion by Mormons who had settled there. The Buchanan administration feared the creation of an autonomous theocracy, but such never occurred and the Utah Expedition resulted in only a few minor skirmishes. In 1858 Alfred Cumming from Georgia was appointed Utah's territorial governor.

15. In 1859 a dispute erupted on San Juan Island in Puget Sound over American and British competing claims of ownership. The so-called Pig War started when an American settler on the island killed a pig that was eating in his garden. The pig belonged to another nearby settler who was an Irishman. This minor event escalated into an international dispute of ownership of the entire island thanks in part to the bravado of William

Harney, the military commander in the area. The Buchanan administration dispatched Scott to the region to try to sooth ruffled feathers. The seventy-three-year-old Scott made the arduous trip, arriving at Puget Sound in October, and soon worked out a joint occupation accommodation with Vancouver Island's governor, James Douglas.

16. Gouverneur Kemble (1786–1875), an arms manufacturer and longtime friend of Scott, served two terms from New York's 4th Congressional District in the late 1830s and early 1840s.

17. James McKay was a congressman from North Carolina and Walter Coles from Virginia.

18. James Chatham Duane (1824–1897) from New York was an 1848 West Point graduate. He had accompanied U.S. forces during the Utah Expedition. He went on to be the chief engineer for the Army of the Potomac.

19. This was Maj. Robert Anderson, who eventually attained the rank of major general. See chapter XXII, note 10.

20. Joseph Holt briefly served as secretary of war in the waning weeks of the Buchanan administration.

21. Senator Isaac Toucey, identified in note 16 above, had previously served as U.S. attorney general and was secretary of the navy in early 1861 in the closing months of the Buchanan administration. James H. Ward had entered the navy in 1823, taught at the Naval Academy, and commanded the frigate *Cumberland* during the war with Mexico. He was involved in helping to plan the navy's role in a solution to the Fort Sumter dilemma. Ward was killed, shot by a sniper, a few months later, while providing close shore support for a Union landing party in the Chesapeake Bay.

22. Adam Jacoby Slemmer (1828–1868) from Pennsylvania graduated from West Point in 1850. He commanded the garrison at Fort Pickens and later rose to the rank of brigadier general in the Union army.

23. George W. Lay (chapter XXIX, note 47) from Virginia resigned from the U.S. Army and joined the Confederacy soon after.

24. James Armstrong (1794–1868) commanded the navy yard at Pensacola, Florida, and would later surrender the post to state officials after the state's secession.

25. Pennsylvanian Israel Vogdes (1816–1889) graduated from West Point in 1837. He was an artillery officer and he participated in the defense of Fort Pickens, being captured with other Union defenders. He was later exchanged and continued to serve meritoriously in the Union cause.

26. James P. Wolfe (1727–1759) was the British general who defeated the French in the French and Indian War. Louis Charles Antoine Desaix (1768–1800) was a general in Napoleon's army who was killed in battle in Italy. Louis Lazare Hoche (1768–1797) was an officer in the French revolutionary army who quickly rose to the rank of general before an untimely death.

27. *Cui bono* is Latin for "who would benefit."

28. Horace Binney (1780–1875) and Joseph Reed Ingersoll (1786–1868) were both successful lawyers and congressmen from Pennsylvania. Binney was the winning attorney in *Vidal v. Girard's Executors,* the famous 1844 case in which the court ruled that schools cannot teach morality without the Bible. Ingersoll's father, Jared, was a delegate in the Continental Congress and the Constitutional Convention.

29. Pelatiah Perit (1785–1864) was a wealthy New York shipping merchant and from 1853 to 1863 president of the New York Chamber of Commerce. Edwards Pierrepont (1817–1892) practiced law in Connecticut and Ohio before moving to New York. In 1857 he was elected superior court judge in New York City. He was later a U.S. attorney and minister to Great Britain. Hamilton Fish (1808–1893) was a U.S. senator and secretary of state in addition to being governor of New York. In 1853, Fish, a longtime friend of Scott, quietly helped raise money for the Headquarters Fund, which went toward the purchase of the only house Scott ever owned. It was located on West Twelfth Street in New York City, and today it serves as the Center for Italian Studies at New York University.

Bibliography

Anderson, Robert. *An Artillery Officer in the Mexican War, 1846–7: Letters of Robert Anderson, Captain 3rd Artillery, U.S.A.* New York: G. P. Putnam's Sons, 1911.

Archer, Mary Roach. "Journal of Major Isaac Roach, 1812–1824." *Pennsylvania Magazine of History and Biography* 17, no. 2 (1893): 129–58.

Army and Navy Chronicle 9, no. 1 (July 4, 1839).

Atkinson, William B, ed. *The Physicians and Surgeons of the United States.* Philadelphia: Charles Robson, 1878.

Barbuto, Richard V. *Niagara 1814: America Invades Canada.* Lawrence: Univ. Press of Kansas, 2000.

Bartlett, Irving H. *John C. Calhoun: A Biography.* New York: W. W. Norton, 1993.

Bauer, K. Jack. *The Mexican War, 1846–1848.* New York: Macmillan, 1974.

———. *Surfboats and Horse Marines: U.S. Naval Operations in the Mexican War, 1846–48.* Annapolis: Naval Institute Press, 1969.

———. *Zachary Taylor: Soldier, Planter, Statesman of the Old Southwest.* Baton Rouge: Louisiana State Univ. Press, 1985.

Biographical Directory of the United States Congress, 1774– Present. http://bioguide.congress.gov/.

Brands, H. W. *Andrew Jackson: His Life and Times.* New York: Doubleday, 2005.

Brock, Robert A. *Miscellaneous Papers, 1672–1865: Now First Printed from the Manuscript in the Collections of the Virginia Historical Society. . . .* Richmond: Virginia Historical Society, 1887.

Brockman, William Everett. *History of the Hume, Kennedy and Brockman Families: In Three Parts.* Washington, D.C.: Charles H. Potter, 1916.

Bromley, J. S., ed. *The New Cambridge Modern History.* 14 vols. Cambridge: Cambridge Univ. Press, 1957–70.

Brown, Harvey E. *The Medical Department of the United States Army from 1775 to 1873: Compiled under the Direction of the Surgeon General. . . .* Washington, D.C.: Surgeon General's Office, 1873.

Bullard, Mary R. *Cumberland Island: A History.* Athens: Univ. of Georgia Press, 2003.

Byron, George Gordon. *The Works of Lord Byron.* Frankfort: H. L. Brœnner, 1837.

Cadwalader Family Papers. Historical Society of Pennsylvania, Philadelphia.

Carnes, Mark C., and John A. Garraty, gen. eds. *American National Biography.* 24 vols. New York: Oxford Univ. Press, 1999.

Chambers, John Whiteclay, II, ed. *The Oxford Companion to American Military History*. Oxford: Oxford Univ. Press. 1999.

Christ, Mark K., and William A. Frazier. *Ready, Booted, and Spurred: Arkansas in the U.S.-Mexican War*. Little Rock, Ark.: Butler Center Books, 2009.

Coffman, Edward M. *The Old Army: A Portrait of the American Army in Peacetime, 1784–1898*. New York: Oxford Univ. Press, 1986.

Colby, Frank Moore, Daniel Coit Gilman, and Harry Thurston Peck, eds. *The New International Encyclopaedia*. Vol. 3. New York: Dodd, Mead, 1903.

Cooper, William J., Jr. *Jefferson Davis, American*. New York: Random House, 2000.

Cromartie, Alan. *Sir Matthew Hale, 1609–1676: Law, Religion and Natural Philosophy*. Cambridge: Cambridge Univ. Press. 1995.

Cruikshank, Ernest, ed. *The Documentary History of the Campaign upon the Niagara Frontier in 1812–14*. 9 vols. Welland, Ont.: Lundy's Lane Historical Society, 1896–1908.

Cutrer, Thomas W. "Daniels, Joseph." *The Handbook of Texas Online*. http://www.tshaonline.org/handbook/online/articles/fda11/. Accessed December 19, 2011. Texas State Historical Association, Denton.

———. *The Mexican War Diary and Correspondence of George B. McClellan*. Baton Rouge: Louisiana State Univ. Press, 2009.

Dabney, Virginius. *Virginia: The New Dominion*. Charlottesville: Univ. Press of Virginia, 1971.

Davis, Jefferson. *The Papers of Jefferson Davis*. Vol. 4. Edited by Lynda L. Crist and Mary S. Dix. Baton Rouge: Louisiana State Univ. Press, 1982.

———. *The Papers of Jefferson Davis*. Vol. 5. Edited by Lynda L. Crist and Mary S. Dix. Baton Rouge: Louisiana State Univ. Press, 1985.

Davis, William C. *Jefferson Davis: The Man and His Hour*. New York: HarperCollins, 1991.

Degler, Carl N. *The Other South: Southern Dissenters in the Nineteenth Century*. New York: Harper & Row, 1974.

Edwards, R. M. *"Down the Tennessee": The Mexican War Reminiscences of an East Tennessee Volunteer*. Edited by Stewart Lillard. Charlotte, N.C.: Loftin, 1997.

Eisenhower, John S. D. *Agent of Destiny: The Life and Times of General Winfield Scott*. New York: Free Press, 1997.

Elliott, Charles Winslow. *Winfield Scott: The Soldier and the Man*. New York: Macmillan, 1937.

Encyclopaedia Britannica Online. http://www.Britannica.com/.

Encyclopedia of Arkansas History and Culture. Central Arkansas Library System. http://www.encyclopediaofarkansas.net/.

Fitzgerald, Thomas W. H. *Ireland and Her People; a Library of Irish Biography: Together with a Popular History of Ancient and Modern Erin.* . . . Chicago: Fitzgerald Book, 1910.

Foreman, Grant. *The Five Civilized Tribes: Cherokee, Chickasaw, Choctaw, Creek, Seminole.* Norman: Univ. of Oklahoma Press, 1934.

Fowler, Will. *Santa Anna of Mexico.* Lincoln: Univ. of Nebraska Press, 2007.

Frazer, Chris. *Bandit Nation: A History of Outlaws and Cultural Struggle in Mexico, 1810–1920.* Lincoln: Univ. of Nebraska, 2006.

Frazier, Donald S., ed. *The United States and Mexico at War.* New York: Macmillan, 1998.

Grant, Ulysses S. *Personal Memoirs of U.S. Grant.* 2 vols. New York: Charles L. Webster, 1885.

Graves, Donald E. "'I Have a Handsome Little Army . . . ': A Re-examination of Winfield Scott's Camp at Buffalo in 1814." In *War Along the Niagara: Essays on the War of 1812 and Its Legacy,* edited by R. Arthur Bowler, 38–52. Youngstown, N.Y.: Old Fort Niagara Association, 1991.

———. *Red Coats and Grey Jackets: The Battle of Chippawa, 5 July 1814.* Toronto: Dundurn Press, 1994.

Greer, James Kimmins. *Texas Ranger: Jack Hays in the Frontier Southwest.* College Station: Texas A&M Univ. Press, 1993.

Hannay, James. "The War of 1812." *Canadian Magazine* 21, no. 4 (Aug. 1903): 344–55.

Hastings, H. *Public Papers of Daniel D. Tompkins, Governor of New York, 1807–1817.* Vol. 3. Albany, N.Y.: J. B. Lyon, 1902.

Heidler, David S., and Jeanne T. Heidler, eds. *Encyclopedia of the War of 1812.* Annapolis: Naval Institute Press, 1997.

Heitman, Francis B. *Historical Register and Dictionary of the United States Army.* 2 vols. 1903. Reprint, Baltimore: Genealogical Publishing, 1994.

Hemphill, J. C. *Men of Mark in South Carolina: Ideals of American Life: A Collection of Biographies of Leading Men of the State.* Washington, D.C.: Men of Mark Publishing, 1907.

Henderson, Timothy J. *A Glorious Defeat: Mexico and Its War with the United States.* New York: Hill and Wang, 2007.

Hetzel, Abner R. *Military Laws of the United States: Including Those Relating to the Army, Marines Corps, Volunteers, Militia, and to Bounty Lands and Pensions.* . . . Washington, D.C.: George Templeton, 1846.

Hickey, Donald R. *The War of 1812: A Forgotten Conflict.* Chicago: Univ. of Illinois Press, 1989.

Hill, Daniel Harvey. *A Fighter from Way Back: The Mexican War Diary of Lt. Daniel Harvey Hill, 4th Artillery, USA.* Edited by Nathaniel Cheairs Hughes Jr. and Timothy D. Johnson. Kent, Ohio: Kent State Univ. Press. 2002.

Hone, Philip. *The Diary of Philip Hone, 1828–1851*. Edited by Allan Nevins. 2 vols. New York: Dodd, Mead, 1927.

Hough, Franklin B. *American Biographical Notes, Being Short Notices of Deceased Persons. . . .* Albany, N.Y.: Joel Munsell, 1875.

Howe, Daniel Walker. *What Hath God Wrought: The Transformation of America, 1815–1848.* New York: Oxford Univ. Press, 2007.

Hughes, Nathaniel Cheairs, Jr. *General William J. Hardee: Old Reliable.* Baton Rouge: Louisiana State Univ. Press, 1992.

Hughes, Nathaniel Cheairs, Jr., and Roy P. Stonesifer Jr. *The Life and Wars of Gideon J. Pillow.* Chapel Hill: Univ. of North Carolina Press, 1993.

Hughes, Nathaniel Cheairs, Jr., and Thomas Clayton Ware. *Theodore O'Hara: Poet Soldier of the Old South.* Knoxville: Univ. of Tennessee Press, 1998.

Index to the Reports of Committees of the House of Representatives for the First Session of the Forty-ninth Congress. 1st sess. Washington, D.C.: Government Printing Office, 1886.

Jay, William. *A Review of the Causes and Consequences of the Mexican War.* Boston: Benjamin B. Mussey, 1849.

Johnson, Timothy D. *A Gallant Little Army: The Mexico City Campaign.* Lawrence: Univ. Press of Kansas, 2007.

———. *Winfield Scott: The Quest for Military Glory.* Lawrence: Univ. Press of Kansas, 1998.

Jones, Howard. *To the Webster-Ashburton Treaty: A Study in Anglo-American Relations, 1783–1843.* Chapel Hill: Univ. of North Carolina Press, 1977.

Judah, Charles, and George Winston Smith. *Chronicles of the Gringos: The U.S. Army in the Mexican War, 1846–1848.* Albuquerque: Univ. of New Mexico Press, 1968.

Kelly, Howard A., and Walter L. Burrage. *American Medical Biographies.* Baltimore: Norman, Remington, 1920.

Kendall, George Wilkins. *Dispatches from the Mexican War.* Edited by Lawrence Delbert Cress. Norman: Univ. of Oklahoma Press, 1999.

Kenyon, J. P., ed. *A Dictionary of British History.* New York: Stein and Day, 1983.

Keyes, Erasmus Darwin. *Fifty Years' Observation of Men and Events, Civil and Military.* New York: Charles Scribner's Sons, 1884.

Lamb, Martha, and Constance Cary Harrison. *History of the City of New York: Its Origin, Rise, and Progress.* Vol. 3. New York: Casimo, 2005.

Lee, Sir Sidney, Sir Leslie Stephen, et al., eds. *The Dictionary of National Biography.* 22 vols. London: Oxford Univ. Press, 1917– .

Levinson, Irving W. *Wars within War: Mexican Guerrillas, Domestic Elites, and the United States of America, 1846–1848.* Fort Worth: Texas Christian Univ. Press, 2005.

Lochemes, M. Frederick. "Robert Walsh: His Story." Ph.D. diss., Catholic Univ. of America, 1941.

Long, George, ed. *The Penny Cyclopedia of the Society for the Diffusion of Useful Knowledge.* London: Charles Knight, 1833–43.

Lossing, Benson John. *The Pictorial Field-Book of the War of 1812; or, Illustrations, by Pen and Pencil, of the History, Biography, Scenery, Relics, and Traditions of the Last War for American Independence.* New York: Harper & Brothers, 1869.

Lubrecht, Peter T. *New Jersey Butterfly Boys in the Civil War: The Hussars of the Union Army.* Charleston, S.C.: History Press. 2011.

MacGillivray, Royce C. *Restoration Historians and the English Civil War.* International Archives of the History of Ideas. New York: Springer, 1975.

Malcomson, Robert. *A Very Brilliant Affair: The Battle of Queenston Heights, 1812.* Annapolis: Naval Institute Press, 2003.

May, Robert E. *John A. Quitman: Old South Crusader.* Baton Rouge: Louisiana State Univ. Press, 1995.

McAlexander, Ulysses Grant. *History of the Thirteenth Regiment United States Infantry: Compiled from Regimental Records and Other Sources.* N.p.: Regimental Press, 1905.

McCaffrey, James M. *Army of Manifest Destiny: The American Soldier in the Mexican War, 1846–1848.* New York: New York Univ. Press, 1992.

Miller, Robert Ryal, ed. *The Mexican War Journal and Letters of Ralph W. Kirkham.* College Station: Texas A&M Univ. Press, 1991.

Morris, John D. *Sword of the Border: Major General Jacob Jennings Brown, 1775–1828.* Kent, Ohio: Kent State Univ. Press, 2000.

M'Sherry, Richard. *El Puchero; or, A Mixed Dish from Mexico, Embracing General Scott's Campaign, with Sketches of Military Life, in Field and Camp, of the Character of the Country, Manners and Ways of the People, etc.* Philadelphia: Lippincott, Grambo, 1850.

Munsell, Joel. *American Ancestry: Giving the Name and Descent, in the Male Line, of Americans Whose Ancestors Settles in the United States Previous to the Declaration of Independence, A.D. 1776.* 2 Vols. Albany, N.Y.: Joel Munsell's Sons, 1887-88.

Norcross, George. *The Centennial Memorial of the Presbytery of Carlisle: A Series of Papers, Historical and Biographical, Relating to the Origin and Growth of Presbyterianism. . . .* Vol. 2. Harrisburg, Pa.: Meyers Printing and Publishing House, 1889.

Ohrt, Wallace. *Defiant Peacemaker: Nicholas Trist in the Mexican War.* College Station: Texas A&M Univ. Press, 1998.

Oswandel, J. Jacob. *Notes of the Mexican War, 1846–1848.* Edited by Timothy D. Johnson and Nathaniel Cheairs Hughes Jr. Knoxville: Univ. of Tennessee Press, 2010.

Pancake, John. *This Destructive War: The British Campaign in the Carolinas, 1780–1782.* Tuscaloosa: Univ. of Alabama Press, 1985.

Peskin, Allan. *Winfield Scott and the Profession of Arms.* Kent, Ohio: Kent State Univ. Press, 2003.

Reid, Elizabeth. *Mayne Reid: A Memoir of His Life.* London: Ward and Downey, 1890.

Reilly, Tom. *War with Mexico! America's Reporters Cover the Battlefront.* Edited by Manley Witten. Lawrence: Univ. Press of Kansas, 2010.

Rives, George Lockhart. *The United States and Mexico, 1821–1848: A History of Relations between the Two Countries from the Independence of Mexico to the Close of the War with the United States.* New York: Charles Scribner's Sons, 1913.

Robarts, William Hugh. *Mexican War Veterans: A Complete Roster of the Regular and Volunteer Troops in the War Between the United States and Mexico, from 1846 to 1848.* Washington, D.C.: A. S. Witherbee, 1887.

Robbins, Richard G. "Prince Michael Vorontsov: Viceroy to the Tsar by Anthony L. H. Rhinelander." Review. *American Historical Review* 96, no. 4 (Oct. 1991): 1243–44.

Ross, Robert B. *The Patriot War.* Detroit: Michigan Pioneer and Historical Society, 1890.

Schom, Alan. *Napoleon Bonaparte.* New York: Harper Collins Publishers, 1997.

Schroeder-Lein, Glenna R. *The Encyclopedia of Civil War Medicine.* Armonk, N.Y.: M. E. Sharpe, 2008.

Skelton, William B. *An American Profession of Arms: The Army Officer Corps, 1784–1864.* Lawrence: Univ. Press of Kansas, 1992.

Smith, Gustavus Woodson. *Company "A" Corps of Engineers, U.S.A., 1846–1848, in the Mexican War.* Edited by Leonne M. Hudson. Kent, Ohio: Kent State Univ. Press. 2001.

Smith, Justin H. *The War with Mexico.* 2 vols. New York: Macmillan, 1919.

Stevens, Kenneth R. *Border Diplomacy: The Caroline and McLeod Affairs in Anglo-American-Canadian Relations, 1837–1842.* Tuscaloosa: Univ. of Alabama Press, 1989.

Sumner, William Hyslop. Papers. Special Collections Research Center. Syracuse University, Syracuse, N.Y.

Thomas, Lately. *Delmonico's: A Century of Splendor.* Boston: Houghton Mifflin, 1967.

Thompson, Jerry. "Winfield Scott's Army of Occupation as Pioneer Alpinists: Epic Ascents of Popocatepetl and Citlaltepetl." *Southwestern Historical Quarterly* 105, no. 4 (April 2002): 549–81.

Transactions of the Medical Association of Georgia. Atlanta: Medical Association of Georgia, 1892.

Trial of Col. Thomas H. Cushing, Before a General Court-Martial, Which Sat at Baton-Rouge, on Charges Preferred Against Him by Brig. Gen. Wade Hampton. Philadelphia: Moses Thomas, 1812.

Tucker, Spencer C., ed. *The Encyclopedia of the Mexican-American War: A Political, Social, and Military History.* 3 vols. Santa Barbara, Calif.: ABC-CLIO, 2013.

———. *The Encyclopedia of the War of 1812: A Political, Social, and Military History.* 3 vols. Santa Barbara, Calif.: ABC-CLIO, 2012.

Turner, Wesley B. *British Generals in the War of 1812: High Command in the Canadas.* Montreal: McGill-Queens Univ. Press, 1999.

Virginia Military Institute Archives website. http://www.vim.edu/archives/.

Wallace, Edward S. *General William Jenkins Worth: Monterey's Forgotten Hero.* Dallas: Southern Methodist Univ. Press, 1953.

Watson, Samuel J. *Jackson's Sword: The Army Officer Corps on the American Frontier, 1810–1821.* Lawrence: Univ. Press of Kansas, 2012.

———. *Peacekeepers and Conquerors: The Army Officer Corps on the American Frontier, 1821–1846.* Lawrence: Univ. Press of Kansas, 2013.

Waugh, John C. *The Class of 1846: From West Point to Appomattox: Stonewall Jackson, George McClellan and Their Brothers.* New York: Warner Books, 1994.

Weigley, Russell F. *History of the United States Army.* Bloomington: Indiana Univ. Press, 1967.

Wert, Jeffry D. *General James Longstreet: The Confederacy's Most Controversial Soldier.* New York: Simon & Schuster, 1993.

Wilcox, Cadmus M. *History of the Mexican War.* Edited by Mary Rachel Wilcox. Washington, D.C.: Church News Publishing, 1892.

Winders, Richard Bruce. *Mr. Polk's Army: The American Military Experience in the Mexican War.* College Station: Texas A&M Univ. Press, 1997.

Index

Biddle, Richard, 144–45, 352n3
Biddle, Thomas, 67, 75, 144, 338n4
Bigottini, Emilia, 120, 348n9
Binney, Horace, 317, 392n28
Black Hawk, 115–16, 118–19, 347n3
Black, Samuel W., 276, 386n4
Blackstone, William, 148–49, 190, 353n10, 357n2
Blair, Francis P., Jr., 228, 368n44
Blair, Francis P., Sr., 368n44
Blair, Montgomery, 368n44
Blake, William, 98, 343n5
Bliss, William W. S., 195, 197, 208, 357n2
Bloodgood, Francis, 62, 366n9
Bloom, Henry, 56, 334n20
Blücher, Gebhard Leberecht von, 84, 340n4
Boerstler, Charles G., 50, 59, 334n11
Bolling, Elizabeth, 341n6
Bomford, George, 18, 61, 329n3, 336n7
Bonaparte, Napoleon, xxvi, xxx, 43, 84, 88, 91, 92, 206, 324n11, 342n4
Boote, William R. 18
Botts, Benjamin, 8, 326n4
Bowlegs, 138, 351n8
Boyd, John Parker, 47–49, 51, 333n4
Brady, Hugh, 75, 76, 79, 140, 159, 339n4
Brant (son), 34, 332n14
Brant, Joseph, 51, 332n14
Breckinridge, John C., 9, 327n14
Brisbane, Arthur, 340n2
Brisbane, James, 80, 340n2
Broadnax, William H., 128, 349n13
Brock, Isaac, 33, 37, 332n11–12
Brook, George Mercer, 215, 362n13
Brooks, Horace, 259, 262, 381n6
Brooks, William T. H., 227, 244, 366n32
Brown, Albert G., 303, 390n10
Brown, Hachaliah, 226
Brown, Jacob, xv, 62, 68–70, 73–77, 82, 83, 111, 145, 297, 329n3, 336n12–14 & 16, 346n7

Brown, James, 187
Buchanan, James, x, xix, 308, 315, 388n2, 390n14, 391n15
Buell, Don Carlos, xviii
Buena Vista, Battle of, 207, 208, 209–10, 215, 359n7
Bulwer, Henry L., 271, 386n1
Burbeck, Henry, 18, 329n3
Burke, Martin John, 250, 378n19
Burnet, Gilbert, xxv, 323n4
Burnett, Ward B., 227, 250–51, 366n33
Burnham, James C., 226, 365n26
Burns, James, 49, 334n9
Burr, Aaron, xiv, 7, 9, 20, 22, 327n8–10, 330n5, 334n10
Butler, Pierce M., 250–51, 379n21
Butler, William O., 280–81, 285, 289, 295, 387n2
Byron, George, 140, 162, 352n12

Cadwalader, George, 209, 233, 236, 240–41, 243–44, 246, 248, 254, 260–62, 264, 284, 286–87, 345n4, 359n6, 369n1
Cadwalader, Thomas, 110, 144–45, 345n4
Caldwell, George A., 261, 382n16
Calhoun, John C., x, 9, 13, 98–99, 124, 327n14, 343n6, 349n6
Caliban, 97, 343n3
Callender, Franklin Dyer, 240, 376n56
Cameron, Simon, 19
Camp, John G., 55
Campbell, George W., 328n10
Campbell, William, 125, 349n9
Campbell, William Bowen, 228, 366n34
Canalizo, Valentín, 224, 365n19
Canova, Antonio, 8, 326n2
Cantey, James W., 265, 386n39
Capron, Erastus A., 250, 378n19
Captain Jacobs, 34–36
Carey, Margaret Eleanor Brisbane, 80, 340n2

Grant, Ulysses, xii, xiii, xiv, xviii, 364n11, 365n22
Grayson, John B., 234, 254, 257, 269, 371n17
Greene, Catherine, 341n13
Greene, Nathaniel, 86, 126, 341n13
Greenway, James, 2–3

Hagan, Robert, 235, 374n41
Hagner, Peter V., 226, 228, 234, 254, 259, 262, 269, 365n23
Hale, Matthew, 148–49, 353n9
Hale, Wiley P., 222, 363n9
Hall, Diminick A., 151, 351n10
Halstead, W. B., 235
Hamilton, Alexander, 8, 271, 305, 390n13
Hamilton, James, 130, 131, 350n16
Hamilton, John C., 304–5, 390n13
Hamilton, Patrick, 271, 386n2
Hamilton, Paul, 28, 331n3
Hamilton, Schuyler, 233, 254, 369n2
Hamilton, William, 373n32
Hammond, John F., 235, 373n36
Hammond, Richard P., 227, 262, 366n33
Hampden, John, 155, 353n2
Hampton, Wade, 20, 24, 25, 27, 28, 330n6
Hancock, Winfield S., xviii
Hanson, Alexander C., 43–44
Hanson, Charles, 245, 377n4
Hardcastle, Edmund LaFayette, 228, 234, 247, 254, 269, 367n42
Hardee, William J., xviii, 350n1
Hardy, Thomas, 11, 12, 328n2
Hargrave, James, 3–4
Harley, Robert, 1st Earl of Oxford, xxv, 323n6
Harney, Benjamin F., 235, 372n22
Harney, William S., 219, 223, 227, 235, 237, 238–39, 243, 246, 251, 306, 362n1, 374n45, 390n15
Harris, Samuel D., 67, 338n3

Harris, Thomas, 227, 366n33
Harrison, William Henry, 32, 156, 181–83, 356n3
Hartford Convention, 71, 338n12
Harvey, John (British soldier), 53
Harvey, John (lieutenant governor of New Brunswick), 174–78, 356n5
Haskell, William T., 222, 228, 363n8
Hawkins, Benjamin, 23, 330n8
Hay, George, 8, 326n7
Hays, John Coffee, 286, 388n7
Head, John F., 235, 373n35
Hebert, Paul O., 262, 385n35
Heileman, Julius Frederick, 18, 131, 329n3, 350n17
Helvetius, 5
Henry, Patrick, 336n10
Henry, Thomas, 228, 366n35
Hetzel, Abner R., 168, 355n13
Hindman, Jacob, 18, 57, 67, 75, 76, 334n8, 335n21
Hitchcock, Ethan Allen, 214, 228, 229, 233, 254, 257, 268, 299, 361n11
Hobbes, Thomas, 147, 352n5
Hobhouse, John, 352n12
Hoche, Louis L., 316, 391n26
Hodge, William L., 204, 206
Hoffman, Saterlee, 250, 378n19
Holder, Levi H., 235, 373n33
Holt, Joseph, 313, 315, 391n20
Homer, 2, 325n2
Hone, Philip, xiv
Hooker, Joseph, xviii, 262, 385n32
Horace, Quintus Horatius Flaccus, 2, 325n3
Houdon, Jean-Antoine, xxiii
House, James, 18, 329n3
Houston, Sam, 371n14, 376n57, 388n7
Howard, Joshua, 251, 261, 264, 379n23
Huger, Benjamin, xi, 234, 254, 256, 259, 262, 269, 370n6
Huger, Daniel, 128, 349n11
Hull, William, 31, 34, 59, 62, 331n4
Humboldt, Alexander von, 85, 340n5

Hume, 5, 155, 353n1
Hyde, Edward, 1st Earl of Clarendon, xxv, 323n3
Hyde, Elizabeth, 262, 384n26

Ingersoll, Charles J., 186–87, 357n4
Ingersoll, Jared, 392n28
Ingersoll, Joseph R., 317, 392n28
Irons, Joseph F., 248, 378n12
Irving, Edward, 8, 326n5
Irving, Washington, 9, 327n11, 355n15
Irwin, James R., 234, 254, 257, 269, 370n9

Jackson, Andrew, x, xiii, xvi, xvii, 9, 20, 81–82, 83, 88, 98, 105–8, 111, 123–24, 133, 135–36, 138–42, 151–54, 155, 193, 212, 295, 297, 306, 311–12, 327n10, 335n2, 343n6, 348n10, 351n9–10, 352n14, 356n3, 357n4, 368n44, 372n21, 377n11, 388n7
Jackson, Henry, 88, 342n16
Jackson, Rachel, 139, 351n9
Jackson, Thomas J., xviii, xxi, 262–63, 355n12, 379n22, 385n36
James II, 153
Jarauta, Calendonio, 286, 388n6–7
Jarero, José María, 222, 363n5
Jay, John, 362n15
Jay, William, 217, 291, 362n15, 388n1
Jefferson, Thomas, 8, 11, 12, 14, 19, 20, 97, 98–99, 100, 126, 190, 198, 326n3, 329n1, 336n10, 380n33
Jenkins, Elisha, 62, 336n9
Jesup, Thomas Sidney, 65, 67, 70, 75, 76, 77, 137–38, 299, 337n19
Johnson, Edward, 262, 383n24
Johnson, Henry, 92–93, 112, 343n6, 347n12
Johnson, Samuel, xxv, xviii, 14, 22, 97–98, 187, 323n7, 340n7
Johnston, Albert Sidney, 306, 384n30, 390n14

Johnston, John Preston, 245, 377n4
Johnston, Joseph E., xviii, 222, 261, 280–81, 364n14, 377n4, 387n8
Jones, Roger ap Catesby, 114, 212, 347n14
Jones, Samuel J., 304, 390n12
Jones, Walter, 14
Jordan, Lewis W., 235, 374n43
Joshua, xxvi
Julius Caesar, xxvi, 353n13

Kearny, Philip, 220, 235, 240, 246, 251, 362n2
Kearsley, Jonathan, 57
Keeney, Charles C., 235, 373n34
Kemble, Gouverneur, 308, 391n16
Kendrick, Henry L., 277, 386n5
Keokuk, 117–20, 347n4
Key, Francis Scott, 335n22, 347n12
Keyes, Erasmus, xiv, 168, 170, 355n11
King, Rufus, 101, 344n11
Kirby, Edmund, 234, 254, 257, 269, 371n19
Knight, Simeon, 19
Kosciusko, Thaddeus, 85, 341n7

Laidley, Theodore T. S., 226, 228, 277, 365n25
Lake Erie, Battle of, 31, 331n1–2
Lamartine, Alphonse Marie Louis, xxvi, xxviii, xxix
Landero, José, 362n14
Laurens, Henry, 126
La Vega, Rómulo Díaz de, 222, 363n5
Lawrence, Cornelius W., 143, 352n2
Lawrence, William, 18
Lawson, Thomas, 235, 254, 372n21
Lay, George W., 228, 233, 254, 257, 269, 314, 368n47, 391n23
Leavenworth, Henry, 67, 70, 76, 338n1
Leonard, Nathaniel, 56, 334n20
Lee, Charles, 92
Lee, Francis, 247
Lee, "Lighthorse" Harry, 342n13

Mason, Winfield (uncle), 2
May, John F., 7
Mayo, John, 103, 344n1
McClellan, George B., xi, xviii, xx, xxi,
    xxii, 234, 254, 269, 350n1, 369n4,
    379n22
McClellan, John, 228, 234, 254, 367n41
McClure, George, 55–56, 59, 61, 73,
    334n18
McCullough v. Maryland, 326n3
McDonald (adjutant general of New
    York militia), 158
McFeely, George, 47, 333n3
McGowan, Samuel, 234, 371n16
McIlvaine, Bloomfield, 80–81
McIntosh, James S., 233, 369n1,
    377n10
McKay, James, 308, 391n17
McKenzie, Samuel, 259, 261, 381n8
McKinstry, Justus, 234, 269, 370n12
McLeod, Alexander, 157, 354n6
McMillan (surgeon), 235
McNeil, John, 67, 70, 75, 338n2
McRee, William, 17, 68, 88, 329n3
McReynolds, Andrew T., 235, 251,
    374n46
McSherry, Richard, 235, 374n44
Mendoza, Nicolas, 245, 277n3
Menominees, 117, 119
Merchant, Charles G., 262, 384n25
Mexico City, xviii; battles around,
    267–68; campaign, xix, xxi
Middleton, Conyers, xxvi, 324n12
Mitchell, Samuel Latham, 14, 328n9
Miller, James (Capt.), 261, 382n12
Miller, James (Col.), 48, 76, 334n7
Miller, John H., 277, 386n6
Mills, Frederick D., 251, 380n31
Molino del Rey, Battle of, xviii,
    256–57, 270, 354n10; casualties,
    381n2
Monroe, James, 83, 98, 144, 198,
    343n6, 346n7
Monterey, Battle of, 200, 210, 358n8

Montesquieu, xxxi
Montgomery, William R., 262, 383n24
Montreal expedition, xv
Moragne, John B., 265, 386n39
Morales, Juan, 361n7, 362n14
Moreau, Jean Victor Marie, 70, 338n10
Morehead, James T., 358n6
Morgan, George W., 241, 243, 250, 264,
    376n57
Morris, Thompson, 249, 378n18
Moses, xxvi
Moultrie, William, 126
Mower, Thomas Gardner, 115, 347n2
Mullany, James Robert, 32, 332n6
Murray, Henry F., 222, 363n9
Murray, William (1st Lord of
    Mansfield), 25, 98, 330n11, 343n5
Myers, Abraham C., 234, 370n10

Napoleon. *See* Bonaparte, Napoleon
Napoleonic strategy and tactics,
    xviii, xix
Nelson, Frederick B., 222, 363n8
Nelson, Horatio, 11, 69, 328n2, 338n9
New Orleans, xiv, xvi, xix, xxii
New York (New York), xx, xxii, 7
Niagara River, xv
Nicholas, John, 61, 80, 336n5
Nicholas, Samuel S., 147, 352n4
Nicoll, Abimael, 18
Noriega, Louis, 222, 363n5
Nourse, Charles J., 346n6

Obando, José María, 222, 363n5
Ogilvie, James, 4
Ogilvie, Peter, 33, 332n9
O'Hara, Theodore, 234, 371n15
Okeechobee, Battle of, 138, 351n6
Oxenstierna, Axel, 101, 343n9

Page, Francis N., 262, 385n34
Page, John, 168, 355n13
Pakenham, Edward, 88
Palo Alto, Battle of, 198, 354n9, 355n13

Wheaton, H. L., 235
Whitelocke, Bulstrode, xxv, 323n2
Wickham, John, 8, 326n3
Wilds, Samuel, 13, 328n8
Wilkinson, James, xiv–xv, 20–22, 51, 53, 55–57, 60, 153, 327n12, 329n5, 335n23, 337n13
William, King of England, 148
Williams, David Rogerson, 28, 331n3
Williams, Thomas, 228, 233, 254, 269, 368n46
Williams, Wilson R., 251, 379n26
Wilson, John Lyde, 132, 350n19
Wilson, John Moryllion, 79, 339n1
Winder, William H., 47, 49–50, 82, 333n4, 340n9, 341n12
Winfield, John (great grandfather), 2
Winnebagoes, 117, 119
Winthrop, Robert C., 171, 303, 356n3, 390n11
Wirt, William, 8, 9, 111, 326n6, 347n11
Withers, Jones M., 281, 284, 387n4
Wolfe, James P., 316, 391n26
Wood, Allen, 250, 379n20

Wood, Eleazer D., 17, 68, 329n3
Wood, George T., 207
Wood, George W. F., 234, 371n13
Woods, Samuel, 261, 383n22
Wool, John E., 33, 159, 299, 332n9
Worcester v. Georgia, 326n6
Woronzow (Mikhail Semenovich Voronstov), 87, 342n14
Worth, William J., 64, 79, 138, 159, 207, 219, 221, 222, 223, 227, 229, 236, 238–39, 243, 246–49, 251, 256–59, 261, 263–66, 276, 295, 337n18, 351n8, 354n8, 360n1–3, 381n2, 389n6
Worth, Winfield Scott, 354n8
Wright, Silas, 292, 388n3
Wyncoop, Francis M., 228, 286, 366n34

Xenophon, xiv, xxvi

Yearwood, William, 222, 363n9
Yeo, James, 60, 73, 74, 335n3
Yorktown, xxi